W0010433

"Paul McGowan is the real deal, 100% inspired, inspiring and a genuine mensch. This book will make you laugh and push you to do something remarkable. Go make a ruckus."

Seth Godin
Author, *This Is Marketing*

For Terri

CHAPTER 1

"I have been through some terrible things in my life,
some of which actually happened."
— *Mark Twain*

MY FAMILY MOVED to Anaheim because my father heard it was the promised land—a new beginning in an affordable and up-and-coming rural suburb of Los Angeles, carved out of acres of sweet orange, walnut, and avocado groves. Sure, car exhaust mingled with the citrus blooms and orchard dust, but it was the gold rush days of the early 1950s: jobs were plentiful, land and homes were new and cheap, and outsiders were welcomed with open arms. Even better, Disneyland had opened just three years before the McGowan clan arrived. Along with my sisters, Sharane and Bobbi, I spent many nights camped out on the front lawn, watching the nightly fireworks displays explode in bristling starbursts of gold, yellow, and red.

It was 1958, and the warm evening air of Southern California was intoxicating. Our development of tract homes—then a new trend—wasn't quite as impressive as the Magic Kingdom, but it was orderly and symmetrical. It was named Gibraltar: a nine-street square carved out of a small patch of the orange groves that surrounded us like green-capped sentinels. Where the orchards' borders ended, our neighborhood streets began. Those orchards and groves, along with the acres of strawberries, the multiple fruit stands, and the occasional egg and dairy farms, offered endless adventure for me and my fellow neighborhood ruffians.

With school out for the summer, I was on my own as soon as the front door closed behind me. My parents, Don and Sue, didn't give a second thought to leaving a ten-year-old boy on his own without plans, guidance, or instructions other than a stern "don't get in trouble." In fact, once out that door I rarely returned home until dinnertime or dark, depending on what kind of trouble we were actually causing. And there was certainly plenty of that. I had the devil in me back then, and shudder to remember some of the stunts we pulled.

On Saturdays I would get up early and ride my bike south on State College to Chapman Avenue, then take a tough uphill climb through the city of Orange with its traffic circle, and finally reach Irvine Park, about 12 miles from my house, by noon. In those days bikes had no gears, heads had no helmets, and cyclists took their chances with traffic. My typical attire was a T-shirt, shorts, and PF Flyers: black canvas high-top sneakers with white rubber soles and white cotton laces, finished off with a round "PF" on the side. In Irvine Park I would meet with school buddies from Placentia and Yorba Linda, to see what kind of mischief we could manage to assuage the summer doldrums. On an average weekend we'd at least roll trashcans into the small lake—their tops would fly off, leaving a swath of half-eaten chicken, brown beer bottles, crumpled napkins, and empty bean cans with their jagged metal lids still attached. Other weekend projects to battle boredom entailed letting the air out of the park ranger's truck tires, hiding behind boulders to scare the crap out of unsuspecting hikers near Rooster Rock, skidding our bikes along dirt trails sternly marked "no bikes," or craftier misdemeanors like my first scrape with the law, one that should have landed me in jail.

It all started innocently enough on a lazy Saturday afternoon. My new best friend, David Wiley—a dark-haired, athletic, alpha-male transplant from Dallas—helped me prepare the bait: overalls stuffed with newspaper, a hoodie sweatshirt with a basketball for a head, and Dad's old boots pinned to the pant cuffs. We hoisted the body out of the garage and dragged it to the edge of the orange grove nearest my house, its lifeless head bouncing along La Palma Ave as twilight approached. The street was empty, so we threw the dummy face-down onto the road and hid amongst the trees, preparing an arsenal of rotting oranges scooped off the fertile ground. Night sounds surrounded us as we tensed in the shadows. Suddenly, the highway turned to daylight. With a loud boomp boomp, a car mangled the torso and screeched to a halt. The body, now crumpled on the asphalt, was lit red by taillights. The car roared away.

"Shit!" said David. "Hit and run!"

"Hang on!" I said. "Here comes another."

The body, twisted on the highway, was again brightly lit as a car swerved to miss it. Doors were flung open. Soon, gasps of horror turned to cries of panic under a hail of oranges, as we pelted the driver and passengers with our stores of orange ammunition.

"What the hell?" cried the driver, shielding his head as he knelt next to the body. "Dammit, this is a dummy!"

Without warning, the sound of a third vehicle paused our barrage of oranges. Tires screeched, doors opened, and bright lights again moved toward the lifeless lump on the road as we prepared our next round of missiles. Suddenly, the world flashed bright red and blue.

"It's the cops!" cried David.

"Run!" I yelled, not daring to look back. Halfway into the orange grove the flashlights started gaining on me, so I hurtled Old Man Niedermeyer's fence and hid in his cactus garden, braving the poking spines. The cops' bright lights played over the orange trees as red and blue washed the grove. I held my breath and exhaled only after they left. David and I would live to see another Saturday.

School wasn't far away. After barely graduating from sixth grade at McFadden Elementary in Placentia, a mostly Hispanic village three miles northeast of Gibraltar, I wound up in Placentia's Kramer Middle School, where I struggled through seventh and eighth grades. I hated school, and I didn't feel any better about it when my parents threatened to send me to Catholic school if I didn't graduate. I didn't take the threat all that seriously—we weren't Catholic, and anyway we couldn't afford private school. But the threat of those mysterious Catholics was ample motivation to scrape by with just Cs and Ds.

I was a goofy-looking kid. It was bad enough that my parents demanded a fresh crewcut every two weeks when my peers were experimenting with grooming; worse was a prominent set of buck teeth that I'd earned by sucking my thumb well into kindergarten. My upper lip couldn't cover my jutting teeth when my mouth was closed, and they didn't begin to straighten out until seventh grade, when orthodontists filled my mouth with painful silver wires and bands, loudly advertised by a metal hoop

3

attached to a flesh-colored elastic headband. Despite all that hardware, I tried to dress like the in crowd—but our family lacked the money to buy stylish clothes. It was the end of the postwar economy, and a decade and a half into the Cold War. The nation was on a growth curve that had yet to trickle down to the up-and-coming middle class. When those soft, checkered Pendleton shirts were all the rage, my mother did her best to make me some by hand, but her generosity backfired: the clothing snobs at my school rolled back the collar of my homemade shirt to expose the lack of an authentic label, then ridiculed me for being too poor to buy "real" clothes.

My main friends at school were the same ones I hung out with from our neighborhood, including David. There was Dennis, the kid that went along with everything: a lanky, stumbly, pigeon-toed redhead who lived a shout away, on the other side of our backyard fence. And Tony, always up for any sort of trouble: a short, fiery, black-haired spitfire driven by the devil (if you listened to my mom) or more likely by the ants in his pants. And of course there was the kid no gang could be without: Mike, teasingly called Mikey—afraid of his own shadow, and hoping for status and acceptance through misadventures. He was made timid by his overbearing father and shy by his ever-perfect mother, who neatly dressed him in pressed new clothing before letting him leave the house. And if those weren't high enough hurdles in a neighborhood of barefoot louts in ragged shorts and T-shirts, Mikey had the misfortune of living next door to the neighborhood curmudgeon, Old Man Niedermeyer.

Late afternoon and most evenings would find David forced to practice piano while the other four of us played tag football on the asphalt circle at the end of our street, Belmont Place. It was our four against the rival gang from Sandalwood Court, or sometimes the toughs from Banyan Place. I wasn't as good at catching the football as Tony, so I wound up quarterbacking while Mikey and Dennis defended the line. At times we had a small audience: my two sisters on our home's tiny oval of Dichondra, the reclusive spinster across the street peeking through her curtains, Mikey's mom inspecting us through their upstairs window, and, without fail, Old Man Niedermeyer. His home was at the eastern curve of the cul-de-sac and from his porch he could see all the way down Belmont Place to Whittier Drive. He was a retired Orange County sheriff and, before that, a Marine. We knew this because the rear window of his blue-and-white 1958 Oldsmobile had been taken over by a menacing skull, with rifles for crossed bones and USMC slogans emblazoned across the top — DEATH BEFORE DISHONOR paired with SEMPER FI.

Niedermeyer was probably a fit man at one time, but he'd long ago fallen into disrepair. His enormous pear-shaped midsection folded over his belt and hung down like a drape. He was large enough to have difficulty walking, forced to swing each leg out before planting his foot down with a thud. But he could move with surprising agility when the situation called for it. If one of our footballs landed on his cactus-ringed property, the unlucky retriever had to be quick or risk that mountain of a man's iron grip and punishment: a phone call to his parents or Niedermeyer's buddies at the sheriff's department. Worse was when the ball landed close to him. If he got it first that was the end of the game. I don't know how many balls he collected over the years, but he certainly had an easy dozen.

Niedermeyer was the target of a great deal of mischief and retribution from our little gang: toilet paper rolls decorating his prized trees, burning paper bags of dog shit on his porch, and always the easy favorite: the doorbell ring and a quick dash for safety. I had never bothered much with him, personally: he'd never caught me in his yard and I'd always managed to escape before the sheriff's arrival. But it wasn't like that for Mikey. He had been marched home by the old man more than a few times, where his father would beat him within an inch of his life. Mikey always talked of revenge but never did anything about it, until one late summer's evening Tony told him to "put up or shut up." I could see Mikey biting his lower lip, holding back tears at the challenge.

"You gonna start crying?" Tony tormented.

I felt sorry for him. Mikey stuttered when he got anxious and that made it all the worse. The other boys would copy his halting speech until Mikey fled for home. I didn't want that to happen again.

5

"Let's egg the old man's house tonight," I proposed.

Egging someone's house was standard practice, especially on Halloween. Each kid would pocket a few eggs from the fridge and together we'd launch a fusillade attack on windows and the front door. But this would be different. I could see Mikey's spirits rise at the thought of laying waste to Old Man Niedermeyer's house, so I wanted to make this the crime of the summer—perhaps the century—a feat that would become neighborhood legend. Instead of pilfering a few eggs from our parents I told the bunch we'd raid Wright's Egg Ranch and fill a shopping bag full. It was a brilliant plan, one that was audacious enough to extract revenge for Mikey and fame for me.

Wright's Egg Ranch was south of us on La Palma Avenue. It was a big place, with row upon row of caged chickens. Most people would visit Wright's through the small retail store in the front, but enterprising young thugs like us could hop a fence and get what we wanted. It was dark and moonless at 9 pm and just a little cold, as it gets near the first of September. The crickets' chorus had slowed due to the chill, but still their million-voice symphony accompanied the stealthy march of we four rogues. I was the first over the fence, so the others hid as I surveyed the scene.

"Come on over," I whispered.

We stalked the darkened rows of cages as quietly as we could, but those chickens seemed easily awakened: their wings flapped and their beaks broadcast scolding squawks as we lifted egg after egg, filling our Alpha Beta shopping bag full. By the time we had gotten to the far end of the row—closest to the Wright's home—our eyes had adjusted so we could see by the swath of bright stars clustered in the Milky Way.

Mikey tapped me on the shoulder. "Let's go, we have enough." I could tell he was scared. I didn't see Tony, but Dennis nodded too. None of us had ever tried anything this daring.

"Shhhh," I cautioned, and motioned with the crook of my finger for the troop to make our exit.

Suddenly the entire chicken yard burst into noise: cackling and feathers flying everywhere. I spun around to see that Tony had thrown one of the eggs at a chicken and was preparing a full barrage. I grabbed his arm and pulled him close.

"Are you nuts?"

Tony broke away and started running back towards the fence, peppering chickens with their eggs, and soon the whole place sounded like an angry mob. The idiot.

"Who the hell's out there?" bellowed a voice just behind us.

It was Mr. Wright. The sudden lights blinded us as we ran for our lives.

"Stop, you little thieves!"

I stumbled into Mikey, who had been running as fast as he could with the bag of eggs. He fell, and his face plowed straight into the yolks of a hundred eggs. I grabbed him by the shirt collar and we sprinted to the fence amidst the cackles and cries of hundreds of agitated chickens, just as Mr. Wright was about to play his trump card.

"Stop or I'll shoot!" he ordered.

Shoot? A gun? Jesus. I considered for the smallest instant following his orders and raising my hands in surrender, but that fence was now within sight. The hell we'd pay for getting caught stealing eggs was too much, and it was every man for himself. Tony and Dennis had already hurdled the fence, so Mikey and I vaulted ourselves as high as we could before tumbling over that barrier head first. I felt the hot searing pain in my legs and butt before I heard the retort of the shotgun. He had shot us, just as promised. Another BOOM! echoed just as we landed on the other side. I could hear Mr. Wright running towards us; soon we'd be back in shotgun range. My legs and butt felt on fire, but I could still run. Was I dying? Bleeding to death? It didn't seem to matter right then, all I could think of was getting away. I felt the back of my jeans once safely away from the egg ranch: sticky and matted with blood. I imagined a gaping flesh wound with spurts of pumping blood like I'd seen in the movies. Tony took a look at my backside after I pulled my pants down.

"Rock salt," he declared, then he and Dennis hightailed it back home.

We'd each told our parents we were spending the night at the others but now we'd need a new story. Dennis and Tony had gotten off without a scratch but Mikey and I were in rough shape. His face and clothing were covered in yellow goo and the back of his fresh-pressed jeans was peppered with holes and caked in blood. I felt awful but didn't know what to do, and figured for his safety he should just go home and get help. I told him my plan: throw my clothes in the trash, use the garden hose to wash out the salt still burning in my legs and butt, and hope not to get caught. Mikey couldn't manage that and 'fessed up to his father. We didn't see him back in the football game until the next summer.

My friends and I struggled with growing up, as I suppose all kids do. We did our best to not get caught for our mischief, and worked hard at elevating our social status at school, but that wasn't all we struggled with. Puberty made me one horny kid—an unfortunate fact when you're an insecure middle-school dork trying to move unnoticed into high school. I watched with envy as the suave guys coolly chatted up every starry-eyed girl in my class. How they managed such poise and confidence was a mystery to me: as soon as I got within ten feet of a pretty girl, my heart pounded, my face flushed, my ears burned, and my throat constricted. I was mortified by the thought they'd uncover my deepest desire: to discover the wonders of sex with them.

I could think of nothing else, and was almost certain that every cool guy and cute girl in my class were having wild sex all the time. By my senior year, in fact, I was convinced that I was the only virgin in my entire high school. The shame I felt of not connecting with girls haunted me, feeding my deepest fears and greatest anxieties. But I had other fantasies that kept my self-esteem from total collapse. Some days I felt deep in my inner being that I was somehow destined for something special—perhaps to be a leader or an inventor, some sort of innovator who might someday change the world—but when the daydreams snapped back to the present, I found my imagination never matched my reality. I was still an uncool kid without a direction or a girlfriend. Choosing a direction seemed important, but it was a distant second to my far more urgent lack of a girlfriend.

CHAPTER 2

IN MY SENIOR YEAR of Valencia High School, an aging collection of buildings near downtown Placentia built in 1933 by the WPA, I had fallen head over heels in love with the cute blonde girl who sat in front of me in science class. Robyn wore her hair in pigtails, secured each day with a different colored bow. Her high rosy cheeks were sprinkled with light brown freckles and her eyes twinkled sky blue. I had never been brave enough to say more than hello to her, but in my heart, I desperately wanted to put a going-steady ring on her finger, the kind wrapped in fluffy yarn. It wouldn't be easy because she liked another guy: Ernesto, a big hulking brute of a football player with slick, shiny black hair, and a blue-and-white '55 Chevy with chrome wheels. He was serious competition, yet there was a glimmer of hope: a lot of girls seemed to like Ernesto. In fact, each day a different girl would leave the school parking lot in his '55 Chevy — the warm California breezes fluttering their hair, music blaring from within, their elbows resting on the open window sills as if neither had a care in the world. Sure, I was jealous of Ernesto's prowess with women, but I was practical about it too. He wasn't a particularly good-looking guy, and certainly nowhere near as bright as I was, but he had two things I did not: confidence and a car. A car, I figured, would buy me the confidence I lacked and provide a reason for Robyn to like me. But, it couldn't be just any car. And it certainly couldn't be my parents' car — the dinky blue Chevy II mom car I learned to drive in — it had to be a real car. A man's car. A leader's car.

Soon enough she came into my life: a 1959 Austin-Healey 3000 red convertible. Her twin tailpipes gently curved upward, toward the trunk. She sat neglected in the far corner of a 20-car lot on Katella Avenue, near the Riverside Freeway. I had begged the salesman for a test drive, but was allowed only to hear the sound of her engine at the tap of the accelerator — a deep, throaty purr that charged me with anxious excitement. There wasn't much to the lot: a forgettable stretch of gray, cracked asphalt with a wooden shack at its center. Draped across the Healey was a fallen string of red-and-white triangular plastic flags, insulting her dignity. I lifted the flags from her once-white leather interior, now parched and cracked by Southern California's relentless sun, and pictured Robyn and me motoring down the highway together. The Healey was the perfect car—not an overcompensating muscle machine like Ernesto's, but a classy ride no one in my school could rival. Robyn, I figured, was a sophisticated lady, so when she saw my red sports car she'd surely fawn over me for a ride. No, this Austin-Healey would soon be mine. She had to be. She was my ticket to a girlfriend.

I knew the Healey had been mistreated and left alone to languish. Maybe it was her lack of a front bumper and passenger-side mirror, or her flat right-front tire. It could also have been her sun-bleached red paint with rusty spots of body cancer, or her persistently malfunctioning door handles, windows, electrical system, and convertible-top mechanism. Whatever the reason, she'd been sitting alone on that lot for months, maybe years, clearly waiting for one person: me. This gorgeous car had my name written all over it. I would make her mine at any cost. This car would *become* me, would define my life, and most importantly would attract the girls, the confidence, and the direction I lacked.

If I could land a job and save the $500 asking price, the Healey would have someone to take care of her and treat her like I knew she deserved— and in return, she would boost my standing in the world and fill that empty spot my teenaged soul yearned for. She was promised to me by Howard Sanders, owner and sole proprietor of Howard's Fine Cars. "No job? No problem!" read the sign in Howard's office window. He assured me that he was a man of his word.

"Look, son, when I say something's going to happen, you can bet your sweet ass it will. If you can scrape together the cash, the car's yours. I'll even throw in a full tank of gas and fix the flat tire. You just come up with that $500."

A sign reading "dishwasher wanted" hung inside the glass front door of a single-story structure of red brick and blue wood, topped with a white neon sign: carl's restaurant. This popular Anaheim drive-in and coffee shop with a full dining room was Carl Karcher's first restaurant, the precursor to his multimillion-dollar hamburger chain, Carl's Jr. The restaurant was close enough to home for me to ride my single-speed silver Schwinn there for the evening shift. I spent that summer washing dishes and saving up $500 for my Austin-Healey 3000. On my way to work and back, I'd stop by the car lot to check on her: broiling in the hot summer sun by day, with Howard's buzzing neon lights attracting millions of moths by night.

My last day at the restaurant, a Friday near the end of summer, ended with a particularly trying night. It was my job to empty the garbage into the alley dumpster, and that night it was already overflowing. Relieved that there was nowhere to dump the pails of burger slime, hamburger wrappers, and half-chewed French fries, I went to my manager, Duke. He was a heavyset, pimpled, knuckle-dragger just out of his teens, a toothpick permanently sticking out the side of his mouth.

"It's full," I reported, hoping to be given my final paycheck and sent home.

I followed him to the dumpster, where he pushed down some of the overflow and demonstrated that there was still plenty of room.

"You're not getting paid until the trash is emptied." The toothpick bobbed up and down to emphasize his point and he turned to go back inside. But a quiet exit was never enough for Duke. "Oh man, here it comes!" he announced. He raised his right leg, pulled down on an imaginary chain, and farted: loud, raspy, and liquid.

Priding myself on being clever, I determined to find a better way to empty that trash and get my last paycheck. My Austin-Healey was at stake, after all. I piled on the trash, then climbed the dumpster's greasy, corrugated-steel sides and balanced myself on one edge. The stench of rotting food and Carl's famous Thousand Island hamburger dressing was almost too much for me. I nearly threw up, but I was determined. *The car.* What horrors would I not face to acquire my scarlet beauty?

A cardboard carton lay atop the garbage. I flattened it, spread it over the mound of steaming trash, climbed as high as I could, balanced myself on the metal edge of that dumpster, and launched myself onto it. The cardboard collapsed and I plunged deep into the muck, sinking all the way to the bottom. My face was covered in a slime of rancid

11

hamburgers. I sputtered to breathe, spitting out a chunk of garbage I'd inhaled on the way down. But I couldn't move—the more I struggled, the deeper I sank. It was like quicksand. I thrust my arms over my head to clear an air passage and tried to swim out, but made no progress. I screamed for help again and again. No answer. My only audience was a brown-and-black cat on the cinder-block wall above me, nonchalantly swishing its tail.

"Get a grip on yourself, McGowan," I told myself. "Deep, slow breathing." Again I felt vomit pushing its way up my windpipe. I swallowed hard. More slowly this time, I inched my way to one side of the dumpster, wading through the wet, sticky trash. Finally, using all my strength, I was able to hoist myself out. I felt like crying. Reeking of trash, dripping with goo, I snuck back into the kitchen in hopes of making it to the bathroom before anyone saw me.

"What the hell happened to you?" Duke bellowed.

Before I had time to make up an answer, I realized that his question had drawn the attention of the entire kitchen. It might have been the gobs of Thousand Island dressing oozing down my face, or the French fries sticking out of my hair. Whatever it was, I can still hear the roar of laughter that erupted after I'd closed the bathroom door. I tried to stick my head under the faucet, but that turned out to be impossible—it was one of those low faucets close to the wash bowl. Nor was that the worst of it. The faucet was stingy and you had to keep pressing to get any water. Hopeless. By the end of my shift, my jeans and shirt had become stiff with dried mayonnaise, ketchup, coffee grounds, and God knows what else—but I had my final paycheck in my back pocket. I got on my bike and headed straight for my Healey.

A few minutes later, I propped my Schwinn against the pole that held up the sign for Howard's Fine Cars. Lit by the blinking red and yellow of that sign, the bike looked sad, as if it knew our partnership was at an end. Moths fluttered in the neon light, and I shooed them off the car. She was damp inside—the night air had condensed in sparkling drops on her black vinyl dash and white leather seats. I cleaned off Robyn's seat first like the proper gentleman I knew I would be, then tended to my own seat before sliding behind the massive steering wheel.

The knurled bumps for the driver's fingers—soon, *my* fingers—felt just right in my hands, ready to command the little two-door around curves. My left hand, still yellow from a mustard stain, clutched the steering wheel as I eased the stick, mock-shifting through the gears. "*Vroom, vroom,*" I mouthed. I jammed the gas pedal to the floor, expertly releasing the clutch with each shift. The tachometer, to the right of the steering shaft, would have been close to redlining, but I'd make sure it never went that far. I vowed to keep a careful eye on every one of my beauty's gauges. She'd never known the tender care I would lavish on her, but we'd bond soon enough. A lone set of headlights approached slowly. Cops! I ducked down, and they passed. No sense getting in trouble now. Tomorrow she'd be mine.

Howard was a man of his word. The right front tire got a new inner tube, and a makeshift mirror was attached to the empty stub on her right front fender. The black vinyl dash and the yellowing seats were clean and somehow shiny. Her windshield's pitted surface sparkled in the bright morning sun, and as I drove my beauty off the lot and into traffic, I honked her horn—how *British* she sounded: reserved, never overbearing. Unlike American horns, with their authoritative dual tones, hers was a single note, almost nasal but still classy—polite yet effective. She was mine now, and she purred contentedly as I revved her higher. I turned my head to hear her perfect pitch, to know when she wanted to be shifted. My hair fluttered in the warm California breeze. At last I was free, my own man. Nothing held me back now from calling Robyn for that date, except my lack of confidence. Perhaps a few weeks of driving my new car would build up my nerve. But for the moment one thing was for certain: I had a new love in my life, one I knew would be faithful even before we started going steady.

My car.

13

CHAPTER 3

IN THE ORANGE COUNTY of the early 1960s — before the concrete and asphalt devoured the orchards and strawberry fields, before the strip malls and fast food chains sprouted like weeds, before the air pollution got so bad that it was hard to see across the street and schools closed for smog alerts, and before skyrocketing property values choked the rural out of the land and made a mockery of the Orange in County — life seemed simpler. But for me that was little more than a respite, a brief lull in a life that would soon be yanked into the maelstrom of change already brewing in that decade. By the fall of 1966, I had somehow managed to rack up five big achievements: being the first kid in my high school's 35-year history to be thrown off Student Council for something besides academics, actually graduating from that same high school, building a hi-fi system that was the envy of my friends, buying a sports car, and not landing in jail.

Outside my world, though, the US was changing rapidly, and not always for the better. The nation was still reeling from President Kennedy's assassination three years earlier, and just a year before that, the Cuban Missile Crisis had brought the world to the brink of nuclear war. In elementary school, my classmates and I practiced ducking under desks and covering our heads to protect them from flying glass, just in case the Soviets decided to drop hydrogen bombs on Los Angeles. By the mid-60s the Cold War was in full swing, and ten years after the Korean War, America was itching for another fight. That itch was being scratched by deploying 385,000 US troops to a small Southeast Asian country we'd never heard of, to fight another proxy war between the US and USSR.

But in 1966, the distant Vietnam War didn't concern me: I was just an 18-year-old kid trying to find his way. One foot was still firmly planted in my parents' world, as the other groped for tenuous footing in an uncertain future. Music bridged those very different worlds. At home, my parents' music — Louis Prima, Keely Smith, Frank Sinatra, Sammy

Davis Jr., and Louis Armstrong—connected me with their generation. Outside, there was an entirely new world to explore: the Beatles, the Rolling Stones, Jefferson Airplane, and Jimi Hendrix would come to define my generation and start a revolution the world is still trying to figure out. Our elders hardly had time to catch their breath before the next wave of objectionable pop music invaded their status quo. But they weren't the only ones—I remember my grandmother Elsie's rants about the free-flowing music of the 1920s. Jazz to her generation was the devil's music—at the core of classical music's ruination—and central to the destruction of conventional white sensibilities. Music of the 1920s, with its undercurrents of racism and attacks on Victorian mores, was thought to be at the heart of society's collapse and the cause of scantily dressed women, blacks mingling with whites, drunkenness, smoking, whoring, infidelity, and the flouting of morals in the face of tradition.

By the fall of 1966 my love affair with the Austin-Healey hadn't dimmed, but it also hadn't resulted in a date with Robyn. I was just too afraid to pick up the phone and ask her out for a ride in my car. What if she said no? It was the thought of rejection I couldn't face. All my hopes and plans had centered around the car, in the hopes she'd ask me for a ride or it might somehow fortify my lagging self-confidence, and so far that hadn't worked. Perhaps Robyn was to blame. She was quite the popular girl, and though she always returned my smile when we passed each other in the park or at the pool that summer, she was never alone. Always there were others vying for her attention.

Undaunted, but disturbed, I contemplated my next moves. It was clear to me after graduating from high school that part of my failure to connect with willing females was that I lacked opportunities for meeting them. Outside of Robyn I really didn't know any other girls, and living at home wasn't exactly putting me in touch with anyone outside my tight little circle of friends. I'd need to find richer hunting grounds if I was to succeed. A solution to this problem—and to another, more pressing problem—soon emerged.

The military draft hung over my head. In those days, every 18-year-old male expected the dreaded letter from the local draft board. Three choices were offered: the Army, prison, or a college deferment. Only the last seemed a reasonable escape route, but even that looked to me like the same kind of prison high school had been—though with the upside of lots more girls. To get a draft deferment you had to be a full-time student, but there were few restrictions on what classes you took. Community college seemed to be the cheapest, easiest means of getting a student deferment.

I enrolled at Fullerton Junior College, a low-cost, 14-acre community college campus on the corner of Lemon Street and Chapman Avenue—the same school I knew Robyn had enrolled in. Like my home town of Anaheim, Fullerton was once an agricultural mecca, and its 22 square miles of orange groves formed the epicenter of production of the Valencia, the most popular juice orange in the world. In 1904 Fullerton had two dirt streets, train tracks running through its middle, and more orange groves than any other city in the US. Sixty-two years later, the only evidence of its agricultural past was the occasional orange, lemon, or avocado tree bristling with fruit in someone's backyard.

Tuition at FJC was free for Californians, so I stuffed my schedule with as many light courses as I could—photography, journalism, and radio—to get me to full-time status. Unlike high school teachers, though, my college professors didn't take attendance, so I could attend the classes I liked and not bother with the rest. It seemed that the only requirements for passing were occasional multiple-choice tests, which were pretty easy even when I didn't study. I wasn't interested in high marks; passing grades were enough to keep me out of the Army.

I set up my class schedule for three days a week: Monday, Wednesday, and Friday. Each morning at 9 am I vaulted over the still frozen shut Austin-Healey's door and into her seat. I loved the sound of that engine coughing to life. I'd mash the gas pedal to the floor when she was cold, crank it for no more than five seconds, then release the pedal. She was good to me, always faithfully firing up with that familiar *vroom* I so loved to hear. I felt a sense of power in that car's purr. In fact, our love affair had grown so deep that she actually began to define me. I was that car and always made a point of parking her where people could see the two of us. She was my best friend, my confidant, my alter ego.

16

As I put the Healey into reverse and adjusted the rearview mirror, I always hoped I'd see Robyn on the sidewalk near my home. I dreamed of offering her a ride, but so far it had never happened.

One morning as I motored to school down North Lemon—a pleasant twin-lane street that cut through the countless blocks of homes and side streets that make up Orange County—I saw flashing red lights in the rearview. Crap.

"License and registration please," said the Fullerton cop. He had a kindly, deep-lined face and sad eyes that made me wonder what pain he'd been through. He left me to sit as he sauntered back to his cruiser. I'd never been stopped before, and I gripped the wheel to calm my trembling. What had I done wrong? Other cars slowed as they passed, familiar faces turning to see if there'd been an accident.

The cop returned. "Your brake lights and taillights don't work." Thankfully, it was daytime, or he'd have noticed that my headlights didn't work, either. It was nothing more than a "fix-it" ticket—no fine, no punishment. All I had to do was get the lights fixed. I crumpled the piece of pink paper, tossed it into the passenger footwell, and continued to school. That was Monday.

On Wednesday, at the same spot on North Lemon, the same cop pulled me over again and wrote another ticket for the same violations. He remembered me from Monday, and this time his eyes weren't so sad.

"But I haven't fixed it yet. I get it—I don't need another reminder," I pleaded. "Just give me some time." It turned out that, when you got a fix-it ticket, you were supposed to stop driving that car until you'd had the problem fixed.

Friday: same place, same cop, same problem, same ticket. This time his eyes displayed disgust; his pursed lips and shaking head told the rest of the story. Had I been as smart as I thought I was, I'd simply have driven down the next street over. Somehow it never occurred to me to just get the lights fixed. But now it had become a sort of game: me vs. cop. Over the next few weeks the passenger footwell filled with balls of crumpled pink paper.

I had bigger worries than those fix-it tickets: I still couldn't hook up with women, even though there were plenty to choose from at school.

17

My angst of rejection was so crippling that I feared I might never meet a willing female. But then something changed—I realized it was me that was the problem, not the availability of women. This depressing revelation sent me right back to the start of my love quest and to Robyn, who still smiled at me whenever we passed each other on campus. I determined to call her and ask for a date, but every time I picked up the phone to dial her number my fingers froze. Once I even got as far as her phone ringing, but when her father answered I slammed down the receiver, terrified of going any further. I just could not force myself to do this. In desperation I shared my frustrations with my best friend, David, who suggested an audacious plan. If I was too afraid to ask Robyn for a date, why couldn't he impersonate me and ask her out? Our voices were close and she'd never talked to me on the phone. The plan had merit.

It was a Monday night in December. The Southern California cool was settling in from an offshore cloud bank, but I couldn't be bothered with the chill as David and I walked the last few steps to my front door. This was to be the moment of reckoning. David picked up the phone in my father's basement office and closed the door behind him. I placed my ear to the door to hear his muffled laugh, his suave sounding banter, his confident demeanor. He was everything I was not, but at least he could do a passable impersonation of my voice. At last I heard the phone's handset lock into its cradle.

"Well?" I asked, almost wishing I hadn't. "How did I do?"

"You did great. You're taking her to the drive-in theater Saturday night."

I had a date with Robyn. She had said yes to me, or at least she thought she had. Whatever. Saturday couldn't come soon enough.

Two days later, on Wednesday, my world suddenly turned upside down: my mother Sue was presented with a warrant for my arrest. I never had followed up on all those tickets, so now I had to face the consequences. I was ordered to appear in court on Friday.

I was still living at home, where my father, Don, ruled the McGowan clan with an iron fist. Dad, a ruggedly handsome man of Scottish descent, was just under six feet tall and of medium build. He had slicked-back hair, bespectacled green eyes, a serious demeanor that could instantly

18

turn to a salesman's practiced smile when it suited him, a trace of scarring on his forehead from a bout with chicken pox, and an ever-present briarwood pipe. But what I remember most was his mood swings. Dad was a manic-depressive who smoothed out life's bumps and dips with alcohol. I rarely knew which father I was addressing: Normal Don—just Dad? Or the brilliant, obsessed man who sometimes compared himself to Jesus? Or the depressed, angry victim everyone took advantage of? That afternoon it was Dad Number Three, who offered me three choices: fix the car, sell the car, or move out of the house—"today."

This was an absolute disaster. Without that Austin-Healey I was nothing. She was all I clung to, my thin lifeline of confidence for my upcoming date with Robyn. Was I supposed to show up at Robyn's house in mom's tiny blue Chevy II? I was nervous enough as it was to go on this date—living the lie that had gotten her to say yes in the first place—but at least I had my sports car to bolster my image. I had no money to fix the car, Dad's demands were pretty clear and not worth testing. I had experimented with his resolve before. Not more than a year ago, following his edict I get a job and start paying room and board, I declared I was leaving home and defiantly packed my suitcase. Dad asked for my key and promptly locked me out of the house for the weekend. He was nothing if not a man of his word.

Depression set in as I made my decision. It tore my heart out to sell my beauty back to Howard for $100 cash, but I did. I handed him the silver ignition key and watched in disbelief as one of his mechanics, a pimple-faced kid younger than me, ground her gears and killed the engine trying to get her to move. I wanted to yank him out of the driver's seat and show him how to be gentle with her, but I bit my lip instead. She was no longer mine.

My mother promptly relieved me of my $100 windfall to cover some money I'd borrowed from her. I refused her kind offer of a ride and walked home from Howard's, past the offices of the Anaheim Bulletin, where I'd worked for two summers and one winter as a cub reporter and photographer and given an assignment that nearly got me locked up. Two years earlier, I had been detained by the Secret Service as a possible threat to presidential candidate Barry Goldwater, after I had scaled the

19

12-foot tall security wall of the Balboa Bay Club to get close enough to snap his picture for the paper. It was there, in front of the newspaper offices, that I stopped and wept in the cool California December. I'd worked so hard to get here, to buy my car, to become the man I always knew I could be—to get a date with Robyn. As I walked home, shoulders slumped, some kids I recognized from high school passed me in their cool cars and honked. I felt mortified. Instead of being a part of the in crowd in my stately sports car, I was alone, dejected, and miserable. I felt ruined, defeated. And what of my date with Robyn on Saturday? I shuddered to even imagine how that would go, what I would say to her, how I would act.

The only cool thing left in my life was my hi-fi. At least I still had that. It was a beauty of a system, and the envy of my friends—especially David, who coveted that audio system. I'd built it myself from scratch, from pieces discarded from my father's do-it-yourself hi-fi. It was my magnum opus: a single cabinet that stood about four feet tall, and 20 inches wide and deep. On top was mounted a turntable I'd lovingly resurrected from Dad's junk pile, and below that was an old Fisher 500 receiver. Its scratched, gold-painted faceplate was peeling, and the tuner didn't work (though the dial lit up), but miraculously, the phono amplifier sounded fine after I replaced the tubes. Farther down the plywood tower was the best part, hidden by a grille cloth cut from an old set of yellow curtains Mom had retired: an 8-inch woofer with a whizzer cone. A woofer is the drive unit that makes bass and, in this case, midrange sounds as well; the whizzer cone—a small, funnel-shaped paper add-on to the center of the woofer—helped reproduce the higher frequencies, such as those produced by snare drums and cymbals. I'd found the speaker in Dad's shop. Although its paper cone had a large rip in it and the whizzer needed repair, some rubber cement and patience put that beauty back together again. Few kids my age had a sound system, and certainly none had one as cool as mine.

After losing the car that afternoon, I locked my bedroom door and curled up in a fetal ball—like a turtle in his protective shell. My only solace was my hi-fi system with the music cranked up: Hendrix, Beatles, Jefferson Airplane. That music system was all I had left and I listened

20

into the wee hours of the night, quietly enough not to wake the family. Safe in my protective shell.

The next day, Dad and I went to the Orange County Courthouse, in Santa Ana. Dressed in my best pants and a pressed shirt, I waited for an hour as criminal after criminal was sentenced to jail terms of various lengths. Their heads were bowed, their eyes glued to the floor, their shoulders drooped—I felt sorry for them as they were handcuffed, then led from the courtroom through a side door.

"Paul McGowan," droned the clerk. She wore pointy tortoiseshell glasses that hung halfway down her nose and were secured by a gold chain. "Fourteen vehicle violations and failure to appear."

"How do you plead?" asked the judge, peering over his own glasses.

"Innocent, I suppose," I said, pulling the Austin-Healey's bill of sale from my pocket and walking to the bench. "The car's been sold, so the question is moot."

He glanced at the document, then looked up. "And of the failures to appear?"

"I didn't know any better, Your Honor. My apologies."

"Then you plead guilty?"

"No sir, I plead ignorance."

"Not in my court," he barked. "Two hundred and fifty dollars or fourteen days in jail."

"I'll take the $250." I was directed to the bailiff, a short, stocky, balding man sitting behind a desk.

"We only take cash," he said.

I looked up at my father, who shook his head. Then, without a word, he turned and walked out of the courtroom. He was just gone. I stood there in disbelief unsure what to do.

"Do you have money?" droned the bailiff.

And that's when it hit me I was going to jail. Me. Paul McGowan, a jailbird abandoned by my family and left to rot like the dozens of others I had just watched led off to the gallows. The bailiff signaled for the other cop to handcuff me. I made one last scan of the courtroom in the hopes my father had changed his mind, but he was nowhere to be seen. I was marched off through the same door that had swallowed

21

all the other criminals before me. How would I ever explain this to Robyn? I couldn't call her, and even if I could, what would I say? That I was standing her up on our first date, because I was too busy being hauled off to jail?

The handcuffs hurt, but standing buck-naked, my arms above my head and my feet spread wide, being sprayed down for lice with a garden insecticide sprayer, hurt worse. I opened my eyes when the spraying stopped to face the intense stare of the man wielding that spray gun. Those eyes told a story I did not want to know as I remained stark naked and spread-eagled, arms raised over my head as he inspected his work longer than needed, hovering near my privates. The eyes may never lie, but it was his lecherous smile I'll never forget. I was the only middle-class white boy in a cell of 15 men. A few looked tough, eyeing me as if planning I don't know what. The others just looked scared, like me. I didn't sleep that night, and was relieved to be taken the next day to the Orange County Jail, where I was outfitted with an orange jumpsuit that smelled like Duke had farted in it, then marched off to a thick metal door with a tiny window in it. Behind the door was a small room with two beds. A single, bare 60-watt bulb on the ceiling provided the only light. In the corner was a metal toilet and washbasin and, along one wall, a metal bunk bed with the thinnest mattress I'd ever seen. Rolled up on one end of the mattress was an army-green wool blanket, and on top of that a yellow-stained gray pillow without a case. I shuddered to think where the stains had come from in this all-male facility.

To a young guy, two weeks behind bars seems like a lifetime. I'd watched old black-and-white prison movies like *The Last Gangster*, with Edward G. Robinson. This was no movie. There was nothing to do but sit on the bed in the little room and try to talk to my cellmate Julio. Just bordering on 17 years old, he had been here before for breaking and entering, a crime for which he claimed innocence. He said it was all just a misunderstanding—a bad rap. His story seemed real enough to me. This time, however, things were worse for him: he'd gotten a job at a gas station, and the owner had caught him stealing from the till. I felt sorry for Julio. He'd had a tough family life: his father left early, and his mother hooked up with a string of men who didn't treat her well. He said he'd had to stand up to them to protect his mother, but now he was out on his own and feared for her safety. The best I could offer him, to show I understood, was tales of my own criminal behavior.

I couldn't have been more than ten years old when Dad decided he wanted to assemble a lie-detector kit. In those days, Heathkit and Eico were the big makers of electronics kits; customers could choose projects to build from their thick catalogs of cool gear. The parts for the lie detector came, and I watched as Dad assembled the case and soldered the parts to the perforated circuit board. He patiently explained to me how it worked by conductivity, measured by a meter on the front panel. The accused would grasp two metal bars, each attached to a wire plugged into the front of the detector, just below the meter. When someone lies, he told me, his heart rate increases and he starts to sweat. The small voltage present on the metal bars would grow stronger with the increased moisture, moving the meter's needle from the green Truth zone into the red Lie zone. I eagerly absorbed this technical information. But when he'd finished assembling the kit, Dad needed to find someone he thought might have something worth lying about, and given my past crimes he knew I was the most likely target in the McGowan household. He didn't have to wait long.

For months I had been making a habit of nicking quarters, dimes, and nickels from my father's dresser, which I then spent on gum and candy. One Saturday afternoon, Dad gathered my sisters and me together. He'd long suspected there was a thief in the house, and over the last few days he'd laid a trap by counting his change. All three McGowan kids were practiced in the art of lying to our parents. After all, if any one of us committed a crime, even a full confession wouldn't prevent us from being punished. Instead, our parents would commend us for our brave truth-telling, then haul us upstairs for a beating anyway: the belt for me, a hairbrush for my sisters.

Dad grilled all three of us about the change missing from his dresser, but when no one 'fessed up he looked straight at me, smiled, then headed to the basement to set up the lie detector. I hurried in the opposite

23

direction, heading for the paint shed outside the garage. I knew the lie detector could detect sweat, so I quickly spread varnish on my hands, then blew on them as hard as I could to dry them before he'd finished setting up the detector.

Dad began the interrogations with me, but the needle remained limply in the green Truth zone. Certain I was the culprit, he was dumbfounded. Next up was the middle child, Sharane, who moved the needle toward the red Lie zone—but in the green it stayed. My innocent little sister, Bobbi, was so scared she was sobbing, her hands wet with tears. You can imagine how hard the needle pegged into the red. Poor kid. My instinct was to own up to the whole thing so she wouldn't swing for my crime, but I knew my father would have beaten me twice as hard: once for the theft, and again for the deception. It was too much, and I was too afraid of him. I reasoned he'd go easy on her, which he did, but the guilt I still feel for my cowardice wasn't worth dodging the belt. To this day, I don't think Bobbi has fully forgiven me.

My story got a laugh out of Julio. When we were released from our cell to stand in line at the cafeteria, he introduced me to his friends as one of the good guys. Three days later, the jailer told me I was to be released. Of course, I thought—my loving mother had come to my rescue.

But she hadn't. There, waiting for me, was David who had covered for me with Robyn. After hearing of my plight he'd again called her and offered my apologies for having to cancel, but at least I was off the hook. He then informed me that he'd paid the remaining $200 fine, and that the price for all his help was my beloved hi-fi system. He'd always lusted after that sound system. It was all I had left in the world and once David demanded his ransom, I was back to having nothing, just like everyone else.

CHAPTER 4

WITHOUT CAR, HI-FI, OR GIRLFRIEND, I was in a pretty low state; it was a struggle just getting back and forth to Fullerton for the few classes I was taking—a risky move since only full-time students were exempt from the draft. But, I figured, I had better things to do than sit bored in too many classes. My terror of the draft seemed to fade into the distance as those seemingly faraway events tend to do; I vaguely hoped my name would be lost in the government shuffle.

With my girlfriend acquisition project on hold for the moment, my empire-building fantasies took center stage. They were never small and almost always audacious: big, boundless dreams of someday making a dent in the universe. Defeating gravity or discovering a new source of energy interested me as much as building a company with thousands of employees or running for President of the United States. But the older I got the more practical my dreams became, which was a good thing because nobody benefits from living in a dream world forever. At some point, your dreams morph into reality by scaling down to the point of attainability. One of my almost-down-to-earth long-term fantasies was to be a famous Hollywood disc jockey with millions of adoring fans and hundreds of fawning females. Yup, this was a persistent one, and it certainly seemed more likely than getting elected president, let alone competing with the likes of Albert Einstein to figure out how gravity really worked.

In the 1960s and '70s, radio DJs were like rock stars, only more powerful; choosing which records to play on the air could make or break a band. The competition to become a rock 'n' roll DJ was fierce, but I was determined to break through those barriers. I knew it would take a lot of work and training, so all through my senior year of high school I spent hours polishing my diction in front of a mirror, and even set up a little homemade DJ studio that broadcast through my hi-fi speakers. I mouthed excited intros to music I heard on the radio, timing my words perfectly to hit "the mark"—the moment the song's intro ended and the singing began.

Few things occupied more of my time than preparing to become a DJ. Polishing my vocal delivery and honing my musical knowledge were only the first steps in achieving my dream of broadcasting to thousands of radio listeners in Orange County, and someday to millions in Los Angeles. First, there was the small task of getting hired—the rest would then fall into place. Fame, I figured, would buy me courage, and get me in the winner's circle. Unfortunately, becoming a DJ wasn't as easy as I'd imagined it would be. Radio stations insisted on an audition tape accompanied by proof of experience. It was a classic catch-22: I couldn't get hired without experience, and I couldn't get experience without getting hired.

My college offered a class in radio broadcasting, which I signed up to take as soon as I enrolled at FJC. The college station was run by Mr. Thompson, a generously proportioned man not much taller than 5 feet. Physically, even Mother Goose would mistake him for Humpty Dumpty, though the similarities ended there. Instead of being a happy egg, Mr. Thompson was gruff with constantly furrowed brows and a twisted scowl of a mouth. I had always assumed he was mistreated as a child or that his wife didn't like him, but more likely the class rumor mill had it right: he was a failed disc jockey who fell into teaching as a last resort. Whatever the truth, Mr. Thompson never let us forget that he was in charge of the Radio Class and we were all lucky to be in it. To his credit, there wasn't one empty seat.

When I registered for Radio Class that spring, it was with the express idea of getting on-air broadcast time. This would be the perfect start to my radio career: with a few years of actual on-air experience and an armful of audition tapes to prove it, I would be well on my way to realizing my dream of building an audience of millions. I just needed that chance at a live microphone, so I would work out the inevitable nervous jitters and hone my craft. I pictured hundreds, if not thousands, of FJC students lounging on the school's grass or gathering in the Student Center patio with their portable radios tuned to my program. I was excited for that first day in Mr. Thompson's class.

26

Radio Class met in a large room featuring 30 desks, lined up in orderly rows facing an elevated, windowed broadcast studio. At first glance this was everything I had hoped for: microphones, turntables, control board, headphones, and a studio monitor—all the equipment you'd want in a radio station. Only one thing was missing: the radio station itself. It turned out that there was no broadcasting transmitter. Instead, aspiring DJs played their tunes and practiced their craft through a loudspeaker playing into the classroom. Worse, there was only one studio and four hours of class time per week. With 30 students, none of us had much hope of extended studio time.

I was miffed by this unexpected turn of events, so a week into the semester I knocked on Mr. Thompson's office door to discuss the situation. "Come in!" he barked.

"I am sorry to bother you, but perhaps I signed up for the wrong class?" I looked around his cramped office for a chair, but there was only room to stand.

Thompson's cold black eyes squinted at me through a forest of papers and books on his cluttered desk. He didn't say a word. His narrowed bushy black brows and tightly scrunched lips said it all.

"I, uh ... I was hoping to get on-air experience. Seems there's only a speaker to play into the class."

"There is no station here," he finally replied, venom dripping from every word. His voice was somehow too deep for his body. "I've been trying for years to get the school to fund a live broadcast station but there's no money. There's a broadcast speaker for your on-air experience and an audience in the class. Take it or leave it."

So that was it. The school didn't have a station and its only class in the broadcasting arts was a grim joke, run by a disgruntled teacher. As far as I was concerned this was a dead-end street, one I'd have to figure a way around if I was to ever close in on my goal of getting in front of millions. For now, I had little choice but to suck it up and attend Mr. Thompson's poor excuse for a broadcasting facility.

Over the next few months I attended class religiously, hoping my assessment was wrong, but the longer I attended the more convinced I became that Radio Class was for losers. One kid was so nervous when he cracked open the microphone for the first time that he froze and stopped breathing. All we heard through the classroom loudspeaker was a gurgling sound, as if he were trying to force out a piece of unchewed chicken caught in his throat. Mr. Thompson lumbered out of his chair, put his face and meaty hands on the studio window, and pounded on the glass for the kid's attention. Unfortunately, it had the opposite effect: instead of snapping out of his fright the lad locked eyes with Thompson through the glass, pleading silently for help as the rest of the class erupted in laughter. I felt badly for him but hadn't a clue what to do.

"Out!" cried Thompson to the boy through the window. "Get out of my studio!"

My new friends in class, Ed and Bill—both second-year veterans of Mr. Thompson's course—came to the rescue. As Thompson mashed his angry face against the window, jabbing his finger into the glass to punctuate his demand, Ed and Bill calmly opened the booth's door, helped the student down the two studio steps, and led him out into the hall to calm him down.

"Who's next?" bellowed Thompson, glaring directly at me. His eyes scrolled down the class seating list. "McGowan," he announced, devouring the moment like a tomcat biting into a squirming sparrow. "Let's see how you do on the air."

'On the air' was Thompson's euphemism for the loudspeaker—the students called it his speaker, but never to his face. I had guessed early on that loudspeaker was a point of serious disappointment for Mr. Thompson. Cal State Fullerton, the competing state college just down the road, had a real radio station and I had always assumed that rankled him to the point of bitterness. It certainly was a sensitive enough point that he required everyone in the class to refer to studio work as an "on-the-air performance."

Still, it was finally my turn in the booth. I loaded the two turntables with tracks of music, each cued up and ready to go on Mr. Thompson's signal—a scowl followed by upturned hands asking "well, what are you waiting for?" There wasn't the best selection of music in the station's small library, mostly Thompson's favorites from a bygone era: Louis Prima, Frank Sinatra, and mercifully, a few Beatles albums. I had practiced being

28

a DJ for a couple of years in the mirror and with my home broadcast studio, so going live on Thompson's speaker was no big deal—something that I believe angered him. He would have relished watching me squirm and freeze up like the last kid, but I offered him no satisfaction. Something in his eyes told me he had it out for me.

Weeks went by, and I soon learned that Ed and Bill shared my frustration with the hopelessness of the situation. Bill was a journalism major who wanted to be a DJ as badly as I did, and Ed was an electrical engineering geek with the same aspirations. Rather than throwing in the towel and accepting Mr. Thompson's class as our only alternative to fame, we decided to circumvent the system. If Mr. Thompson couldn't get the school to fund a radio station for him, maybe we could build it ourselves. Within days we hatched a plan to approach the Fullerton Junior College administration about starting a campus radio station. A real station.

Fullerton JC occupied a typical California campus of one-story buildings, loosely connected by sidewalks and strips of grass and decorated with orderly rows of institutionally landscaped planters. At the center of the campus was the William Boyce Library, a beige, one-story cement building that looked like a department store. Shading the library's main entrance was a small portico, supported on the right by a red brick wall festooned with flyers and posters, and on the left by a stucco wall with a scrawny ivy vine trying to climb up it. In this utilitarian building, the school regents met once a month to consider student requests. To be awarded a slot at the regents' speaking platform, we had to petition the office of the college president.

This tedious process began at the desk of the president's secretary, Mrs. Hayworth, a bored-looking middle-aged woman who'd probably heard every story and seen every sort of student malarkey. Once past her desk, a written request would rise through several more levels of bureaucracy until, at last, it wound up—round robin style—back on that same desk for one last approval. A week after we first approached her, we were granted permission to enter the library's windowed conference room, where three dark-suited men heard one student petition after another. Some wanted new classes added, while others petitioned the

29

board to let them form a club or society on campus: the Spanish Club, the Art Society, the Chess Group, or even Students Opposing the War.

Our proposal to build a student-funded campus radio station was something they'd never heard before. I was the point man for the pitch, and explained to the regents how other schools, such as Fullerton State College, had an actual radio station but our fine institution did not. FJC was missing out, I told the group. A campus radio station would put community and the school first, announcing class schedules, promoting school events, and keeping FJC students in the know. This part of the pitch we had little intention of honoring—all we really wanted to do was play rock 'n' roll music—but I figured they'd be hard-pressed to turn us down. Besides, we were offering to fund it ourselves. With only a minimum of discussion, and a footnote for Mrs. Hayworth to ask Mr. Thompson what he thought, the regents tentatively agreed to give us a room in the Student Center for broadcasting, so long as we supplied all the equipment and obtained a broadcast license from the Federal Communications Commission.

That sounded simple enough. Ed had already built an AM transmitter that used a Sears guitar amplifier as its front end and a single big vacuum tube for its output. I knew enough electronics from my stereo-building days to construct a control board with turntables and a microphone. We were ready to go, except for that pesky FCC license.

The regional Federal Communications office was located in an imposing, cement-gray, multi-story government building in downtown Santa Ana, the seat of government for the 34 cities of Orange County. Other than my tangle with the courthouse just down the street, and my resulting three days in county jail, I'd never had to deal with government, so I figured it would be a snap to fill out some forms and get a broadcast license.

Two weeks and five visits to the FCC later, Bill and I were getting discouraged. Instead of government making our lives easier and handing out commercial broadcasting licenses to aspiring station owners like us, they wanted large sums of money just for the application. To make matters worse, we hardly got past the yawning receptionist, who eyed our youthful appearance and lack of credentials with disgust, and suggested we have our attorney contact the FCC to apply for the license. Our attorney?

Just when we were about to give up, I had an idea. On our last visit to the FCC, we'd managed to score an audience with a staff engineer named Milton Answorth—a short, balding, scarecrow-skinny, bespectacled man with a nervous tic in his right eye that I couldn't stop staring at. Hats in hand, Bill and I pestered a younger version of the first receptionist for another meeting with this engineer. Though she seemed more interested in chewing a piece of gum than in dealing with us, she relented and we were allowed to meet with Milton one last time.

Milton hardly remembered our previous visit, but he ushered us into his cramped office. After reminding him of our quest for a broadcast license, I waved my hands at the endless volumes of rules and regulations that lined one wall of the room. "What kind of broadcast license could we get without all of that?" I asked. Milton's right eye disappeared and reappeared several times before he pulled from the shelf a thick Britannica-like book covered in blue vinyl. He thumbed through the pages until he found what he was looking for, then pointed to a paragraph. "That kind."

It was a license for a low-power signal—about a quarter of a watt—with a broadcast radius of less than 20 feet. Ed's transmitter was a thousand times more powerful and could easily cover more than a mile. Clearly, using it would be illegal, but mere technicalities had never stopped me before. Besides, who was going to check up on us? The college regents?

"Can you make a copy of this license and sign it for us?" I asked.

"Sure," Milton said.

Damned if we didn't have an official-looking FCC license. There, next to the standard bearing FCC seal of red, yellow, white and blue, featuring an eagle grasping lightning bolts in its talons, soaring above twin transmitter towers, was scribbled "Milton Answorth, FCC Engineer." We were counting on it looking just official enough to bamboozle college administrators, who, we were sure, wouldn't know one transmitter level from another. The only danger would be Mr. Thompson, who might spot the phony license if he had enough engineering knowledge. With fingers crossed and hopes high, we returned to the regents with all the necessary paperwork. Everything hinged on Mr. Thompson and the regents not knowing the technical details of what they were looking at.

They didn't. Near the end of the 1968 school year, we launched KFJC with 250 watts of AM power at 95kHz, smack dab between the two most famous rock stations in Los Angeles, 93 KHJ and 98 KFWB. I had the honor of being first on the air at our new station, and the first record I played was the Hollies' "Bus Stop." I was officially a DJ. Live, on the air, not broadcasting through a damned loudspeaker.

As soon as KFJC went live, Ed, Bill and I—along with a handful of others in Mr. Thompson's radio course—stopped attending his biweekly class. Running a live radio broadcast from the Student Center from 7 am until 9 pm was far more exciting than playacting. And that was just the beginning of the exodus: within a few days his classroom was nearly empty, and we had a long waitlist of eager DJ candidates.

Our little studio was located in a windowed corner of the campus Student Center, in a small cubicle that used to serve as a ticket counter for live events. From the disc jockey's perch in front of my homemade plywood control board, on-air personalities could look out over the sunny courtyard and play to the students. Ed had fashioned a little outdoor speaker powered by a radio playing the station, and often small throngs of students crowded the glass for a look at us. We were stars as far as the students were concerned, but Mr. Thompson didn't buy it. He could often be seen lurking under a nearby eave, staring at the small station with a determined look on his face. More than once a cold shroud of dread flooded over me as I saw him in the shadows with his arms folded atop his belly, his dark eyes peering through bristly brows and narrowing towards the downward corners of his clenched lips. He was definitely out to get me, but so far nothing had happened and we were still on the air.

Ed, Bill, and I were worried. If Mr. Thompson somehow got hold of our station license and had enough engineering chops to figure out we'd pulled the wool over the regents' eyes, we'd be shut down or even wind up in jail. Illegally broadcasting on the commercial radio band was a violation of federal law, not to mention the fact that we intentionally defrauded the college. If they found out what really happened I could only imagine what they would do to us.

There were rumors spreading that Thompson was on the warpath, hell-bent on shutting down our little enterprise. He had been seen canvassing the school grounds with a transistor radio to check the station's range. We knew he wasn't an engineer, but he also wasn't an idiot. A one-quarter watt radio station was legal and we had an official FCC license to prove it. Our 250-watt station, however, was 1,000 times more powerful than legally permitted. The problem was coverage: if there was too much, Thompson could prove the discrepancy. Ed, our resident engineer, set out to measure the station's range. To our horror, he discovered that we were blanketing a good bit of the town of Fullerton. Something had to change, and fast. Ed's discovery came late on a Friday afternoon. By lunchtime Saturday he had detuned the transmitter to cover no more than the school parking lot — still illegal because we couldn't go more than 20 feet, but within the bounds of what we gambled would not get us caught. We wiped our collective brows, hoping we had caught the problem in time.

The following week was mercifully quiet, but then Friday rolled around. I had come in early, to tidy up the albums and check the control board, when I noticed a white van parked in the middle of the Student Center patio. This was odd because I had never seen a vehicle parked in the courtyard before. Even stranger was the set of ominous looking antennae perched atop the van's roof and the short, nearsighted wisp of a man holding a meter inches from his face. I was trying to figure out why he looked familiar when he turned and looked right at me. It was Milton from the FCC. A shot of raw adrenaline shot up my back and stood my hair on end. Jesus. I hightailed it to the bank of black pay telephones lined up along the Student Center wall and fumbled to insert a dime.

"Ed," I hissed. "The FCC is here, what do I do?"

"Pull the plug on the transmitter. Now!"

I dove under the station's counter holding up the control board, yanking out the AC plug on the Sears guitar amplifier that was acting as our modulator.

33

"What the…" cried the on-air jock, Randy, as the music ground to a sickening halt.

Next was the transmitter itself. As its one glowing yellow power tube dimmed, my pulse slowed enough to catch my breath. I promptly bonked my head on the counter, nearly knocking myself unconscious, but for the moment we were technically not illegal. I rubbed my bruised forehead and peeked out the window to see if Milton was still there.

He was, as was Mr. Thompson, along with the president of the college. The two were speaking quickly and gesticulating wildly, and Milton was scribbling something on his notepad. I knew the jig was up: our days as live broadcasters were at an end. I had been the mastermind behind the station, the point man, the one person they could easily pin the blame on. It would be me they'd come looking for, perhaps with another warrant for my arrest. Only this time, it wouldn't be the Orange County Jail. Visions of Leavenworth, Kansas flashed through my mind, but I had no intention of hanging around to find out what was going to happen. I snuck out the back of the Student Center, hopped in my car—now a beat-up blue and white 1955 Chevy four-door I had earned with weekends spent photographing weddings—and headed home, dreading what surely would come on Monday. That's when my whole world turned upside-down again. David Wiley was waiting for me at home, and as I drove up, he handed me a letter from the draft board, revoking my student deferment for lack of a full-time class schedule. He had received an identical letter.

"Pack your bags," he said. "We're going to Canada."

CHAPTER 5

BY THE MID-1960s, as the policing action in Vietnam heated up to a full-blown war, our country's northern border had become the accepted escape route for draft-dodging young American males. For a time it was easy to leave the States for Canada, until the influx became so great that the Canadian government began requiring proof of a US military discharge. That rule was eventually rescinded in May 1969, a year after my deferral was canceled, when Canadian immigration officials announced that they would no longer ask immigration applicants their military status if they showed up at the border. There's no official estimate of how many draft dodgers and deserters entered Canada during the Vietnam War, though unofficial estimates range from 30,000 to 40,000. In fact, in 1971 and 1972, Canada accepted more immigrants from the US than from any other country.

David's invitation to drop everything and flee the United States couldn't have come at a better time in my life: my radio station had just imploded, I was without a girlfriend, and living under my parents' roof, subject to all their rules, wasn't working for me. I was going nowhere fast and this trip felt like an open door into the future. That Saturday, I left home with ten bucks in my pocket, along with an Enco gas credit card "borrowed" from my mother. David and I loaded up my hoodless Chevy Bel Air with our few worldly possessions. At six that evening, we headed north on US Highway 101. Neither of us had said a word to anyone.

Once we hit the open road, we felt as if a weight was lifted from our sagging shoulders. The feds and the school might be hot on my trail, but I didn't care. I was on an adventure and would soon leave the United States behind. If they really wanted me they'd have to cross the border to get me. I was a desperado now: a free man heading north, out of harm's way. It felt exhilarating.

As the evening's twilight purple cooled the warm day, we sped up the 101, leaving downtown Los Angeles and passing cities like Thousand

Oaks and Woodland Hills, which then still resembled their names, before dropping down the steep Conejo Grade into Camarillo and getting our first view of the Central California coast. It was May 1968, a few days after my 20th birthday, and we rode with the windows down as far north as Santa Barbara, where we stopped for a tank of 38¢ a gallon gas. Neither of us had thought this trip through. Necessities like food, clean clothing, and shelter hadn't crossed our minds. Stuffed in the trunk and back seat was an odd collection of two teenage boys' meager possessions: my photo enlarger, two sets of clothing, David's electric piano, a few coats, shoes, an assortment of David's books, and a can opener. Between us, we had my mother's gas card and less than $30. It was 1,300 miles from Los Angeles to Vancouver, Canada. We would survive the first leg of our journey on boiled spaghetti noodles sauced with ketchup packets hijacked from fast-food restaurants.

By morning, we'd reached San Francisco's Golden Gate Park. It was a warm Sunday, and we found street parking near the corner of Haight and Ashbury streets. The buildings there were old wooden structures built in the late Victorian era, jammed together like dominos stood on end. On one corner was the Unique Men's Shop, which looked as if it once sold formal suits and hats; now there was only a "closed" sign. Everywhere we looked were kids our age sitting on the sidewalk, bobbing their heads to music or milling about aimlessly. There were guys in brightly colored shirts and strings of beads, their hair as long as a girl's. Braless women in see-through blouses wore laurels of flowers in their hair. Few wore shoes, and even fewer seemed to have bathed recently. The aromas of body odor, incense, and patchouli oil was as thick as the pot smoke permeating the air. Recorded music blared from open doors and live versions from street corner buskers. People played bells or tambourines on what seemed like every inch of sidewalk. As we stood in wonder, an endless parade of cars, VW vans, buses, motorcycles, bikes, and scooters inched by us on Haight Street, past the Boot Hook, The Bookstore Café, Loyal Liquors, The Juke Box, and so many hole-in-the-wall record stores I lost count.

We'd landed at the epicenter of one of the greatest countercultural revolutions the modern world has ever known. Though we were about a

36

year late for the Summer of Love, the streets were still filled with plenty of love and even more hippies. Dazed by the spectacle, we wandered the neighborhood for an hour. Then we became aware of a rising sound, like a distant chant at a football game. Drums and tambourines kept time as voices rose and fell, repeating an unintelligible phrase. The noise seemed to come from nearby Golden Gate Park, a place we'd wanted to visit anyway. We moved close enough to hear what was being chanted.

"The Dead! The Dead! The Dead!" shouted a ragtag scrum of shoeless longhairs heading for the park. Expecting to see a casket and funeral parade, we followed them to a narrow strip of grass called the Panhandle, where, to our surprise, a stage had been set up. A Sunday-afternoon concert in the park—cool! Apparently, there was a group with Dead in their name. I asked one glassy-gazed guy who was weaving back and forth who these Dead musicians were.

"Grateful, man...the Grateful Dead," he mumbled. He closed his bloodshot eyes.

Within an hour we were at the front of the stage, buried in a sea of undulating bodies. A girl with a red scarf and a necklace of wooden beads puked right in front of me, then lay on her back, her hair mired in vomit, fondling a flower and grinning insanely at the sky.

A tall, bearded guy on our right handed a joint to David, who took a long drag before handing it to me. I had never smoked pot, and nearly coughed up several pieces of my lung before handing it back. I had no idea what to expect. Friends had described hallucinations, monsters flying in the air—all the crazy stuff that, I learned later, loosely applied to LSD experiences. I felt nothing from that first hit.

When the Grateful Dead walked onstage, I was taken aback. The musicians looked as if they'd just walked out of the crowd. Instead of the matching suits and fancy getups I'd seen British Invasion bands wear on television, the Dead wore jeans and flowered shirts, and looked as if they might have just gotten out of bed. This was the most casual live act I'd ever witnessed—yet as soon as they started playing, I was entranced. First, a riff—just guitars. Then a harmonica entered. The crowd was already swaying. To my surprise, I realized they were playing an old blues song by Sonny Boy Williamson, "Good Morning Little School Girl."

I'd never heard such music. I was still in love with the Beatles' older songs, had dabbled in Jefferson Airplane, and was slowly getting used to *Sgt. Pepper's Lonely Hearts Club Band*. But this was different. There weren't any short hit songs with clearly defined beginnings and ends. And if I was befuddled by the nonstop progress of *Sgt. Pepper's*, in which each song flowed seamlessly into the next, these guys were taking it to a new level. When they got tired of playing one song, they'd start the next without so much as a break—long riffs of good music, like jazz.

I suddenly became aware of a gnawing in my stomach like I'd never known. I was ravenous, and my mouth was so dry I could hardly move my tongue. Had someone offered me lawn clippings, I think I might have happily eaten them. A young woman dressed like a gypsy, with hairy armpits and legs, spun and twirled to the music while holding a basket. She pirouetted her way down the space between me and the stage, handing out cookies and flowers. I passed on the flowers but took a cookie—two, actually. They were the best cookies I'd ever eaten.

Two hours later—or was it a lifetime?—the concert was over. All I could think about was sleep. David and I found a spot on a knoll in the park, propped ourselves against a tree, and passed out. When I awoke, it was dark, but the park wasn't deserted. Strange sounds came from all corners of the expanse of grass around us—hoots and howls like wolves on the loose, but clearly emanating from humans. It was the strangest night of my life. I'd spent nights outside before, camped out in my backyard or on the occasional camping trip with my family, but nothing like this. It felt as if we'd entered a strange jungle where alien creatures roamed, and God only knew what sorts of mischief they were up to. The distant scream of a girl—was that terror or a rave review? Unearthly chanting. Dogs barking, some howling. I shivered and started second-guessing my decision to leave home. Becoming a wanted desperado, fleeing the law, and escaping the mess I had created had all seemed so glorious at the time, but now I wasn't so sure. I thought about telling David I had changed my mind. It was a fun idea, but what the hell were we doing leaving the country? This seemed like madness. As I rolled around the options in my head, it felt like I was at the junction of two dead-end streets. The first was the Army. If I stayed anywhere in the United States I would eventually be drafted, a fate I was determined to avoid. If I returned home to regroup with a new plan I would likely be tossed in jail for violating federal law. At a minimum I'd be thrown out of school and would be forced to suffer the damnation—and domination—of my parents. Neither option seemed good. This was my big chance to escape: the Army, the feds, my parents, my mistakes. No, I decided, I was committed to a life on the lam. This was the new me, for better or for worse.

I fell asleep frightened. When the yellow glow of morning sparkled on the dew-soaked grass, David and I turned the car north and high-tailed it out of there.

Chapter 6

San Francisco, Geyserville, Cloverdale, Avenue of the Giants, the Russian River, the Columbia River Gorge—I had never seen such natural beauty. My experience of California had been disappearing orange groves and proliferating strip malls. The wildernesses of Northern California, Oregon, and Washington were revelations: redwood trees big enough to drive through; streams that were green, wet, robust, and full of life. We found apple trees and blueberry bushes along the highway and harvested more than we could eat, just for the joy of eating free fruit in a land of plenty.

Finally, we arrived in Bellingham, Washington, the Red Carpet City—the northernmost city in the contiguous United States, just 17 miles south of the Canadian border. We were soon to be in the real land of the free, with no draft hanging over our heads and no feds on our tail. I finally felt free and had gotten over my angst of leaving home. Adventure called and I was excited. As Bellingham disappeared in the rearview mirror, we saluted it with our middle fingers, mocking the homeland we were soon to leave. Before us, our new home beckoned: Canada.

I can only imagine what the Canadian border guards thought of us: two 20-year-old American males in a beat-up '55 Chevy with California plates and no hood. Everything we owned was in that car, with the trunk stuffed full and the back seat piled high enough to block our view out the rear window. The floor of the car had served as our trash can, and neither of us had showered in more than a week. The interview process didn't last long; within an hour, we were photographed, fingerprinted, and turned away.

Depressed, tired, hungry, and not sure what to do next, we dragged our tails back to Bellingham. A port city on Bellingham Bay, in the shadow of Mount Baker, Bellingham is both a ski destination and home to Western Washington State College. It's a quaint and quiet place whose economy back then was based on the college, ferry rides to the San Juan Islands, paper mills, and agricultural product processing, particularly frozen corn and berries.

It was raining when we arrived—as we were soon to find out, it always rained in Bellingham. The sky looked as gloomy as we felt. I had been driving as David struggled to open a can of kidney beans. We were stopped for a red light at the top of a hill, and I watched the rain splash against the street's gray cobblestones, small rivulets between the stones growing into curbside rivers. There was nothing exciting about this rain—no lightning, no bursts or dry spells, just constant, gray, unstoppable rain that lulled me into melancholy as we aimlessly chatted about our next moves. Out of nowhere, I heard an odd noise—a whirring sound I couldn't identify. I looked to my left and saw a powder-blue, big-finned, 1960 Chevy Impala skidding toward us over the cobblestones, the driver waving his hands in warning.

"Oh shit!" was all I had time to say before he crashed into our front fender, on the driver's side. We spun around and hit a street lamp, which crushed David's passenger side door and splattered red beans all over his face. My trusty '55 Chevy—our home—was done for, totaled. The other driver, another 20-year-old, was uninsured, but he offered to house and feed us. We took him up on the offer.

We hadn't anywhere else to go but Bellingham and so we decided to stay, at least until we could come up with new plans. Within a month's time we had rented a large, three-story Victorian house on Indian Street (with a promissory note to a hungry landlord) and become slum lords, renting rooms to students at Western Washington State College. I found a job as a darkroom tech at a local portrait studio called Russ Cliff Photography, where I learned a great deal about darkroom work, while David drove a truck for Larrabee State Park, emptying garbage cans.

By this time, I'd contacted my parents to let them know where we were and that we were okay—things they'd already concluded from the trail of credit card receipts they'd received from Mom's stolen gas card. I promised to pay back every cent once I got back on my feet, which smoothed Mom's ruffled feathers but not Dad's. The only thing he said to me was: "I don't talk to thieves." Mom was far more forgiving and told me to call my friend Bill from the campus radio station. He'd been trying to reach me ever since my sudden departure. Turns out things weren't quite as bad as I had imagined. The FCC had confiscated the transmitter, made Ed tear down the station's antenna—a long wire strung across the Student Center's rooftop—and they both got a good finger wagging scolding from the school's president. But there was no warrant for my arrest.

As summer waned and fall slipped into winter, I found Bellingham increasingly depressing. Its overcast skies, bone-numbing cold, and constant rain seemed to match the mood of the general population, and eventually my own. I missed the sunshine of California, and I never felt part of the Pacific Northwest. The people were different here. Unlike laid-back, carefree Southern Californians, Washingtonians seemed to be serious, studious, and intent, without a ready smile to brighten a stranger's day. It was as if the constant cold and wet kept their spirits wrapped in thick outer shells, that could be thawed out only by long conversations and hot coffee.

One afternoon, on a chilled winter day, David invited me to hang out at a community gathering organized by some of his newfound churchgoing friends. I don't know what sparked it, but David had suddenly found religion, and he was determined that I see the same light that had inspired him. I had no interest in religion, but accepted his invitation because there was sure to be free food. It was as dull as I'd expected—until I saw a beautiful young girl walking straight toward me after talking with David. She had brown, short-cropped hair, big eyes, and the sweetest smile I'd ever seen.

"You're David's friend?"

At least, I think that's what she said. Anyway, I nodded yes. I think I would have answered yes to anything she asked.

She smiled at me for what seemed an eternity.

"Call me tomorrow," she whispered, and stuffed a crumpled piece of paper into my hand. I suddenly realized that my mouth was hanging open and that I'd stopped breathing. My mind was as frozen as my mouth. I was convinced she'd think me mute, or stupid, or both. The laughter in her blue eyes nodded in acknowledgment of my unspoken acceptance,

42

and she melted back into the crowd as if she'd never appeared. My spirit raced with possibilities. My life had just changed. Through no effort of my own, a girl had paid attention to me, and she was cute — really cute. In fact, I thought she was the most beautiful creature I'd ever laid eyes on. The rest of the day felt like a lifetime, as my mind raced with endless scenarios, endlessly squashed — I didn't dare dream too big, for fear of disappointment. What if she wanted something other than what I'd dreamt of my entire pubescent life? What if, when I called, her father answered the phone? I didn't even know her name.

But when I called the next day, it was she who picked up. "Hello?" When I asked for her name, she said "Donna," but slowly, teasingly, as if it were a well-kept secret. She chatted away, but I don't remember much more than that she was 18 and wanted to meet me at David's and my place for dinner the next night. Then she hung up. A miracle.

I told David what had taken place, and that she wanted to come to our house. When he realized that she was a member of his church group, he was horrified and, flapping his finger in my face, told me to be on my best behavior. I promised I would, but begged him to be somewhere else tomorrow night, so I'd have the house to myself — a request he begrudgingly granted with a slam of the front door.

I served Donna a dinner of spaghetti and sauce out of a can — an upgrade from the boiled noodles and ketchup packs David and I had wolfed down on our journey north. As we emptied our plates, we awkwardly chatted about our lives. But after I rinsed off the dishes, she asked to see my room. I climbed the narrow stairway to my loft in the attic of our old Victorian, with her following close behind. My trembling hand unlocked the bedroom door. Donna feigned interest as I showed her my oddly shaped room: the sloping walls formed by five differently angled sections of the pitched roof, pierced by two pairs of dormer windows on opposing walls. Between those walls, a large central dormer sheltered my bed — a sheet of plywood supported at each corner by a cinder block, and a mattress without a box spring. I don't remember what we talked about, or for how long, but as we sat on the bed I tried my best approximation of cool, calm, and collected.

"You're a virgin?" She giggled.

"Uh, yeah … I …"

Without warning, she pulled me down and leaped on top of me, pinning my arms against the bed, her hips pressing hard against my jeans. Within moments I was no longer a virgin. To my surprise—and at first, delight—we went at it again—and again, and again, until I desperately wanted no more.

"This never happened," Donna whispered. She buttoned up her blouse and headed downstairs. It was late, and I worried about her getting home safely.

She put up one hand in protest. "I'm okay, but I have to be home by ten. Don't call me." She left.

I did call her after that, many times, but I never spoke to her or saw her again. She appeared out of nowhere, ended my unwanted celibacy, and took with her my virginity as reward.

Bellingham had been good to me, but still—the rain. I missed the dryness and warm sunshine of Southern California, and I had already achieved a lifelong goal—in spades. So after having gotten my first adventure away from home, I said goodbye to David, put my thumb out, and hitchhiked back to Anaheim.

Chapter 7

THE DRAFT STILL HUNG over my head, but after months of no communication from the draft board other than the original letter, informing me of my new status as a potential draftee, I blew it off as something that would probably never happen. I had moved back home but my father's patience for his freeloading son was growing short. That January, Dad declared I had 30 days of free rent remaining before I would either start covering expenses or be booted out of the McGowan home. The clock was ticking; the pressure was on. I had been homeless once before, living out of my car with David, and I didn't relish the thought of repeating that experience. I needed a job and none made more sense than being a disc jockey, a skill I already had under my belt from my days at our college pirate radio station.

During my brief tenure at KFJC I had made a number of air checks —taped radio shows without most of the music, but including all of my announcements, intros, and outros, and some examples of segues from record to record. Armed with my air-check tape, I hit the streets and within a few weeks of knocking on doors I found employment at an older, sleepy, background-music station, KTBT FM, in Garden Grove. The station had just been converted to a new broadcast format that was exactly what I was looking for.

In the late 1960s, FM radio was just coming on the scene as a source of rock and pop music, instead of the background and occasional classical music they'd been previously broadcasting. FM was largely a phenomenon of at-home listening, and not much of one at that—monaural AM radio ruled the road, because most cars still had only AM radios. Most FM stereo stations broadcast background music, as KTBT had done, while many others simply simulcast the same programming as the AM station that owned them. Then a revolution in FM programming swept the country: album-oriented rock (AOR). For my generation, AOR was a revelation that fit our desire to break free of the status quo established by AM Top 40 radio: a short playlist of two-and-a-half-minute singles played over and over, separated by endless commercials. But AOR stations played new music that had never been released as singles, individual tracks that could be as long as 30 minutes, or entire albums. Instead of fast-talking DJs driving hard to keep listeners on the edge of their seats with jingles and the latest pop songs, AOR played long blocks of music—typically three tracks in a row, without interruption, in what were called sets—and the announcers spoke quietly, without rushing, without exaggerated voices. Enterprising businesspeople began buying up FM stations, and the AM stations were glad to get them off their books. That turned out to be shortsighted on the part of the AM station owners, many of whom went out of business as their listeners left the overcrowded commercial bombardment of Top 40 AM for the less frenetic pace of the AOR stations: less talk, more music, fewer commercials. In less than a decade, FM listenership overtook AM. It was the end of the AM era.

I was lucky to find work at KTBT in the middle of its transition from AM to FM. It was the right job at the right time—with my limited experience and unseasoned skills, an established station would have been unlikely to hire me. Also, there were plenty of experienced radio pros in AM, but the entire field of FM AOR, which required very different skills, was new. My gig at KTBT was midnight to 6 am, the graveyard shift, and at first I loved it. I played the music I was closest to and felt the admiration and respect of a growing number of fans who liked my musical choices and segues. One of the hallmarks of the first AOR formats was what was called freeform radio: DJs chose their own tunes to play, sequencing them according to a theme or rhythm or pattern. For example, I might begin with a track from the Who's *Tommy* and, as the track faded out on "can you hear me, can you hear me, me, me ..." I might have overlapped it with Jimmy Page's opening guitar riff from Led Zeppelin's "Whole Lotta Love," then finished the set with a quieter track that spoke of love, like the Beatles' classic "Julia." Some jocks were masters of the art of the set—after half an hour of music, in a seamless flow of tracks played without interruption, you realized that every song was related in some way to all the others in that set. Today, the playlists on most AOR or Classic Rock stations are fully automated and without soul or anything reminiscent of a human's touch. It's a shame—FM radio's golden era of freeform was a treasure trove for music lovers, the likes of which isn't often heard anymore.

At KTBT I gravitated toward the long-play versions of album hits: Led Zeppelin's "Dazed and Confused," Iron Butterfly's "In-A-Gadda-Da-Vida," and the Doors' "Light My Fire." These were loved by KTBT listeners—who referred to the station as "Underground 94"—and I cranked the music as loud as the studio monitors would allow. For three months, I was in musical heaven and the gig came with one big job perk: getting laid. From my earliest days of wanting to be a radio personality, that primal male urge hadn't left me, though by now, thankfully, I was far less obsessed. I met Wendy through KTBT's request line. She was tall, blonde, freckled, smart, cool, and kind of a fox—someone I enjoyed being with. We'd have sex on the floor of the program director's office, and smoke pot during my graveyard shift. Life seemed pretty complete. I had a girlfriend and a job with a paycheck—and that job was playing my favorite records from midnight to six.

One Saturday morning I awoke just before noon, having worked until six that morning. My mother gave me the list of chores I had to complete in return for living at home, then handed me an ominous-looking, plain brown envelope. It had the look of the federal government all over it, including a return address from the Selective Service Department. I opened it. "Order to Report for Induction," the paper read. I'd been drafted. In two weeks, I had to report to the induction center in Los Angeles. My world was suddenly dark. The Vietnam War was in full swing. By that month, March 1969, American troop levels had swollen to 543,000, the highest point they would reach in that war. In those days, if you were drafted, your term of service was two years—unless you went to Vietnam, which everyone did. A tour in 'Nam meant you'd be out in 18 months—or sooner, in a body bag. By this time, 33,641 American soldiers had come home in body bags with countless more Vietnamese, from North and South, suffering the same fate in a proxy

47

war between two superpowers, with no winner in sight.

I did not want to be troop #543,001. But I did have one ace in my back pocket: my local Army recruiter. Army recruiters offered an enticing package: if you signed up for three years, they guaranteed job placement once you got in. That seemed like a reasonable compromise. So, rather than waiting for draft day, I went to downtown Anaheim to see what I could arrange. The recruitment office was nearly empty, and a smartly dressed Army man, Sgt. Hopkins, was happy to help me. He didn't look like Howard of Howard's Fine Cars, but he had the same toothy grin, the same easy self-assuredness. Sgt. Hopkins was built like a muscled brick wall: short-cropped hair, tanned skin, muscles rippling in his neck as he adjusted his tie. He offered me a Coke and a donut, and said he wanted to know all about my life. He seemed fascinated and encouraged me to tell him everything. I handed him my draft notice.

He chuckled and handed it back. "You're smart, Paul," he said. "You let me take care of things, and I'll make sure you get exactly what you want." I told him I was a DJ and a photographer. I'd seen wartime photos by journalists in the field of battle, but that held little interest for me. Spinning records and entertaining the troops seemed right up my alley, and I told him so.

Sgt. Hopkins pored over his books and said there wasn't a job opening for a disc jockey, but he had something even better: a Radio Relay Carrier Attendant. "Hell, with your background in electronics, you're a shoo-in." He patted me on the back.

This was my lucky day. My new best friend explained that I'd have to remain Stateside, and hoped I wouldn't be too disappointed at not having to wear a uniform. In fact, I'd be living in a government-funded apartment traveling from transmitter site to transmitter site, checking meters and making sure the Army's telecommunications systems were in proper working order.

"Just don't tell anyone about your live-in girlfriend," he winked.

He said I'd have to wear civilian clothes and climb tall towers in the middle of the forest across the country, and there would be no chance of deployment to Vietnam. Oh darn.

This all sounded perfectly acceptable. It would cost me only another year of my life, and I'd be on easy street. The guarantee of a safe, cushy, Stateside Army job was only a signature away. Life was looking up.

CHAPTER 8

GOVERNMENTS AND POLITICIANS have long used the media to portray war in a light favorable to their political agendas. During World War II both the Office of War Information and Hollywood produced patriotic films, as rallying cries to affirm a sense of national purpose. Films of all kinds in that era emphasized patriotism and the value of individual sacrifice. They portrayed WWII as a people's war, typically featuring a group of men from diverse ethnic and economic backgrounds thrown together in the army, tested on the battlefield, and molded into a dedicated fighting unit.

While that approach was effective in World War II, it didn't work in the late 1960s — not because the government had any less desire to paint a rosy picture of the war effort in Southeast Asia, but because of a fundamental shift in home entertainment. Whereas once books, newspapers, movies, and radio had slowly molded the nation's attitudes over months and years, television's instant access, piped into millions of homes in real time, threw a monkey wrench into the government's carefully crafted propaganda machine. As the Federal Government painted one picture of the war, the media were busily painting a very different one. The war in Vietnam was the first American war to be viewed by the public from their living-room armchairs, and what they saw upset them. Unlike the sanitized propaganda of newsreels and Hollywood fluff in earlier times, war's true horrors were now watched over dinner, and they turned many viewers' stomachs — and more importantly, changed their minds.

Many Americans felt betrayed by Washington for withholding or deliberately manipulating information about the progress of the war. What they saw on their TVs or heard on their radios was a significantly less optimistic version of the war than the politicians had been painting. Coverage of atrocities, such as the massacre of hundreds of Vietnamese civilians by US troops at My Lai, galvanized the nation.

But it wasn't only television that was pounding nails in the coffin of the war effort. Activist musicians produced a growing number of albums in the 1960s to express their dissent and plant seeds of rebellion that would eventually help end the war in Vietnam. Songs like Creedence Clearwater Revival's "Fortunate Son," along with John Lennon's "Give Peace a Chance" and "Imagine," played through car radios and home stereos. My generation had been encouraged to "tune in, turn on, and drop out." And we did. As a result of the intense media coverage and the barrage of anti-war songs, public pressure to withdraw from Vietnam mounted until the government began to withdraw troops, in July 1969. Before it was over, in March 1975, 2.5 million South Vietnamese and 58,000 Americans would lose their lives.

Though the seeds of change to end the conflict had been sown, for me the Vietnam War was very much in full swing. I was inducted into the US Army in March 1969, on a depressing Monday morning. Rain was forecast for the afternoon, and the clouds were already gathering to threaten the March dryness of Los Angeles. The Selective Service Department occupied the first and second floors of an ugly concrete-block building with twin American flags fluttering above its glass door. I'd seen government drab before, at the DMV and the Santa Ana court-house, but this was a new low, one that matched my own mood. The hallway floors were tiled in tan, puke-colored linoleum flecked with green, and the cement walls were two-tone: green rose from the peeling brown molding halfway up, where it met an off-white that extended to the ceiling, an amalgam of decaying, tobacco-yellow acoustic tiles. Signs led to lines that led to more lines. "Hurry up and wait" was the running joke.

The Selective Service System's deferment program allowed college students to stay in school, the politically connected to join the reserves, and the economically well-off to pay physicians to exempt them. This meant that the men most likely to be drafted and sent to fight on the front lines were of lower socioeconomic class. Between 1964 and 1973, from a total of 27 million eligible men, the US military drafted 2.2 million. Although only 25 percent of the military force in the combat zones were draftees, the system of conscription caused many young men like me to volunteer, trading an extra year of our lives for guaranteed job training. Most of the young men being inducted that Monday morning had volunteered for that reason.

There was a lot of joking in the halls as we nervously waited our turns to fill out papers and get a two-minute psychiatric evaluation. Two minutes. I'd been to shrinks before, accompanying my father when he sought treatment for his bipolar disorder. This was something quite different. When I stepped into the Army psychiatrist's small cubicle he didn't look up, but just pointed to a single folding metal chair. I sat. The only indication that he was anything other than a file clerk was his white lab coat.

"McGowan?"

I nodded.

"Ever had any mental problems?"

Friends had coached me to say yes, but I'd already figured out the futility of it all. Half an hour earlier, I'd been given a hearing test. Tones were played into headphones, and you were supposed to signal yes or no if you could hear them. I didn't put them on, and never touched the answer switch. I passed: "Hearing: excellent."

The shrink stamped my papers "passed" based on that single question to me. I then joined a group of inductees who'd been gathered into a large room and ordered to strip down. There we were in two long lines: a hundred frightened, pimpled boys, 19 and 20 years old, fat and skinny, white, yellow, brown, black, close-cropped or long-haired, tall or short or average height, mustached, clean-shaven, or bearded. A hundred swingin' dicks, looking silly and stripped of our identities: the sweatered preppy, the ducktailed leather-vest cool guy, the nerd with wire-rimmed glasses, the trembling mama's boy, the wife beater, the pressed-white-shirt-and-tie overachiever, the delusional hopeful with a note from Mom to go easy on him.

There were two white-coated doctors, one per line of hairy, naked boys. One by one, the doc stopped in front of each boy, slipped a gloved hand under his balls, then pressed his middle finger hard just short of the anus and ordered him to cough. On to the next boy, and the next, and on to the end of the line. No change of gloves. I had no idea how

52

foul a hundred naked young men could smell—a combination of Jade East, Old Spice, pee, fear, and BO.

Of 100 of us, not one was rejected. We got dressed, and soon each group was herded, single file, down a long dim corridor that led to the rear of the building and outside. The promised rain had spent itself and slowed to a gentle mist—wet enough to keep the windshield wipers of two Greyhound Scenicruisers busy. One by one we entered the silver and red-white-and-blue bus with the dog on the side like cattle to the slaughter.

"Keep moving. All the way to the back," barked a tough-looking man in a soldier's uniform, holding a clipboard. "All the way to the back," he repeated. "Take the next seat."

The pneumatic sigh of the front door closing signaled our departure, and we pulled away from the Selective Service loading dock. We were 50 scared, anxious, excited, questioning young men heading north on US 101, the same road I'd taken to gain my freedom from the very thing that had now befallen me. Dying in a bullshit war in the jungles of Vietnam was what I'd feared most and had tried to avoid by moving to Canada, yet here I was, bouncing down the Ventura Freeway, whizzing past the same brown Woodland Hills, the ocean blue of Camarillo, the quaintness of Santa Barbara, just as I had less than a year before.

We were being bused to Fort Ord, a military base on the California coast, a few miles north of some of the most valued real estate in the country: Carmel by the Sea. Fort Ord's 28,000 acres of wind-blown sand dunes, coastal fog, pampas grass, Monterey pines, and thick mats of low-growing vegetation would be our home for the next eight weeks. I didn't know it at the time, but five years earlier outbreaks of deadly spinal meningitis had closed this basic-training facility. It was now said to be free of infection, but just barely. They still maintained a vigilant eye for another outbreak. Lucky us. Fort Ord processed 1,000 recruits a week: a testosterone-filled factory whose drill sergeants had eight weeks to strip fat, build muscles, eliminate personality, command obedience, and scare the shit out of every mother's son—a challenge they seemed to sadistically relish.

The 99 other young men I'd begun with exited the buses and lined

53

up outside what was called the Butcher Shop—a series of one-story green buildings designed to process men for combat. A line formed at one door. We said goodbye to our street clothes and were given a bundle of ill-fitting uniforms, then herded into the barber shop where carefully coiffed locks piled unceremoniously on the floor. Until that moment, it had never occurred to me just how closely our identities were intertwined with our choices in fashion and grooming. Stripped of those identifiers, we looked remarkably the same—a fact not lost on the military.

In our stiff and ill-fitting uniforms, our shaved-raw heads under unfamiliar green caps, our feet in unbending combat boots, and our street clothes stuffed in a brown sack under one arm, we did our best to line up outside the Butcher Shop in some semblance of order. It wasn't working out too well until a short, stocky Army guy in a uniform started yelling at us. Screaming, actually. None of us knew who he was, though I assumed he was one of the terrifying drill sergeants we'd heard about on the bus. In fact, it was all any of us could talk about though none of us had a clue what the truth was. We'd heard that drill sergeants had the power of life and death over their charges. They would be our slave masters and constant tormentors over the next eight weeks of basic training.

"Maggots!" this guy screamed. "Line up and shut the fuck up!"

Not another word was uttered as we clumsily attempted to form a line and avoid eye contact with this guy. Whoever he was he certainly had succeeded in terrifying me and everyone else in that line.

"You see this?" he bellowed, pointing at a yellow stripe on his arm. All eyes cautiously turned toward him, then quickly away, for fear of drawing his attention. "This stripe means I own you." He paced up and down the line, glaring into each face as each owner's eyes desperately looked away. "I am not your drill sergeant," he announced. "But it doesn't matter, because you are all maggots, the lowliest creatures on the face of this godforsaken earth. Anyone here, anyone at all, tells you what to do—where to shit, where to sit, where to go, when to breathe—you do it. Is that understood?"

54

"Yes sir!" we shouted.

"Sir?" he raged. "Sir? I am no officer. I work for a living. You DO NOT call me sir! Do I make myself clear?"

We hadn't a clue what to call him instead. He got a muddled "Yes!"

To the Army, we were, officially, maggots — the scum of the earth, lower than dirt. It seemed that maggots did what they were commanded to do by anyone of higher rank, and that meant everyone on the base. Worms, apparently, outranked us.

Eighty of us were then peeled from the original 100, herded into the back of a tall green vehicle the size of a dump truck, and ordered to seat ourselves on one of four long, gray benches, one along each side of the cattle-car stake-rack-truck and two down the middle. We sat and faced each other, 20 to a bench. The vehicle ground its gears, belched a plume of foul black smoke, and we wormed our way out of the reception area and headed up a winding hill. We drove past ceremonial cannons, flagpoles, squares of men marching with rifles on their shoulders, and little green Army jeeps like the ones I'd seen in World War II movies.

I was frightened in a way I had never felt before. It wasn't the same sense of foreboding as when I went to jail or even at the approach of my father as he pulled from his pant loops the belt that was destined for my bare ass. No, this was a scared that was new to me. Perhaps it was the feeling of permanence, of suddenly being asked to perform as an adult under the very real threat of being killed. But more likely it was the fright of the unknown, of what waited for us all atop that lonely looking hill the truck was heading to.

Chapter 9

Basic training at Fort Ord took place in a series of three-story, cement-block buildings in an area known as The Hill, a grassy knoll overlooking the ocean. Each barrack had a dormitory bay, mess hall, exercise yard, and administrative office to organize 80 recruits into companies. Mine was Company B, 3rd Battalion, 4th Basic Combat Training Brigade, abbreviated B-3-4. To prevent us from straying too far from "home," a maggot tag—a white stripe labeled B-3-4—was sewn above our nametags.

We stumbled out of the cattle truck and milled about the exercise yard, unsure what to do, on the lookout for our drill sergeant. We were scared to death. None of us knew what lay ahead, only that the stories we'd heard probably didn't describe in vivid enough detail the hell we'd just entered. All any of us knew came from other clueless recruits' tales of evil drill sergeants. These stories, shared on the bus ride and while waiting for haircuts and uniforms, had built up the drill sergeants to near-mythical status—they were Caligula, Attila the Hun, the Hydra, or maybe all three. Already, fear of the unknown was breaking us down into puddles of confusion and dread. We jumped at the slightest noise, craned our necks at anything moving. What kind of monster would this man be? We assumed he'd be a combat veteran—a trained killer—someone who'd not only seen the horrors of war but had very likely caused some of them. We assumed he'd be capable of any atrocity, willing to crush the life out of anyone he didn't like. After all, we'd all heard that trainees had died in basic training, pushed over the edge by overzealous drill sergeants. None of us wanted to find out if those stories were true.

All our speculation abruptly ended when a short, stocky, determined man marched directly toward us with an athlete's gait. We stared as he approached, our nervous chatter quickly dying away to a burning silence. I don't remember breathing.

It was, indeed, our drill sergeant—a thickset, burly Japanese man with piercing brown eyes and a hard-set mouth that could easily sneer when the eyes willed it. On his head was a Smokey the Bear hat, its leather strap tight against the underside of his chin. In his hand was a short stick, a baton—it looked like a riding crop. This was Sergeant Ito, and we would soon learn that he was one mean son of a bitch, a dictator with a hair-trigger temper who would exercise absolute control over us with unforgiving rules and punishments meted out with sadistic pleasure.

Sgt. Ito did not utter a word; his piercing eyes, his hands, and his pointing baton did all the talking as he lined us up in two rows. We stood at stiff attention, our jaws clenched shut, eyes staring straight ahead, barely breathing for fear of being singled out. Ito slowly walked up and down the line, stopping in front of each trembling recruit, his face inches away. He seemed to examine our souls in the greatest detail, drilling down deep into the pool of darkness within each man in turn. Even before he reached me, I could feel his probing energy, growing in intensity with each step. All at once, it was just Ito and me. The world seemed to stop. I held my breath. All I could hear was his slow, calculated, nasal breathing—the muted inhalation, the slight whistle on exhalation, a hint of garlic. His eyes challenged mine to waver from staring straight ahead past him, to stare into his face. I held firm, but he saw right through me: he cut through all my bullshit in one silent, ten-second interview. He knew—and I knew he knew—that I would never challenge him. He could kill me with a snap of his finger, and I didn't imagine for a moment that he'd hesitate to do so. He owned me.

Inside the faceless barrack were two perfectly straight rows of bunk beds on a floor of polished concrete. At the foot of each bunk was a double trunk, to contain the meager possessions of two maggots. The beds were thin slabs of mattress atop gray steel springs stretched between the side rails of the bedframe. Covering each mattress was an olive-drab blanket stretched so tightly that Ito could bounce a coin off it, and he often did. At each end of the barrack were bathrooms: two rows of ten white toilets sitting in the open, opposite the same number of stainless-steel sinks attached to the walls. At the very back was an open shower stall with 20 nozzles, 10 per side, aimed down at rows of once-white floor tiles.

57

Mornings began at 4 am, when Ito rattled his baton across the bunk beds: time for maggots to get up. We were out the door by 4:15 — no time for a shit, shower, or shave. You didn't want to be last in line. Last was usually some poor kid who was mentally slow or physically fat. Ito loved the fat ones: slow-moving, pimpled objects of his evil pleasures.

"You fat-assed motherfucker!" he'd bellow. The rest of us couldn't help but watch — like you do at a car wreck, glad it's not you. "You're wasting our time. Everyone on your team is ready to run — aren't you, maggots?"

"Yes, Drill Sergeant!"

But oh my God, we didn't want to run. Not at that time in the morning. Not when Monterey's bone-chilling fog gripped the very ground we daily pounded into submission. Not in our heavy combat boots. Not after only four hours of sleep.

"Drop for a hundred," he'd say, disgust in his voice and the devil in his eye. The poor kid would usually struggle through 20 push-ups before collapsing. Ito's gleaming black boot would then push the squealing kid onto his back as he ordered him to hold up the wall while the rest of us finished the push-ups. Holding up the wall was a particularly grim form of punishment: back propped against the wall in a half-crouch, arms stretched out straight in front of you. Within a minute, your legs start shaking to the point of collapse. This morning ritual took place before our pre-breakfast five-mile wake-up run in combat boots.

This routine continued for weeks until May 10 rolled around, my 21st birthday — almost halfway through basic. The day before had been particularly hard, fighting to stay awake in personal hygiene class as we were taught Army protocol for wiping our asses: six tissue squares folded twice, plus instructions on what to do if your finger punched through. Really. As I lay in my bunk that morning, waiting for Ito's baton to strike, I wept. Happy Birthday, Paul, I thought.

A 21st birthday is supposed to be a rite of passage filled with alcohol, friends and merriment. All I could revel in was the sound of 39 men snoring and the approaching footsteps of Sgt. Ito, who could turn on me at any time. I was so unnerved by Ito that I tried to stay in the background as much as possible, hoping never to be noticed. But today didn't feel right. God help me if he found out it was my birthday. There'd

58

be no telling what pain and torture he'd inflict.

"McGowan!" He walked straight up to me, as I scrambled to my feet and stood statute-still, clad only in T-shirt and skivvies.

Jesus, I thought. He knows.

"It's your birthday, maggot," he sneered.

The hair on the back of my neck shot straight up and my face instantly felt on fire. Ito had already demonstrated an amazing talent for inventive torture and punishment. One night, after lights out, some idiot had stolen Ito's whistle and paraded up and down the hall, blowing it as loudly as he could. There was hell to pay that night. For the next two hours, out in the exercise yard, we rolled on our backs, legs and arms extended skyward, yelling: "I am a dying cockroach!" until we were hoarse. When we could roll no more, we ran around the outside of the barrack singing: "Two old ladies lying in bed, one rolled over to the other and said, I want to be an Airborne Ranger!" It ended only when it was time to line up for morning PE and our five-mile run.

But today was my birthday.

"Yes, Drill Sergeant!"

"Report to the kitchen for KP."

I hightailed it out of there, thankful for the seemingly light punishment for having been born.

Even the privates in charge of the Kitchen Police could command maggots to do their bidding, and they weren't shy about it. I figured I'd be peeling spuds, but the Army had mechanized that job: a spinning barrel of sandpaper removed the outer skins. There were worse tasks for maggots, and the worst was cleaning the grease trap, where the dregs of institutional cooking wound their way down and coagulated in a gray, putrid, gelatinous clump. This was far more disgusting than the rotting Thousand Island dressing and half-digested fries I'd cleaned up at Carl's to get my first car.

The trap was deep. I had to pull off my boots and socks and wade ankle-deep in the chunky muck. As I scraped the sides with a putty knife, one of the cooks came out for a smoke.

"Drafted?" he asked, exhaling a ring of blue.

"RA," I replied. Reserve Army—not drafted, precisely.

"What the hell'd ya do that for?"

"Got a cushy job ahead of me," I gloated. "31B."

"Bummer."

"At least I don't have to go to 'Nam."

He almost inhaled the cigarette, trying to catch his breath from laughing so hard.

"Who the hell told you that? The recruiter?"

I had a bad feeling.

"Hey!" he yelled for the other cooks to come over. "Dummy here is a 31B and thinks he's not going to 'Nam. RA, too!"

The laughter from the three angered me from deep inside. The picture was suddenly coming in clear. The recruiter who'd befriended me, cared about me, fed me donuts and Cokes—he'd screwed me. I just didn't know how as yet. I felt nauseous and started to shake.

"Wha…what do you mean?"

"You don't know? 31Bs are the guys with the radio calling in air strikes. You know, the long whip antenna the snipers aim for?"

Now I understood. I'd swallowed the recruiter's lie whole. He'd seen me coming. I was sure that he and his fellow recruiters had had a good laugh after I left. I'd been an idiot. Boiling mad, I wanted to kick someone, but I had no one to get mad at but myself. I probably couldn't have gotten a more dangerous job if I'd been drafted. Not only that—draftees sent to 'Nam were out in as few as 18 months. RAs were in for the full 36.

I stood ankle-deep in the greasy waste of 80 men, surrounded by flies, overflowing dumpsters, and cigarette butts, as I was ridiculed for being a sucker, a first-class fool. So Dad was right about my being a failure—that hurt burned deep. I wasn't worth much in my own eyes, and evidently even less in the eyes of those laughing at me.

Then and there, in the middle of KP, I decided I'd had enough. The Army had screwed me over, and it was time to leave. If the Army didn't want the sick, the injured, or the crazy, I would become all three.

That night at 10 o'clock, after being discharged from KP, I quietly walked to the front of the barrack, lay down on the grass, and closed my eyes.

It wasn't much of a plan, but it was the best I had. I would hypnotize myself, a skill I'd played around with in my teens. I'd hypnotize myself to appear comatose, they'd send me to the hospital, and from there I'd...well, I'd wing it.

Not ten minutes into the process of calming myself with slow, controlled breathing and relaxing each set of muscles in turn, focusing first on my toes and working my way up my body, I heard the voice of Sgt. Ito. I wasn't ready.

"Troop!" he yelled, and kicked me in the ribs. I kept my eyes shut and didn't flinch. Too late to turn back now.

Silence. I heard him mutter "Jesus" and hurry off.

I could feel my pulse raging in my ears. Now what? I didn't dare open my eyes or move. If he caught me faking it, he'd run me around the barracks until I collapsed. Or died. He was capable of that. Then, just for the hell of it, he'd kick my corpse. No, I was done with this torture. I was committed.

I could hear a group of fellow maggots approaching, at Ito's insistence.

"Maybe he fell out of the window and broke his neck?" one of them wondered.

I felt fingers digging under my ribs and legs. I was hoisted into the air and carried up the stairs. The bright lights of the dayroom glared through my clenched eyelids, and Tommy Roe's godawful "Dizzy" was playing.

I heard the bark of First Sergeant Anders's baritone: "What's this maggot doing in my dayroom?"

"Found him outside. I couldn't wake him," said Sgt. Ito.

"I'll wake him." I could hear Anders approaching. I was done for. Then it got very quiet. He must have been examining me.

"Dammit," said Anders. "Call an ambulance."

What? Was I bleeding? I couldn't open my eyes. I was suddenly in a cold sweat.

"Everyone out of the room!" yelled Ito.

I could hear them whispering out in the hall. They thought I had spinal meningitis. Oh, sweet Jesus. What had I done?

The emergency room doc made quick work of me. He broke open a capsule of ammonia nitrate and held it under my nose until I gagged and opened my eyes. I blinked at the bright examining light and started babbling in my finest crazy talk.

"Save it, kid," said the doc. He turned to his orderly. "Get him ready for Ward E20."

CHAPTER 10

WARD E20 OF SILAS B. HAYS HOSPITAL was for people who suffered from serious mental illnesses. It was a drab and dreary wing with some 30 cots, as well as offices, locked patient rooms, and a meeting area. The walls were the same two-tone concrete I'd seen in the LA induction center, but were white and blue instead of gray and green.

On Ward E20, screams pierced the night; orderlies armed with hypodermic needles rushed to sedate the screamers. An unrestrained guy next to me talked in his sleep constantly, recounting over and over some horrible chase scene unfolding in his head. I dared not sleep, scared he would try to strangle me. These were real soldiers. They'd been in combat and had returned as shadows of themselves. To this day, I can't imagine the horrors that had scarred their souls. Ward E20 brought the reality of war home, and it shook me to my core.

In 1969 no one had heard of post-traumatic stress disorder (PTSD), though for centuries its symptoms have been known by various names, such as shell shock. It wasn't until 1980, five years after the end of the Vietnam War, that PTSD was officially recognized as a mental health condition. Among the men who survived combat in Vietnam, one long-term medical consequence of PTSD was a doubled death rate after the war—mostly from suicide or a slower version via drugs and alcohol. PTSD has also been found to exacerbate chronic conditions such as cancer, nervous-system disorders, and musculoskeletal problems, on top of symptoms like nightmares, intrusive memories, and hypervigilance.

In my weeks on Ward E20 I saw this acted out daily; soldiers cried constantly or shook so badly that they rolled off chairs onto the floor, writhing in psychic pain. Instead of helping these men recover, the Army tolerated them until they were discharged—if they weren't career soldiers, without compensation or access to mental health facilities. My travails seemed meaningless compared to these poor guys. They were trapped in a place they didn't want to be and victims of events beyond their control. My resolve to continue acting out this farce I had thrust myself into remained strong, though I wasn't sure if I'd gone from the frying pan into the fire. At least I wasn't on an express train to Vietnam for a job I never signed up for.

My new home was a long, two-tone hall half the length of a football field, with rows of patient rooms on both sides. Midway, the hall opened out into a central meeting area comprising a sort of multipurpose dining area and lounge. We were still all dressed alike, but here the uniform was a sheer examining gown of white linen, open at the back, and Army-issue slippers. We took our meals promptly at 8 am, noon, and 6 pm. They came prepackaged on metal trays stacked on trolleys, pushed by orderlies in olive-drab work clothes with badges hung around their necks. On one wall of the central area were two doors with the names of the resident psychiatrists: Anderson and Wardley, both captains; on the opposite wall was an opening with a counter like you'd find at a McDonald's. This was the drug dispensary. Though I hadn't seen a doctor since being admitted to E20, each morning I stood in line at the prescription window in my little open-back dressing gown, feeling like a total idiot. When I reached the window, an orderly looked up my name, handed me a small Dixie cup in which rattled some unknown, unexplained pills, then watched as I downed them.

Whatever those pills were, the first dose almost literally paralyzed me. It felt as if an 800-pound gorilla was sitting on my chest. I struggled to breathe, and for a few moments I thought I was dying. I said a prayer—kind of a cheat because I have never been religious, but when you look death in the eye…"God, please. Help me make it through this night. I swear I will never do anything bad again. Just make this feeling go away. Please."

Before the war, I'd seen some good people paralyzed. Automobile accidents had changed the lives of a few high school classmates, forever relegating them to a wheelchair. Now I knew what they felt like. My mind raced but was trapped inside my body, which was paralyzed by the drugs. I may as well have been chained to my bed. The next morning, and every morning after that, the pills went under my tongue, then wound up in the trashcan.

64

"Hey!" someone behind me said one morning, as I leaned over the trash-can. I thought I'd been caught. When I turned, I saw a guy in an examining gown like mine, with bloodshot eyes. "Can I have them, instead?"

Tom was a tall, gangly guy with the start of a head of bushy brown hair, a face full of freckles, and stubby, fat cauliflower ears that were squared off at the top. He was as sane as I was, but he liked the drugs. He told me that they were like the heroin he'd taken on the streets of San Francisco before being drafted.

He filled me in on the E20s. It turned out that about a third of us were faking it, trying to get a Section 8 discharge from the Army that would declare us mentally unfit for service. The rest were in serious need of mental help. More importantly to me, Tom revealed that the ward was run by an iron-fisted, 300-pound sadist named Eric. Tom and our little group of fakers called him Tiny. Of course.

Tiny's life's mission was control: unquestioned dominance of E20 and everyone in it. Nothing escaped Tiny and no one could miss him. As he walked down the hall with his ever-present clipboard, he took up nearly half its width. Like the other ward workers he wore an olive-drab, waist-length lab coat and carried a pocketful of pens, and the same jangly set of ID cards hung by a chain around his neck. But Tiny also had a long, thin, silver bosun's pipe that made a shrill piercing noise. He blew it often. Tiny's size meant that he couldn't move quickly—if a patient who was being transferred in or out of a room got loose or began misbehaving, Tiny's face would turn bright purple as he blasted his whistle at ear-shattering volumes. Help would soon arrive, with Tiny huffing and puffing right behind. Woe to the escaped or misbehaving patient when Tiny did arrive. I saw him ram the head of one weeping, out-of-control patient into his sweaty armpit and drag him back to solitary confinement. Later, after that patient had tried to hang himself with his bedsheet, Tiny ridiculed him for botching the job. I had no desire to tangle with Tiny, but I had trouble keeping my eyes off him. Under his left eye was a mole unlike any I'd ever seen: black, and big enough to partially block his vision. Out of its center curled a single thick black hair.

In my first few weeks on Ward E20, a routine was established. Every other day, like all the other patients, I met with a psychiatrist for 30 minutes, during which I further embroidered the fiction of my insanity. Later in the day, in the quiet of the lounge, our faker's group would compare notes, whispering what lies we'd told the shrinks. Tom's story was that if he wasn't discharged, he'd kill himself—or someone else. Mine was simpler. I said I couldn't control myself, and crapped my pants every time the drill sergeant yelled at me or even looked at me. I was too embarrassed to continue on as one of the guys—I knew I couldn't face combat. Looking back, I'm amazed I never came up with anything better.

My shrink, Captain Anderson, was a bone-thin guy of 30 or so, with a thick head of black hair that extended down his forehead in a bushy V to meet his arched eyebrows. He peered at me over half-rimmed glasses and scowled. From the questions he asked and the looks he gave me, I figured he had little doubt that I was faking it, but for some reason he never called me out—and I sure as hell wasn't going to tell him the truth and be sent back to Sgt. Ito's basic training shitstorm. An unspoken truce seemed to be in place. I began to hope; if we kept playing our little game every other day, sooner or later I'd be discharged.

But as the weeks dragged on and nothing happened, and I began to worry that I'd wind up living in this cuckoo's nest for the rest of my three-year hitch, Sgt. Ito and Vietnam started not to seem so bad. Then, a miracle. I was told there was an urgent call for me. As I picked up the ward's telephone, Tiny stood nearby; arms folded, his mole scrunched against his squinted left eye, its single black hair touching his narrowed, disapproving brow. I turned away. I was frightened of this guy and I knew if he suspected I was a faker—even if just for a moment—there would be hell to pay. I was supposed to be nuts.

"Hello," I said in a small voice, expecting my mother. But it was Wendy, my girlfriend from KTBT.

"Can you get out of there?" she whispered. "Maybe for a couple of hours? I'm in Monterey."

Wendy's was the last voice I'd expected to hear. But I played it cool, pretending that I was talking to my mom. I hung up and Tiny escorted me back to the lounge. He didn't give any indication he suspected wrongdoing—not yet, anyway. But this guy was notorious for uncovering hidden plots. I had learned from Tom and the others that Tiny's word was respected by the shrinks. If he suspected one of the patients was a faker, he could get them discharged and returned to active duty. He was one mean dude.

Escape from E20 was simple. There were no locked doors. The uniforms we'd arrived in were stashed in a closet off the cafeteria, kept in stapled-shut shopping bags of brown paper, our names and companies scrawled across them with a felt-tipped pen. Tom had agreed to cover for me in case Tiny or one of the orderlies asked, so I felt reasonably secure in leaving, though I knew the consequences for going AWOL: jail time or perhaps worse. I changed into my uniform in a bathroom just inside the ward's door and just slipped out the door, headed for the gates of Fort Ord. No one stopped or questioned me though I was as nervous as a cat tiptoeing through broken glass. It felt like all eyes were upon me and what if the sentry at the gates of Fort Ord asked for my papers? Was I supposed to even have papers? An ID? I had just escaped from the Army's looney bin without ID, or even a clue as to where I was going or how I would get there. The hammering in my chest made it hard to breathe as I approached the main gates of the base, but it was then I noticed the smartly uniformed gate guards were paying attention to the cars that entered the gates, not so much the foot traffic. There was a steady stream of green-suited soldiers coming and going through a side gate and they seemed oblivious to the guards. I fell in with a loud talking group of three and, head down and eyes glued to the sidewalk, waltzed right out the front of Fort Ord as if it was something I had done a hundred times in the past. Suddenly, I was free, back in the outside world, breathing the cool, moist breezes of Monterey Bay. I caught a free Army shuttle to downtown Monterey and got off near Fisherman's Wharf—close enough to hear the bark and chatter of the harbor seals sprawled across the rock jetty next to the pier and marina.

***

Wendy looked gorgeous. She was now a hippie in a peasant blouse, with her strawberry-blonde hair adorned with beads. She'd rented a motel room, where we showered together, then rolled around in bed till late afternoon. Between bouts of lust, we laughed, reminisced, and she caught me up on news from home. Though I'd been gone only a few weeks, it seemed a lifetime ago that I'd been running free, and Wendy brought it all back to me. God, this felt good. To be back with someone I knew, to laugh, to feel free, unshackled from the screams of Sgt. Ito, the demands of basic training, and the jarring experience of being yanked out of the clueless bliss of youth, shoved into the serious business of removing my personality, and prepped to blindly follow orders.

We moved from Wendy's rented motel room to a bench on Cannery Row. The waning afternoon sun felt good on my face. The whole experience of the past few weeks seemed like a dream, and a bad one at that. Had I really just gone through being tricked by a recruiter into trading a year of my life for a lie, followed by induction into the army, tortured by Ito, KP, faking spinal meningitis, and escaping the Fort Ord Looney Bin? That whole world seemed a million miles from me as I held Wendy's hand and watched the seals bicker over their rock perch. But an afternoon together was all I could afford. Soon it was time to go back, to ensure that I wouldn't miss the lineup for dinner. As Wendy walked me to the bus terminal near the far end of Cannery Row, she handed me a small, thin joint as a going-away present. I gratefully accepted it, kissed her goodbye, and snuck back onto Ward E20.

When Tiny began work the next morning, he knew something had happened. I could see it in his beady brown eyes, and that damned mole quivered like a compass needle with each scowl of distrust. Suspicious, he followed me around, but I knew he had no evidence. At least I hoped he hadn't found any. I've never been good at hiding the contents of my soul from the outside world, so I was careful not to make eye contact with him.

Tom, however, had coaxed my secret out of me. I gloated over my adventure and showed him the joint. We promptly repaired to the ward's small bathroom to smoke it, exhaling out the window into the trash area behind the ward, certain we were getting away with high crimes. Suddenly, the bathroom door flew open with a loud bang and toppled

68

me off the toilet seat. Oh shit! There was Tiny, his catlike grin displaying his silver tooth. He grabbed me by the arm, lifted me off the floor, and slammed me against the wall.

"You're dead meat, maggot!"

I don't think I have ever been as frightened as I was at that very moment. The jig was up and now Tiny knew our game. It wouldn't be long before he figured out how I got that joint and put two and two together with Wendy's phone call. Tom and I were both fakers in the ward and now he had us by the short hairs. Would he call the MPs and have us hauled off to jail that afternoon? Possession of marijuana was a serious offence in the military, and I could just imagine Tiny's glee in watching the two of us dragged out of his ward in handcuffs.

Tiny marched us down the hall, one beefy hand gripping each of our necks, and threw us into separate locked rooms normally reserved for patients who might hurt themselves. It was the closest thing on the ward to a holding cell before the executioner's arrival. I spent a sleepless night worrying about the next day's consequences, running the scenarios through my head: jail, dishonorable discharge, maybe Leavenworth. My bright idea of escaping basic training had turned into a nightmare scenario that I could have avoided with just a little less Paul McGowan. Dammit. I felt bad about being me, real bad, and I fretted all night, promising myself I'd do better if only I could get out of this jam with my skin intact. Really. I wouldn't let anything like this happen again. I promised myself. If only ...

At 6 am Tiny flung open my door and crooked a meaty, tobacco-yellowed index finger at me. I followed, the lump in my throat so big I could not swallow. When we got to Capt. Anderson's office, Tom was already there, standing at attention near the door. Not a good sign, but at least there weren't any MPs ready with handcuffs. Tiny pointed to two chairs. On the floor next to each was a stapled-shut, brown paper shopping bag with each of our names written in felt-tipped marker. We sat.

Capt. Anderson arrived and started yelling. "You two knuckleheads were weeks from a discharge, but then you violated my trust. Did you think I didn't know your game? It's over. You're both reassigned to start basic over again. Now get the hell out of my office before I change my mind and have you both sent to prison."

Not only had I put myself through hell in Ward E20, but I was right back where I started from having lost my fight to get out of the Army. It would be eight more weeks of basic training, but at least I knew what to expect with basic and felt better prepared to handle whatever they threw at me. I could make it through basic with my skin and personality intact—small compensation for being screwed by the Army in the first place, but, at least I wasn't headed to prison. I still had time to figure out an escape plan from Vietnam. I'd just have to bide my time and seize the next opportunity when it came.

I got through the eight weeks relatively unscathed before I was shipped off to Fort Gordon, in Augusta, Georgia—a hot, sweaty, humid, nasty armpit of a place. There I received 14 more weeks of advanced 31B training—not calling in air strikes, but sitting in the back of an Army truck, relaying radio signals to field telephones. In this program, every 14 weeks, a new group of trainees graduated and was sent to Vietnam. No exceptions. But because I'd faked spinal meningitis, landing me in the looney bin, I'd somehow short-circuited the Army's administrative rigor and got lost in the system. The Army was a stacked deck, but now I was a wild card they didn't know how to play.

Fourteen weeks, fourteen graduation classes, and 1,399 graduates of the Army's course in fixing things went to Vietnam. Graduate 1,400 got orders to take an all-expenses-paid trip to Stuttgart, Germany, courtesy of the US Army.

CHAPTER 11

As A 21-YEAR-OLD soldier in the US Army, I was excited to be landing in a foreign country. Other than one quick trip to Tijuana to buy fireworks when I was supposed to be in class — a trip that made me the first member in 34 years to be thrown off the high school Student Council for anything but academic probation — I'd never traveled outside the US. My concept of "over there" consisted of whatever vague notions I'd learned from the few pages of high school history I'd read of World War II, and from Hemingway's *A Farewell to Arms* (wrong war).

But as my United Boeing 747 lowered its landing gear and extended its flaps, about to land at Frankfurt International Airport, I was more interested in the view outside the aircraft's little oval window than I was in the history of what was to be my new home. Germany seemed a treasure waiting to be discovered and I was eager to see what it had to offer, aside from the obvious: good-looking women, great beer, and sizzling bratwurst. My mental pictures of the country were a hodgepodge of images from colorful travel calendars, interspersed with wartime newsreels depicting the rubble of cities bombed in the 1940s.

I was thankful to see that, two decades later, much that had been destroyed had been rebuilt and renewed. Below me were carpets of green and yellow fields split by a twisting ribbon of blue — the mighty Main, its banks lined with hundreds of modern steel-and-glass buildings. Frankfurt am Main was the economic and financial powerhouse of West Germany, spreading alongside those colorful fields all the way to the horizon, in a seemingly endless parade of streets and buildings.

By rail I traveled from Frankfurt to Stuttgart, a city nestled among the small hills of the fertile Neckar River valley, an hour from the Black Forest and even nearer to the vineyards of the ancient German territory of Württemberg. The valley runs north and south of Stuttgart, and is the only region of Germany that specializes in red wine. I was assigned to live and work in Patch Barracks, an old German Army facility that, until 1952, had been called the Kurmärker Kaserne. In World War II it had served as the headquarters and barracks for the Wehrmacht's Seventh Panzer Division, once commanded by General Erwin Rommel, aka the Desert Fox.

My new home in the Signal Brigade was behind barbed wire and guarded gates that kept us in and visitors out. It was a colorless and depressing place, but it wasn't Southeast Asia. Inside the compound were rows of identical three-story cement buildings, gray with orderly rows of white-trimmed windows; each held several hundred soldiers and their few possessions. Our accommodations were sparse: a bunk bed, a stand-up locker with a combination lock, and, on all three floors, a single community bathroom at each end of the building. I was assigned a top bunk in a barracks I shared with 20 roommates. The prized bottom bunk was occupied by a soldier I only ever knew by his last name. Tucci was from Philadelphia, and he liked to get high on whatever was close at hand: hash, pot, alcohol, LSD, reds, whites—even gasoline fumes. Apparently, you can get quite a buzz from inhaling gasoline—until you pass out, which was what happened to Tucci. When he fell face first into a pool of gas he'd been inhaling, his face was scarred for life. He seemed proud of it, as if it were a cool tattoo, but it left one side of his long, gaunt face pockmarked bright red, as if he'd pressed it onto a hot griddle. Tucci was my bunkmate, so the job of helpful guide fell to him.

The first thing Tucci told me to be wary of in Patch Barracks was race: "The blacks," he said, "have their own music and their culture, and they don't like us whiteys." Tucci told me that knifings were common. I didn't believe him, but it soon became clear he was right about one thing: Patch Barracks was loosely segregated. Each evening, as music pounded out of the dorms that were mostly African-American, I lay awake in my bunk and listened to the good stuff—like James Brown chanting "Say It Loud—I'm Black and I'm Proud."

I hadn't had much experience with racial prejudice. My high school class was a mix of Hispanics and Caucasians, with a few African-Americans sprinkled in for good measure. Perhaps it was because my school was predominately Hispanic (putting me and my crowd in the minority), or the fact I was friends with one of the more popular African-Americans, Tony, that I never really noticed a racial divide like

72

I did in Georgia and again here in Germany. Still, I didn't like it and was torn between buying into it or breaking with my new bunkmates. In the end I fell into the same trap as everyone else, a daily groove that began each morning at 6 am with breakfast in the central mess hall: white guys on one side, African-Americans on the other.

During the day we worked on our trucks or did other assigned jobs. Mine was to help our team of five, led by our crew chief Sgt. Adams, wash our two-and-a-half-ton truck, called a deuce and a half. Then we had to make sure all the equipment inside the metal house set up on the truck's bed was operational, tuned, and ready for combat at all times. Somehow, the Army made sure that job took all day; we all knew we were just killing time.

But weekends were mine. I mined Stuttgart, riding its public transportation system of streetcars, buses, and taxis, enjoying the beer and brats, and ogling the women—who seemed pretty uninterested in me, and in GIs in general. There was sightseeing, too. Stuttgart is filled with castles, parks, and history, but there wasn't enough to keep me busy. Before long, boredom set in, at least until I discovered hash.

Hashish is a concentrated resin made from the powdered, flowering tops of female cannabis plants, and was said to have been mixed with the sweat of the harvesters and camel dung. It's a lot stronger than weed, and the guys in our barracks smoked a lot of it: red hash, black hash, blonde hash, and sometimes green hash. To get high, they used a community water pipe—a bong. Because hash can be harsh on the throat and lungs, they filled the bottom of the bong's bowl with red wine, to filter and cool the smoke before they inhaled it. Aficionados would have replaced the wine every few days, but my barrack prided itself on "letting it ride," it being common knowledge that several months' worth of absorbed hash residues would get everyone even higher. The red wine in that bong had long since turned black.

I was invited to take my first hit of hash from this bong. Burning in the small bowl was a lump of Afghani black hash—black because of its black cannabis buds, high levels of CBD and THC, and because it was laced with opium. Within moments, I thought I was falling over. The few times before this that I'd smoked a joint, I'd gotten high, but

73

this was unlike any of those experiences. The world seemed to bend sideways, and there was a constant loud buzzing in my ears. Paranoia swept through me. Was I being watched? Were people whispering things about me? Voices sounded amplified, lights shone too brightly, and I felt a little sick. I was greatly relieved when, after what seemed a lifetime but was probably no more than an hour or two, the effects finally lessened.

I'd had it easy. Sgt. Wyatt, a mid-level noncommissioned officer, was the dorm manager in charge of our section of the barracks. Wyatt was pigeon-toed and overweight, with baby-like facial features. He hated that we smoked hash and threatened to turn us in if he ever caught us, which he did only once. Late one Saturday night, the barrack door burst open and Wyatt stumbled in, just as the community bong was being fired up. Normally we'd have panicked, but Wyatt was obviously drunk. We tried to ignore him, but...

"I caught you!" he bellowed, pointing an unsteady finger at the bong.

"You're drunk," said Tucci, who hated Wyatt, the Army, and everything military—as did almost all the grunts in our barracks. "Besides," he said, talking through a cloud of blue smoke, "we're not smoking anything. We're drinking wine."

Tucci disassembled the bong and pretended to drink from it. "Want some?" he said, offering the bowl to Wyatt. His eyes burned with hatred and anger. Tucci claimed to have been a successful auto mechanic back in Philly, one who'd lost a golden opportunity to own his own garage and hit it big. He blamed this loss on the military, on the draft, and now on Sgt. Wyatt.

Wyatt downed the entire bowlful of black, hash-soaked wine. I had never seen projectile vomiting before, but a few seconds later Wyatt dropped the bowl—it shattered—and violently spewed its former contents against the wall. Rumor had it that he was rushed to the hospital, where his stomach was pumped, but we could never verify that. Several in our barrack speculated that Wyatt died that night, but surely that was only a bad rumor. Whatever happened to Sgt. Wyatt, we never saw him again. A few weeks later, Tucci got high on something, rammed Patch Barracks' front gate with an Army truck, and nearly killed a sentry. We never saw him again, either. I immediately claimed the bottom bunk for myself, but it was an uneasy victory. Tucci was a friend who had brought a bit of levity and a rebellious spark to this otherwise dismal, depressing place. Stuttgart's constant overcast skies, viewed through the camp's barbed wire fencing high atop its prison-like walls, were a constant reminder to me that I was here against my will. I had been lied to by the Army and was now forced to spin my wheels, doing nothing of value. My excitement of landing in a new country and seeing Europe for the first time faded over my time in the Signal Brigade. Still, I reminded myself, it could be worse. I could be in Southeast Asia along with several hundred thousand other troops, wanting little more than to just get home alive. Germany may not have been a picnic, but it certainly wasn't the hell hole it could have been.

CHAPTER 12

AS THE RED MORNING sun peeked over sleeping Stuttgart and tinted our gray barracks pink, our convoy of 20 deuce-and-a-half trucks and 20 support vehicles drove through the gate and into the empty streets, headed for the autobahn. We were going on my first field readiness test.

Our mission was to provide telephone communications for NATO forces deployed in mock war games. We'd provide those communications through our mobile network, relaying the telephone messages of field commanders in the heat of battle. Via microwave transmissions, each truck could wirelessly receive and transmit up to 24 telephone messages simultaneously from and to other trucks, from as much as five miles away. With the trucks daisy-chained, a long-distance telephone network could be deployed in a battle zone within a matter of hours.

I was actually excited to be going on a field trip. Anything was better than being locked up behind the camp's tall stone walls, and bouncing in our truck along the autobahn's green belt felt freeing: the wind from the open window brushed briskly through my crewcut and whistled past my ears. Four hours and 150 miles later, the convoy pulled off the road near Hohenfels, at the edge of the Schwarzwald (the Black Forest), a place I'd only heard of in stories and legends. It felt like an adventure. The Schwarzwald is 93 miles long, from the High Rhine in the south to the hilly Kraichgau in the north. This dank, dense, thickly wooded area got its name from the tall conifers that block most of the light before it reaches the forest floor. Add castles, cuckoo clocks, and tiny villages, and you've got the setting for real-life fairy tales. According to legend, the Brothers Grimm were inspired by this forest when they collected and published peasant tales such as *Hansel and Gretel*, *Rapunzel*, and *Sleeping Beauty*—fairy tales, yes, but when read in the Grimms' original versions, not for young children or the faint of heart.

I stepped down from the truck's tall cab and wandered to the edge of the road to have a look. Green. Everything was green—the grasses, the trees, the fields. Compared to the brown of Southern California, this place was so green I was convinced it had never seen a dry spell in its entire history—and, judging from the overcast skies and the light mist just starting to fall, we were unlikely to see one soon. Riding in the truck's high cab, I'd seen nearby homes and villages nestled in small yards or fields carved out of the Schwarzwald and connected by winding two-lane roads. This was not the Germany I was familiar with—the big city of Stuttgart. It was gorgeous countryside, and I loved its sweet heather and scent of fresh clover. This was the Germany I had hoped for, unlike the bland of Stuttgart and the confining walls of Patch Barracks. Finally, I got to breathe in Germany's beauty.

We climbed back in the truck and, coordinates in hand, each team arrived at its destination and set up camp: a four-man tent, a microwave antenna, and a generator trailer. Our team included our esteemed leader Sgt. Adams, me, and two other grunts. Adams was a pudgy, bookish guy with Ben Franklin glasses who'd already earned an undergraduate degree; he'd joined the Army to take advantage of the GI bill, to pay his way through grad school when he got out. My job was to help set up the antenna and ground the truck by pounding a few copper rods into the dirt—tough work in hard soil, but a necessary one for the safety of the truck. The rods in place, my next task was to connect them to the truck and generator. But on that day, the gnawing in my stomach was apparently more important, so I took a break for some hot food: a can of C-Ration beef stew heated on the exhaust header of the power generator and opened with a P-38 can opener—the only Army implement that ever impressed me, for its effectiveness, compact design, and cleverness.

Adams was in the truck's cabin, setting up the communications rig as the other two grunts snoozed in the tent. I was alone at the very back of the truck, standing on the tailgate, thinking that it seemed a convenient place from which to take a whiz. I unzipped, whipped out Willy, and let fly.

Electricity flows where there's a path for it to travel. If it's left alone, like in an unused battery, it's nothing more than stored energy until it's connected to something. Our truck and its generator weren't much

77

different from a big battery. The electrical generator we'd towed provided the power to run the radios and light the inside of the truck's rear enclosure, as the power lines do in our homes. The big difference between a truck and a house is that the house is connected to the earth. The truck sits on rubber wheels that insulate it from any electrical connection. In short, a truck or a car is not grounded.

But as I watched my stream of piss arc toward the forest floor, these most basic of electrical concepts escaped me — as did the fact that I hadn't finished grounding our truck. I learned that day that human urine is a reasonably good conductor of electricity. The moment my stream struck the ground, 120 volts knocked me off my feet and hurled me through the cabin's open door. I lay there, my Willy frazzled and totally exposed. I was shaking and in my head was ringing as if I were inside a bell. It felt like a giant hand had picked me up, violently shaken the bejesus out of me, and then hurled my limp body onto the back of the truck.

Sgt. Adams calmly glanced at me and smiled. "Forget to ground the truck?"

I got through nearly a year of this assignment before the gloom became almost unbearable. It wasn't just the drab of Army green that had gotten to me, or the daily grind of washing trucks and twiddling my thumbs. I was still scared about being moved out to Vietnam. Every month a new list of Signal Corp members rotated out of Germany and headed straight for Vietnam. Of the several thousand or so that were part of my brigade an easy 100 a month were assigned to 'Nam. It hadn't escaped me that I was one of only a very few grunts who had yet to be rotated out. It was time for me to take action. I could no longer ignore the inevitable like I had before getting drafted. I needed a new job. Quickly.

But aside from photography, I wasn't qualified for anything other than being a radio DJ. The Army did have a radio station connected to the Armed Forces Network, better known as AFN, a worldwide network that provided a touch of home for US soldiers around the world. AFN Europe was the only English-language broadcast service in Central Europe, and its civilian audience far outnumbered the several hundred thousand Americans the broadcasts were intended to reach. Though there were no official rating services at the time, I later learned that AFN Europe went out to an audience of 20 million.

In Stuttgart, AFN's studios were located above an elementary school in Robinson Barracks, in the Burgholzhof community, nestled in the northern Stuttgart district of Bad Cannstatt. I'd made friends with one of the station's lifers, Staff Sergeant Tom Tucker. He wasn't very tall, had slight features and a hawk nose, and wore big dark-rimmed glasses. I made sure that Tom, who hosted a network country-music show called 1500 to Nashville, auditioned my on-air tape from California, and I pestered him daily about switching jobs. After about a month of my constant badgering, he agreed to get me an interview. I couldn't have been more excited. This was a chance to escape the grind and depression of Patch Barracks and get a job that I not only wanted, but one that would keep me off the front lines calling in air strikes. It was a perfect opportunity and, if I could get in, a legal maneuver the army would support me in. Everything I did, every thought I had, was now focused with laser-like attention on scoring that job as a DJ and getting into AFN. It was my best hope at a dream job and the perfect solution to the looming problem of Vietnam.

Unlike most radio stations, which hired on-air staff for their talent and entertainment value, AFN didn't seem to care if you were good on air. They wanted to know that you could properly pronounce cities, countries, and names in the news: an avalanche at Val-d'Isère, France; the Boğaziçi Bridge; Guyana; the Soyuz 9 spacecraft. This skill seemed useless, since DJs didn't announce the news—that came from a feed out of AFN headquarters, in Frankfurt—but the Army was set in its ways. I learned the pronunciations, and was thrilled to learn I passed the audition and was approved for transfer to my dream job. It would take several weeks for the military to process the papers and get me transferred out of the Signal Corp and into the Armed Forces Network. I woke up each morning with a renewed sense of vim and vigor. Life was good again.

And then the axe fell. I received orders for Vietnam, orders that superseded my transfer.

CHAPTER 13

WHAT WAS WRONG WITH ME? Every great plan, every one of my brilliant brainstorms, seemed to end poorly. I was always a day late and a dollar short and now I would be heading off to Vietnam despite being so close to getting what I wanted. The taste of a near victory was still sweet in my mouth. I couldn't take this sitting down. Hell, I couldn't take this standing up. I had to do something.

Fortunately, or unfortunately depending on one's viewpoint, this all felt familiar. When I'd received my draft notice, a year before, I'd taken the plunge and enlisted with a recruiter's guarantee. I could do the same now. Older and cagier now—or at least, better clued in to how the military actually works—I could choose to sign up for another three years, in exchange for an ironclad guarantee of working as a DJ in Europe and an immediate release of my old contract. The price would be high. Another year in the military stacked on top of the two I still owed them. It would be as if I was starting from scratch. And what of the recruiter's promise? The first guy had lied through his teeth. I wasn't about to make the same mistake twice. This time I had done my homework and met with a military-supplied attorney who assured me the contract could not be broken by the Army.

"It's as legal as your first one," he counseled. "Only this time you're signing up for the right thing."

It was true. Reviewing my original recruitment contract, he pointed out they had guaranteed me exactly what I had been assigned to do: a 31B, Radio Relay and Carrier Attendant. Only the recruiter's verbal description of what that job entailed had been a lie. Now, wiser and with proper legal counsel, all I had to do was sign over another year of my life and be guaranteed a job spinning records in Europe for the next three years. It was a big decision, one I had only a single weekend to ponder before committing to the deal.

I asked my friends for advice and was told in no uncertain terms I was nuts to even consider the move.

"What are you," said my new bunkmate Jeremy, "a lifer or something? Go to 'Nam and you're back on the streets in 18 months. Eighteen months! You can do that."

But I didn't think I could. No, this was too much. I had tried for the quick fix, the brass ring, the easy solution one too many times — and each decision had ended poorly: the car, the fix-it tickets, Canada, ignoring the draft. It was time for me to take a good hard look at my life. I needed to get away from the barracks and Stuttgart, to clear my head and make my decision.

I had heard of a beautiful waterfall not more than 30 minutes by train. It seemed like an ideal spot to get some distance and perspective. I packed my trusty hash pipe and a 35mm film can full of Lebanese Red in a knapsack, along with a little lunch: a few German semmel rolls, light brown crusty ovals that flowered into fluffy white bread when cracked open; a cold bratwurst still slathered in freckled German mustard saved from lunch the day before; and a few bottles of sparkling Spezi, a popular beverage melding Coke and orange cola. Soon I was on the train heading south to Bad Urach. This small town of spas and tourists is located in the beautiful Maisen Valley, a narrow cut of land nestled at the foot of the Swabian Alps: a mountain range in Baden-Württemberg, bounded by the Danube River in the southeast and the upper Neckar River in the northwest. Summer was nearing its end, yet in this lush valley the carpet of yellow rapeseed flowers was just beginning to falter. In its place bright green underbrush anxiously waited its turn. Alongside the train's tracks was the Brühlbach, a meandering stream nourishing bright green moss clinging to a bed of limestone. Bad Urach was right out of a picture book of quintessential German towns: a lovely little village that couldn't have been more than a few streets big. Its buildings were plaster white, trimmed in brown inlaid wooden patterns and capped with steep tall red roofs, and everywhere there were tourists taking pictures and ogling at the sights of this tiny burg. But I had come here to get away from it all — to sit high atop a mountain and figure out my next move.

I traipsed past the village spa center where tourists and locals frolicked in the warm volcanic waters and refreshed themselves with strong-

81

scented mineral-infused vapors. None of them seemed to have as heavy a burden weighing them down as I did. Their fading laughter made me feel all the gloomier as I hiked away from them on the footpath, along the Brühlbach stream fed from the waterfall above. It was crowded when I got to the falls, with perhaps 20 or so tourists craning their necks at the 100-foot free-falling water cascading over rocks and moss to crash in a bridal veil of enveloping white mist. A crowd was the last thing I wanted. At the bottom of the falls, partially hidden from view by the fog of obscuring water wetting everyone and everything, was a set of steps that no one in the crowd seemed to have noticed. After nearly half an hour's climb I found myself high above the waterfall's roar in a meadow fed by the gentle flow of the Brühlbach's headwaters. There wasn't a soul to see. It was perfect.

With my back nestled against a smooth boulder close to the stream's serenade I stuffed my pipe with a few crumbles of bright red hash and blew clouds of blue smoke into the air. Soon a calmness came over me and I felt as much a part of nature as the stream, the flowers, the harvesting insects, and the warm rock on my back. I closed my eyes and tried to imagine starting over in the army. Three more years. To an antsy 22-year-old three years seems like a lifetime. And it was a lifetime to me, but then I weighed my choices. There was the quick way out: stay alive for the next 18 months in Vietnam and be home to restart my life where I had left off, as a broke DJ trying to figure out what the hell I was doing and where I was going. Or, make the investment of another three years and graduate from this prison sentence with high marks and radio experience at one of the largest networks in the world. When I thought of it that way it didn't seem quite so bad. Still, three long years. I ran the problem again, looked at it every way from Sunday, and kept coming back to the same conclusion. I wasn't going to listen to my friends. I would make my own decision, and perhaps for the first time in my life I wouldn't take the easy way out. I would invest the time and make it work. I hated that decision, but I knew I couldn't keep making the same mistakes over and over again.

And so there, high atop a mountain in Germany I stared up at the azure sky and made my decision. No more quick fixes. No more brass rings to grab. No more shortcuts. I would man up, take my licks, and invest the next three years of my life as a disc jockey for Uncle Sam.

My few Army friends were horrified. They called me a traitor, a lifer, a sucker for giving in to the military, which we all hated for having robbed us of our freedom. They all thought I'd taken the easy way out, which was exactly the opposite of what I knew to be true. On my last day at Patch Barracks, not one person I knew said goodbye or even met my eye. I was an untouchable. This depressed me, because I was more than a little afraid that they were right. But by then I'd already signed the papers. The Army's contract cut both ways. They couldn't welch on the deal and, once I signed it, I couldn't get out of it. I hoped this move would turn out better than my previous disasters.

At least I now had hope … again.

CHAPTER 14

WITHIN WEEKS OF my new contract I had been reassigned to AFN Stuttgart. Unlike Patch Barracks there was no housing for AFN personnel. Instead, the Army provided extra pay for soldiers to live "on the economy" in rented apartments or houses. My extra allowance wasn't much—just a few hundred bucks—but between that extra pay and a little savings I'd managed to stash away there was enough to afford a beat-up old VW van for transportation and a small apartment in Ludwigsburg, 20 minutes north of Stuttgart. The blue and white VW van had been owned by one of the soldiers at Patch Barracks and he had outfitted it for camping with an add-on gasoline powered heater fueled from the vee-dub's gas tank, a set of homemade wooden cabinets, and under the floor mats custom welded metal compartments with latched covers for storing small camping items. My new home was a two-room loft above a shoe repair store with a simple kitchen in the living room and a bedroom just big enough for a small bed. Though it wasn't much, it sure beat the barracks. Suddenly, life got a whole lot better and I was feeling vindicated for my decision to sign up for another three years of Army life.

The programming of the Armed Forces Network was eclectic, much like National Public Radio's lineup today. Each broadcast hour began with five minutes of live network news, followed by that hour's program. There was something for just about everyone's taste: country, classical, variety, rock, music, and magazine-style news programs.

I worked the afternoon on-air shift, 3 to 6 pm, playing pop music—mostly bubblegum, like the Osmonds' "One Bad Apple," the Bee Gees' "How Can You Mend a Broken Heart," and Tony Orlando and Dawn's "Knock Three Times"—then spent the rest of the work day recording public service announcements and doing mundane station chores. This was a major improvement over washing trucks and twiddling my fingers in the Signal Corp. Armed with the knowledge I could not be ordered to Vietnam, I was doing pretty well. My biggest challenge was figuring out a way to spend the next three years of my life not going stark raving mad from the mind-numbing routines of Army drudgery, the radio station, and keeping my nose clean. I had been warned first by the recruiter I had signed my contract with, then by my new commanding officer at AFN, that the radio station gig was a privileged one. Expectations for on-air personalities were extremely high — higher than for just about anyone else in the Army. AFN personnel were expected to maintain the highest standards of conduct and personal grooming habits if they were to be trusted on the air. Failure to abide by these rules was the one way the military could retract their contract with me. Violating any of the unwritten rules at AFN carried the potential of being dismissed from duty and sent back to ... well, no one quite seemed to know what would happen because apparently no one had ever broken the rules at AFN. It all made sense, if only from the military's perspective. I was never very good at following orders, so I determined it'd be best to lay low and not be seen. My plan was to spend as much of my free time as I could manage away from the Army: attending rock concerts, making a few friends, and inevitably in the 70s culture, doing lots of drugs.

Maybe I just like living on the edge. Given my commanding officer's warning to maintain the highest military standards at all times, it always felt a bit daring when I roamed around the seedier parts of German culture doing my best to fit in. It was certainly exciting if not foolhardy. I had time on my hands and an itch to be a part of this new European hippie culture that seemed everywhere. It wasn't long before I began filling my nights and weekends with hash. It was easy to score — it took only a few minutes of hanging around on a downtown side street to catch the eye of some shady-looking guy with shoulder-length hair who would sell me what I wanted. Which I did. Often. The way I figured it, what the Army didn't see didn't matter. As long as our two worlds never met I would be okay.

While I was pretty comfortable with hash I was always tempted to try something stronger, like LSD — acid — a powerful drug that came in many forms and potencies: Orange Sunshine, Purple Haze, Windowpane, etc. All varieties were said to have one thing in common: they grabbed hold of your mind and body for eight hours or more and

85

took you on a wild ride from which there was no escape until the next morning. Some varieties were said to be wilder—more dangerous—than others. The smart guys began with a drop of one of the gentler strains in liquid form, usually Blotter Acid or Windowpane, soaked into a matrix of paper or plastic.

Unfortunately, those street smarts were learned in hindsight.

I had befriended a German drug dealer who seemed to take a liking to me. His name was Joachim, a tall, slender twenty-something with long, stringy sable hair, a big black walrus mustache that weighed down his upper lip, and gentle hazel eyes. I had bought plenty of hash from Joachim and he always treated me fairly, so a kind of trust had developed between us. I'd find Joachim outside a popular disco in Stuttgart called Cinderella, a loud and garish affair in the basement of an old building accessed by a long stairwell that smelled like stale piss and fresh vomit. The dance floor was surrounded by mirrors and bright lights, and the music was loud and unending. The few times I ventured into the hall in search of female companionship I felt lost and unwanted. My short army haircut, the fact that I cannot dance, and my nervousness around beautiful women all conspired to make me feel uncomfortable and out of place. I wasn't the only one: there were almost no GIs in there which, I figured, was a good thing. The further from any contact with the Army the safer I was. Instead, a steady stream of partygoing young Germans danced and drank the night away, unaware of me and just as uncaring. My real companionship, it turned out, was outside and around the corner, where my buddy Joachim suggested that if I really wanted to get into the German culture and feel included, I should take a trip—and not one involving trains, planes, or automobiles. He'd get me some of the good stuff. But not just any LSD. It had to be strong and pure, a claim that as I think about it now ran counter to common sense. Joachim's advice was simple: "Strong means pure. Go pure for your first time." Well, jeez. Who doesn't want pure? What the hell did I know?

I followed my friend's advice and went whole hog, downing a hit of Orange Sunshine: strong LSD cut with strychnine to intensify the experience. But intense doesn't adequately describe what happens when that drug took hold. It began with a wavy motion—curtains over the closed windows began undulating in a nonexistent breeze. Outside, leaves or bushes started moving without benefit of wind. Soon, the ground itself, and fixed objects on it, tilted, lights brightened to an unbearable glare, and the colors of everything changed. Sounds became distorted and magnified, as if run through an aural funhouse mirror, and the normally wide world shrank until it felt like a tight bubble around me. That's when the paranoia crept in. I felt trapped, unable to extinguish or reroute thoughts and emotions I might normally ignore. The paranoia in turn fed self-doubt, until my protective shields of ego, motivations, accepted norms, and cherished beliefs were stripped bare to reveal the basic defining stories: who I am, what the world is. Then the paranoia passed, the self-doubt healed, my mind felt unshackled and my spirit could fly—and possibility seemed endless.

On that first trip, after the paranoia passed, I spent the next few hours on the floor of Joachim's apartment with six other German trippers, listening over and over to side one of Led Zeppelin's II on a record player that, at the end of the side, automatically played its four songs again. Somehow, three fellow acid-travelers and I crawled up off the floor and stumbled into someone's Volkswagen Beetle. Our intention was to get out of that little apartment and go to a park, but the driver was so stoned he couldn't keep track of where the road was, much less where we were headed. Each of us—two in the front, two in the back—had to focus on the part of the road nearest him to help navigate. We could just barely do it. It's a miracle we didn't kill anyone, or ourselves.

I was thankful I survived that evening, but I wanted to keep my distance from hallucinogens without giving up getting high. Joachim's advice had brought me fresh insight into feeling more into the German culture, though it was hardly the culture most folks would have thought of as normal for a twenty-something on his first trip to Europe. But, this was the 70s and a time when it seemed like everyone my age was getting deep into music and drugs. I certainly didn't want to be left out, but acid was a bit too strong and unnerving for anything more than the occasional trip. To stay a part of the German youth scene on a full-time basis, I figured I'd be better off going back to what first got me into the culture: hash. It was an expensive pastime hard to maintain on a serviceman's pay, surely a problem in need of a budding entrepreneur like me. Joachim and his fellow businessmen would have to find a new source for their revenue—I would soon find myself in competition with them.

The economic model of the street-drug trade was simple: wholesalers purchase large amounts at low costs and retail smaller amounts at higher costs. To become a drug czar, I'd have to travel to the wholesale marketplace—Amsterdam. I'd never been there, something I'd have to fix if I truly wanted to flourish and fit into this new culture. My old best friend, David, who'd bailed me out of jail by buying my hi-fi system, and who I'd said goodbye to in Bellingham, Washington, gave me just the excuse I needed. He had also wound up in the Army—and, miraculously, was also in Germany. David had been sent to Wildflecken, at the border of northwestern Bavaria and southern Hesse, one of the coldest, highest-altitude US Army bases in all of Germany. He was miserable there, so had applied for a transfer to the Seventh Army Choir in sunny Heidelberg, but as of yet he was still stuck in the bitter cold of his rocky prison. I convinced him to take a few days' leave and travel with me in my VW van to Amsterdam, where we would pool our resources and score a kilo of hash on the cheap.

It was good to connect with David again. He'd gotten disinterested in the religious kick he'd been on and had found himself immersed in the same drug culture as me, only where he was forced to live it was even harder to get access to hash. In contrast to the easy access I had in Stuttgart, he'd have to travel nearly 100 miles to find his version of Joachim. He was more than excited to solve that problem and head into another adventure with me—this time, to become a drug king and my partner in crime.

CHAPTER 15

AMSTERDAM WAS A CITY alive with canals, boats, flowers, hippies, unpronounceable words, gorgeous women, and, above all, bicycles. I don't know that I have ever seen so many bikes on city streets, before or since. I loved the culture I saw and felt more at home here. Instead of the neatly organized precision housing of Germany, Amsterdam's residences were an eclectic mélange of tall and short; skinny and fat; straight and leaning; brick and stone crammed together without so much as a hair's breadth between them. Row upon row of many-windowed dwellings erupted out of the brick-lined canals serving the city as blood to a body. Streets and bridges crossed hundreds of waterway veins splitting neighborhoods, parks, and civic buildings into city life islands. And everywhere there were boats, bikes, trees and the occasional car crowding the edges of what little dry land remained. Perhaps best of all, Dutch people smiled wider than Germans and there was a palpable if mysterious frivolity in the Amsterdam air. But we were here on business and I couldn't let our attention wander. With our mission foremost in our minds, a roll of cash, and dressed in our best hippie tie-dyed shirts to look the part of dope buyers, we hit the streets.

As in Germany, a nod of the head, a wink, a grunt, or a shady look was all it took to attract the people who most interested us. Hash dealers carried samples of their wares inside their long coats, which they opened for inspection like a hot-watch merchant. They had Lebanese Blonde and Red, Afghani Black, and Moroccan Green to choose from, but all of those were too expensive. The people trying to sell it seemed like they saw us coming, and the prices they were offering were nearly the same as what Joachim and the others in Germany were asking. We guessed we stood out like sore thumbs: two short-haired Americans in search of a deal on hash. We weren't really getting anywhere and got discouraged, but kept with it until late that afternoon, after we had ventured into Amsterdam's famous red-light district where women displayed their wares in windows along the street. A particularly sleazy-looking Dutch guy with scraggly, unkempt hair, a pockmarked face, hip boots, and a rawhide vest with leather tassels was standing alongside one of the windows where the prostitutes worked. He was leaning up against the side of the building smoking a cigarette. He yanked his head to the side beckoning us to go into the alley beside the storefront. He was either trying to get us hooked up with women or hash, but clearly, he was up to no good.

"Americans?" he asked in a gruff smoker's voice.

We owned up to our citizenship as quietly as we could and did our best to look like seasoned buyers, rejecting his high-priced offering of Afghani black, his better deal of Lebanese Red, and his final deal for sweet blonde from an unknown region. Just as we were getting ready to bail, his thin-lipped smile turned into that knowing secret look: the quick raising of the eyebrows, the slight upturn of the corners of the mouth. He said he could fix us up with something extraordinary—white hash—for the right price. He said we were obviously savvy buyers and he wouldn't offer this to just anyone, but because this was our lucky day, because we were there at the right time, he was going to give us the deal of the day.

I'd never heard of white hash, but it sounded exotic and looked the part: a pristine white, oily slab, about an inch thick. Before long, we'd bought a kilo of white hash from him and saved $1,000—our first wholesale purchase. Now all we had to do was smuggle it out of Holland and back into Germany.

We carefully buried the slab in a little metal compartment under the van's floor mats the car's previous owners had installed for camping supplies, changed our clothing from colorful hippie to conservative tourist, then passed through customs near Veldhuizen, on the Dutch side. Then it was on to the place that gave us the willies: the border crossing at Knauheide. More than a few Americans had been busted there on their way back into West Germany, and we didn't want to be next. If we were caught smuggling drugs into Germany, it would mean an instant German prison sentence, not to mention what the Army would do to us afterwards.

The short few miles between the Dutch crossing and the German border had us both questioning what the hell we were doing. It's one thing to come up with grand ideas like stealing my mother's credit card and driving my '55 Chevy to Canada to escape the draft, yet quite another to try smuggling drugs into another country. We knew the Germans were tough on drug dealers. What had we been thinking? Maybe we just hadn't. But now, we were trapped between two countries with a kilo of hashish hidden in the floorboards of my VW van. Did we imagine that we were the first to try this and that the Germans would be as clueless as we had apparently been? The drumbeat in my chest was paralyzing. David and I considered pulling over to the side of the road and chucking our contraband, but the slim chance of success and the thought of cheap hash outweighed any commonsense move we might have had in us. Luck had been by our side in the past; perhaps she'd hover over us again.

The line of cars inched toward the lowered gate at Knauheide, where two green-suited West German cops, one on each side of the vehicle about to pass through the gate, questioned drivers and passengers alike. Occasionally one of them signaled a car to pull into a parking area, where teams of cops waited to thoroughly inspect the vehicle, in search of contraband. As we approached, my pulse raced. The cop on my side of the car didn't look much older than I was, but his pinched, precision-trimmed mustache and intense gaze had a steely authority that shook me. These cops were serious and it was too late to turn back now. I think if I had seen just how serious they were I would have never attempted to smuggle drugs into the country. Oh, shit. Now it was our turn. We inched up to the gate and I rolled down my window and smiled my most innocent face.

"American?" Of course, he already knew this—my van's green US Army plates. He hardly looked at our IDs. He was more interested in the back of the van.

"Aus!" he ordered. We stepped out of the van. This was not good. In fact, this couldn't be worse. Most of the traffic had been let through to journey on. Only a few had been stopped and now they demanded we get out.

The first cop kept an eye on us as the second, flashlight in hand, rummaged through the van's cabinets, glove compartment, engine area, and under its seats. The back of my neck felt as if it were on fire. The two cops spoke quietly to each other. Then the second cop got in the van, fired it up, and pulled it into the holding area. David and I were marched across the road, into a building, down a hall, and into a small, cramped waiting room with a locked and windowed door. Here were six other frightened people: a young couple with a baby, two long-haired Dutch hippies who looked like drug dealers, and an old Middle Eastern man who yelled at the guard every time the door opened. I felt like puking.

David and I sat nearest the door, on a hard wooden bench, awaiting what we assumed would be a trip to jail. The thought of being locked up petrified me. I promised myself that if only we were let go, I'd go straight and toe the line—a promise of questionable validity, and one I'd already broken in Ward E20 and knew had little sway, even if there was someone actually listening in on my soul. The door opened, and in walked a big, mean-looking bull of a West German cop. He had to be almost six foot six, with the body of a weightlifter. His expression was that of a butcher hacking apart a side of beef. None of us dared to meet his gaze as he strode straight to the Dutch hippies and handcuffed both of them. The door's lock clicked shut behind them, and the rest of us stood at the window and watched as he marched the hippies down the hall. I had never really given any thought to how the condemned must feel as their date with the gallows neared. Every sound must be amplified. Every outside motion—even the landing of a robin on the window or the buzzing of a fly—would draw rapt attention. The ticks of distant clocks must sound like drumbeats as every second draws the doomed closer to their maker. The guard would soon come for David and me and march us down the green mile. It was only a matter of time.

Our holding cell was deathly still for the next half an hour. My eyes were fixed on the floor, wondering what crimes the others in the room were guilty of. Then the inevitable: the bull came for us, but without handcuffs. I felt a glimmer of hope in an otherwise desperate situation. David and I were led down the same hall as the Dutch hippies and into a room with a single wooden table. A smartly uniformed woman with a thick German accent spoke to us in English.

"Is this yours?"

On the bench was my backpack, its top flap open.

"Yes," I said.

She emptied the contents onto the bench. Nearly $1,000 in cash, a small glass bong, a pack of red rolling papers bearing the iconic portrait of the Zig-Zag man, a butane lighter, my leather pouch full of hash pipes, a half-eaten sandwich, and a map of Amsterdam with the drug-dealing part of town circled. But no kilo of hash.

"You know it is illegal to bring drugs into Germany?"

We nodded. I kept my hands behind me so she couldn't see how badly they were shaking. I was certain the very next thing she'd pull out was that kilo. My father used the same tactic: he'd bring forward just a little bit of evidence and demand I tell him the truth, the whole story. That gave me a chance to come clean and cleanse my soul before he whipped me for the crime. He believed that if he could coax the truth out of me I'd be the better man for it, and perhaps he was right. But I never gave in, preferring to take my chances that the evidence he had was little more than conjecture. I was right more often than wrong.

She conferred with the guard and the two nodded in agreement. It was at that moment I knew we were toast. Done for, destined to rot in jail. I swallowed hard as she approached, certain she would pull out that block of white hash which would seal our fate. And then she stopped mid-stride as a loud clanging permeated the air. I could hear doors opening in other parts of the building, and lots of people shouting. Suddenly the rear door to our little room burst open and one of the guards who had stopped us ran in. He yelled something in German that caused them both to drop our stuff, pull their weapons from their black leather holsters, and sprint after him out the door.

"What the hell's going on?" asked David.

Through the open door we could hear more shouting and other alarm bells. David bravely stuck his head out the door, then motioned for me to do the same.

"There's the van," he hissed.

The open rear door faced the parking lot where the van sat untended. Something was going on at the border crossing gate 100 feet to the south of us. A big semi-truck was stopped, its cab doors wide open, and its driver lay facedown on the asphalt with his hands over his head. The young guard with the thin mustache was holding a gun on him and screaming something while the other guards swarmed over the truck's cab and trailer. No one was paying the slightest attention to David or me. David shrugged his shoulders, headed out the door towards the van, then motioned for me to scoop up the contents of my pack and join him.

I stuffed everything on the table into the pack, and by the time I was out that back door David was dangling the VW's keys in front of me.

"Yeah, but we can't just …" I whispered, nervous as hell at what David was contemplating.

David grabbed the pack, opened the van's side door and flung it in, then tossed me the keys.

"Come on, man!"

Jesus. Now we were going to be fugitives too? My hands were wet and cold. This wasn't a game, and it sure wasn't TV. This was real. If they started shooting at us like Mr. Wright at the egg ranch, it sure as hell wouldn't be rock salt hitting us.

"Come on, come on!" hissed David.

I was frozen in place. David was ready to hightail it out of there while the semi-truck bust was distracting everyone. Now there was more shouting, more guards had weapons drawn, and at least ten people had been pulled out of the truck and shoved face-down on the roadway.

"McGowan!" David yelled from inside the van.

My feet refused to move. I was trapped. The keys for our escape were in my clenched hand, but the courage to flee was missing.

"Aus, aus!" The same cop who'd rummaged through the van restrained a kneeling prisoner with one hand while waving at us with the other, as if to clear away a swarm of flies.

What did this mean? Was he signaling for us to leave? "Aus" meant out, I knew. I looked to David and he was nodding his head yes. Yes, we should get out?

"Aus, aus!" He seemed to be motioning for us just to leave the area. It was then I noticed his hand was not waving towards the open road, as I had wanted to believe, but instead back at the opened door of the interrogation room.

"Come on, McGowan!" David yelled.

My right foot began to inch towards the van.

"Halt!" the guard yelled, unable to move closer because his prisoner was still kneeling.

It was too late. I found myself stumbling into the driver's seat and fumbling with the keys, even as the cop yelled for backup. Jesus. Now or never.

"Do it!" yelled David.

I mashed the clutch to the floor, cranked the engine, and we rolled backward on the lot's slight incline. Now the cop was waving his hands at the others and pointing at us.

"Now!" ordered David.

I let the clutch fly and we lurched forward a few feet, leaving the cop and his prisoner engulfed in a puff of blue smoke before the engine died.

"Now, now, now!" David's eyes were as big as dinner plates.

I felt like I was going to throw up, but got the van started again and we began moving away from the melee, the cop screaming unintelligible words. Within 30 seconds the chaos faded into the distance and we kept moving as fast as that old VW van could manage: away from the border, away from the shouting and guns and blue flashing lights. I constantly checked the rearview mirror, looking for flashing blue lights. But no one followed us.

"Take that road," demanded David.

An offramp pointed towards some little town, and we exited there to find a hiding spot just north of the road. We parked the van and shut off its engine to wait. We hardly spoke a word, both of us frozen in our seats, afraid to even move, let alone discuss what had just happened. I was sure I had soiled myself. Was there an all-points bulletin for the Germans to be on the lookout for us? Had they written down our license plate? It wasn't until darkness rolled in and the evening moisture laid a thick carpet over the van that we inched our way back onto the highway and headed home, alone in the right lane of the Autobahn. We spent more time staring in the rearview mirror than watching the road ahead.

Back in West Germany, still watchful at every moment in the rearview mirror, before we got to Wildflecken, we fired up a bowl of that rare white hash, our hard-won prize, the material that came close to landing us in a German jail cell for the better part of our lives. It was like smoking sawdust. Nothing. Our hearts sank. We'd been robbed. That sleazy Dutch guy. We then bickered over who should have known better, which of us should have spotted the fraud, but in the end we both had to swallow a meal of crow. We chucked our worthless blocks of nothing in the trash — though I saved a small nugget in my leather bag of hash pipes. A reminder to pay more attention in the future.

CHAPTER 16

A FEW MONTHS AFTER our failed attempt at becoming hash dealers, David called to tell me he'd gotten his wish: he'd been reassigned to the Seventh Army Choir in Heidelberg, at last escaping the lonely cold of Wildflecken. Excited, he said he had something to show me, but didn't want to talk about it over the phone. I was anxious to reconnect with David. He was still my best friend and the only real connection with the world I once knew. So I drove the 60 miles to Heidelberg, where we would celebrate his reassignment. This was a great moment for David and I was happy for my friend. We'd been through a lot together, though much of it was trouble. This was instead a happy moment, a joyous occasion and one to be celebrated properly.

Heidelberg is one of the oldest cities in Germany, a picturesque university town along the Neckar River in the shadow of the thousand-year-old Heidelberg Castle. I met David in Old Town, among a collection of bars, shops, and restaurants near the Heiliggeistkirche (Church of the Holy Spirit), a massive church with a tall tower that looks out over the city. David had picked a little hole in the wall, the Wirtshaus zum Nepomuk, a traditional German eatery with animal heads on the walls and busty women in classic white blouses, black flowered pinafores, and frilly aprons slinging food and beer. Following a dinner of Wiener schnitzel, pommes frites, and a mixed-vegetable salad, we drove to the student district and parked on a quiet side street, where David showed me his secret: an oozing, oily, heavy black lump about the size of a tennis ball. Reverently, he told me that it was the finest black hash in the world. He didn't own the lump outright; he'd bought into it as one might buy into a collective. "This'll kick your ass," he said.

I smoked one bowl. He was right. Despite my tolerance for cannabis, now well-established through months of daily toking, that black hash did as advertised. We sat in the back of the van stupefied, unable even to turn the radio on. I had smoked a lot of dope up to that point but nothing anywhere close to the strength of that black opium-laced ball of oily clay. Within seconds I knew it was too much and it would soon overwhelm me in an uncomfortable way. Big hits of ultra-strong cannabis and I never did well together. Smaller doses were easier on my system and I enjoyed the slow build up to a nice buzz but this...this was through the roof strong and I started to panic. I needed some air, perhaps even to get out of the van and stumble around to try and break its mighty grip on me. I felt myself hyperventilate and worked to calm myself: slow, controlled breathing. This wouldn't last for too long, I counseled myself.

Then, without warning, the street filled with lights: blue, flashing, bright, and white. We heard car doors flung open—not the doors of my van, but of two other cars, in front and in back of us. It was the West German police. Ice shot up my spine, and my hash-induced haze was immediately replaced by ultra-alertness. I did the only thing I could think of; ignoring David's pleadings, I threw the ball of hash out the window. He was deeply in debt for that ball, but at the moment that seemed the least of our problems.

The van's doors were flung open, and a flashlight blinded us. Angry shouting in German. They knew we were Americans from the van's green US plates, and from the fact that neither of us understood a word they said. They pulled us from the van and threw us to the ground. A boot—it might have been a knee—pressed on my back kept my face smushed against the pavement, which smelled of beer and piss. The police searched the van and found only my leather bag, stuffed full of old pipes and my little keepsake of "white hash." That was all they needed. We were handcuffed and taken to jail. This wasn't something we'd easily escape. We were in the custody of police. Real police. Police who had the goods on us and apparently had every intention of making sure we'd not go down this route again. I don't think I've ever been so scared as I was at that moment.

My three nights in jail when I was 18 were like a vacation compared to this. That California jail was a single room with twin beds, a bathroom, a bare light bulb, and a small window that let a bit of light in. This cold, dank West German holding cell was a windowless place of cement and steel, with two metal bed-benches affixed to the cement wall by a hinge and hanging on two chains, one at each end. No blanket or pillow, just the cold black steel of the bench to sit or lie on. The only light was what came through the cell bars from the guard's room, and the toilet was an ice-cold metal bowl without a seat. No toilet paper either. This was the real deal, the stuff you read about in books but never happens to you. A darkness spread over me, a cold and enveloping weight which I had never known. This wasn't the jail cell of a kid found guilty of not showing up for vehicle violations, the kind who could be bailed out by a friend for a couple of hundred dollars. No, this was now an international incident that involved the German police and soon the United States Army. Hell, maybe even the American Embassy. This was bad. Really bad.

The lights dimmed to a bare glow at around 10 pm. We tried to get some sleep before whatever storm of punishment or torture we were sure the morning would bring, but the truth was I couldn't close my eyes. I was bone-scared of what was about to occur. This was actually happening, not a bad dream or a scary movie: German police, drugs, and prison. Doomsday neared. I could feel it and hear its approach with each tick and tock of the clock outside our cell, echoing off the cement walls, bringing us ever closer to our fate like the doomed man I almost was at the border crossing.

What seemed like an eternity later, we were startled by screams and yells echoing through the cells. David and I looked at each other wide-eyed. Suddenly, the lights came up hard and bright. Two cops dragged in a drunken man and threw him, sobbing and pleading, into the single wooden chair that sat in the middle of the main room outside our cell. This room couldn't have been more than ten feet square—David and I were close enough to both of them that we backed as far away as we could from our cell's bars.

The bright lights blinded the prisoner. The two cops blew cigarette smoke in his face. Neither of us understood enough German to figure out what they wanted, but they wanted it badly—they screamed menacingly at the poor guy, their spittle running down his face. When he didn't answer, they started to beat him, at first with the backs of their hands. The prisoner tried to cover his face, but they didn't stop. One pulled a black, wooden baton from his belt. They thrashed the guy badly, then left him to sob and bleed on the floor as they paused for another smoke. When the bigger cop noticed that David and I were watching all this, his lip curled in anger. He pointed at us and demanded something in German. I looked away, shaking so violently I was afraid I'd piss my pants. The cops then picked up the battered man and hauled him out the door they'd come in through. The lights dimmed.

CHAPTER 17

TROUBLE AND I are close enough partners that I'm happiest when we maintain a comfortable distance. Lying on a cold steel slab in that dark Heidelberg jail cell, I feared we might have just gotten married. I'd always been able to wriggle my way out of jams before, but I doubted that would work this time. This was real. I was in German custody and soon would be handed over to the military police. When you cross the military and they catch your sorry ass, it's usually a quick ride to the gallows.

Why hadn't I honored the promise I'd made to myself when the West German border guards didn't arrest us—that henceforth I would toe the line? More to the point, hadn't I been through enough to know that the three-year investment I made by signing that contract with the Army, guaranteeing my radio job and European address, was only going to work if I kept my nose clean? That the military could not only take what little freedom I had away from me, but could put my butt in a prison cell awful enough to make 18 months in Vietnam look like a walk in the park? What was wrong with me?

We spent what seemed to be an eternity in that cell until the same loud-barking, thick-necked, cauliflower-eared cop who'd beaten the drunk in the middle of the night came for us. The cell doors were unlocked and we were escorted down a narrow antiseptic-reeking hall into a white windowless room, then ordered to sit. There wasn't even a clock to mark the passage of time but I saw through a small window that it was now nighttime. We waited for yet another eternity to pass. At last I saw a familiar uniform: the starched green of Army class A. COLLINS was written on his name tag and by the sound of his voice I knew it must be Jim Collins, the host of a popular program on AFN called "The Stateside Sound Survey," a version of DJ Casey Kasem's American Top 40. I was relieved it wasn't some bull of a Military Police wielding a baton and handcuffs, especially when I learned Jim was taking me to AFN headquarters.

On the 30-minute drive through stop-and-start evening Frankfurt traffic I did my best to answer Jim's questions without owning up to any wrongdoing. Apparently, the entire network had gotten wind of my arrest, the first such incident in the three decades of AFN Europe's operation. Jim seemed genuinely excited to hear my story, which no doubt he'd relay to every member of the AFN staff eager for news of my Bonnie and Clyde debacle. I was infamous now, something I desperately wanted not to be.

Jim, doing his best to pay me back for the juicy tidbits of my arrest, shared with me the few details he knew of my future. I would not be returning to my job in Stuttgart, that much was certain. My DJ gig was over and the Army was in the process of packing up my things and shipping them to Frankfurt. There I would remain under house arrest, until the Army Criminal Investigation Division could analyze the evidence held by the West German police and schedule a court-martial—surely a prelude, I imagined, to throwing me in the clink and tossing the key in the Rhine.

We soon arrived at AFN Frankfurt's headquarters, a modern multi-story glass-and-cement structure at Bertramstraße 6, not too far from downtown Frankfurt. Jim escorted me past the security guard with a knowing nod and showed me to my room: a bunk in the upstairs dormitory.

"You have orders not to leave this building," he said. "Let me know if you need anything. There's a restaurant downstairs."

Jim seemed genuinely concerned and I wished I could return his kindness, but I felt like a worthless schmuck. I was an outcast now, having soiled the reputation of the network. All I could do was curl up in my protective shell and go to bed, hoping for a good night's sleep before morning rolled around.

I was awakened by the searing glare of eastern light through the tall dormitory windows. It was quiet inside the dorms: the only sound I could detect was the steady rush from the air conditioning system. By 9 am my fellow DJs had dutifully gone to their respective jobs and I was left alone, a prisoner in a huge building I didn't yet know. I showered and dressed in the same clothes I had arrived in, then wandered the halls of AFN's network headquarters to get a feel for the place. Unlike AFN Stuttgart, a remodeled set of rooms above an elementary school, the Germans had built AFN Frankfurt as a top-notch broadcast facility. Its cluster of modern glass and acoustic tiled on-air studios were state-of-the-art rooms suspended on springs for sound isolation, in a quadrangle with circular windows that included the main control room, newsroom, production studio, and broadcast studio. It was real downtown radio, and I'd never seen anything like it. In the building's basement was the restaurant and bar Jim had told me of. I suppose if one had to be under house arrest this wasn't so bad, but still I was a lost soul—busted, dishonored, ready for court-martial, and overdue for prison. I tried to strike up conversations with some of the AFNers drinking beer after work, but while they were all courteous to me—painfully aware of who I was and gently prying for more details than the rumor mill had supplied—there was a palpable ocean's distance between us. I was an untouchable celebrity in the same way Clyde Barrows must have been. Few would make eye contact with me. I ate alone, I drank alone. In between I wandered the halls like an unnoticed spirit, watching the DJs do their shows.

Twenty four hours after my release from the German Polizei I found myself face-to-face in the office of a short, stocky, crewcut bear of a man: First Sergeant Roberts.

"Tell me what happened," he growled as I stood pole-straight, eyes locked on the wall behind his desk.

"I guess I was in the wrong place at the wrong time, First Sergeant," I said trying hard to keep my voice from shaking. "My friend had a little pipe and I smoked some of it. It was wrong and I am sorry."

I expected a verbal tirade but instead he leaned back in his wooden desk chair and lit a briarwood pipe. I snatched a quick glance and noticed it was the same type as my father's: a simple L shape with a black plastic mouthpiece and a dark brown, heavily grained wooden bowl rimmed in silver. He sucked on it three times to get it lit, and it made the same noises my dad's ritual did.

"Son," he said looking off in the distance, "I won't lie to you. You're in a shitload of trouble. Whether the dope was yours or your buddy's doesn't really matter. If CID comes back with a positive match for THC, I am afraid there's no place for you at AFN. I'll do what I can to get another assignment if you manage to show me you're a good soldier while we wait."

"Thank you, First Sergeant."

"Keep a low profile and do not under any circumstances leave this building. I will trust you to be a man of your word. It'll be a few months before we know what the investigators find."

"I won't violate your trust," I promised, and I meant it. There was no way I was going to try and sneak out of the building.

"Good luck, son."

Now my path was clear. I was free to wander the building and await my fate. If the CID came back with a positive result from the residue in my pipes, or if there was any THC in that chunk of white hash, I was a goner.

After a week of laying low, as the First Sergeant had advised, I was getting restless. There were no books to read and no television to watch. I had read every throwaway magazine and newspaper in the building's lobby three times before I started hanging around the newsroom. There, the editors and copywriters collected news stories from the world's wire services and recorded audio feeds from the three major networks in the States. The editors would gather at long wooden desks in front of old-fashioned typewriters, using yellow Crayon-tip paper-wrapped China markers to assemble the hourly 5-minute newscasts broadcast by AFN 24 hours a day. Everywhere there were news clippings and stories tossed about, in a clutter familiar to me from my days as a cub photographer at the Anaheim Bulletin. No one seemed to pay much attention to me, so the newsroom became a sort of sanctuary where I could hang out and read up on the news. A few of the on-air newscasters were civilians, as was their director David Minot, and they didn't much care about my situation. Unlike the soldiers they would actually talk to me, which is how I met veteran AFN newscaster Milt Fullerton. Milt was a civilian journalist who had worked for United Press International and ABC News before becoming AFN's lead anchor. He had a sad sort of face, a downturned mouth and woeful puppy dog eyes decorated with arched brows, as if he was always surprised. After hearing my story Milt felt sorry for me and started assigning me little tasks, like tidying up the newsroom or helping him gather stories from the newswires. Soon I was spending most of my day puttering around the newsroom and helping out where I could. It was certainly better than moping aimlessly through AFN's corridors.

"Doesn't anyone talk to you?" he asked one day, probably out of mild curiosity.

"Not until the investigation is over," I said. "I think they're all afraid I'll taint them with my criminality. I feel like a leper."

"I know someone who might be able to help people feel more comfortable around you," he said. "I'll have a word with Win."

Goodwin Hale "Win" White was a tall, lanky, DJ from Hartford, Connecticut. He was always smartly dressed in a crisp pressed uniform with a perfectly knotted tie, his jacket always buttoned, and his hair neatly trimmed. Win was the host of the network program *Underground*, the only AOR-style music permitted over Army airwaves. He also filled in for the newscasters when someone was ill. Win was one of AFN's superstars, and for good reason. College-educated, erudite, well-spoken, and always by-the-book in appearance, manners, and attitude, Win was the model soldier the Army wanted me to emulate. He was their golden-haired boy and AFN's management loved him. I had seen Win in my aimless wanderings often enough—his tall, perfect pose was hard to miss. I had also done my best to keep out of his way, worried he'd scold me and then launch into a lecture like those door-to-door missionaries people hide from. Milt figured Win might be the perfect soldier to help me straighten up and fly right and made a formal introduction. Win returned my tepid handshake with a confident grip, a welcoming smile, and a promise to help with whatever I needed. Instead of that uncomfortable distance between me and every other soldier in the station, Win actually seemed interested in me. Whenever we passed each other in the hall he made a point of stopping whatever he was doing and asked how I was, often introducing me to others with him. He seemed genuinely thoughtful and generous to a fault, and I was thankful for his efforts.

Maybe Win had it all figured out. He was smart, energetic, brimming with confidence, and respected by everyone that knew him. Yes, this is how I wanted to be, like Win. I had had enough of trouble and felt ready to turn my life around. Perhaps if I got another chance, Win might help steer me towards the same positive lodestar that seemed to guide his charmed life. I had no desire to be a perfect soldier but I sure as hell wanted to be like Win. Finally, I had a role model I could hope to emulate.

One evening as I wandered the station's halls, depressed about my status as prisoner, Win White cornered me.

"You and me need to talk," he said, commanding me to follow him into an unused recording studio, then locking the door behind us.

This didn't feel right. Win was an intense man, and his sharp cobalt eyes seemed to bore right through me as if I had no secrets from him. Maybe he finally felt it was time to lecture me or perhaps threaten me lest I contaminate the others in the station. He seemed protective like that. I really wanted to be in his good graces in the hopes some of him would rub off on me but by the look on his concerned face, this was building up to be more of a finger wagging lecture or a friendly warning behind locked doors. At least he was thoughtful enough not to berate me in front of the others.

"You got busted for dope," he said, looking deep in my eyes for the truth. "Did you do it?"

Shit. Same question First Sergeant Roberts asked me. Now what? My game plan all along was to proclaim my innocence in spite of the overwhelming evidence to the contrary. Should I just spoon-feed Win the same line of crap I had offered the First Sergeant? On the one hand if I was ever to get help from Win it could only work if we were honest with each other—like a shrink and patient relationship. On the other hand, if I should even so much as hint that I was guilty, it was off to prison for me without waiting on the criminal investigators. No, I couldn't answer him truthfully. He'd simply have to figure it out for himself.

"Bullshit," he replied to my denial.

My glimmer of hope evaporated. The one person in the outfit that could have helped pull me up by my bootstraps and teach me to fly right saw right through me. Figures.

From inside his smartly pressed uniform coat Win pulled out a slim glass pipe that had turned all the colors of the rainbow, right at the point where flame met glass and hash. What the hell? He proceeded to light that pipe, inhaled deeply, then handed it to me as he pursed his lips and choked on the trapped smoke in his lungs. He was grinning from ear to ear. I just held the pipe without taking a toke. It felt like a trap.

"What?" I asked him.

He just giggled, then took another toke before marching over to the room's thermostat and turning up the ventilation system to high. Win had everyone fooled, including me. It turned out that no one else at AFN Frankfurt knew about his double life: I was the only person that he was absolutely certain was as corrupt and as much a rebel as he was. Win befriended me because of my dope bust, not despite it. It was he who convinced Milt Fullerton to let me work in the newsroom so I wouldn't go stir crazy. I could not believe what I was hearing. This was incredible. A rebel in the midst of all these perfect soldiers and Win had them all buffaloed. He was razor smart in a way I could only hope to become. Instead of outwardly fighting the military he worked from within, giving them every indication he played their game while all the while controlling every aspect of the situation. By day he was a model soldier who had the run of the place. By night he was an acid-dropping, dope-smoking lunatic just as desperate to get out of the Army as I was. We bonded instantly and Win set about taking charge of my life. He spoke to the First Sergeant and got my house arrest lifted by promising to be responsible for my rehabilitation into the military mindset. He then got me an 8-hour a day gig running the master control board for the network, so I had something to do besides wander the halls.

Night after night he would "check me out" of the AFN facility for rehabilitation that consisted of bringing me to his apartment, where we smoked hash or on occasion dropped acid and listened to the Firesign Theatre—a group of four radio actors whose surreal, off-the-wall comedy sketches made political statements and mocked the establishment. This was much to the disgust of Win's wife Sharyl, who barely tolerated him, let alone me. Win took me on as his ward and I learned a great deal from him over the next few months. He coached me on how to control the situation rather than letting it control me. He told me how to figure out what each person's motivations were and generously serve them, without depriving myself of what I wanted. It all seemed so clear to Win, my new mentor.

Over the next few months life began to return to normal as I felt stronger and more empowered, though the threat of prison still loomed large over me. Though I did my best to fit in with daily life as if nothing had ever happened, I was always looking over my shoulder, panicked the axe would fall and I would be hauled off to prison.

Soon, the day of reckoning was upon me. I was summoned to stand at attention in front of AFN's commanding officer, a no-nonsense lieutenant colonel by the name of Harold Roeder. Commander Roeder scared me so badly that all I remember of him, other than his name, was his classic crew cut and brilliant green eyes. The look in those intense jade daggers will live on in my memory for eternity. The colonel hated me. He was a real military man, a soldier's soldier, and proud of it. I imagine he considered me the worst example of a GI he'd ever had the misfortune of commanding. In fact, I am sure of it. His stabbing cold orbs pierced my soul without saying a word, Sgt. Ito style. He circled me in an ever-tightening spiral as I stood at stiff attention—close enough now that his sneer of hot breath singed me and strangled my breathing. His intense gaze seemed microscopic, examining my every hair follicle, inexorably drawing out my darkest anxieties and laying them bare. I was helpless in his presence. He held my life in his hands. He toyed with it, weighing his options: should I live or die? I could feel my carotid artery pulse under my tightly-knotted black tie and starched-white dress shirt. Win had made certain my uniform was pressed and cleaned to the nines. I hoped the colonel wouldn't ask me any questions—my parched mouth probably wouldn't work.

"You are a disgrace to this outfit," said the colonel, his eyes emerald snipers, his breath still smelling of that turkey sandwich he must have had for lunch; Dijon for certain. Yes, there it was—that deep hatred, not at all disguised. "I am not sure what to do with you. The CID has analyzed the evidence and couldn't find any measurable THC."

It was unthinkable to smile when standing at stiff attention. But inside, I was grinning in joy.

"You and I both know that's BULLSHIT," he screamed that last word so loudly my ear rang. "You had a pouch full of hash pipes, and the investigators couldn't find anything. You're one lucky son of a bitch. If it wasn't for the recommendations of First Sergeant Roberts and Specialist White—both of whom assure me you're a changed man—your sorry ass would be behind bars. Instead, I'm shipping you as far away from here as I can. Munich."

I suddenly realized that he had no choice but to keep me in AFN. I had a contract that guaranteed my job for the next three years and, unless I was convicted of a crime, there was nothing he could do about it. The contract. That damned contract that I had stressed over for so long was now saving my bacon. I was thrilled but couldn't show it.

The colonel inched even closer and put his face within millimeters of mine. The hiss of his breath rattled through his nasal hairs. "Listen, you little prick," he whispered, before raising his voice so loud his spittle covered me and my ears rang even louder, "If I so much as see your name cross my desk again, I will personally make it my life's mission to put you behind bars. One way or the other, we will make a soldier of you. Do I make myself clear?"

"Sir! Yes, sir!"

CHAPTER 18

MUNICH, THE CAPITAL and largest city of the southern German state of Bavaria, sits some 30 miles north of the Bavarian Alps, on the edge of a high plain called the Alpine Foreland. With its warm, inviting, music-filled ambiance and beer-swilling, fun-loving citizens, Munich was a godsend for me. Instead of the cold and colorless places and people of Frankfurt or even Stuttgart, southern Germany was more like California than anywhere I had ever been. Mostly sunny weather coupled with smiling people, including tons of hippies and musicians, made me feel right at home. I was here to make a fresh start, to get my act together and see if I couldn't make it through my last two years of servitude without getting in trouble. It would be an opportunity to apply some of my newfound skills from Win White: maintain an outward appearance of conformity, encourage others around me, and secure a semblance of control over my immediate situation.

AFN Munich operated out of a beautiful villa on Kaulbachstraße that had previously belonged to Adolf Wagner, a district governor of the Nazi Party. After the war, many villas and mansions were taken over by the American military, and the Kaulbach was one of the finest: the size of a department store, it's four stories tall and has a ballroom. Frescos adorn the interior walls of this magnificent structure, which were mercifully covered in protective plywood before the Army moved in.

No splendid palace is complete without its gardens, and the Kaulbach Villa was no exception. Its trellised grounds were bursting with flowers, grasses, two fountains, and a miniature version of the Munich Monopteros, a neoclassical circular colonnade that sits in the middle of the nearby Englischer Gardens. The Kaulbach's landscaping was maintained by the groundskeeper, Yaki, a short, gruff, gnarled little man; and the house itself by Frau Singer, a gentle, shy, German woman.

Yaki appeared to be second in command of the house under the iron thumb rule of Irmy, the ever-scowling station's front desk receptionist, and the woman he nervously referred to as Frau Tito. With a wave of her hand she unloaded me off to Yaki to escort me to my room. "All comoonist gone," he declared—referring to the fact there were no longer any US servicemen still living in the Kaulbach—as I followed him in lockstep. To Yaki, I would soon learn, everyone was a communist, including all the Kaulbach's past residents. A refugee from communist Yugoslavia, which Marshal Tito then ruled as dictator, Yaki had been a Chetnik, one of the rebel guerrilla fighters who'd tried but failed to oust Tito. After the war Yaki had narrowly escaped and eventually made his way to Germany, where ever since he'd worked as a gardener and handyman, taking the place of the Kaulbach's former German handyman, who Frau Tito had fired for fraternizing with the female help. Now, he was the Virgil to my Dante for my new life in Munich.

On the top floor of the Kaulbach Mansion were the original owner's many bedrooms, long ago turned into living quarters for AFN staff during AFN Munich's heyday just after World War II. With my worldly possessions in hand I followed the old Yugoslavian up three flights of stairs to the end of a long hall, and waited as he fumbled to open my room. It was the corner suite—a huge expanse, originally the Kaulbach's master bedroom. Except for the Army-issue metal lockers, it was the most luxurious living space I'd ever seen. Ornate, two-story-tall, colonnade windows at the corner of the room dwarfed the single military-issue one-man bed and desk. The view outside those windows had me in awe. To the south I could see another walled villa that Yaki told me was an exclusive girls' school with its own lush grounds: a spouting fountain in the center of a perfectly coifed graveled walkway, bisected by a circular path that wound around manicured gardens bright with flowered streams of red and yellows—and all topped off with iridescent grass shaded by the leafed canopies of old trees. Out my westerly window sprawled the Kaulbach's gardens, with their own fountain just at the end of a long gravel courtyard. The courtyard bordered a stretch of curved stone stairs leading up to the villa's plaster-white deck, where summer concerts were once held in the home's glory days.

I'd gone from an Army-style barracks in Frankfurt to regal splendor in southern Bavaria. Even better, I was the only actual resident of the entire 30-room villa—the rest of the AFN staff were married or civilians who lived in off-site housing. When 5 pm rolled around, the Kaulbach Villa was left to one person: me.

My job at AFN Munich was nearly the same as it had been in Stuttgart. I had the morning show, so I had to be in uniform and on the air by 6 am I wasn't in possession of an alarm clock, but I got reasonably good at dragging myself out of bed as the morning sun lit the gardens and flooded my room with its golden hues. Sometimes it was a close call, though — more than once I was still buttoning my shirt as I wished the listeners of Munich a good morning. Without fail, Yaki would stand just outside the studio, peering through the glass to make sure I was on schedule and doing my job. Every time I ran even moderately late I would get a headshake and a scowl out of the old rebel guerilla fighter, and he'd point a threatening index finger to the clock above the control console. I would smile and hold my palms up, as if there wasn't much I could do about it — my way of acknowledging his concerns without being judgmental. Day after day this ritual played out, until I decided to play a little game with Yaki: regardless of when I actually got up, I'd make a point of getting to the studio with only seconds to spare, just to see the look on Yaki's face. I could sense within him a playfulness: just the slightest hint of a smile when he didn't think I noticed. It wasn't long before he and I had become friends of a sort, something I realized as soon as he elevated me to the tongue-in-cheek nickname "Nazi" at a time when everyone else was, to Yaki, only a "comoonist." Anyway, Yaki was a smart old guy and it didn't take him long before he guessed I was toying with him. Soon afterwards, I was awakened one morning with a loud bam bam bam on my door and Yaki's loud bark.

"Nazi!" he yelled. "Raus!"

What the hell? I cracked open the door and peered out into the dimly lit hall. Yaki pointed at his watch and through blurry eyes I could see it was 5 am He clenched his jaw and nodded his head before traipsing back down the hall. The game was over: he knew I was up an hour before my show, so arriving 30 seconds before air wouldn't work anymore. He had me on that one, and thus we started our own early morning ritual. Without fail, 5 days a week, at 5 am sharp, I could expect three loud bangs on my door, accompanied by his signature wake-up call: "Nazi! Raus!"

Within a few weeks I'd adapted to Munich, which I found far more hospitable than orderly Frankfurt. Southern Bavaria and I clicked. Young, energetic, and full of life, Munich was like a breath of fresh air. The Germany I'd recently experienced was stiff and conservative. Frankfurt shops closed early in the evening; with rare exceptions, everything closed by 9 pm, after which few people were out and about. Munich was the opposite: by 9 pm, its night life was just getting started.

Schwabing, where most of Munich's youth did their partying, is bisected by major boulevards on each side: Leopoldstraße to the south and Ludwigstraße to the north. Downtown was filled with concert venues, nightclubs, buskers, and dance halls. The festivities lasted into the wee hours each night. I quickly got hooked on the scene, but being accepted by the people took longer. As a GI in a foreign country, I found it hard to make new friends. My Army-mandated short hair, in a city filled with men with shoulder-length locks, made me stand out as just another American guy trying to crash the party scene. My Army friends in Stuttgart and Frankfurt had worn long-haired wigs to disguise their GI status, which I guess worked until you were caught—or, if you got lucky, when you undressed in front of a woman. That wasn't for me, especially considering how I'd ended up in Munich in the first place. My commanding officer had made it painfully clear—screaming in my ear while I stood at attention—that if I were to get in trouble with the Army again it was over. I had no reason to believe he wouldn't have taken the greatest of pleasures seeing me thrown in jail for the simplest of infractions of Army law, like wearing my hair long or getting caught parading around town in a long-haired wig. It was a dangerous thought, I decided, and I had been through enough trouble already.

I only had two years to go before my discharge from the military—18 months if I got lucky enough for a European out—and I wanted to make sure I was released unscathed as a free man. Yet, I still had to figure out a way to get accepted into the German crowd of musicians, hippies, and girls—otherwise this once-in-a-lifetime opportunity would pass me right by. Looking like a clean-cut American GI wasn't going to cut it with this crowd. No, if I was going to fool anyone, it wouldn't be people I wanted to get to know better—it would be the Army. I just had to figure out a plan that would satisfy both requirements: grow my hair long and keep the military happy, just like Win had taught me.

After a good deal of thought amid a strong desire to get involved in the local musician scene, I concocted what I believed was a brilliant scheme: let my hair grow long, put up my locks in bobby pins, and cover them with a short-haired wig. This seemed like the perfect solution. During the workday I would wear my short hair wig around the radio station. To the Army I would seem perfectly groomed at all times: a model soldier that never had to be reminded to get a haircut—a real Win White move. At night I'd remove the bobby pins and let 'er fly. It was a risky move, yes, but the two sergeants I worked with, "Uncle Vic" and Sgt. John, were clueless DJs and almost never paid attention to me. They went about their daily chores as if I didn't exist. Even the station's civilian manager, Neil Fontaine, was so obsessed with his own career that I hardly ever saw him at work. It seemed like the perfect plan, and best of all, it worked.

It wasn't long before I was accepted into Munich's music subculture, partly because of my longer hair and my nightly forays into Munich's music scene, but mostly because I lived in a mansion—a mansion with a recording studio. When the workday ended at Kaulbach Villa, a stream of uniformed AFN staff exited the front door as, through the back door, the night shift of unruly, long-haired musicians and hippies entered. We were ready to party, smoke dope, play music—and have me record everything, from their demo albums to interviews that we would later air on AFN's network.

The AFN recording studio was in the second-floor ballroom, a huge space of about 1,000 square feet, with a two-story ceiling and a beautifully hand-carved wooden balcony around its perimeter. I always imagined guests in the early 1900s standing along this balcony, drinks in hand, watching as dancers waltzed to Johann Strauss II's "The Beautiful Blue Danube." Near the ballroom's double-wide entrance doors was a production studio, with a window looking out onto the dance floor.

Microphone connectors fed the mixing board in the production studio, where two tape recorders were at the ready. While the ballroom had been there since the villa's completion in 1889, the recording studio was an add-on by the US forces who took over the facility in 1945. I can only imagine the recordings they must have made of bands and small ensembles following World War II. For me and my musician friends, the setup was perfect. I just had to be careful. If my superiors discovered the villa's nighttime transition from sedate Army radio station to wild party-mode, with half of Munich's artists and musicians invading the place, it'd be bad news for me. Fortunately, the AFN staff entered and left the building like clockwork. All of them, that is, except Yaki. Yaki was a wild card and he didn't approve of anything that was going on nights in the Kaulbach Villa. I took it upon myself to get to know him well enough to predict what he would and wouldn't do. I certainly didn't need him ratting me out.

Over the next few months he and I would chat about "stuff" on weekends as he raked the gravel to perfection and trimmed the mansion's rose and lilac bushes. I did my best to pry into his personal life as much as was polite, but he never let me in, so I started ribbing him about his boss Irmy — Frau Tito — implying the two of them were having an affair. His eyes would flare wide and he'd playfully threaten me with pruning shears or chase me off with a rake.

One lazy Saturday morning, as I quietly munched a bowl of milk and cereal in the villa's cavernous basement kitchen, I heard some scratching noises from inside the tunnel. During the war years the Germans had built a network of tunnels connecting many of the larger homes together. These escape routes had been sealed off with cement barriers by Allied troops following the war, but a portion of the Kaulbach's tunnel remained. In the very back of the kitchen and dining area was a tall metal door with a long lever clasp that covered what remained of the tunnel. It sounded to me like an animal might be inside, something that didn't seem too unlikely since the tunnel still went under the gardens and ended at the miniature Monopteros. I pulled up the latch and stuck my head into the blackness. There was only silence.

"Hello?" I asked into the dark.

I swear I could hear more shuffling, perhaps a whisper. I searched for the light switch, only to be startled half to death by the dim outline of Yaki.

"Nazi," he hissed. "Go."

This was completely unexpected and I had no idea what to say, but as my eyes adjusted to the darkness I could see another form pressed against the tunnel wall, as if trying to melt into it. The housekeeper, Frau Singer. I smiled at Yaki, gave him a thumbs up, and gently latched the door. I knew from that moment on that my secret was safe with Yaki, just as his was with me.

CHAPTER 19

As my hair lengthened over the next year and I got to know and work with more musicians, I was offered the job of hosting *Underground*, AFN's one-hour weekly AOR show of music and interviews with musicians, once hosted by my buddy Win White, who had come to my rescue in Frankfurt. This was my first network show that would reach AFN's huge 20 million strong audience throughout most of Western Europe and the Benelux, and the offer was quite a vindication given where I had started after being released from that German jail cell. Finally, the Army trusted me enough — or more likely had forgotten me enough — to let me host an actual network broadcast. *Underground* was a big deal. Interviews on the show were with some of the biggest names in music: Zappa, America, Humble Pie, Cat Stevens, Fleetwood Mac, Procol Harum, Led Zeppelin. They came to AFN's microphones because the station's audience of 20 million listeners was the largest in Europe. Each week, I not only got the opportunity to interview these stars but also got free VIP tickets to their concerts. It was the most coveted show on AFN's network for those of us interested in rock and roll music, and I was certain Win White was responsible for my getting the gig.

Summer nights in Munich are rich with outdoor activities. The beer halls and restaurants overflowed onto the sidewalks, buskers performed on street corners in the hopes of picking up a few Deutschmarks or the occasional lump of hash, and everywhere there are warm lights, sweet smelling flowers, and a gaiety not seen in the dark of winter. Weekend concerts by major acts were commonplace at the Circus Krone; it had been built in 1919, but during World War II it had been wrecked by Allied bombing.

It was June 4, 1971 when one of those concerts changed the shape of my life. I waved my VIP pass to the ticket checker outside Circus Krone, where keyboardist Keith Emerson, bassist Greg Lake, and drummer Carl Palmer, better known as Emerson, Lake, & Palmer and later as ELP, were giving their first concert in Munich. ELP was a big deal in the 1970s—they eventually scored nine gold records in the US and sold 48 million albums worldwide. Their music was dominated by Emerson's flamboyant playing of the Hammond organ, piano, and Moog synthesizer. I had read reviews of the Moog in industry magazines like Billboard. The synthesizer was claimed to be the next stage of musical evolution: a device so advanced it would forever change the way music was played, obviating the need for traditional instruments like guitars and drums. This was a wild claim I wanted to investigate for myself.

The Moog synthesizer is an electronic instrument that can produce just about any sound imaginable, and many that aren't. A skillful operator can adjust its many knobs, switches, and patch cords to mimic the sound of any acoustic or electric instrument. Back then, Moog synthesizers were large, expensive, complex machines used by only a few musicians, including Keith Emerson, Pink Floyd, Curved Air, and the Beatles. Over time they would become more affordable and easier to use, eventually providing the basis for nearly every modern recording.

I knew about synths from the increasing number of recordings that featured them, but had never actually heard or seen one performed live. I struggled to imagine how a collection of wires, lights, patch cords, and knobs could produce the new sounds I had heard on numerous records: Walter Carlos' *Switched on Bach*, the Doors' *Strange Days*, Simon and Garfunkel's *Bookends*, and the Beatles' *Abbey Road*. This was technology new to me and I was on pins and needles anticipating the evening's concert. I had hoped to get an interview with keyboardist Emerson for AFN, but their tour dates had them moving from city to city at a breakneck pace. Their promoter got me in to see the sold-out concert instead. I had to see what all the synthesizer hoopla was about. Were they just hype and fluff, or real technology that might someday change the face of music?

The Krone is a theatre in the round. It seats about 3,000 people in ever-widening rows moving upwards from its center round stage. It was designed primarily as a circus: the elephants, tigers, and clowns would enter through a narrow passageway, like players emerging from the locker room onto the field at a football game, then burst onto the circular floor to perform their acts. When the Krone hosts concerts, that same red-carpeted ground level stage elevates into a raised platform where the band is displayed in a 360° stage. There isn't a bad seat in the house. I had scored a front view seat, three tiers above the floor and eye level with the stage. The band's mixing console was just in front of me, so I knew there would be no better sound than right where I sat. If this synthesizer was anything close to the excited reviews I had been reading, then this was my best chance to get a firsthand view.

In the seats to my right were two young blonde German women, who seemed more intent on chatting to each other than on paying attention to anything on the stage, but the concert had yet to start. On my left was a glassy-eyed German with shoulder-length hair, a heavy overcoat, and a hash pipe at the ready. And on the stage was a set of drums facing the biggest machine I had ever seen: a Moog Synthesizer. It was a stack of multiple black boxes taller than a man, with a tangle of wires bristling off its front like an old-time telephone switchboard and a dizzying array of blinking lights. Below it was a small keyboard and to the side were multiple stacks of PA speakers, a Hammond B3 organ, and a vocal microphone. The longhair next to me offered his pipe — red Lebanese, a very up kind of high — and I inhaled deeply, coughing and sputtering from the power of its smoke. The lights dimmed and the crowd's chaotic chatter turned to a concerted buzz of anticipation until the three musicians walked out on stage. Every person in that auditorium rose to their feet as if on cue — their applause was deafening.

On that warm June evening, under the tent-like ribbed ceiling of Circus Krone, my world was shaken as I watched Keith Emerson do battle with that huge box of flashing lights, wires, and knobs. As Lake and Palmer sat idly by in the middle of their hit song "Lucky Man," Emerson proceeded to mesmerize me and 3,000 stoned Germans with music and sounds none of us had ever heard. Just the sheer power of the instrument made me speechless. Far-reaching glissandos that stretched from the lowest bass to the highest treble roller-coastered up and down the scales in stunning, sweeping panoramas of sound. It was unfathomable to me that the sounds made by this collection of wires, lights, and circuits could grab hold of my soul, but grab it they did. At that moment, I knew not only that I had to understand how this machine worked, but that I had to master its technology and someday build my own. How could I not? From my home-built hi-fi system to our cobbled together college pirate radio station, the way I uncovered the mystery of technology was to jump in feet first and become one with it.

All too soon, ELP's encore ended, the music stopped, and the house lights came up. The show was sadly over. I somehow threaded my way through the hordes of exiting concertgoers and plodded home, still in a dreamlike state. The evening was gorgeous, as Munich often is in summer. It was almost midnight, but the air was still richly sweetened with the scents of flowers, some blossoming from vines covering the sides of buildings, others growing in hanging baskets, and still others erupting from the bright floral displays that fringed the outdoor cafes and beer halls along the way back to Kaulbach Villa. My mind swirled with questions about how a box of electronics could make such sounds, though I soon realized that the answers would not come quickly or easily.

The next day, I was approached by a major record producer and song-writer—my friend, Pete Bellotte—who wanted me to schedule a couple interviews on AFN's *Weekend World*, a magazine-style show like NPR's *Weekend Edition*. Producers and publicists who wanted to get their acts in front of AFN's 20 million listeners often struck deals with DJs: a chance to interview a big star, in exchange for a second interview with a lesser-known performer. Pete, who was close to Elton John, offered me an exclusive interview and the worldwide premiere of John's newest single, "Rocket Man," in exchange for an interview with a relatively unknown Italian performer by the name of Giorgio Moroder. I agreed, primarily because what little I knew of Moroder involved synthesizers. He'd just released "Son of My Father," a bouncy pop tune that became a local German hit, and whose melody line was played on a Moog. Moroder was a man I had to meet, and I was excited to do so.

Moroder's studio, Musicland, was in the basement of the Arabella Haus, a large Munich hotel. Instead of AFN's one- and two-track tape recorders, Moroder's state-of-the-art studio had a beautiful deck that could record on 16 tracks: enough to separately capture instruments and voices, so that one musician could sound like many—which is what Moroder did. He had a walrus mustache, intense brown eyes, a flop of

120

dark hair, would wear a necktie and T-shirt, and laughed as easily as he breathed. We became instant friends. I helped Giorgio acquire the stereo equipment he wanted from the US Army PX, and he let me play with his Moog and use his studio. It was a deal made in heaven.

Musicland made Giorgio money not just from his one hit song, but from his cover versions of others' hits. Germans loved American pop music, especially bubblegum, but preferred to hear it sung in German. Giorgio hired studio musicians to copy American hits note for note, then replaced their lyrics with German translations sung by German singers. It was a lucrative business for him, but he detested it. A talented musician, he didn't want to churn out covers; he wanted to set the world on fire with his own music — a new style that would eventually be called disco.

I felt Giorgio's pain of being trapped in a life he couldn't control and struggled to change. Despite my wonderful accommodations at the Kaulbach Villa, my acceptance into the Munich music scene, and my new job as the host of AFN's *Underground*, I was still trapped in the Army without a way home. I had about eight months left on my contract and could not shake the feeling that despite all the good fortune I had come to enjoy in Munich, this was not my home, or my job, or what I wanted to be doing in life. I was antsy to start my career in something — anything of my choosing. I just wanted to be set free to find my own way, instead of just making the best of a situation I had been forced into. Each day was painful and I found myself increasingly homesick. I scheduled a leave of absence to spend some time with my family in California. It had been three years since my last visit. Maybe some family time would cure my depression.

CHAPTER 20

I GOT UP EARLY and caught the train to Frankfurt's international airport. My flight back to California would be through New York's JFK airport, then on to LAX and a week's leave—a short break from the radio station and the Army. Mostly the Army. Grandma Elsie, my mother's mother, had died after a tough final few years, debilitated by a stroke that paralyzed the left side of her body and robbed her of all words but one: "shit." Elsie had been an investor, and she left my parents enough money for them to buy a 33-foot Tollycraft cabin cruiser and a fixer-upper home in Lido Island, a swanky neighborhood they'd long dreamed of living in.

Mom invited me to spend the week on the new boat, on a cruise to the warm waters of Mexico. It would be just me and the next oldest McGowan, Sharane, because the youngest, Bobbi, was somehow uninterested. Sister Sharane picked me up at Los Angeles International Airport, and we drove from there straight to Newport Beach. I knew little of boats, but Mom had told me a few things about their new one. It was powered by twin diesel engines and had a flying bridge: a perch above the main cabin, where sweeping views of the rolling ocean helped the captain guide her safely.

Sharane and I were still searching for Slip 27 when we saw Mom waving her arm.

"There it is!" Sharane announced.

The boat was a beauty: gloss-white with a mahogany deck, chrome railings at bow and stern, and a blue stripe at the waterline; its snappy white-and-blue flag fluttered in the warm sea breeze. A miniature version of the boat, a dinghy, was raised on davits at the stern, and could be easily lowered for trips ashore while the cruiser rested at anchor. Stenciled onto the side of the flying bridge was the vessel's name: Heaven Bound.

We climbed from the pier onto her deck. Mom hugged us both, but looked worried. She lowered her voice. "Dad's ..." she bit her lower lip, "in one of his moods."

Mom never liked to face Dad's manic states head on. Instead, she tried to soften them, calling them moods or periods, hoping they'd pass and life could return to normal. The family had taken part in interventions and therapy for Dad's alcoholism and manic-depression, both of which were getting worse. He'd recently landed in the hospital—drunk, he'd fallen into the engine room of Heaven Bound and cut himself badly. The doctors scolded him for having stopped taking lithium, a prescription drug that smoothed out his manic-depressive swings and lessened his thirst for alcohol. But he hated taking lithium because it robbed him of his creative streaks. In his opinion, it was better to smooth out the peaks and fill in the valleys with "a few" drinks. After his fall, hospitalization, and more than 30 stitches to close the deep gash in his leg, he'd promised to take his medication again—a promise he hadn't kept, if Mom's worried face was any indication. Sharane and I looked at each other and rolled our eyes.

I'd had high hopes for spending time with Dad in the quiet environment of a vacation cruise. When he was on an even keel (so to speak), Dad was a pleasure to be around. He was not only a musician, inventor, writer, salesman, and electronic engineer; he was, at core, an intellectual, a voracious reader of the philosophy and mathematics of P.D. Ouspensky, George Gurdjieff, and Bertrand Russell, as well as such sci-fi writers as Isaac Asimov, Arthur C. Clarke, and even L. Ron Hubbard. He was also an artist—an expert wood sculptor of the human form, and an oil painter. He even ventured into firing his own mosaic tiles to create the massive ceramic works that filled our home. But what met me on that boat was not that version of my father—instead, I was about to share a week's cruise with a man possessed by an affliction he could neither end nor control.

Dad was waiting for us in the cabin. It was lunchtime, and already there was a tumbler of gin on the table: straight up in a juice glass, no ice. He wore a frumpy blue captain's cap with a shiny black bill; embroidered on the front was an anchor surrounded by a yellow garland crest. His eyes were already bloodshot, and the look on his face sent shivers down my spine. That look was all too familiar: dominating, with a thin, forced

123

smile, his mouth open just enough to show his yellowed, pipe-stained teeth—and a fixed stare that followed my every move, like a hunter sizing up his prey. This was the dad who frightened me: unpredictable, ready for a fight, and determined to win any argument.

On the table in front of him was a neat stack of paper and three pens. "There are just a few rules we need to go over before we begin," he growled. No "Hello," no "How ya doin'?" even though we hadn't seen each other in almost three years. I clenched my jaw for what I knew was coming.

Printed on the papers was a manifesto. It declared that he was the Captain of Heaven Bound, and that all its passengers would be under his command, heed his every word, obey his every command, and perform their duties without question. Each point was spelled out in detail, like a legal contract. We were commanded to sign our names, swearing our allegiance to the Captain, or leave the boat. Sharane and I walked out in silence with exactly that in mind. Neither of us had any desire to play his game, or to spend time with him on that boat in his present condition. In hindsight we should have just gotten back in the car and headed home.

Mom shot Dad a wicked look and quickly followed us. "I am so sorry," she said. "It'll pass." When she pleaded with me, Mom's big brown eyes were hard to resist.

I'm hardly the first guy to think of his mother as a saint, but Sue McGowan, however clueless she might have seemed at times, had a huge heart. There was nothing she wouldn't do for her family, including tolerating her husband when he was in one of his "moods." She convinced us to stay and assured us that we wouldn't have to sign his manifesto. When we agreed, she walked back into the cabin and slammed its tiny door behind her. We could hear harsh words, but neither of us wanted to listen. So we sat on the bow, dangling our feet over the edge, enjoying the sun and sea.

We set off an hour later; Dad was at the helm, briarwood pipe clenched firmly in his teeth, blue captain's cap pointed straight ahead as we turned south out of Newport Bay en route to Ensenada, Mexico. The journey was pleasant enough, and even my tendency to get seasick seemed to

124

abate as we passed Tijuana, then entered All Saints Bay and Ensenada's sheltered harbor, on the western shore of Baja California. We anchored near a buoy that Dad rented for a few pesos from a toothy, smiling Mexican man, adorned in a big sombrero that he kept on his head with a cinch strap, like the Lone Ranger's. Dinner that night was actually fun. Mom made tacos in honor of where we were, and Sharane and I shared a glass of wine. Mom and Dad focused more on tequila, but the conversation was good and we felt at home. The cabin was small; my parents took the twin beds inside, while Sharane and I lay on cots out on the deck, staring up at the sea of stars, lulled to sleep by the sounds of lapping waves and the distant barking of harbor seals.

Near midnight I was awakened by the sound of someone rummaging through the cabinet under the sink, where the booze was kept. It was Dad, and he was already drunk. I entered through the cabin door and stood not more than a few feet from him. He hardly noticed me at all until I spoke.

"You okay?"

"Hi, Paul," he slurred. "Just need another..." He fumbled among the bottles.

"Dad, I think you've had enough. Let me help you back to bed."

He seemed drunk enough not to care, and let me lock my arm in his and help him back through the little cabin door.

I knew his alcoholism was beyond his control. I wasn't angry at him, but I was angry: at the alcoholism itself, and at all the liquor aboard—the stuff that had a grip on his soul and wouldn't let go. Without thinking, I tossed every bottle of gin, tequila, bourbon, and wine overboard. Then I made sure it was all gone—nothing left in the small propane fridge, no obvious hidden stashes. I went back to my cot and fell back asleep.

By the time the warm morning sun woke me, I could smell breakfast. I rolled over and saw Mom puttering about in the small galley—and, to my surprise, Dad was climbing up the metal ladder hung over the port side. He'd gotten up early, taken the dinghy to shore, bought a new supply of booze, returned to the Heaven Bound, and stored it all in the cabinet—all without a word to anyone. I sighed deeply, rolled over, and closed my eyes.

After breakfast, Dad declared that we would head for the Islas de Todos Santos, two small, uninhabited islands. Why we were going there was a mystery, but I'd learned that to avoid an argument, it was better not to ask. Last night's deep-sixing of Dad's booze aside, I was committed to going along with the plan of enjoying a pleasant family cruise and keeping a low profile.

The Islas de Todos Santos are about 20 miles off the coast, just outside All Saints Bay. Back then they had no docks, or any other means of accommodating boats the size of Heaven Bound. As I was later to learn, the islands are best known to surfers—some of the biggest waves that strike anywhere on the coast of North America make landfall there. With the islands looming on the horizon, Dad idled the twin engines and announced that he was going to try to run the Heaven Bound ashore—we could then have a picnic lunch, with no one else around. "Our own island," he mused, "all to ourselves!" As he maneuvered the cruiser, pointing its bow straight at one island, I ducked under the flying bridge and opened the liquor cabinet. As I suspected: a nearly empty tequila bottle. Jesus.

As we neared land, we could see the impossibility of his plan. Instead of being edged with sandy beaches, the island was actually a walled fortress: a coastline of eroded gray rock that seemed to jut straight out of the water, before flattening out into a grassy plateau ten or so feet above the waves. This was madness.

"No!" I commanded, hands on hips. "This is crazy, Dad. You're not driving this boat onto that island."

Once, in an argument with Dad when I was 15, I'd gotten so angry that I'd shoved him in the chest, and he'd tumbled backward and fallen in a heap. His face first registered shock, then sadness. I had expected anger—I could have lived with anger—but his sadness was almost too much to bear. It made me want never to do anything like that again—but here I was, standing up to him. Again. And I was scared, without a plan.

My biggest nightmare was that Dad would now defy me by pushing the twin throttles forward to maximum speed and keep heading straight

126

for the rocks. But he surprised me again: he pulled back on the throttles, climbed down from the flying bridge, walked to the dinghy, lowered it to the water, and stepped in. We watched in disbelief as, without oars or sail, he drifted away toward the island. The Heaven Bound itself was only a few hundred yards from the island—we could see the swells cresting into huge breakers that crashed into the rocks, forcing mountains of white foam up the cliff face. Helpless, we watched Dad—captain's cap firmly stuck to his head, briarwood pipe resolutely clenched in his teeth—as each swell lifted the dinghy high before it disappeared in the following trough, then suddenly crested the next wave, getting ever closer to shore. All at once he flipped over. The dinghy was upside down, Dad clinging to its side—captain's cap gone, but pipe still in his mouth.

Mom screamed. Sharane panicked. It was up to me to save him. I had never piloted a boat, but I'd been around them enough to understand that the Heaven Bound could be steered only when it was moving—without motion, the rudder was as useless as a hand wave. Big motorboats steered with their engines at slow speeds and their rudder at higher speeds. Using the left and right throttles, I tried to position the cruiser's bow perpendicular to the waves, so that we could proceed forward, toward Dad, until we were close enough for Sharane to throw him a rope. But each swell lifted the Heaven Bound and drove it sideways, toward the shore. To keep our distance from the rocks, I had to put the twin screws hard in reverse and back the boat up—then quickly turn the craft toward Dad again and jam the throttles forward before the next swell drove us sideways again.

Back and forth we went. My senses on ultra-high, I took little short breaths between moments of panic—not only was Dad at risk, but so was everyone on the cruiser. All the while, the swells kept pushing us closer to the rock walls of the island along with Dad. I thought of calling the Coast Guard on the boat's radio, but quickly quashed that idea. First, the US Coast Guard wouldn't enter the territorial waters of another country to rescue us, and even if they would, neither they nor their Mexican counterparts would arrive in time. Ensenada was at least an hour away, San Diego much farther—and in ten minutes or less Dad would be smashed against the rocks.

"Paul!" cried Sharane, but it was too late. I had jammed the boat's propellers in reverse just as the next monster swell picked up her stern and the tip of the green and white wave washed over Heaven Bound, nearly sweeping Mom and Sharane over the edge.

"Hang on!" I hollered from the flying bridge, gunning the boat's engines forward, right at Dad, before the next swell lifted us onto the rocks.

Sharane scurried along the boat's narrow starboard walkway towards the bow holding onto the silver railing with one hand, and gripping a red and white life buoy in the other.

"Dad!" she cried across the water just as Heaven Bound dipped and nearly dumped her into the water.

It was now or never.

"Throw it!" I cried, then plunged Heaven Bound's throttles into full reverse to climb back up that immense wall of water before the sea's oncoming surge rolled us over like Dad's dinghy.

He caught the life preserver just before disappearing under the water again. The engines shook and their sound overwhelmed us as we backed over the sea mountain so I could keep the rear of the boat pointed into the ocean's rolling onslaught.

"There!" said Sharane, pointing at Dad as he bobbed over the wave's crest, arms wrapped around the life buoy. We had enough speed to keep backing away from the island and I rushed to help Sharane haul Dad aboard.

Cold, wet, and probably sobered up, Dad stomped down into the cabin without another word. I turned the Heaven Bound north and headed back to Newport Beach.

Clearly, family was a diversion that didn't soothe the ache in my soul. I had imagined that in my three-year absence my father and my relationship would have magically healed itself but on this trip I came to understood the truth. Dad was who he was and there was nothing I could do to change him. I was truly on my own. The strings that held me to the nest were long ago broken, but I hadn't felt the cord cut and still clung to my 23-year-old childhood bonds. Like it or not, I was an adult, and it was probably about time I started acting like one, though I recoiled from the thought. Adult smacked of my parents and at the moment that was not who I wanted to be.

CHAPTER 21

FOR AMERICANS LIVING in Germany in the 1970s, finding English-language films to watch was a challenge. About the only opportunities were at US Army bases, which were popular venues for GIs and civilians alike, frequently with long lines of moviegoers waiting to get in. Late one Friday night in the winter of 1972, in Munich, a few Army buddies and I went to see *When Dinosaurs Ruled the Earth*, a cheesy 1970 British thriller. After the film, as we stood outside having a smoke, my coat collar snapped tight against the last cold of a fading winter, another group of Americans spotted us and introduced themselves. Among them was a cute blonde: not too tall, with perfect curves and a few freckles near her nose. I made eye contact. She smiled back.

Hungry, we all agreed to meet at a McDonald's, then a novelty in Munich; the fast-food chain had just started to expand beyond the States. Over burgers, fries, and a Coke, I learned that her name was Terri and that she was from California, not more than 30 miles from where I was raised. She and ten of her California friends had rented a ski house in Pettneu, Austria, for the winter, and had driven the two-and-a-half hours to Munich for a bit of nightlife and a movie. I was smitten by her beauty and her…well, her spirit. Call it a vibe: an unspoken beauty and intelligence that came from within her and connected with me on a level we all know when we feel it, but one that's nearly impossible to limit to a category. I had never met anyone that touched me so deeply.

I was still quite shy around girls, but we bonded anyway—not because I suddenly became brave, but because Terri made it easy by starting the conversation and keeping it going. We talked of music, skiing, and California—and of how we'd missed the Woodstock Music Festival, the single musical event that did more to change the hearts and minds of American youth than almost any other. But 1969 was the year I'd gone into the Army and Terri had graduated from high school.

Terri returned to Austria with her entourage, and I went back to my day-to-day life at AFN and the Kaulbach Villa: a morning show called *The Dawn Patrol* at 6 am, station duties throughout the day, and musicians, hippies, and drugs flooding the studios at night. I was coming up on less than a year left to go before my hitch was up, days I was counting down with eager anticipation.

As spring's morning chill ebbed and summer's warmth took over, I had two very pleasant surprises. First, Terri returned to Munich and we started hooking up on a daily basis—and second, I got a call from a concert promoter who was organizing a four-day, Woodstock-like music festival. It would be called the Second British Rock Meeting—apparently, I'd missed the first—and would be held on a small island in Germersheim, Germany. The acts would include an impressive list of rock's best groups: Deep Purple, Black Sabbath, Pink Floyd, Uriah Heep, Status Quo, Fleetwood Mac, Rod Stewart, Rory Gallagher, Curved Air, Humble Pie, the Kinks, Billy Joel, Savoy Brown, Spencer Davis Group, and the Strawbs. To pull so many groups together, the festival's organizers had to guarantee an audience of at least 100,000, which meant they'd need lots of publicity. There was no better publicity outlet than AFN, and no one more likely to help them promote it than I.

We cut a deal. In exchange for publicizing the event to AFN's 20 million listeners, they would permit me to record all four days of the show, for later broadcast on AFN, and would provide everything I needed other than the recording equipment itself. The deal was signed, and the show promoters loaned me an old Volkswagen bus to outfit as a mobile control room, complete with mixing board and tape decks. We had two weeks to prepare, and Terri agreed to join the crew. Life was very much looking up. But first I had to build a recording studio in that borrowed VW van.

The Kaulbach Villa studio had given me plenty of recording experience. All I needed for Germersheim was a lot of blank tape, two extremely expensive Ampex stereo tape recorders, a mixing board, and a bunch of microphones. The station had everything but the board, but that wasn't a problem. Though it had been a continent away and already seemed a lifetime ago, I'd already designed and built a control board for KFJC, the pirate radio station Ed, Bill, and I had put together in college.

With only days to spare I finished building the board, then headed to Germersheim with Terri and two friends as crew.

Germersheim is a sleepy German town a few hundred miles northwest of Munich, near the French border in the Rhineland, where the mighty Rhine River winds through the green bosom of Germany's industrial center. Just north of town, where the river straightens out, is an oxbow. This abandoned meander of the Rhine, called the Lingenfelder Altrhein, loops around to form Insel Grün (Island Green), a 20-acre splash of pristine farmland accessible by only a single road, Hafenstrasse. Learning that this peaceful island pasture would soon be overrun by 100,000 concertgoers got the city elders up in arms: horrified, they banned the expected hordes from entering the area. The panicked promoters pleaded with the city, and eventually convinced them that containing everything at the concert site was better than letting 100,000 angry fans overrun the city. Two days before the festival was to open, on May 20, 1972, the ban was reluctantly lifted. Crowds flooded Island Green for four days of music and debauchery that none of us will ever forget, or likely repeat.

The organizers of the Second British Rock Meeting were Marcel Avram and Marek Lieberberg of Mama Concerts, a promotional group that was founded in 1968 and would later become one of the biggest concert promoters in Europe. They weren't able to hold things together very well. When our own motley recording crew arrived on May 18, two days before the festival opened, trouble was already brewing. The crowd had swelled beyond 100,000 young people, many of them GIs. All were camped out on Island Green in a makeshift tent city, having demolished the fence that was supposed to keep them in orderly groups. It looked like half of Germany was there, entrenched in mud and pasture. Hafenstrasse — the only road — was hopelessly clogged with cars; concertgoers were shuttled in by caravans of police buses.

Enough portable toilets for 50,000 people — not 100,000 — were lined up alongside the stage, close to the only sources of food and clean water. Drugs were everywhere; by the time the first band took the stage, more than 200 people had been taken to the hospital to be treated for overdoses. Another several hundred were treated for glass splinters in their feet from the thousands of broken beer bottles. It was chaos.

There were two performance stages at Germersheim, and between acts my crew had to move quickly to set up our gear: a few microphones and transformer-coupled direct-inject devices that tapped off the signal going into the loudspeaker, connected directly to the performing band's amplifiers. I was behind the stages in the VW van, running the mixing board and keeping the tape machines fed. Over the course of several days, as act after act played, the 100,000 wild, stoned, and drunken Germans and GIs seemed to get only rowdier.

At one point one of my favorite groups, Uriah Heep, was onstage wailing away, to the delight of the crowd. Their signature hit, "Gypsy," with its soaring synth and raucous guitar licks, had everyone on their feet, and the uproar was so loud it nearly drowned out this very loud band. Soon people started charging the stage, and one guy threw a piece of fruit that hit drummer Lee Kerslake in the nuts. That only infuriated the crowd, which began to riot. Tents were trampled, and the fence between stage and audience collapsed. Food, bottles, mud, and God knows what else were hurled at the Heep, who managed to finish their set, but they left the stage in a huff, without an encore.

The last day of the festival was to be the most exciting. No bands played the entire morning and afternoon, as crews dismantled the two stages to create a single, bigger stage, and rewired the sound system for what would later become known as Quadraphonic sound—an early version of what today we call surround sound. The act everyone had waited for, Pink Floyd, was on tap for 8 pm, just as dusk fell.

I was keyed up as well, cleaning the tape recorder heads and making sure everything was in place for that evening and the most important recording I would ever make. Pink Floyd was already an ascending phenomenon, and by far the biggest act of the Rock Meeting. Today they can boast of 16 gold, 13 platinum, and 10 multi-platinum albums. Their seminal releases, *The Wall* and *The Dark Side of the Moon*, are two of the best sellers in the history of recording. In fact, *Dark Side* would be on Billboard's Top 200 Albums Chart for a record 736 weeks. (It finally dropped off the charts 15 years later, in 1988.)

As night fell, I could feel the crowd's excitement. Roadies and stagehands scurried over the newly constructed wooden platform that Pink Floyd would soon stand on. My crew and I were ready. Then the promoters, Marcel and Marek, accompanied by a silent, heavyweight guy, meekly approached the van to let me know that I would not be recording the Floyd, despite the fact that we had a signed contract to the contrary. All my angry outbursts, my jumping up and down in frustration, were to no avail. Pink Floyd had no wish to be recorded, and that was that. To make sure I didn't attempt to make a pirate recording, they posted the heavyweight guy just outside the van.

Terri and I were crushed. Recording Pink Floyd had been one of the primary motivations for my agreeing to do the job in the first place. Depressed and upset, we dragged ourselves out to the crowd, where the promoters had reserved an area for us to enjoy the show, perched slightly above the noisy, muddy throng.

The lights dimmed, and all went surprisingly quiet except for an anxious buzz rippling through the crowd. Then Pink Floyd walked onstage. It was May 22, 1972, and they played, in full surround sound, an early version of the music that would become their next album: *The Dark Side of the Moon*. It remains one of the more remarkable concerts I have ever seen or heard. Unlike every other group I'd heard in concert, this one didn't speak a word. They played the entire album without breaks—a single continuous work of linked songs, through-composed and improvised passages blowing through the audience as if we all traveled together through space. During their set, not one member of the crowd acted poorly. The music, the surround sound, the warm May night, the slight breeze fluttering the many flags—all combined to make the magic that only music can make.

To this day, I'm thankful that Pink Floyd's management stopped me from recording the concert. Had I been stuck inside that cramped van, listening through a pair of little monitor speakers to a pale facsimile of the music, I'd have missed one of the great musical events in the history of rock—or, at least, of my own life. And though I didn't know it at the time, the seed of an idea had just been planted, which would one day blossom into my life's work: to find a way to build home stereo equipment capable of rendering music as clean and dynamic as the live event itself.

CHAPTER 22

WITH THE CONCERT over and the teeming masses of unkempt hippies and hungover GIs heading back to their respective homes, we packed up the VW and headed back to Munich, with a quick stop at AFN Frankfurt to drop off some of the unused recording tapes and say hi to Win at AFN Frankfurt. It was good to see him again. He was now a short-timer getting ready for his exit out of the service and back into the real world he'd come from in Connecticut. I had tracked him down in the corner of the newsroom as he prepared for the top of the hour broadcast. We hugged and laughed, and I thanked him for the opportunity to host *Underground*.

"Look at you," he said, staring at my neat hair and pressed uniform.

I winked and lifted up the corner of my short hair wig.

"Good man!" laughed Win and slapped me on the back.

"Is that McGowan?" came the voice of Milt Fullerton.

It was good to see them both but it was time to head back to Munich; Terri and her two friends were waiting in the van out in the parking lot. On the final leg of the journey home I had plenty of time to think. I'd passed the three-year mark of my time in the Army, with less than a year still to go. It was an exciting time in my life, but I still felt like a prisoner, and I was anxious to embrace my destiny outside the service — I was sure now that it would involve music, synthesizers, and the recording and reproduction of sound. The days ticked by slowly, as if my eyes were glued to a clock.

Life in Munich settled back to normal for a few weeks until I received a call from my old friend Pete Bellotte, who'd introduced me to Elton John and Giorgio Moroder. Seems Pete had arranged a meeting with Giorgio and me on a project he really wanted to present in person — they had time that afternoon at the studio, and of course I agreed.

Giorgio's studio, Musicland, was located in the basement of the Arabella Hotel, less than two miles northeast of the Kaulbach Mansion — an easy walk through the Englischer Gardens. It was a crisp Sunday morning near the end of spring. I zipped my windbreaker and was thankful for its pockets to guard my hands as I wound my way through the Garden's twisting, turning, tree-lined paths. It was quiet that Sunday, as Munich doesn't really get moving until midmorning on the Sabbath. I crossed an arched wooden bridge over a gentle flowing stream by a small grassy rise, near one of my favorite lunch spots. I never went in for fancy lunches: just a loaf of crisp French bread, a hunk of sharp local cheese, a bottle of Munich's best Hefeweizen, and the shade of a tree were the perfect summer companions.

I stepped off the pathway and cut across the expanse of grass to circle the Monopteros, an old ten-column circular structure topped with the green and blue of weathered copper. The low easterly light just cleared the trees and cast its long shadow on the small rise of lawn the Monopteros sat upon. Terri and I had once spent a chilly gray morning under its roof, waiting for sunrise to peek through the smallest of openings in the trees lining the Isar river to the east. The park was deserted that early morning and it felt like we owned the acres of green that spread before us. With our backs propped against a marble column and her hands held tightly in mine, we snuggled under a warm blanket and talked of our future plans. Our conversation was stopped by a distant cacophony of baying and howling, growing louder by the second. To our surprise and delight, just cresting a small hill to the west of us were dozens of light brown beagles—white of chest with saddles of black—howling and running in a tight pack at the urgings of a shepherd's crooked staff. He was alone and wore a long white beard, a Peter Pan hat, and dark lederhosen with a white shirt. The whole scene was straight out of a picture book. We sat mesmerized, trying to keep our jaws from dropping as the herd of hounds—floppy ears and all—covered the land, and then faded around a corner like it had all been a dream. Only their distant howls and bays broke the silent morning before we were again alone with our own thoughts and dreams.

The pleasure of that memory cut through the morning chill as I passed by another fond remembrance, the Beer Garden—or as the locals liked to call it, The Mini Hofbräuhaus—a group of picnic benches alongside a beer hall hiding in a tight clump of trees just off the walking path. I had spent many a fine afternoon here, enjoying a mug of draft beer and a crusty semmel roll oozing with spicy brown mustard. I laughed, remembering this was where I had first come after my ordeal with the colonel in Frankfurt. I hadn't yet gotten my pay transferred and found myself with only a few Deutsche Marks salvaged from the bottom of an old drawer—just enough for lunch at the beer garden. I was famished and feeling pretty low after what I had been through at the hands of AFN's colonel, but the sun was shining, the birds were singing, I was in a beautiful city—away from the trouble—and I had a fresh, cold, German beer and sweet bread roll to make things better. As I raised the glass to my lips for that first sip—the best any beer has to offer—a passing seagull decided to take a shit: its white effluent splattered first across the table, covering my semmel roll and my hand, then the last of it plopped into my beer. Its aim couldn't have been better. Seriously?

Remembering that low point in my life, and thinking of how far I had come since that day, made me feel pretty good about where we were and how much both Terri and I adored this city. Munich felt like home to us. Of all the cities we'd ever been to, Munich was special—a place we both had begun to consider permanently calling home after leaving the Army. I had no clue how we'd make a living here, but that didn't matter. We'd find a way. I had already applied for what was known as a European Out. Soldiers in non-critical jobs were eligible to leave the service six months early and stay in Europe for up to a year without a visa, and the Army would still cover the cost of a one-way ticket home. It was a sweet deal and my fingers were crossed I'd be approved.

After a few more minutes I could see the Arabella Hotel, and I was excited to hear what news Pete and Giorgio were about to share with me. Perhaps another shot at a really big act. I had always coveted a chance to interview Led Zeppelin and I knew Pete was somehow connected to their management. Maybe, just maybe…

Pete met me in the hotel lobby and escorted me downstairs to the basement where Giorgio was waiting. They had a proposal they thought

I'd be interested in, but it wasn't interviewing Led Zeppelin. Turns out Giorgio had discovered a young singer named Donna Summer and wanted to produce her career, something he couldn't do while continuing to crank out knockoffs of English-language hits. He didn't want to face making a German-language version of the next "Tie a Yellow Ribbon," and I didn't blame him. Top 40 bubblegum rock was unworthy of his musical talents.

It wasn't unworthy of mine, though. Pete and Giorgio proposed that, over the next few months, they would build a new recording studio. Their main studio, Musicland, would go on to record more musically interesting artists: Led Zeppelin, Queen, Rolling Stones, Electric Light Orchestra, Marc Bolan and T. Rex, Deep Purple, Freddie Mercury, Sweet, Elton John — and Donna Summer. They asked if I wanted to run the proposed new studio, producing and recording German covers for a share of the profits. It took me about two microseconds to make up my mind. This was the chance of a lifetime to realize a long-held dream: to be involved in music's creation and control the quality of its reproduction. This was it, the culmination of everything in my life up to this magic moment. All the trouble, angst, close calls, missed opportunities, disapproving commanders, parents, all of it, to somehow arrive here with a life fulfilling opportunity few on Earth would ever be offered. The big leagues, finally.

With a handshake, the deal was made. If my application for a European out was accepted, and it looked promising, I could be released six months early — just in time to take advantage of Giorgio and Pete's offer to run their new studio. I don't think I had ever been as excited and pumped up as I felt on that day. My career was now set. I would finally be able to craft magic.

Terri and I, now a committed couple, scoured the Munich outskirts for a suitable home for the studio and for us. We visited dozens of potential homes for lease before we stumbled on the place of our dreams in Grünwald, a small municipality along the Isar River nestled a few miles southwest of downtown Munich. Like the Black Forest where I had spent time in on my training mission with the Signal Corp, Grünwald was buried deep in the green of lush forest. Our real estate agent Joachim, a short, balding, rotund man with ruddy red cheeks, drove Terri and me around in his little four-door BMW through Grünwald's twisting roads until we reached a narrow cobblestone driveway, flanked on both sides with tall white trees topped with green.

Joachim had said it was a villa, though neither Terri nor I were quite sure what that meant to our real estate agent. The only villas I was familiar with were the Kaulbach and picture-book Italian estates with bubbling fountains, occupied by rich, fashion-forward, good-looking people. We motored up the curving driveway to find a white stucco two-level home, set back against a pair of the largest weeping willow trees I had ever seen. Its dark, shingled, angled roof met three brick chimneys that rose out of the structure like fingers pointing heavenward. Inside the home, white marble and plaster-white walls mirrored the structure's exterior feel. In the middle of the entry a curving staircase rose to the upper level, and to the rear of the main room double sliding glass doors led out to the gardens. We were in love. It was indeed a villa, and it even had a stone fountain surrounded by manicured beds of flowers. For the briefest of moments I thought of wrestling Yaki away from AFN to tend those gardens. He'd like that, I imagined. Below the main level was a finished basement perfect for a recording studio. It was everything we had hoped for, and it was available.

With approval from Giorgio and Pete, we signed a lease on that beautiful villa. Here they would build us a studio in the basement, and here we would be happy. Finally, our dream of making music and living like kings in the heart of Europe was about to come true.

Now I had only a month to go before my early out and the start of our new life. I don't think I had been that excited and charged with energy since David's and my shot at freedom in our attempt to cross the Canadian border. The thoughts of being released from the Army as a free man in fewer than 30 days, starting a new life with Terri at our villa in Germany, and making recordings for Giorgio and Pete filled my every waking moment. I couldn't have wiped the grin from my face if I tried.

It was a Wednesday morning, just before the 9 am network news break and the end of my morning program, the *Dawn Patrol*. As I pulled my headphones off I noticed Yaki pacing outside the studio glass. This

139

was a bit unusual for Yaki as he normally would check on me before the start of my show.

"Nazi," he whispered. "Trouble." His head motioned for me to go downstairs.

Yaki knew something was up and wanted to warn me in advance. I jammed upstairs to my room and changed out of my sloppy fatigues and into my pressed uniform— always at the ready, just in case I had to present myself to the station manager. It was a smart policy to look my best when the occasion called for it—something I had learned from Win White. Dressed and ready for anything that might come my way, I presented myself at Irmy's desk. She shook her head as if I had done something wrong and pointed to the station manager's closed door.

"Come in," barked a voice I didn't recognize.

As the door creaked open, my soul fled my body and left my feet glued to the floor. It was the Colonel, AFN's commanding officer—the same commander who'd told me that if he ever saw my name come across his desk again, he'd make it his life's mission to make sure I landed in the brig, or worse. The guy hated me.

I stood at attention before him, thankful I was wearing my finest Class A uniform, with my shoes polished to a bright gleam, long hair neatly hidden under my shorthaired wig, and eyes glued straight ahead.

"I thought you and I had an understanding," he barked. His hair was trimmed so close that his sidewalls gleamed white.

"I—"

"No one told you to speak, asshole!"

He got up from behind the massive mahogany desk belonging to AFN Munich's civilian manager, Neil Fontaine, and moved within inches of my face, just like he had in Frankfurt. Sgt. Ito style. His eyes scanned my facial features searching for something. I hadn't a clue what he was up to, but was sure he could smell the fear I must have been radiating.

"Remove the wig," he said.

Dammit. There I stood, my hair pinned up like a woman's and that wig in my hand. How could he have known? I had only showed it to Win…wait…Milt Fullerton had seen me too. I'd never given him a second thought. He was the first person to take pity on me when I was under house arrest and had gone out of his way to help. Whatever had happened didn't matter now.

"You look like an idiot," the CO said. "You are a fucking idiot."

With my hair in bobby pins, I felt like one.

"You have been a pain in my ass one too many times. I've tolerated your bullcrap because you're a good announcer. But now it's over, you little prick. You have six months left in the service, and that gives me the right to fix your attitude once and for all."

"Sir, respectfully, I am scheduled to be released in a few days here in Germany."

"Yes, I know. I've rescinded that order. You're being transferred to Fort Benning, Georgia, tomorrow. I should put you in the brig as I promised, but I am convinced this will be worse."

I'd just signed a five-year lease on a house, and had a handshake agreement with Giorgio Moroder and Pete Bellotte, but now it was clear that this CO had absolute control over my life. It was intolerable. My panic turned to anger, welled up, and burst out of my mouth.

"Sir, if you don't let me out as agreed, I will burn down this network!"

Silence. Immediately, I wished I could take back those words. But there they hung in the air. I could almost see them. I could certainly see them in the expression on the CO's face.

To my surprise, he didn't explode. But why should he have? He had me by the short hairs and knew it. He was relishing every second of this meeting, toying with me as a cat with a mouse.

"The commanding officer in Fort Benning, a personal friend of mine, has assured me that your life there will be a living hell. You're not going to burn anything down, son. I'm going to light my own fire under your skinny little ass and put you on an airplane tomorrow morning at 0600 hours, and we are done. Dismissed."

He was true to his word. The next morning, my singed ass was on a plane flying to the States. My personal effects had been unceremoniously scooped up by a moving company and were already on their way to Columbus, Georgia, in a large box.

I hadn't had time to say goodbye to anyone but Terri, who was so angry at me she could hardly speak. To this day, she's never forgiven me for blowing that gig. It was to be our life's work, and now we'd have to start again from scratch. It was just gone—our hopes and dreams of a recording studio and a life with musicians dashed.

Now, all that remained was another six months in the Army. And this time, it would be at one of the toughest military bases the Army could serve up: Ft. Benning, Georgia, home of the United States Army Airborne Rangers and the 1st Battalion, 507th Infantry. The real Army.

CHAPTER 23

MY OFFICIAL CRIME against the military? Long hair. The real crime? Disobedience. The military can't tolerate independent thinking or breaking the rules — not when the next order given a soldier might well put his or her life at risk. I understood the necessity of obedience in wartime but that didn't mean I had to like it, or agree to be part of it. As far as I was concerned, the only war going on in Europe in 1972 was between me and the Army, and I'd just lost. Defeat meant an all-expenses-paid trip back to Georgia, where my AFN CO had promised me six months of living hell. But that wasn't the worst of it. From the moment Pete and Giorgio made us the offer of that recording studio, both Terri and I believed our life's path was set. We were on track to build our future around music, something we both wanted badly. In those brief few seconds it took me to remove my short-hair wig, our dreams were crushed, and we were back to square one without a pot to piss in.

Terri left Germany about the same time I did and met me in New York's JFK airport, and together we flew to Georgia. She was still pissed at me. As the plane descended toward the Columbus airport, I was heartened to see a thick carpet of forest below — it was a pale reminder of Germany's lush forests, which I'd always loved. But when I got off the plane, the heat and humidity told a different story: I was no longer in the Black Forest, something I seemed to have conveniently forgotten since my last days in Augusta.

The largest state east of the Mississippi, with Florida to the south and Alabama to the west across the Chattahoochee River, Georgia was then mostly forested — tangles of slash, spruce, and Virginia pine, broken by stands of sycamore and gnarled oaks fighting for territory. With all that Southern sunshine and humidity, you'd think trees would thrive — but unlike Germany's moist forest floors nurturing trees to grow, Georgia's forests looked as if they were struggling, as they spread more sideways than straight up. From what I could tell, Georgia's trees grew at about the same rate that Georgians moved in the midday heat: slowly and steadily. Why they didn't grow like Germany's forests was a mystery to me. Maybe it was the stranglehold of kudzu, that invasive Japanese species of pea vine that continues to steadily consume the Southeastern US. Or Georgia's red clay soil. Or the insects—millions of creeping, buzzing, hungry bugs working through the nearly dry mats of forest floor, while those with wings swarmed through the thick haze of humidity, all searching for food, mates, or me. Mostly me. But, whatever the reason, this certainly wasn't where I had just left. I was back again in the deep South, steeling myself for six months of threatened hell.

Shortly after arriving in Georgia, Terri and I paid $900 for a rusted 1962 Ford Falcon that Terri named Bessie. Bessie's exterior had once been red but was now a faded Pepto-Bismol pink. Her cracked, white-and-red seats of pleated vinyl had also faded. She ran okay—her little inline six-cylinder engine shuddered as she started to move, but at highway speeds we hardly noticed. We bought Bessie at a used-car lot that was little more than a square patch of asphalt trimmed with colored plastic ribbons hanging limply in the windless heat. The lot was Bubba's, whose motto was ominous: We won't steer you wrong.

We left Bubba's with a full tank of gas, began looking for a place to rent, and found one that day—a small shack in a neighborhood called Wynton. Instead of the neat, orderly enclaves of tidy houses we'd come to feel at home with in Munich, our gray-and-pink two-bedroom on Ninth Street, a block from the scorched brown grass surrounding the Abiding Faith Baptist Church, was a ramshackle, clapboard frame house with no foundation. In California I'd been accustomed to houses built on cement slabs, but our rental, like so many other Southern homes, was perched atop short, gray, foot-high wooden pilings, as if the builders had anticipated a flood. In fact, when I knelt down outside to look under the place, through the ranks of pilings I could see all the way to the backyard and to the neighbors' houses on both sides. A stoop of two dirty-white steps led up to the front door. The front yard was little more than parched dirt, with the occasional tuft of crabgrass. Ahhh, home.

When I'd been put on the plane to the States, my instructions from AFN's commander were clear: "Report to the base commander as soon as you land in Georgia." He'd sent me to Fort Benning to straighten me

144

out, but hadn't accounted for the Army bureaucracy, which foils the best efforts of everyone, well-and ill-intentioned alike, to get anything done.

When I arrived at Fort Benning, I reported not to the base commander as I had been instructed to do—hey, it's still me—but to the admissions clerk, who was like me a lowly grunt. I was betting on the notion that my commander hadn't put anything in my records about his disciplinary actions, since I was never officially reprimanded. My guess was he'd sent a personal note to the commander but skipped Army bureaucracy. I was right. The clerk read my orders without so much as a flinch, then pulled out a thick book of military job classifications.

"Says here you're a 71B, Broadcast Specialist," he said with a Southern twang.

"Yep."

"There's only one slot open for that." He stamped my orders, then sent me to the base hospital.

I wasn't sick this time: the only job then open for a 71B at Fort Benning, Georgia, was at Martin Community Hospital. I was to take charge of the Martin Community Network, nicknamed the Bedpan Network—a radio station whose programming was piped into the patients' pillow speakers. Perhaps this was a blessing in disguise. I'd always thought that radio should be broadcast live, rich in programming that suited the audience. I believe that radio audiences should be honored by those of us who produce broadcasts. Listeners almost always have a choice of stations; by choosing one over another, they give DJs and stations intimate access to their homes and lives. I'd seen background-music stations that existed for no other reason than to fill dead air, and that had always bothered me because it seemed such a waste. The idea of a literally captive audience listening through pillow speakers seemed like an opportunity to produce programming that might ease the burdens of people who were suffering, or in pain, or just bored. No one wants to be confined to a hospital bed.

So, with high expectations, for my first day on the job I dressed in my finest military threads, polished my shoes, and even cut my hair, then waved goodbye to Terri as she sat on the stoop of our little house. Bessie seemed in fine working order as I drove north on Fort Benning

Road, toward the base. It was still early morning—the heat of the day had yet to set in, but I could already tell by the buzz of the cicadas that it would be oppressive. Just past Custer Road, the entrance to Fort Benning was isolated in a clearing among trees. The guard asked for my papers, looked at them, and pointed me toward 10th Division Road, where I would find Martin Community Hospital; the door to the Bedpan Network was in the basement. On opening the door I was met by a tall, frumpy-looking private: Lou.

"You the new supervisor?"

"I guess." I introduced myself and shook his hand. He ushered me inside.

What I saw depressed me beyond words. The hospital's radio station was little more than a 20-by-10-foot room with a ceiling of yellowing acoustic tile and a single buzzing fluorescent light fixture. At the center of the room was a control board with an empty microphone stand, and two turntables without tonearms or cartridges. An isolation window separated this control room from what looked to be a recording studio of about the same dimensions. Without a mike or the ability to play records, what, exactly, was the Bedpan Network set up to do?

"I don't get it."

Lou jerked his thumb at an equipment rack that stood in one corner. Stacked in it were six AM radio tuners, each tuned to a different station, all turned on. These six tuners fed the hospital's system of pillow speakers—patients could select among them with a bedside switch. That was it.

I looked at Lou. "What's our job?"

On his face was a look of fatalistic gloom. "We sit here."

If I had balked at spinning my wheels in the Signal Corp—washing trucks and playing soldier—this was two steps lower on the "I want to stab myself with an ice pick to feel anything" ladder. Six months of twiddling my thumbs. Truly, this was going to be hell.

CHAPTER 24

MY NEW CHARGE at the Bedpan Network, Lou, turned out to be doing more or less what I'd done when I was drafted. He wanted out of the Army any way he could, and his conscientious-objector status seemed to be working for him. The Army didn't know what to do with him, so here he sat, waiting for release. And they'd put me in charge of him which, at the time, seemed like a golden opportunity. I had just lost the best career opportunity of my life, gotten thrown out of Europe, nearly imprisoned—multiple times—for taking advantage of golden opportunities, yet I didn't want to stop taking advantage of the opportunities that came my way, nor did I want to hide behind my failures. I just needed to be a little more careful with my choices. Successful people move forward when chance favors circumstance.

Monday through Friday, we were required to arrive at the studio by 8 am and stay till 5 pm. During those hours our job was to sit there and do literally nothing. I asked Lou why we should show up at all, but then it hit me: if we were caught abandoning our post, we would be Absent Without Leave. Punishment for going AWOL ranged from a scolding and a fine to jail time and a dishonorable discharge.

Lou had noticed that the Sergeant Major of the hospital made it his business to check on the Bedpan Network at precisely 3 pm each Friday. To be on the safe side, it wasn't long before we agreed to split the shift: Lou would do mornings till lunch, when I would relieve him. If either of us was ever questioned about the other's whereabouts, we'd make some excuse, then call him and tell him to scramble back. It was a perfect plan, and already I had a good reason for it.

Within days of my arrival at Fort Benning, I'd applied for a position at WCLS, the local Columbus rock'n'roll station. They wanted me to take the drive slot—the time with the peak listening audience, from 6 pm to midnight—and I agreed. The only hitch was that I had to get permission from the Army to work a second job, permission that the officer in charge, a skinny bespectacled lieutenant that looked like he'd just gotten out of high school, by the name of Robbins, quickly denied for no apparent reason.

"You're already working at the hospital radio station. Just do a good job there," he said, dismissing me as if I were a gnat.

Undaunted by a mere denial of my request, especially by this guy, my solution was a simple one: I'd broadcast under an assumed name, and the Army would hopefully never be the wiser.

I called myself Christopher Robin.

While I DJ'd at night Terri was waitressing at Shoney's Big Boy, a nationwide chain of sit-down restaurants that served hamburgers and coffee. Outside was their trademark, a larger-than-life statue of Big Boy himself: a chubby 12-year-old in red-and-white-checked overalls with a sweeping cowlick of blond hair, pinched at the top like the crest of a wave, holding up a double cheeseburger. Terri worked hard at Shoney's, for a ridiculous thirty-five cents an hour. Her tips were meager; nonetheless, over time, she filled jar after jar with quarters, dimes, nickels, and pennies saved for our eventual release from Georgia and our journey back to California.

Evenings found me at WCLS, marking time. This was Top 40: two-and-a-half-minute songs interspersed with station jingles and ads to the point of boredom. I sedated myself by smoking a fat joint before each shift, and sometimes a few more before it was over.

The station was owned by Charlie Parish, a classic old Southern dude: skinny, white hair coiffed like Col. Sanders's, and an accent as thick as the Georgia humidity. Charlie fancied himself everybody's friend—a Southern good ol' boy who expected deference from his employees even as he pretended to be their pal. Nonetheless, most of the station employees were Southern-raised, and addressed him as "Mr. Parish" or "Sir." I decided to take his apparent offer of familiarity at face value.

"Mind if I just call you Charlie?" I asked him a few weeks after we'd met.

His eyes narrowed but I just ignored them.

Charlie and I got along well enough but he was always a bit wary of me, often warning that I should be on my best behavior while working alone in the desolation of the station's transmitter. During daytime hours WCLS broadcast from their downtown studios where Charlie kept a watchful eye on his wards. But when night fell the studio moved to the transmitter house, a lonely wooden shack in the middle of a cow pasture. From 6 pm to midnight each night, that shack was my hangout.

"I am trusting you out there alone, Christopher Robin," he'd say, never calling me by my real name. "Don't let me catch you smoking them drugs."

Charlie was convinced all young males smoked pot and one of the questions on my employment application and later my face-to-face interview with Charlie had been about the use of drugs—which I of course denied.

"I don't allow no drug smokin' in my station," Charlie announced near the end of our interview. "I got a good nose for such stuff and there'll be no monkey business. Ya hear?"

I wasn't completely sure about Charlie and his ability to smell pot smoke because he was about as straight-laced as anyone I'd ever met. I suspected he wouldn't have known weed from a burning cowpat but I didn't know for sure.

One evening about 9 pm, I'd just finished huffing down a particularly fat joint of a nice Jamaican blend—my second of the evening—and the shack was filled with thick blue smoke, which ordinarily would never have been a problem because I was always alone. Without warning Charlie walked in on a surprise visit, waving the smoke away, and asked if something was on fire. I assured him nothing was on fire and came up with some cockamamie story about the farmer the station shared the field with burning manure—a story that seemed to set well with him but only just for a moment.

"Christopher Robin," he growled. "I caught you red-handed this time." Suddenly, I was sure that I was DJing my last show.

He slowly walked over to the studio console, then stood there a while, still engulfed in a haze of blue smoke. I continued playing records, jingles, and commercials as if nothing was wrong. I didn't know what else to do. He may have caught me red-handed, but out of a sense of duty to the station I figured he'd want me to finish my shift before I handed him my keys. During one song he pulled from his pocket a small, folded-up piece of white paper and, as if to heighten the suspense, slowly and carefully opened it. Inside was a single red pill.

"I caught you," he said. "It's a red devil."

I think he must have meant a red—Seconal, a barbiturate. But I didn't do reds. I picked up the pill and sniffed it. It was a Red Hot, a common cinnamon candy. I broke it open and held it for Charlie to sniff. Poor Charlie realized he'd been wrong and left the station, walking back through the mist of pot smoke.

Life in Columbus was pretty normal. For me, it was nights at WCLS, masquerading as Christopher Robin, and afternoons in the hospital basement helping Lou work on his conscientious objector release, doing nothing at the Bedpan Network, and pretending to be a soldier. For Terri, it was waitressing at Shoney's Big Boy and getting us ready to make the big move out of Georgia, back to California and "the world"—civilian life.

Near the end of our six months in Georgia, we had a surprise visitor: my old best friend David showed up, looking for a room. He'd gotten out of the Army, grown his hair long, and wrapped his forehead in a red bandanna. He looked like a hippie.

After our big drug bust, David's time in the Army had been hard. I'd heard that he'd dropped a big dose of acid and drifted off to mental parts unknown, never to fully return. Taking street acid was like playing Russian roulette—bad trips often left their victims permanently damaged, and God only knows what else was in that big hit David had taken.

David felt he was back to normal, but he wasn't—his often vacant stare worried me. But I couldn't do much besides offer him a place to stay, food to eat, and some understanding. After all, he was like a brother. David had again found religion, of a sort. At the time, he was anything but spiritual, but someone had convinced him that if he chanted Namu Myōhō Renge Kyō over and over, then rang a gong, great material wealth and good fortune would come to him. David was convinced that his chanting was keeping his car running and money flowing in. The only evidence of a money stream were the jars of hard-earned tip

150

change Terri generously gave him out of the goodness of her heart—but David's beat-up old VW van kept chugging along, and that was a sort of miracle. So before he left, we bought the van for $500 and gave him our car Bessie. We then invested another $500 for a local mechanic to rebuild the vee-dub's tired 4-cylinder engine. We knew the trip to California would be long, and we didn't have enough money to stay in motels along the way. The van would be perfect for roadside overnight stays. Plus, after the engine rebuild, we'd have reliable transportation to start our new life together. Our possessions were minimal: clothing, a small stereo, a camera, a pregnant cat named Mama, and David's van.

I was released from the Army at noon on a Friday in December. Georgia's summer heat had gone, and the morning had been a gray pallor, with frost on the ground. I couldn't be happier to be leaving Georgia and the Army, but it felt bittersweet. At the time I wasn't considering all the positive aspects of my four-year tour: meeting Giorgio and all the other musicians, attending the Pink Floyd concert and countless others, traveling in Europe, finding new friends—and, best of all, meeting Terri and not getting killed in Vietnam. All I felt was anger and bitterness at the loss of four years of my life.

My one charge at the hospital station, Lou, drove over that morning at my invitation. We talked of his ongoing efforts at getting out of the Army, a never-ending string of endless paperwork and denials. I told him I was sorry. I knew how it felt to be trapped in the Army's green muck and wished him luck. Though Terri tried to stop me, and Lou did the opposite, I piled all my military gear—boots, shoes, hats, shirts, uniforms—in the middle of our dirt driveway, poured gasoline over them, tossed a lit match, and the three of us watched as the black smoke rose into the humid Georgia air. It would be another week before Terri and I hit the road for California. Until then, I took a grim pleasure in driving, every day, over the charred remains of my years in the Army, as if I could grind away those memories.

Meanwhile, we needed to get out of Georgia. Our VW bus was loaded up with everything we had, including a cardboard box for Mama Cat. She was looking pretty fat, ready to have those kittens. Our first stop was the laundromat. Wanting to scrub every speck of Georgia dust

151

from our lives, we filled five washing machines, got them running, then went out to grab a last bite of Columbus food. When we returned, we discovered that some desperate person had emptied the machines and vanished with all our clothes.

Terri looked at me in utter disbelief and laughed. "Time to go."

CHAPTER 25

THE MOST DIRECT route out of Columbus was Interstate 10 West. We motored along it into darkening clouds that threatened rain. Alone on the highway, we drove straight toward what looked like a black wall—dense towers of cumulonimbus clouds with flat, anvil-like tops. They looked like a slow-motion atomic bomb blast.

At first, it was exciting. Huge raindrops began to splatter against the windshield, and soon the van's weak little wipers were struggling to clear what seemed like vertical standing pools of water. Suddenly, we were in the middle of a flooded road: as we plugged along, slower and slower, the bus shook and rattled. Then, above the noise of the rain on the roof, we heard strange noises from the back of the van: Mama Cat was giving birth. By now the wipers were almost useless—I could barely see the road. Terri urged me to pull over, but there was no shoulder on either side of the highway, just a ditch filled with rushing water. To keep from being rear-ended, we continued to creep along. Then big blobs of something began smacking the windshield like tiny grapes.

Bam! Bam! Bam! Some of the things, whatever they were, disintegrated on contact with the glass, leaving smears of red that made it even harder to see the road. Now gusts of wind were shoving the bus from side to side, but they also blew gaps in the rain, and we could see the road ahead. It was covered in little white lumps, and they seemed to be jumping. Afraid that whatever they were would damage the van, I felt I had no choice but to stop in the middle of I-10. I got out to look and through the heavy deluge of unending rain I saw something I will never forget.

Frogs. Thousands—maybe tens of thousands—of tiny white frogs were hopping, scurrying, and crawling from the ditch on one side of the highway, across the pavement, to the ditch on the other side. They seemed oblivious to the tsunami of water, to the van, to us. Drenched, cold, and shaken, I hopped back in the driver's seat and told Terri.

She covered her mouth in horror. "We can't run over them!"

"And we can't sit here in the middle of the interstate and have someone plow into our back end, either." I put the van in gear and inched forward. Terri went back to help Mama Cat, who was crying again. She'd given birth to five kittens, all still wet. As we crept forward, frogs crunched under the tires and continued to hit the windshield, with a sound like popping corn. Crunch. Crunch. Smack!

All at once it was over. The clouds broke, the rain stopped, the frogs vanished, and what was left of that day's sun lit the way ahead, down the perfectly dry highway. I glanced in the rearview at the black wall of clouds, and hoped that most of the frogs had made it across the highway. We hated having to kill so many animals that were just trying to stay alive, but we'd had little choice.

Onward we plowed through two-lane highways, billboards offering a comfortable night's rest at motels we couldn't afford, and scrumptious meals we longed to eat. We were living on the few dollars we had left from my last paycheck from the radio station, and the last jar of Terri's tip money, so our provisions were a few cans of beans; cold, uncooked Top Ramen made edible by soaking the dried noodles and powdered flavor packs in tepid water inside the empty bean cans; and not a lot else. Our nighttime accommodations were a few blankets we'd managed to buy at a secondhand store along the way. Our pillows were rolled up dirty jeans we'd gotten at the same store, and we were lulled to sleep at night by the sound of kittens mewing for Mama's milk.

Just outside El Paso, Texas, Terri climbed up a small ridge and posed for a picture next to a big sign welcoming us to New Mexico. Texas had been a rough drive in our old Volkswagen bus: hot and dusty, with endless miles of nothingness broken only by the occasional cavalcade of soot-belching trucks roaring past us as if we were standing still. To us, the end of the Texas Panhandle and our entry into New Mexico meant our trip to California was more than half over. Our traveling cat hotel was getting on our nerves, and we were anxious to park the van and get a decent night's sleep in a real bed.

A few hours of travel later we were low on gas, so I pulled into a tiny nothing of a town called Lordsburg: a dot on the map along the interstate. It was hot that day, I guessed more than 100°, and I was glad for the awning shading the cement island of gas pumps as I filled the vee-dub's tank. Terri reached into her back pocket for the few traveler's checks we had left. Nothing. In a panic we ripped everything out of the van but the cats, and still came up empty. We were flat broke, stuck in the middle of nowhere with six cats, no food, and only a little water. Where had the money gone? It must have dropped out of her back pocket when she climbed that small rise in front of the sign back at the state line. It was the only possibility.

By this time the station attendant had lumbered out of his air-conditioned shack. He was tall and lanky like Ichabod Crane, with cauliflower ears and a shovel face to match.

"You folks got trouble?" he asked.

I explained the situation and my plan to drive back and find the lost wallet. An iffy plan if I ever heard one, but he bought it on one condition.

"You leave the little lady behind just so's I know ya'll'll come back."

Terri's eyes widened into saucers but she knew the score, and with head down and a wave goodbye, she dutifully followed Ichabod into his lair, steeling herself for the four-hour wait.

For the next two hours of drive time I contemplated what our options might be. The odds of finding that little blue folded checkbook of traveler's checks seemed like a thousand to one. If I didn't find it, then what? About 50 miles from the Texas border, hypnotized by the endless black ribbon stretching into asphalt infinity, I was suddenly yanked out of my stupor when the van lurched up on its right wheel and ripped the steering wheel from my grasp. I regained control and pulled over to the side of the road to see what had happened. Nothing much. The little silver moon hubcap that once covered the wheel's lug nuts was missing, but otherwise everything looked in order.

Undaunted, I continued and, as if heaven-directed, I spotted the little blue checkbook on the other side of the road right where Terri had perched for the picture. It was the kind of miracle that comes only sparingly in a lifetime. I couldn't believe our good luck. I grabbed the checkbook and headed straight back to Lordsburg, eager to scoop Terri up and get out of this God-forsaken stretch of desert. Ninety minutes of driving got me close, but with 50 miles to go a new problem erupted: a

155

chirping sound from that right front tire, as if a bird had been trapped and was trying to call for help. Something was wrong, but it would have to wait. Poor Terri had already been sitting in that guy's ten-by-ten shack for four hours.

Her bright smile upon my return made the whole trip worthwhile. With the van's gas tank once again full and our dwindling funds safely tucked away, we motored out of Lordsburg, but we didn't get far before the VW started bucking and bouncing like a freshly castrated steer. No sooner had we come to a stop on the side of the busy highway than that chirping front wheel simply fell off the van. The front passenger side of the car kneeled down as if in prayer, settling on the pavement with a thunk.

Terri stayed with the car and the cats as I hoofed it back to Ichabod's station, broiling under the unrelenting New Mexico sun.

"You folks got trouble again?" he asked, as if this sort of thing happened on a daily basis.

I explained our predicament and asked him for help.

"I'll call my buddy Ed. Ed'll fix yer wheel."

Ed turned out to be a rather short man, barely reaching the bottom of my chin, but he was a fierce bowling ball of fiery energy. He owned the local tow-and-repair garage, simply named "Ed's Garage," and from the looks of the busy shop—filled with out-of-state automobiles in various states of repair—he did pretty well fixing the misfortunes of the steady stream of travelers trying to pass unscathed through this little dusty wart of a town.

He towed our sad little van and all her contents to just outside his garage—next to a 55-gallon drum where early arriving mechanics warmed themselves burning the previous day's trash—and let us know it would be a matter of days and many hundreds of dollars to get the wheel fixed with salvaged parts—money and time we didn't have, but we really didn't have an alternative either. Ed demanded that we pay in advance and then wait for the parts and repair to take place. The little cash we had was just enough for gas to get home, so instead I bartered with him: my beloved Hasselblad camera and my Kenwood stereo—nearly everything we had of value—in exchange for fixing that

156

broken wheel with a junkyard part. After further pleas, Ed allowed us to spend the night in the van, as we had nowhere else to go. At least he didn't charge us rent for squatting on his property, though I could sense that he was thinking about it.

It was bitter cold in the high desert those many nights. We shivered under the thin wool blanket and Mama Cat did her best to warm her five kittens. As I lay next to Terri and listened to her gently rhythmic sleeping sounds and the steady drone of the distant highway, I bit my lower lip and tried hard not to cry.

CHAPTER 26

BY THE TIME TERRI and I and our six cats arrived in Southern California, we'd spent what little money we'd managed to save. Flat broke, we continued living out of the van and at my parents' house—a relatively uncomfortable situation since Terri and I were living together out of wedlock, something neither of our parents approved of. But we were free of the Army and loving it, despite our poverty and hardship.

Before escaping Georgia, I'd written to Pete and Giorgio to see if perhaps their offer of a recording studio was still open. Sadly, no, they'd found someone else. We were truly starting over. It was time to claw our way back into the world of music, and the only way I knew to do that was radio. I sent audition tapes to radio stations up and down the California coast, and two in the central part of the state wrote back with job offers: KSEE in Santa Maria and KSLY in San Luis Obispo. I knew nothing about either place, but Santa Maria was 30 miles closer, so that's where we went.

Santa Maria is 160 miles north of Los Angeles on US Highway 101, in a fertile valley bounded on three sides by the Santa Lucia and San Rafael mountains, and to the west by the Pacific Ocean. It was a sleepy agricultural town of 100,000 with two main streets, Broadway and Main, surrounded by tract homes, strip malls, and big farms. The climate was generally sunny, with fog in the morning and afternoon winds that ripped across the plowed fields and tinted the sky brown. That dust was from the valley's rich soil, deposited by thousands of years of flooding by the Santa Maria River, which winds through its basin until it reaches the sand dunes of Oceano and Guadalupe, then empties into the Pacific. There wasn't a lot to Santa Maria other than its agriculture and a few traditions unique to the valley. Locals point with pride to their signature barbecue: tri-tip beef slow-roasted over chips of local oak, served with pinquitos—small pink beans indigenous to the valley, each about the size of a shelled peanut—swimming in a peppery brown sauce. Santa Maria–style barbecue could be found all over the city: in shopping center parking lots, the rich, meaty smoke pouring from food trucks and trailers, and in restaurants like the Far Western Tavern, which then was just west of Santa Maria, in Guadalupe.

Terri disliked Santa Maria from the moment we set foot on her soil, and it wasn't really to my taste either. The constant afternoon winds that slammed doors shut and piled debris against fences, the uninspired architecture of strip malls and tract homes, and the town's distance from anything resembling culture left us both feeling empty. I was so desperate to get hired at something — anything — and settle into a normal life, so I could start working on rebuilding my dreams, making up time lost in my four years of servitude, that I'd grabbed the job at KSEE despite Terri's protestations that we should at least look at the job in San Luis Obispo, 30 miles further north. I figured that Santa Maria would be little more than a quick stopover: we'd save some money, and after maybe six months move to greener pastures. At least we were back in California, and would soon be able to put a roof over our heads and food on the table.

I'd recorded my audition tape at WCLS, in Georgia, which of course meant that when Tom Edwards, KSEE's program director, listened to it, he heard a DJ named Christopher Robin. I was anxious to leave that moniker and persona behind in Georgia, but Tom had hired me because he needed a jock with some personality for his AM station's afternoon-drive Top 40 slot. He figured that Christopher Robin would be just the thing. I reluctantly agreed to continue to play the part, figuring that it wasn't really too awful a job. I worked from ten in the morning until six at night, Monday through Friday, with weekends off.

I had never stopped dreaming my grand dreams, nor had I lost the burning desire to build something that could put a dent in the world, but I didn't yet know what that might be. In Munich I believed it would be a career working with musicians in a recording studio, until that idea was snuffed out by the colonel and my own stupidity. But that was six months ago, and I'd had time to recover and mentally confirm that my work would somehow be tied to music. After all, it was something I kept circling back to: my home-built hi-fi, radio, concerts, musicians, and recording studios. I knew music was where I wanted to go; I just didn't know how. Then, an idea struck me: what about synthesizers?

I'd been hooked on synths ever since that Emerson, Lake & Palmer concert in Munich two years earlier. Would it be possible to build my own? And, if I could, what would it look like? How would it be better? The idea of building a new instrument to radically change the world of musical synthesizers flashed in front of me. Within an instant I knew exactly what I wanted to do for the rest of my life: build the biggest, baddest synthesizer the world had ever known. Now I was back in the game, excited to the point of giddiness. But first I'd have to work out a few details.

For starters, I didn't actually know how synths worked—I'd have to learn the secrets of how complicated electronic machines could make music. That didn't seem so hard—not at that very moment—as my imagination built that machine. I could see it! I could visualize everything about it: how it looked, how it operated, how it was different than anything that had ever been built before. I would make it more like a piano than what Moogs were back then: single note keyboards. In my mind my machine would revolutionize the musical synthesizer market and change music for the better. It was so real to me that I could hear it play, feel my fingers caressing its keys, actually see how its control panel was laid out, and pictured how it would be used. That I knew nothing about the inner workings of synthesizers, and very little about physics, musical theory, or electrical engineering, didn't faze me, which is likely a good thing. If I'd had any idea how difficult the challenge actually was, I might not have tried at all.

Knowledge is essential, but sometimes, so are ignorance and gut instinct. Here's what I was up against. On a piano, you can strike as many keys as you have fingers, to play chords: three or more musical tones sounded simultaneously. An 88-key piano has more than 200 strings—three strings for each treble note, two for each upper-bass note, and one string for each lower-bass note—and 88 hammers to strike those strings. When a key is struck, its note sounds from within the piano's wooden case, which is shaped to amplify that sound.

160

Musical synths of the early 1970s, however, were one-note wonders: the keys on their piano-like keyboards could only be pressed one at a time. And while a piano string vibrates when struck, synthesizers use the electronic equivalent, an oscillator, to create notes. Oscillators are complicated and expensive electronic circuits that make only steady-state frequencies or sounds. Musically interesting or satisfying note sounds are shaped by arrays of circuits: filters, amplifiers, and envelope generators. Having 88 oscillators activated by 88 electronic piano hammers, along with many other individual sound modifiers, would result in a machine of unwieldy size and complexity. Instead, synthesizers had only one or two note generators, filters, and amplifiers. All of this meant that a synthesizer could make only one sort of sound quality or tonality at a time, and only a single note's worth of that tonality could be played at a time.

Needless to say, these severe limitations frustrated musicians. Using a synthesizer required a kind of drudgery previously unknown in music. Walter Carlos, the master musician who'd made the most popular recording of synthesized music ever released, *Switched-On Bach*, created it using only a single-note Moog synthesizer. J.S. Bach's complex polyphonic music demands that many notes be played at a time. To create his recording, Carlos had to laboriously build up layers of harmonies and counterpoint note by note, using a multitrack tape recorder to build the final "performances" of Bach's works the way you make tiramisu, one layer atop another—though even that analogy is misleadingly simplistic. What Carlos had to do was more like creating an old-fashioned player-piano roll by punching into the paper roll, by hand, the hole that represented each note. And those were only the pitches—determining the quality and tonality of the actual sound of each pitch took far longer. Carlos spent thousands of hours over many months making *Switched-On Bach*.

Understanding these limitations was the key to my invention, so I constructed a new kind of instrument in my mind. Building 88 complete synthesizers was out of the question, but it might be feasible to build ten. After all, no keyboard player can strike more than ten notes at a time: one per finger. I set out to build what I already saw clearly in my mind: the world's first polyphonic synthesizer, one able to play multiple simultaneous sounds. To do so, I formed a company of one person—me—and named it Infinitizer.

CHAPTER 27

NO SOONER HAD we started Infinitizer than Terri and I rented and settled into our first house that would soon become the headquarters of our new company: a three-bedroom tract home on Las Flores Street, near Allen Hancock Junior College. Houses in our neighborhood were look-alikes with stucco exteriors, wood-shingled roofs, and tiny front and back yards fenced off from the neighbors, California style. Our place wasn't much to look at from the inside, either: yellow shag wall-to-wall carpeting and, in the kitchen, speckled green linoleum curling at the edges near the back, where Mama Cat and her five offspring traipsed in and out through the slightly ajar door. We had little furniture: a few pillows, a pair of loudspeakers, an amp and turntable, a waterbed, a couch we'd found on the curb, and a huge wooden cable spool used as a table.

Infinitizer and my synth design consumed every waking moment I wasn't on-air at KSEE. I had to learn as much as I could about electronics, physics, and music, in an era before the Internet, Wikipedia, or even personal computers. (IBM wouldn't launch their first PC until 1981.) I copied, borrowed, absorbed, and assimilated every scrap of relevant information I could find about these varied disciplines. I gradually learned how synthesizers worked, and for my own first instrument I drew up detailed plans that covered our cable-spool table.

To build a prototype and finance the manufacture of production units, though, I needed money I didn't have. In fact, Terri and I were already struggling on our meager hourly salaries—mine as a Top 40 DJ, hers as a drugstore photo finisher—and resorted to some less-than-honorable means to make ends meet: rigging our electric meter to run backward, and figuring out how to turn the gas, phone, and cable TV back on after they'd been shut off for nonpayment. But that just bought us time—it wasn't going to pay for the parts I needed to build Infinitizers. I needed investment capital, so I began shopping the plans around town.

The first place I tried seemed a natural fit: the local bank. Armed with a business plan showing first-year sales of $1 million, a firm handshake, and a big smile, I met with the bank's loan manager, Sheri Bryant. She was kind, and generous with her time. We spent the better part of a morning going over facts and figures, until it became clear to me that banks don't lend money to people who are financial risks — at least, they didn't back then. After all, it's not the bank's money that's loaned out: the bank has to be sure that its depositors' funds will be safe and make a profit, which is why they require collateral of a value in excess of the loan amount, as well as a proven ability to pay back loans. I had none of this. Hell, if I did have any of that I wouldn't have needed the bank in the first place. But that's another story.

Sheri offered a glimmer of hope. If I had firm purchase orders, the bank might consider lending me enough to build the products already ordered, which would be just enough to steer me away from what was beginning to look like a dead end. But who would take a flyer and cut a purchase order for an expensive electronic device, not a single unit of which had been produced? My ideal customer had to be someone who was as passionate about synthesizers as I was.

And so I took another risk: I wrote a letter to Walter Carlos, offering him a crack at being my first customer. It was 20 pages long, including hand-drawn diagrams and schematics, and I sent it care of his producer, Rachel Elkind. To my shock and delight, Carlos sent a detailed reply with suggestions for improvements, along with his assurance that, if his suggestions were implemented, he'd buy the first unit off my production line. The owner of the first Infinitizer would be the most famous synthesizer player on the planet.

It still wasn't enough to secure a loan. As far as the bank was concerned, I had a promise — not even an order, let alone payment — for a single production unit. But for me, Carlos's letter was encouraging enough that I kept trying. With his letter, and my own complete conviction in my eventual success, I approached local supermarket magnate Lawson Williams, whom I'd met through a pot-smoking friend: Williams's son, Jeff. In exchange for a $10,000 investment, Jeff would become the proud owner of half of Infinitizer — something that excited him almost as much as it did me. The arrangement would be simple: Jeff, who considered himself an astute businessman — he had successfully sold ounces of pot to friends—would leave dental school to run Infinitizer while I headed up product development and sales. We starry-eyed young bucks were ready to show the world a thing or two.

Lawson, crusty and business-savvy, was apparently less than thrilled with the idea of his son dropping out of school to run a ragtag company with some hippie DJ. Glaring at me as if I'd just violated his daughter, he chewed up my dream and spit it out, telling me how many businesses fail and reminding me I had never owned a business or even run one. It wasn't till Jeff pleaded with him—promising that he wouldn't drop out of dental school and would let me run everything, remaining in Infinitizer only as a silent partner—that Lawson gave in and wrote out a check. We were funded. Jeff and I were partners in my most exciting adventure so far.

Flying high, I felt like a millionaire … minus a few zeros. I had a real company checkbook, letterhead, business cards, and the title of Company President. I immediately invested all but $500 of our $10,000: $9,000 into a subcontractor, CyCo Electronics, who would build all our products; and $500 in a pound of fine pot, for inspiration.

CHAPTER 28

I CONTINUED TO WORK on building Infinitizer into a giant company that could join the ranks of such musical electronics standard-bearers as Moog and ARP—the two 800-pound gorillas in the industry—but I was still a full-time employee of a Top 40 radio station—or, rather, Christopher Robin was. Monday through Friday, 10 am to 6 pm, I was either on the air or in the production studio, knocking out advertising spots for local businesses. I couldn't wait for 6 o'clock—within seconds, I was out the station door to do what really motivated me: build the world's first polyphonic musical synthesizer. It was rare that I crawled into our waterbed before 1 am or stayed there past 6 am.

Meanwhile, my subcontractor Eric Yatzel, owner of CyCo Electronics, was hard at work building the first fully functional Infinitizer prototype: an 88-key synth mounted on a piece of plywood. CyCo occupied a former convenience mart behind a strip mall on the west side of Santa Maria. The only way in was through the rear door—the space behind the dingy storefront window was piled high with boxes and trash, and the glass front door was chained shut. An old sign read "closed" in faded red letters, dangling at a precarious angle off the inside of the door. If you cupped your hands around your eyes and leaned in to peer through the dirty glass, you might see the glare of Eric's bench light as he hunched over the circuit boards he was soldering. Often Eric was so intent on work he neither heard my knocking nor would he answer the phone. That was okay by me, because I'd rather have him hard at work than keeping me in the loop. Over the next few months, as Eric hand-wired the circuits, his partner Jim crafted the schematics, and I designed a printed-circuit board to replace all that tedious work, the prototype circuit that would command the keyboard seemed to be nearing completion.

One cool, Santa Maria–style morning I arrived at Eric's shop just as the sun's golden spell burned through the hex of gray fog. It looked like it might just be a beautiful Saturday and, if we were lucky, one without the afternoon gales that launched the freshly plowed strawberry fields into the sky to blot out the blue. I squinted through the door to see Eric's hunched form. His nearsightedness gave him a look of intensity when he worked on circuits, his face mere inches from the board. He didn't respond to my knock. Perhaps the music he played from a pair of homemade speakers was too loud. I moved for a better view and saw something that brightened my morning more than the sun's challenge to the fog. The keyboard! Apparently it had finally arrived and was being connected to the circuit. I rapped my knuckles on the glass until they hurt, and eventually Eric's head lifted. He let me in the shop and I went right for the keyboard. There it was: the 88 white and black plastic ivories that would soon make our future and change the world of music forever. No longer would a keyboardist like Keith Emerson have to play music with one hand tied behind his back. With the Infinitizer, all ten fingers could tickle those keys and make music as it had never before been made on a synthesizer. A wisp of solder-smoke covered Eric before he put the iron down and flicked on the circuit's power supply.

"Give it a try," he said, switching the small desktop music system over to the synth.

My hand shook as I gingerly pressed a single key, worried I might break the spell or damage the device. C…middle C played through his bench speaker. It didn't sound like a piano. No, it sounded like a single tone, the kind I'd fall asleep to when the TV stations finished their broadcast day and all that remained on the screen was a target that looked like an LP cut into quarters: the image of a Native American chief at the top, grid patterns and smaller circles around the edges. Just a tone, a single tone activated by my index finger. Then another: this time discordant, as my middle finger held down the D. My smile was so big it dented my cheeks. I don't play the keyboard but I know enough to make chords. Now, for the first time in electronic music history, all ten keys of a synthesizer could make independent notes. I could only imagine how Walter Carlos would react once he laid hands on this miracle machine. This was history in the making and I knew all we had invested in time, money, and dreams was about to come to fruition.

There was plenty of work left to do. That early model keyboard could only produce pure sine wave tones. Still to come were the tone modifiers like filters, amplifiers, and modulators that would shape those tones into facsimiles of real instruments, or whatever inventive sounds the new owner of an Infinitizer might dream up. With this new device the sky was the limit. It worked, dammit. All my worries and doubts vanished in the first few seconds of playing those keys. Now, there was nothing standing in our way of building the world's first polyphonic musical synthesizer, other than a lot of hard work and an equal amount of good luck. But, we had done it!

I went home to tell Terri the news — we were so excited we jumped up and down, and I gave her a little spin. The look on her face was one of pure joy, the kind you get when everything goes just right. It doesn't come often, but when it does it's a feeling worth cherishing for a lifetime. Now we would just have to hang on until Eric and Jim finished the keyboard so we could dive into the tougher parts of the design: building those ten note modifiers and figuring out a way to synchronize them together. I had already amassed a sheaf of drawings and schematics to go over with Jim and Eric, and I couldn't wait to get moving.

After another month I was even more anxious to get it ready for trial, to see the progress of the note modifiers and perhaps play with the keyboard again — and most of all, to show Terri. I didn't see much progress on Eric's bench on subsequent visits, so I asked him if the other parts ordered with Jeff's and my original $9,000 investment had been delivered — it had been a few months. Eric assured me they were on the way, and that I had no reason to worry. Things were going slower than planned, but all was well. I heard his words, but for some reason I didn't get a warm and fuzzy feeling from them. I worried. Despite the progress of the keyboard in these last few months, something in Eric had changed. When we'd begun our relationship of contractor and subcontractor, this short, rotund man with thick fingers, bushy black eyebrows, and a dour expression was quick to order parts and beat his completion deadlines. He was a pleasure to work with. We'd often meet for coffee and sandwiches at Pappy's, a local hangout on the east side of the US 101 freeway, near the Orcutt turnoff. Our design consultant and Eric's partner, Jim Childress, an electrical engineer at nearby Vandenberg Air Force Base, was always there too, and the three of us would conspire to bring innovation to the musical-instrument business.

After a while, though, Jim stopped coming to Pappy's — busy with other projects, he said — and Eric slowly cooled toward me. Often I drank my coffee alone, glancing up each time Pappy's front door opened, in hopes one of them had found the time. I had those schematics of the note modifiers with me for every meeting but I didn't get to share them, and finally I just dropped them off at Eric's shop. He promised to share them with Jim and get back to me, but I never heard anything more. Progress on the prototype seemed to have stalled, but Eric always had a good reason and I desperately wanted to believe him. Every time I visited Eric's shop I fired up that keyboard and played the notes all at once. It was infectious, and I left filled with hope. We'd get through this.

The best thing I could do in the meantime was to work even harder, which meant spending less time at the only job that paid the bills: being Christopher Robin at KSEE, a job I really wanted to grow out of and move on.

Sometimes life hands us what we're looking for, as long as we're open to change. KXFM, a local FM station down on its luck, was looking for new leadership to increase its audience and ad revenues and that was a job that really interested me. KXFM was owned by Paul Hallock and Leonard Kesselman. Hallock, tall and gregarious with sweeping hand gestures, always wore cowboy boots and flashed the practiced smile of a politician. Once a successful and wealthy real-estate developer in the California Bay Area, he'd never wanted to own a radio station. Kesselman, Hallock's attorney and longtime friend, dabbled in radio stations when he wasn't lawyering. Leo, as we came to call him, had long, stringy, greasy black hair covering sagging shoulders that seemed weary of supporting his pear-like body. He had few social graces. If the weather got too hot or cold, Leo would often drop his shorts or pants in the middle of the KXFM offices and change into something more comfortable, to the embarrassment of whoever was present — often Janet, the front-office receptionist. Or Leo and I would be talking and,

169

without a pause in his flow of words, he'd chomp down on the butt of his ever-present cigar and drop trou.

Leo had rescued KXFM and its AM sister station KZON from bankruptcy with a short-term loan from Hallock, then threatened to extend the loan to the fifth of Never. "If you want your money back," he announced to Hallock, "you better get down to Santa Maria and straighten out the stations."

So Hallock had rolled into town in his cowboy boots and Cadillac, peeling off cash from a wad in his pocket like a big-time Vegas gambler, hoping to quickly make the two stations profitable. His first job was to get the FM station in the black. He hired me as its program director and I was thrilled. The pay was better than I had ever made and the music and format more to my liking.

KXFM's programming was AOR, the kind of music I loved and listened to: Led Zeppelin, Humble Pie, Peter Frampton, Iron Butterfly, the Rolling Stones, and Genesis. And for years, I'd lusted after a job as an FM program director. The PD was in charge of what music was played—and when and why. It was a rare chance to turn a floundering FM station into a world-class source of music for my community, a chance I was granted and did my best at for what seemed months on end.

But, despite the chance to craft better programming in the hopes of gaining audience share, KXFM wasn't making money, and it wasn't clear that even the best programming in the world could save it. We tried—Lord knows we tried—but it was too little too late, given the state of its financial affairs. Paychecks started bouncing, including mine. Things got worse when a surprise inspection by the Federal Communications Commission turned up a number of equipment violations, including the turntable preamplifiers, whose noise specifications were way out of whack. When the volume control of the station's mixing console was turned up to play a record, a loud hiss was broadcast along with the music. The FCC had the power to shut down our entire operation if improvements weren't made. Hallock and Leo couldn't make payroll, let alone buy new equipment, and in desperation they turned to me.

"You know about this electronic stuff, right?"

I nodded.

"Tell me what the parts cost to build new…thingamajigs, and help save us."

I didn't have a clue what to do, or how a phono preamplifier worked—but had my ignorance stopped me from designing parts for the world's most complicated synthesizer? I knew I could figure it out.

Besides, I now seemed to have some time on my hands. At CyCo, the building of the prototype Infinitizer had come to a halt. I'd arrive at the back door of Eric's shop at 9 am—he was an early riser—but increasingly, he wasn't there. Sometimes his little white Toyota pickup was parked nearby, but he still wouldn't answer the door. Jim still seemed to be avoiding me, too. Something was very wrong.

With little more I could contribute to the Infinitizer's progress, I worked on building a phono preamplifier for KXFM. It was work I could bury myself in, and I did. After all, it would save the station, which would save my job. Head down, soldering iron hot, I worked at the big round cable-spool table in our living room. Still, I couldn't help feeling that my future empire was crumbling, along with my life's work on the Infinitizer.

Then, out of the blue, Eric asked me to meet him at Pappy's for coffee. We hadn't met there in weeks, but any hopes I had of hearing good news were dashed as soon as I saw his face. His eyes never left his coffee cup as he announced, in a monotone barely above a whisper: "The money's gone…" He couldn't say where. The work had stopped. He was closing the shop, moving out to the Mojave Desert and leaving me holding the bag. I couldn't believe what I was hearing. With those words it seemed that my entire future—everything I'd worked for, dreamed of, gambled with, had confidence in—was suddenly gone. Once again. This was getting old.

With the help of his father's lawyer, Jeff Williams and I eventually won a judgment against Eric, but it was meaningless: there would be no blood from that turnip.

With my company up in smoke and the radio stations still on shaky ground I needed some time alone. On a cloudless, blustery day that defied my mood, I drove west, past Guadalupe, to the windswept dunes that met the Pacific, and watched the sandpipers pecking the sand for

171

food. I envied them. These birds didn't have the weight of the world on their shoulders. They weren't trying to conquer anything. They hadn't been taken to the cleaners, their dreams shattered. They just ran around, scooping up tiny crustaceans, their three-toed footprints vanishing under each incoming wave.

I'd failed, and I'd let down everyone who'd trusted me. Maybe my father was right when he told me that his highest hope for me was that I not land in prison. I'd almost managed to convince myself he was wrong about me, and now this—maybe I was a failure as a son and a human being. I wasn't practical in the way he was, the way I hoped I would become. I was a dreamer, and he'd warned me that dreamers fail because they can't bring themselves down to face reality. His words bit deeper because I knew that he, too, was a dreamer, and knew what he was talking about.

More than once, Dad had dreamed big—of inventing things like his hands-free intercom; of becoming an independent business owner by selling green dye for yellowing lawns; of being a successful investor in the Twentieth Century Motor Car Corporation, would-be manufacturers of a futuristic three-wheeled car, the Dale, that never went into production; of wealth that would free him from middle-class doldrums; of being a painter, a sculptor. In Dad's eyes, he'd failed at every one of these. He wanted things to be different for me. And now here I was, merely the next Don Quixote of the McGowan Clan, destined to joust windmills and play out my life as if success and fulfillment would come my way simply because I wished it to.

What had made me believe I had the chops to build the world's first polyphonic synthesizer? I had no education, no degree, nothing but chutzpah and a dream. I felt like a fraud. Should I start over looking for another round of financing when the first had been blown to waste? Who in this small community would take another chance on me? I am not sure I would have. I sat on the beach alone and wept.

And what about Terri—after this humiliation, how could I face her? Terri had believed in me, encouraging me to plow through the difficulties, the pain, the denials, the hardships. She'd somehow made ends meet when we had no money, stood by me, and told me my vision was a

172

good one—even after our dreams of working with Giorgio Moroder and living in Europe had been snuffed out. And here we were again. I wept some more.

A cloud passed in front of the sun, blocking the little warmth I hadn't realized I was feeling until it was gone. The wind picked up, as it does near Guadalupe, and tugged at my long hair, which flapped like a limp sail. I had no idea what to do. I couldn't avoid the fact that I'd failed, but what pained me most at that moment was the thought of having to tell Terri that Infinitizer was over.

Then my grief turned to anger. Eric had spent the money my partner Jeff's father had invested, and we were the ones left penniless. He was moving to the desert—as if becoming a loner in the great emptiness of the Mojave would somehow cleanse him of guilt. But it was his fault, not mine. Asshole. I could rest on that. It would be my story—my explanation for what had happened. Surely, once they knew the truth, those who'd trusted me wouldn't blame me. It wasn't I who'd taken the money. It was out of my control—we'd been robbed. No. Eric's deceit would not push me into the ground.

The cloud moved on, and the low sun warmed my face. Half convinced by my own shifting of the blame onto Eric, I took the returning sunlight as a sign to soldier on. But as I brushed sand off my pants and turned toward my tired old VW Beetle, sitting alone in the parking lot, I somehow let go of my anger at Eric. I suppose articulating his treachery didn't make me feel absolved, just worse—like doubling down on what had gone wrong. After all, it was I who'd thrust the money into his hands, with no instructions or backup plan. I was the one who'd abdicated responsibility. I was the one who spent $500 of our loan on a pound of pot when what I needed was a clear head. This was my fault, my failure.

Once again, I'd made a mistake, but this time I was determined to learn from the experience. I still dreamt big dreams. I wanted to build, create, explore technology, and embrace—even create—change, so I could put that long-sought dent in the world. I wanted to figure out how anything and everything worked, then make it better. It's what got me out of bed in the morning. My work would be to build my dreams and ideas, and somehow figure out a way to make money doing it. Travel, vacations, camping trips, and other diversions would be respites from the work of realizing those dreams, not the object of those dreams. My life would be my work and my family.

I wanted to be a wide-eyed entrepreneur, but feared I was only an irrepressible fool. Standing there alone next to my dilapidated Beetle in the empty parking lot of Guadalupe Beach, the salty sea wind buffeting my clothes and face, I proclaimed myself an irrepressible entrepreneur—one who understood that what's worse than failing is not to try again. I wiped away my tears and took a deep breath. I was at the beginning once again, and it wasn't looking like a clean slate. My dreams of the Munich recording studio were dashed, replaced with building synthesizers, and now that too was at an end. I had to pick myself up by my bootstraps and try again, starting from scratch.

Somehow, giving myself permission to be an entrepreneur—to know that was in my blood—gave me the courage to try again. I felt ready to jump off the proverbial cliff—risky, yes, but now I was sure I could put together an airplane on the way down and coax it to fly.

That just left one question: doing what?

CHAPTER 29

DESPITE MY PEP talk on Guadalupe Beach, the real world didn't miraculously go away. Terri's and my only sources of income were our jobs — mine depended on a radio station in financial trouble, and it was up to me to build the equipment it needed to stay afloat. This was a temporary situation, a hurdle, a bump in the road to rebuilding my crumbled business and future — yet I hadn't any clue what that new future would look like. So, in the meantime, we had to stay afloat and the sooner I could move past this briar patch the quicker we could move on.

The radio station needed new equipment that could pass FCC muster and it was up to me to figure out the quickest path to getting it built. I copied a circuit from a book and cobbled together a phono preamplifier, built inside a Roi-Tan cigar box and powered by two nine-volt batteries. It wasn't pretty, but it worked with my own turntable, as well as with the test equipment of Jim Mussel, the station's engineer. But apparently, measuring well wasn't enough. Jim, an introverted man who looked like Super Mario, walrus mustache and all, demanded that my prototype also sound good. He recommended that I take it to Norm Little, a respected local stereo guru who owned Ball Waterbeds, a retail outlet that advertised on KXFM.

Norm was short, with a neat mustache and a hearty laugh, the intensity of his brown eyes tempered by a welcoming smile. He seemed anxious to offer his services as a sound-quality expert, at least until he saw my cigar box. Eyes wide, he leaned back from it in distaste, then laughed.

"You are not hooking that thing up to my stereo."

I felt crushed, and probably looked it.

"But I'll bet Stan wouldn't mind," Norm reassured me. "He likes all that crazy do-it-yourself stuff and can tell you if it sounds any good."

Stan Warren worked for Ball, installing waterbeds, and Norm introduced us. Tall, lean, slightly hunched, with longish, sandy-blond hair and a mustache, Stan grunted his acceptance of my request and gave me his home address. He and his wife, Gwen, lived in a small, rickety, one-bedroom clapboard house in Orcutt, a one-street community just south of Santa Maria. The first thing I saw on entering their living room was a couch and two big speakers. In front of the couch was a turntable, mounted on a wooden stand whose four legs disappeared through holes cut in the wooden floor. They went all the way down into the foundation, Stan told me, to better isolate the turntable from vibrations in the floor and the rest of the house. I thought he was kidding.

In those days, everyone had a pair of speakers in their living rooms—mine were shoved up against a wall, the stereo equipment stacked on the floor between them. What made Stan's system unique, in my eyes, was its complete dominance of the space. The entire living room was devoted to sound: speakers, turntable, and multiple silver boxes, and running across the floor between them, cables and wires everywhere.

Stan hooked up my cigar-box phono preamp to his turntable and played a few records, switching between his own preamp, a Dynaco Pat 4, and my Roi-Tan battery-powered Wonder. Each time he switched to the cigar box, he grunted and nodded in approval. Soon we were done—he approved my prototype for use in the station. I went home, built the preamps, this time with AC plugs, installed four of them in KXFM's studio, and they passed the FCC tests with flying colors. I thought no more about it. My job, and the station, were temporarily saved from elimination.

A week after the collapse of Infinitizer, there was a knock on my front door. It was Stan.

"Got a minute?"

I invited him in. Never one for idle chat, he plunked a wad of cash on my table.

"I just sold my van. Here's $500. I want to buy half your company."

I blinked. "What company?" Did he mean Infinitizer? The one that had just collapsed? Did he expect his $500 would replace the $10K we'd just lost?

"The new one that's going to build that phono preamp you brought to my house. It's better than anything I've ever heard, and I think we can sell those."

176

"The cigar box?"

"Yeah. We'll make a nice case for it, add a line cord for power, put our new name on it. Paul and Stan Audio. PS Audio, for short."

"Okay," I said. All I could see was that $500 in cash sitting on the table. I forced myself to look at Stan. "Who would buy these boxes?"

"Audiophiles."

And, just like that, I went from being lost in the woods without a map to passing through the tollbooth of my life's future highway.

CHAPTER 30

I HAD NEVER HEARD the term audiophile before, but it wouldn't take me long to meet them. An audiophile is like an oenophile—a wine connoisseur. Both develop skills to enhance their enjoyment of a sensory experience: audiophiles, to reproduce the recorded sound of the original performance as closely as possible; oenophiles, to refine their tastes for ever subtler, ever more nuanced wines. Both terms comprise a wide range of specialized knowledge and experience. Oenophiles can be casual wine sippers who know a good wine from bad, or master sommeliers who can identify by taste alone the type of grape, where it was grown, even the year. Audiophiles range from committed home enthusiasts to veteran experts who, by listening alone, can identify problems in setup, equipment, cabling, even the components' inner circuitry.

But in 1974, the only audiophile I'd ever met was my new partner, Stan Warren. His speakers were homemade and his humble electronics were good, but they were hardly state of the art, even by the audiophile standards of 1974. Still, music sounded much better through Stan's system than through mine: fuller, clearer, and, on some recordings, with bass I'd never heard before—bass that actually moved his unsteady wooden floor.

As I began to immerse myself in this new world of high-end audio—the term self-described audiophiles prefer—I continued working at KXFM. By day I earned my meager living as a program director and disc jockey, and at night I worked with Stan, building the phono preamp—we adopted its casual nickname, the Cigar Box Wonder—into what we hoped might become a marketable product: something audiophiles would want because it made their records sound better. This was a big leap for me, a disc jockey who had aspired to build the world's coolest synthesizer before crashing and burning. I hadn't known much about synths when I started that project but over time, study, and a lot of work I became an expert at their operation and design. I had to. It was the only way to get where I needed to go. Now it would be stereos

I put my mind and energies towards, a sizeable shift in focus into a field I again knew next to nothing about. At least this time I had a guide through the wilderness. Though Stan knew little of circuits and electronics, he at least understood the inner details of the community we were planning on building products for. The big question in both our minds was whether or not we had the chops to pull this off: me with the electronic knowledge, Stan with the audiophile experience and listening skills.

The job of the phono preamplifier is twofold. First, it accepts an input signal from a turntable's needle and cartridge, amplifies it, then outputs it at a higher level to a preamplifier. Phono preamplifiers of the day were built into existing equipment, such as receivers and integrated amplifiers. What made the Cigar Box Wonder special was that it was a standalone device, one of the first to focus on a single task: to amplify what was trapped in a record's groove and pass that along to a receiver or stereo system. We hoped that customers would accept the inconvenience of a standalone device that sounded better than any phono preamp built into the audio products then available.

The phono preamp's other job is to reverse the considerable equalization applied to the signal during the cutting process, to get more information out of a vinyl disc with less noise. This latter task is done by implementing an equalization curve developed by the Recording Industry Association of America and called the RIAA curve, and it's part of what made possible the creation of the 331⁄3 rpm long-playing record, or LP.

Records struggle with any number of challenges: limitations in dynamic range, frequency bandwidth, and playing time; noise from surface blemishes and warps; and heat generated by the rubbing of the moving groove against the stylus. But major difficulties with playing time and noise had been addressed the year I was born, 1948. Before then, records were made of shellac or vinyl but were spun at a much higher speed, with shorter playing times and higher noise levels than we accept today. These 78 rpm records were everywhere, in ten-inch and twelve-inch versions, but they were scratchy and noisy, and had maximum playing times of only 3 minutes per ten-inch side or 5 minutes per twelve-inch side. A recording of Beethoven's *Ninth Symphony* took up 7 twelve-inch 78s—that's a lot of interruptions of the music, even with the automatic record changers of the day.

The LP solved most of these problems with some novel engineering: the RIAA curve and the microgroove. Instead of the giant sewing-machine needles typically used to play 78s, a tiny diamond stylus was shaped to fit the spiral grooves of equally tiny width stamped into each side of these new LPs. Many more revolutions of microgroove could be packed onto a side than the more than twice as wide groove of a 78, and this, combined with the LP's much slower speed of rotation, extended the maximum feasible playing time from 5 to 25 minutes. However, there was a problem. Because low frequencies—bass—recorded at the same volume level require far greater lateral deviations of the groove than do higher frequencies, the bass frequencies' level had to be lowered relative to the highs. This problem was known well before the introduction of the LP, but its solution varied from record company to record company. By the time the LP was launched, there were over 100 different ways to reduce the level of lower frequencies relative to higher frequencies. These were called equalization (EQ) curves; the RIAA curve was the one that, eventually, became the industry standard.

The idea was simple enough. During the cutting of the original lacquer—from which, several generations of copies later, finished LPs would ultimately be stamped—a filter was used to reduce the volume level of the lowest frequencies. Then, when the record was played, a reverse filter was used to restore those frequencies to their original level to be amplified and sent on to the speakers. What the RIAA curve did was twofold: standardize the filter characteristics, then add a second filter that cut and boosted the high frequencies. Thus, within a few years of Columbia Record's launch of the LP in 1948, it would soon feature both the new microgroove and the RIAA curve. The extended playing time of 25 minutes per side, coupled with higher sound quality, lower noise, and fewer ticks and pops (because, during playback of the amplified high frequencies, the phono preamp did the opposite and lowered that same frequency band), the LP was and remains the standard of high-fidelity vinyl used to this day.

In the early 1960s, console stereos were the rage. They had everything:

a record changer, preamp and power amp, speakers, and even a place to store records. But already in the 1950s, audio pioneers such as Sydney Harman, Frank McIntosh, Avery Fisher, H.H. Scott, and Saul Marantz had begun to separate the console stereo into its component pieces, each boasting better sound than the collection of parts it came from. The idea of a separate component dedicated to maximizing the performance of a single task, one that had previously been built into a larger component that also did many other tasks, extended the relatively recent idea of separate components that had begun in the "hi-fi" era of the 1950s and by the early 1970s, was coming into its own. The advantage of separates is that designers can focus on building a device that does only one thing, but does it better than anything else. To appeal to audiophiles, Stan and I proposed to take the philosophy a step further. Our Cigar Box Wonder amplified the record player's signal traced by the stylus, and with a quality of sound improved enough that even untrained ears could appreciate it.

With a few months' work, Stan and I managed to condense the Cigar Box Wonder into a metal case—a small silver box about half the size of a six-pack of English muffins, with walnut endcaps. It looked official enough and on Stan's stereo system it sounded even better than the original circuit. But, was it good enough? Good enough to build a company around? To commit our lives and futures to?

We were charged up and ready for the biggest challenge of all: an audition on Norm's stereo. This time, I hoped Norm wouldn't laugh. Our futures depended on that.

CHAPTER 31

THE FATEFUL MORNING of our new product's reckoning at Norm's house started out with fog, as it often does along the Central California Coast. Inland heat from the state's Central Valley coaxed the offshore moisture across the dunes to wet the Deergrass, Giant Wildrye, Valley Sedge, and Purple Needlegrass that colored the land and scented the air once the sun broke through and burned off the fog.

My nerves were all a jumble that morning, but Stan counseled calm as we hopped into his army-gray Volkswagen Beetle.

"We have to know how the preamp stacks up against the best there is. It'll be what it'll be," he said, always the pragmatist.

I didn't share his confidence. This first test of our new phono preamp was a make or break moment for me. Did we have a product to sell or not? I was too new to the idea of selling electronic boxes to audiophiles and hadn't any way to judge whether this was just another wild hair scheme or a path worth following towards success. So far, my track record of business successes wasn't all that good.

Norm lived in an off-the-shelf, three-bedroom, single-story tract house in an area west of Santa Maria called Tanglewood, at the edge of the fog, near the old Cabrillo Highway. His living room was a bit dark, and it took a moment for my eyes to adjust as Stan and I entered the house. When they did, I saw speakers lined up along one wall—more speakers in one place than I'd imagined possible. They started at the floor and mounted upward like a temple to the audio gods.

The first thing I could identify was a pair of massive Cerwin-Vega subwoofers with 18-inch drivers, personally built for Norm by the owner of the company, Gene Czerwinski. On top of these beasts sat tall, wide, angled panels of midrange speaker drivers from a company called Janszen. These electrostatically controlled drivers looked nothing like speakers—they were more like window panes. Stacked atop the Janszens were the oddest-looking contraptions imaginable: Ionovac horn tweeters that produced a blue flame when music was played. They made sound by varying the air pressure with high-energy electrical plasma. It was the plasma that glowed blue.

Those were only the speakers. Driving them was a stack of glowing Audio Research tube amplifiers, a tube preamplifier, and a tube crossover to send the three frequency bandwidths to the appropriate speakers. Feeding all of that was a turntable whose cartridge was installed in a strange-looking tonearm that traced the groove in a straight line across the record surface, rather than the arc described by a standard pivoted tonearm. And of course, there were wires and cables everywhere. Norm had one other tweak to further the enjoyment of his hi-fi system, something I hadn't seen since my Army days in Germany: a freezer full of hash that he wasn't shy about sharing with fellow audiophiles.

Once powered up, tubes lit and the needle dropped in the groove: the opening bass notes floated free of the speakers, as if the instrument's own amp and speakers were in the room. The sound was effortlessly powerful. Stevie Wonder began singing "Living for the City," from his album *Innervisions*. I'd played the song many times at home, but now realized I'd never actually heard it—not like this. I could feel the low-bass notes in my toes, and I don't mean that figuratively. With each note, I could feel the vibrations from the speakers through the floor—something I'd felt only once before, at Stan's house. But Stan had a suspended wooden floor—Norm's house was built on a concrete slab.

Although I'd read that Wonder had played all the instruments himself and multitracked the entire album, similar to the way Walter Carlos had assembled *Switched-On Bach*, that process was never clear when I listened at home. Now, listening to "Living for the City" through this dazzling collection of wires, boxes, subwoofers, and flaming blue tweeters, I heard for the first time that the opening bass line vibrating the floor was from a single-note Moog synthesizer—I guessed a Mini Moog. I could tell because Moogs have a distinctly fat, rich sound, like a bullfrog's bellow. It wasn't as if I couldn't tell it was a keyboard bass line on my meager home system—I just couldn't identify its size or tonal character as easily as I could through Norm's system. Each bass note was articulated, and the filter's boowa-wa attack was lush, rich in gushing overtones. The underlying ring of the Fender Rhodes electric piano that also begins this track sounded like the chime of a tubular doorbell through Norm's system; through my system, it sounded like a nondescript electric piano. Then the cymbal crashed—so loudly that I was startled. I hadn't even noticed it through Stan's or my speakers. But with Norm's system, it was as if my ears were only inches from the actual cymbals: big, splashy, and loud, instead of homogenous and lost in the musical *mêlée* of "Living for the City."

There was more. Kick-drum whacks and snare-drum strokes snapped with a presence I hadn't known were on the recording. The deep, rich, lush notes; the feeling of singers singing to us in the same room we listened to them in; electric-bass notes that went deeper than I'd ever heard from a record; highs that floated in the air, divorced from the positions of the speakers, as if produced in Norm's room by the instruments themselves—the reproduction of music by Norm's system was so far removed from anything I'd ever heard from my home system that I didn't know what to think. As we continued to listen, I was in something like a state of shock. It was suddenly clear to me that my system hadn't been giving me anywhere close to all the music my records actually contained. Worse, after listening to Norm's stereo, I realized that what I was accustomed to hearing from my setup sounded artificial by comparison, like looking at the world through cloudy, rose-tinted glasses: appealing, but misleading, and definitely not true to life.

When at last it was time to replace the phono stage in Norm's Audio Research SP3 phono preamplifier with Stan's and my little box, I was beyond nervous. I hoped the magic I'd just experienced wouldn't stop, but from the first needle drop, I could hear that the game was over. Where once there had been life and beauty in the music, now we heard the opposite—a two-dimensional cardboard cutout of the original, living, three-dimensional event. It was like switching from a home stereo system to a decent clock radio. The ringing and extended sound I'd just heard around each struck string was gone. How could one version of the same basic circuitry—a collection of wires, capacitors, tubes, and transistors—succeed at making magic and another one fail, if both preamplifiers measured the same on test gear?

I had expected a miracle that day, but instead, got the booby prize. Our dreams of building our futures around the little box of electronics seemed more distant now than at any time before. With our tails tucked, we got back in Stan's little VW Beetle and putted home without saying a word to each other.

CHAPTER 32

AFTER DAYS OF DESPAIR, Stan and I rallied. We realized that the Audio Research preamp that had beaten us cost ten times more than we were planning to charge for our Wonder, and that Bill Johnson, ARC's owner and chief designer, had many more years of experience than we did. As well, that preamp used vacuum tubes rather than the solid-state devices we had used. We assured ourselves that there must be a way to engineer a solution. We went to work, but soon discovered that replicating the quality of sound we'd heard at Norm's was easier said than done.

Electronic circuits perform specific functions: transforming the wiggles in an LP's groove into electrical impulses, or amplifying those impulses to send them to a pair of speakers, or translating those impulses into sound waves. Such circuits may be similar in the way they work but can be very different in the way they sound.

Our first lesson in the sounds of electronic parts came from the very core of my prototype's circuit: an operational amplifier, or op-amp. When I began to design the phono preamp, I had no idea how such things actually worked. The book I'd turned to for help had been published just that year: *The IC Op-Amp Cookbook* by Walter G. Jung, an engineer at the semiconductor manufacturing company Analog Devices. In it, Jung describes a phono preamplifier circuit using an op-amp designed as an integrated circuit (IC). Each IC op-amp is a rectangle of black plastic about the size of a shirt button, with eight exposed silver legs: one row of four on each side. It looks like a headless Lego spider. Jung's original circuit diagram called for a specific type of op-amp that I had no easy way of getting. After some study, I learned that the type of op-amp wasn't all that important, because all op-amps perform the same basic functions. When sent into an op-amp hooked up to three or four resistors and a power supply, such as the pair of 9-volt transistor-radio batteries I ended up using, a small input signal from a microphone or a turntable would come out much louder at the other end. This increase in loudness, called gain, depended on little more than the values of the external resistors. Jung often referred to op-amps as functional building blocks, which was true as far as it went.

I didn't have the type of op-amp called for in Jung's book: the 741. But for general-purpose amplification, as in audio, just about any brand or type of op-amp was said to perform about the same as any other. KXFM's engineer, Jim Mussel, happened to have samples of a new type of op-amp he'd read about in a technical paper. It was called the 709, and Jim said it would be perfect for my project. So instead of the 741 op-amp called for in Jung's book, I built that first phono preamp with the 709. It turned out to be of critical importance. Had I used the 741, I have no doubt that PS Audio would never have come into existence, and my life would have taken a very different path.

The 709 was designed in the early 1970s by an engineering rebel, Robert John Widlar (1937–1991). With his iconic Van Dyke beard, wiry unkempt hair, and intense cutting eyes, Bob was a wild man. He's still remembered among engineers and marketing people for a classic photograph of him offering the Widlar Salute—right hand up, middle finger extended, the classic fuck you—under this headline: "Digital? 'Every idiot can count to one.'" The Widlar Salute eventually found its way into the print ads of his employer, National Semiconductor, featuring a full-page ad of a fist flipping the bird with this headline in bold type: "Our message to the competition is simple and straightforward." The paragraphs of ad copy, widely believed to have been written by Widlar himself, go on in a similar vein: "We've had it with namby-pamby, blue-sky advertising. From now on, National doesn't pussyfoot. We're going to take on the rest of the semiconductor industry and let the chips fall where they may." I assume the pun was intended.

Widlar was known as the enfant terrible of Silicon Valley for his legendary all-night drinking binges, his penchant for fighting when drunk, and his refusal to fit into the accepted mold of the quiet, nerdy, pencil-pushing, pocket-protected engineer of the late 1960s. The world remembers Widlar not for his drinking and carousing, but because he was a genius single-handedly responsible for an entire generation of advanced linear analog electronics. His designs are still with us today in the forms of op-amps, linear regulators, and even the very fabrication processes used to make integrated circuits. Bo Lojek, author of *History of Semi-conductor Engineering*, described Bob as "more artist than engineer…in the environment where Human Relations departments define what engineers can and cannot comment about, it is very unlikely that we will see his kind again."

As Stan and I began experimenting with different parts, one of the first we replaced was Widlar's 709 op-amp. After all, Jung's book had specified the 741, so in the 741 went. The new op-amp measured identically to the old, so we had no reason to believe it would sound any different. Boy, were we wrong. With the 741 op-amp, the Cigar Box Wonder sounded like mush. Cymbals lost their shine, sounding like they'd been struck with sticks wrapped in gauze. The blat of horns lost the upper grit and glare that help distinguish a trumpet from a trombone. The all-important soundstage, which had spread out behind the speakers with the 709, had moved forward and narrowed—now it sounded trapped between the speakers and us. Shocked, we learned a valuable lesson: nothing in a circuit could be taken for granted.

It was all in the details. We had to learn which parts of a circuit affected which aspects of sound. The bass, treble, and midrange responses might measure flat, but they wouldn't always sound flat. This puzzled Stan and me. We didn't yet understand that not everything we could hear was being measured by our instruments, and might not be able to be measured at all. Even today, much of what we hear can't yet be measured: much more research needs to be done into the human ear's perception of sound waves, and the neural processes the brain subjects those sound waves to so that they can be experienced in the mind as sound—which is, ultimately, not a physical but a mental phenomenon.

But it wasn't just better-sounding bass or treble we had to try for. There were subtler details: clarity, or how distinctly each instrument or voice rises out of the fabric of the sound to stand on its own; openness, or how detached instruments and voices seem to be from each other, instead of being scrunched together like sounds in a crowded room; and quality of soundstage, or the illusion that voices and instruments are being presented in a space extending behind, between, and beyond the outer side panels of a pair of speakers—a three-dimensional sound field that seems to exist independently of the positions of the speakers themselves.

At Norm's, we'd heard this beauty and this magic. But now we were lost in the wilderness without a guide. I remember one particularly depressing evening after finishing a listening and design session. I had managed to convince myself that we were on the right track, so I felt good plowing through night after night of tweaking. We had made good progress with changing parts and retuning the circuit, but our futures still hung on our abilities to make this simple, low-cost circuit of mine outperform units a magnitude more expensive. We were two amateur hacks trying to build better equipment than masters in the field with far more money in their pockets and experience under their belts. I said goodnight to Stan and looked around for Gwen. She'd long since gone to bed, so I left. The door to their little shack clicked shut behind me, and for just a moment I stood on the wooden porch, looking at my sad little VW listing towards the passenger side. There were no sidewalks in Orcutt, but in front of Stan's untended briar patch of mowed weeds lay a ditch that ran the length of South Gray Street. An impenetrable cloud of ashen ocean moisture was heading our way, illuminated by a crescent moon high in the evening sky.

It was cold, and I hadn't thought to bring a coat. I folded my arms around me for warmth and slowly walked to the car, my head filled with doubts. What the hell were we doing? I'd already invested months of our lives into this project, only to discover that the challenges were even greater than inventing a new synth. Musical instruments were straightforward designs. They worked or they didn't. They played the right notes or the wrong notes. They were measurable and easy enough to get right or fix what was wrong. But this audiophile stuff seemed maddening. We had to learn a new set of skills just to know how deep the cesspool was that we had managed to get ourselves into. Had I made the right choice accepting Stan's $500? It wasn't too late to just throw the towel in and admit I was in over my head. Perhaps I should rally back on my synth idea and leave the stereos to Stan.

Leaning against the cold car, I got even more chilled. The fog had moved in following its steady march, and now blanketed me like a scene out of Victorian London.

"Evening," came a friendly voice out of the mist.

It was an older man walking a dog. He was hunched over, in the way old men fold to gravity's incessant pull. His legs were stiff and he shuffled to induce forward motion. His patient dog kept looking back for assurance.

"Fog's coming in again," he observed.

"Yup."

We both looked at the rolling darkness threatening pea soup.

"Looks like ye got the weight of the world on ya," he said. "Tough times?"

"Yeah, we're struggling."

"Good!" his eyes lit up as if he'd just stepped in front of a bonfire. "I miss my struggles. They got me out of bed in the morning and lit a fire in my belly. Now all I got left is moving these legs."

He smiled, tipped his head, and shuffled down the street, disappearing in a gray jacket of fog. I smiled too, and got in my car before the soup got too thick to drive home. We had a lot of work left to do on that preamp.

CHAPTER 33

STAN AND HIS WIFE Gwen's small house in Orcutt became our unofficial headquarters because of his stereo system. Evenings, weekends, and sometimes even lunch breaks found the two of us ensconced in his living room sketching new circuit ideas, arguing over the merits of parts and designs, and endlessly listening to the same tracks of music to compare one notion to another. On the hot days we sweltered because opening the windows and doors impacted sound quality and on the cold days we shivered as Stan's feeble wall heater struggled to keep up.

Fully committed now but without a clear path to financial reward, we spent every spare hour learning, tweaking, listening, redesigning, and listening again, trying to figure out how to engineer audio magic so we could build and sell our own version of it. We didn't know it at the time, but we were learning a skill that few people had back then: the ability to correlate what we heard with changes in electronic circuitry—changes that didn't register on traditional measures of sound quality like distortion or frequency response. At that point, little research had been done into how we perceive sound. After six months of this, we were closer to the sound of our ideal—the sound of live, unamplified music as if the musician were in the room.

But now I had even fewer hours to spare. I'd taken a second job, as an electronic technician at a company that occupied an old barrel-bowl airplane hangar on Skyway Drive, near the local airport. In 1942, the Army Corps of Engineers had developed 3,600 acres that would become known as the Santa Maria Army Air Field, to train advanced pilots in the operation of the Lockheed P-38 Lightning fighter plane. Soon after the war, the old air base became the present Santa Maria Public Airport, and the city leased the Army Air Corps' wooden hangars to private companies. Among those was AV-Alarm Corp, which made products to frighten away birds.

AV-Alarm's chief bird-scarer was the brilliant John L. Stewart—we called him Dr. Stewart—who had a PhD in electrical engineering.

Stewart was athletic, with a wrestler's short, stocky frame, his usually intense facial expressions emphasized by his white crewcut. He'd designed electronic circuits and outdoor amplification and speaker systems that mimicked the alarm calls of some bird species, then founded AV-Alarm to manufacture and sell them. AV's customers were anyone who didn't want birds nearby—airports and vineyards in particular. Dr. Stewart had been looking for a part-time electronics technician, and I seemed to fit the bill. Weekends and evenings would find me upstairs in the hangar, wiping bird shit from the cases of broken alarms and repairing their electronics.

What most attracted me to the job was not bird-scaring but AV-Alarm itself. The 20,000-square-foot facility was a manufacturing mecca, with all the tools needed to make bird alarms—and stereo gear. All the necessary metal-forming equipment was here: punch presses, drill presses, bending brakes, and even silk-screening equipment for lettering and labeling. Stewart watched every penny he spent on materials and manufacturing. To keep costs down, his crew built AV's own horn speakers and made their own magnets and enclosures—even printed-circuit boards.

The deal I made with Stewart was a simple one: I would keep his customers' bird alarms running, in exchange for evening and weekend access to the shop and its tools. Here, Stan and I could hand-build our products with little more investment than the raw materials needed for cases and the parts to stuff into them. But even with access to a fully equipped factory, at the rate we were going, it was obvious to me that it would take us a year of Sundays to complete the product, and maybe even that wouldn't do it. We needed more time to put into the Cigar Box Wonder, and the only way I could think of finding those hours was to quit KXFM and devote myself full time to PS Audio.

Terri and I still struggled to put food on the table. She was working two full-time jobs: as a photo finisher at night, and as a rock 'n' roll DJ at KXFM during the day, even though the station was hanging by only the thinnest of shoestrings. And here I was, about to propose that I no longer bring home a paycheck at all, and instead work full-time at PS

Audio, which had yet to make a cent and had no prospects of making money any time soon. I figured this would not go down well with Terri.

I took her to dinner at Pappy's Coffee Shop, but avoided the booth where Eric had told me that Infinitizer was over. Even in the harsh fluorescent light of Pappy's, Terri looked as radiant as the day we'd met, her golden curls falling to her shoulders. Still, I was nervous. As we shared a burger and drank coffee, I detailed Stan's and my slow progress redesigning our preamp, and my frustration with working full-time at KXFM while trying to keep PS Audio alive. I told her the only way PS could succeed was if I threw myself at it with all my energy. Either I gave up the dream of PS Audio and muddled along as a PD and DJ for the rest of my life, or I dropped everything and made a go of it—as I saw it, it had to be one or the other. "We're nearly broke now—what do we have to lose?"

She said nothing for a while, staring at the black pool in her coffee cup and swirling it with a spoon. "How will we pay the rent? Food?"

"I don't know, but we'll figure something out. It can't get a lot worse."

After a moment she smiled. It was the smile I'd first seen in Munich, the smile that lit up that cold night and drew me to the beautiful lady standing in line at the movie theater.

"Okay Paul. Let's go for it."

I'm pretty sure I cried. I'm crying as I write this.

I now realize how different our lives would be today if Terri had said "No," or even "Maybe." I don't know how many spouses would have said "Yes" and encouraged me to push forward, at the risk of uncertainty, failure, poverty, and even bankruptcy. Few people are blessed with such a life partner—but I needed only this one, Terri, to set me free. I quit KXFM the next day.

Despite my cavalier assurance of "it can't get a lot worse," things did get worse. A lot worse. Fast. We went directly from barely making ends meet to flat broke, and our lives started unraveling. We were two months late on the rent. Food money got scarce. Increasingly, we relied on my parents to keep us afloat. Terri's mother had been widowed decades ago and did her best to raise her two girls as a single working mom. It didn't help that my mother kept asking why I couldn't just be a normal person and get a job.

"But Mom, I have this dream," I would plead.

"Me, too," she would say, "a dream that my son can support his family and not wind up living in a cardboard box. What's wrong with just getting another job?"

We had reached a new low point that dove deeper than I could ever have imagined. When it was just the two of us traveling across the country with our six cats and dilapidated VW van—flat broke but at least with a clean slate—poverty seemed somehow more acceptable. We were just out of the Army, our families were anxious to see us, and life looked like a spotlight shining on the horizon, filled with the promise of unexplored good fortune. But now we were committed to an entrepreneurial career path that increasingly looked like another dead-end street, one we had already traveled down before. We were doing our best to maintain an optimistic outlook, but it was getting more difficult by the day. Terri and I were our strongest advocates for our life's path but even we harbored growing inner doubts. We'd have to get some relief soon or once again, change course and start over, a prospect neither of us wanted but both feared.

CHAPTER 34

ENTREPRENEURS, FOOLS, and gamblers have something in common: they tend to ignore well-intentioned advice when it doesn't match the direction of their forward march. Both Terri and I were convinced we could succeed, despite our family's pleadings and the mounting odds against us. Whether our continued commitment to the new venture stemmed from hubris, stubbornness, or simply an undying belief in ourselves didn't matter. We would not be deterred from clearing poverty's hurdle.

We hatched a plan using the one asset we could tap to support us: my record albums. Over the years, I had accumulated a collection that now numbered in the thousands, including many first editions that I'd gotten through the radio station—some promo copies, some from the artists themselves. The idea of giving up my records was gut-wrenching, but every Saturday and Sunday afternoon, Terri and I loaded up the VW bug with a few boxes of albums and headed for the Nipomo Swap Meet. We sold nothing for less than $1, and many went for $5 or more, at a time when the list price of a new LP was $5.98. It put food on the table and kept the eviction notices at bay. Things were looking up and progress at the new company was steadily creeping forward.

Though we were broke, we weren't yet living out of a cardboard box. Our clean, sparsely furnished three-bedroom rental on the south end of town hadn't acquired many improvements since the days of Infinitizer, but it was a happy home, shared with our six cats. At the far end of our living room, sitting on yellow shag carpeting, was a huge, paisley-patterned, foam-rubber pillow next to a table lamp—the companion table was on our list of someday purchases. Under the living room's picture window was a double-stacked row of albums and a new pair of loudspeakers, while my amp and turntable sat on the shelf above the albums. Our spare bedroom had been converted into a photo darkroom, and the guest room had morphed into an art and sewing room for Terri. While it wasn't luxurious, it was a welcome respite from the struggles of starting a new company, and of clawing our way through the challenges of everyday living without a steady income.

On weekends and evenings, when sales at the swap meet had been good enough to squeeze out a little extra cash for groceries, we'd invite friends over to savor barbecued chicken, lathered in Santa Maria Style barbecue sauce and served with generous helpings of Terri's pinquito beans and fresh green salad. The constant westerly Santa Maria winds had been particularly brutal that summer, coloring the eastern sky with clouds of brown stripped from the freshly plowed sugar beet fields. It was a Friday, and those fierce afternoon gales had mercifully taken a welcome break. As the sun set over the dunes, the twilight air was still warm enough for shorts and T-shirts. The last of the chicken breasts—lightly blackened and crunchy on the outside, moist and tender on the inside—came off the grill and landed on our guests' paper plates to the serenade of bottle caps popping off cold beer bottles. It was a lovely evening, but as midnight approached the ocean's cool blanketed the Santa Maria Valley and our friends said their goodnights. Terri and I slipped under the warm covers of our heated waterbed and soon fell fast asleep to the floating bed's gentle waves.

Early that morning I was awakened by the sound of a catfight in the living room, but I was too tired to get up and throw them all outdoors. In what seemed like the next moment, I smelled smoke and leaped out of our waterbed, leaving poor Terri bobbing in my wake. A cat had knocked over the table lamp, and its bare bulb had ignited the pillow. If I'd had my wits about me, I'd have smothered the fire with a blanket. Instead, I panicked. All I could think to do was to get the burning pillow out of the house. As I dragged it out the front door, it left behind a trail of molten, burning foam rubber. The carpet covering the suspended wood floor caught fire like kindling, and in less than a minute the entire living room was burning, the flames reaching to the ceiling.

I darted through the inferno back to the bedroom—singeing my crotch hairs in the process—and screamed at Terri to get outside through the back door but she was already on it. Once outdoors, we pulled the garden hose around the corner of the house, but it was just a few inches too short. It was hopeless. By the time the fire department arrived, they could do little but keep the crowds at bay. Our home and what few possessions we had managed to accumulate vanished in less time than it takes to get a quart of milk at 7-Eleven. The fire was so hot that the plastic turn signal lights on our Volkswagen Beetle began to melt, so we had to push it from the driveway out into the street. Everything in our home was a total loss, and even worse, our cats scattered to the winds, never to return again.

That afternoon, while we were still dazed, confused, and in shock, Stan drove over and offered to let us stay with him until we could get back on our feet. His little wooden shack in Orcutt couldn't have been more than 500 square feet—just a living room, a kitchen, a bedroom, and an oversized storage closet—but he cleared out the closet to create a makeshift bedroom. It was better than the cardboard box of my Mom's worst jitters, but not by much. We'd been at low points before, but with the house burned to the ground along with our only source of income—my remaining album collection—we were scraping bottom.

All that remained after the fire was a few things we'd stored in the detached garage: a box of old tape recordings from the British Rock Festival, my prototypes of the Infinitizer synthesizer, a few odds and ends, and some old clothes. A week after the fire leveled our home, we lost most of that as well, when some local arsonists decided to torch the garage for kicks. Fortunately our neighbor, wielding his garden hose, was able to keep the flames at bay until the fire department arrived, but all they could salvage was the tapes. We were left with the clothes on our backs, our aging VW Beetle, and a smoke-covered box of recording tapes.

Life was testing us. We knew this was just the kind of situation where most people would call it a day, but we would not be deterred. We may have been fools, and at times we were gamblers, but above all we were entrepreneurs—which meant tenaciously hanging onto our vision, like climbers on the side of a cliff.

CHAPTER 35

LIFE AT STAN and Gwen's tiny house wasn't easy, but at least we had a roof over our heads because of their kind generosity. I still had my part-time job as an electronics tech at AV-Alarm, but that was only covering PS Audio's rent. Terri continued to work her two jobs. The remaining albums we were counting on to sell at the swap meet had been consumed in the fire, so I extended my entrepreneurial roots to become a pot dealer. It was risky business, because the only way to make any money in the marijuana trade was to deal in pounds of the leafy bush, not just ounces. This meant that every second Saturday of the month I'd motor north to San Francisco and pick up ten pounds of Columbian Gold, sometimes a few bundles of Thai Sticks, and on occasion, a bit of golden Honey Oil for resale back in Santa Maria. I had gotten the semi-weekly run down to a science: a steady 55 miles an hour in the right lane, short hair, borrowed baby car seat in the rear, and only one steady customer on both ends of the transaction. This arrangement kept Stan and I supplied with all the pot we could consume, as well as the extra income Terri and I needed to make ends meet.

As 1974 came to an end, Stan and I had reached a point in our design skills where our phono preamp was close in sound quality to the one built into Norm's Audio Research SP3, which in those days retailed for $600 ($2,830 in today's dollars). It was time for us to hit the marketplace and see how we'd do.

In those days most mass-market stereo gear—receivers, cheap turntables, boomy loudspeakers—was sold by a chain of stores called Pacific Stereo as well by a few mail order places like Warehouse Sounds in San Luis Obispo, California. High-end audio equipment was sold by specialty stores like LA's Jonas Miller, Santa Ana's Absolute Audio, and NYC's Lyric Hi-Fi. But high-end dealers only did business with established audio companies, such as Audio Research, Klipsch, Magnepan, Infinity, JBL, etc. They had no interest in two hicks from Santa Maria with a few phono preamps and a lot of hopes and dreams. They refused to even listen to our pitch.

Undaunted, we decided to go it alone by taking out an ad in one of the nationwide hi-fi magazines. We chose *Audio* because we were broke and they'd give us credit—the much larger *Stereo Review* would not. We began with a one-sixth-page ad with the headline "rediscover your records," a picture of our phono preamplifier—which, strangely enough, we'd given no other name than simply "phono preamplifier"—and something that, as far as we knew, no one in the stereo business had ever offered: a full money-back guarantee. We had no clue about how this would go over, but hoped that our asking price of $59.95 was low enough that even unhappy customers wouldn't return it.

We waited with breathless anticipation for the ad to be published and get what we hoped would be a tsunami of orders. Three months after placing our first ad, the April 1975 issue of *Audio Magazine* hit the newsstands but instead of orders we began receiving mail-in questions: How would our little box work with a particular preamp? Would it be compatible with their phono cartridge? How did the money-back guarantee work? Who were we, anyway? By the time we'd received a dozen letters, it was clear that the sooner we responded, the quicker we might make some sales. The job fell to me—neither Stan nor I owned a typewriter, but Dr. Stewart and AV-Alarm did.

I'd grown up with loudly clacking manual typewriters, and my time as a cub reporter and photographer at the *Anaheim Bulletin* had taught me that veteran reporters—tough men with cigarettes hanging out of their mouths—pounded out stories at high speed on tall black Smith Coronas, Remingtons, and Underwoods, using only two fingers. Dr. Stewart's typewriter wasn't one of those stalwart machines. He loved new toys, and sitting in the front office was a brand-new, baby blue IBM Selectric II with a cassette-tape drive on which you could record text, then auto-type it by pressing Play. It was a thing of beauty with styling by the American industrial designer Eliot Noyes, who collaborated with the famous designer Charles Eames, of Eames Chair fame, to sculpt a uniquely gorgeous piece of technology. The Selectric and its automated technology was perfect for answering our growing pile of letters. On the Selectric's cassette machine, Stan and I recorded a standard opening paragraph, which would begin typing when I pressed Play. The recording paused after "Dear" so that we could thank each customer by name for writing to us—I would type in the name, then press Play again, and the Selectric would finish typing the opening paragraph. The machine would then pause for me to answer the letter writer's questions, hunt-and-peck style. I would then press Play again to auto-type our canned final paragraph and our closing: "Happy Listening, Paul and Stan."

The Selectric made it easy to answer every letter within 24 hours of receipt. In the month following the publication of our first ad in *Audio*, we received nearly 100 letters—and our first orders. Orders at first arrived in ones and twos, and then in a torrent. Within another month we had 200 orders for our phono preamp, with more arriving every day.

A follow-up ad had already been scheduled for the next issue of *Audio*, but there was a problem: we'd never actually built a production unit. It was a matter of cash flow—we had none. We hadn't had the money to pay for the ad, never mind build units of the product it advertised. But suddenly, with 200 checks in hand, each one for $59.95, everything changed. Our parts cost was about $30 per unit, and since we had no employees, our labor was free. Our monetization scheme was a mail-order version of today's crowdfunding programs, the difference being that our customers were unaware of it. They became unintended shareholders.

We ordered PC boards and parts. AV-Alarm had all the machinery we needed to build the cases: a metal shear to cut the aluminum sheets; a foot-operated kick punch to knock out the holes, one at a time, for the connectors, power cord, and front-panel LED; a bending brake to shape the pre-anodized aluminum front panel and bottom wrap; a silkscreen setup to letter the front and rear panels; a table saw to cut the walnut end panels, our only attempt at style; and a pneumatic rivet gun and screwdriver to put everything together. Stan and I, along with Rick Cullen, an engineer friend of Stan's who became a minor partner in the business, handmade the first 500 phono preamplifiers, stuffing and soldering every part into the PCB, hand-wiring the connectors, and testing, packing, and shipping the finished products. Occasionally we were helped by AV-Alarm's production manager, Bill Abplanalp, who would eventually become our first employee and who, I'm happy to say, still works with us today, more than 45 years later.

For the moment, at least, we were in business, but I still worried about the ad's money-back guarantee. We'd spent every nickel of our advance orders on parts, metal, walnut, and packaging. What would we do if lots of buyers decided to return our product? Sure enough, only a few weeks later, the first return hit our shipping dock—the front door of our newly rented home. With dread in our hearts, we opened the box to find the returned unit and a note requesting a refund of the buyer's $59.95:

> Dear PS Audio:
>
> I received the phono preamplifier and immediately connected it to my Kenwood integrated, but was disheartened to note your unit destroyed my system's imaging. Where formerly I could close my eyes and easily point to the left and right speaker, with the PS unit, the speakers disappear. Please refund my money.

This customer didn't know it, but his letter was the greatest encouragement we could have asked for: with huge smiles on our faces, we wrote him a refund check for $59.95.

That disappearing-speaker trick, you see, was something Stan and I had labored for months to achieve. One of the hallmarks of a true high-end stereo system seems, at first, counterintuitive: its ability to present a seamless field of sound that seems to come not from the speakers themselves, but from the entire room. The orchestra or band should occupy a space behind the speakers that spreads not only between those speakers, but to the left and right past their outer side panels—an aural image, or soundstage, that's far deeper, wider, and taller than the speakers. A system's ability to perform this seemingly magical feat depends on the combined qualities of its electronic components and loudspeakers, how those speakers are positioned, and the acoustic properties of the room. People hearing a properly set-up high-end audio system for the first time are often shocked that the large or small speakers—which must be pushing sound out of their front panels directly at the listener—can somehow seem to disappear as the sources of the sound. This is one reason many audiophiles turn the lights down low when listening: to heighten the illusion that the music is being created not by hardware, but by musicians playing in their room.

Within our first six months of business, Stan and I realized that in charging only $59.95 for a product whose parts cost $30, we'd screwed up. Each unit required two hours of labor to build, and even paying an assembler a meager living wage of $8 per hour (the minimum wage was then $2 per hour), we would be over budget and make no profit. We'd built these boxes out of our love for what we were doing, and in hopes of changing the world a bit and making a modest living while doing it. We were energized and excited by the fact that we'd gotten even close to the performance of the far more expensive Audio Research SP3 with a product costing only a tenth as much. Profit had never been high on our list of goals, and getting rich hadn't been part of the scheme—in fact, we mocked manufacturers who valued profit more than fidelity to the music. In our view, expensive hi-fi gear was fine, so long as the retail price and manufacturing costs remained in a proper relationship—which meant that there actually was a relationship.

In an attempt to get our budget under control, we soon doubled the retail price, to a whopping $119.95. That covered our expenses, barely, but it left no room at all for dealers, who routinely doubled a product's wholesale cost to set their retail prices.

We didn't know it at the time but we were headed down the slippery slopes of a poorly managed business that so many startups go through. If we weren't careful, we'd wind up in the same place the majority of small businesses eventually land: bankruptcy court.

CHAPTER 36

DESPITE BEING A full year into the business, our progress towards building a sustainably profitable enterprise—one that paid Stan and me a living wage and served the needs of our customer base—was moving forward at a snail's pace. Neither of us was able to take a salary from the operation, so we were supplementing our living expenses by other means: me by dealing pot, and Stan with his dwindling savings.

Already we had outgrown our borrowed space at AV-Alarm and rented a tiny office in the Stowell Shopping Center north of the airport. Our new headquarters wasn't large, perhaps no more than 500 square feet, and we outfitted the place with two workbenches resurrected from old wooden doors Stan's father, Del, found behind a dumpster. PS Audio's only entrance was a retail style glass door tucked out of sight in a small alcove across from the California state resale board charged with collecting sales tax. Del had also resuscitated a brown, peeling, vinyl covered desk which served as our office and accounting area when we weren't building products on the benches. We also had two employees by this time, Lowell and Jeff, both friends of Stan who were themselves audiophiles and thrilled to be working for $8 an hour building phono preamplifiers.

The trappings of new digs and employees wasn't helping our bottom line and we were losing money at the rate of a small leak: slow and steady, without obvious warning flags. From our narrow vantage point the quickest path to financial solvency was to sell more units. It hadn't yet occurred to us that no amount of sales would help if we paid more to build the products than we were selling them for. Greater sales, we reasoned, would bring in more revenue and provide the mortar to patch the growing cracks in our fledgling business, and hopefully bring a measure of stability to an unsteady vocation. Our path forward, then, was a single-minded endeavor with only one goal. Sell more units.

Increasing sales levels inevitably requires reaching a larger audience of potential buyers. We couldn't afford advertising, which left only one avenue open: a review in one of the high-end stereo magazines. In the mid-1970s, buyers of mainstream stereo equipment read reviews in *Stereo Review*, *High Fidelity*, *Audio*, and *Consumer Reports*. Audiophiles mostly shunned these large-circulation magazines because their reviewers never listened to the gear they were passing judgment on. Instead, the mainstream publications fostered a culture of measurements as a means of ranking audio gear, using numbers, charts and graphs to explain emotional responses to music. That didn't sit well with audiophiles, who demanded a more hands-on approach like what they saw in car magazines, where reviewers test-drove new vehicles and offered their opinions on how well the cars drove. The growing resentment of these established publications led to the formation of two smaller journals, *Stereophile* and *The Absolute Sound*. *Stereophile* was founded in 1962 and run by a cantankerous audio reviewer based in Great Barrington, Massachusetts, J. Gordon Holt; *The Absolute Sound* launched in 1973 and was owned and operated by a New Yorker, Harry Pearson. Holt and Pearson told it as they saw it, often writing scathing reviews of components that didn't meet their high standards. Audiophiles loved them.

Because we believed it was imperative to sell more units, we were convinced we needed a positive review in a high-end audio magazine, and we knew of no audio reviewer better known or more widely read than Pearson, universally known as HP. HP rarely praised components, but when he did, it was often effusive—to the delight of the manufacturer and readers alike. Although Stan and I pinned our hopes on a positive review from HP, we knew that he could just as easily pan our phono preamplifier, and orders would dry up. It was a calculated risk.

Meeting Harry Pearson in person was almost as difficult as being invited to the White House. He lived in the sleepy but wealthy little town of Sea Cliff, New York—nestled on the North Shore of Long Island—in an old Victorian house on Prospect Avenue. A highly educated man who had at one time been a reporter for *Newsday*, HP was an avid concertgoer whose knowledge of music, audio, and the fine arts seemed encyclopedic. I tried for months to wangle an audience with him before I caught a break: a fellow manufacturer mentioned that Harry "liked pot," and that turned out to be enough for me to get my foot in the door by eventually supplying him with a bit of Columbian Gold. Apparently, we struck up a good friendship over the phone—a few months of conversations later, Stan and I were invited to Sea Cliff.

We boarded a United Airlines flight to New York's JFK airport and arrived late that evening, tired, hungry, and in need of a hotel. We hadn't thought to book anything in advance—it was New York, after all, the biggest city in the United States. How hard could it be to get a hotel? Outside the terminal we moved through the 30-minute cab line and threw our luggage into the trunk of a battered old Yellow Cab, as instructed by the blue-uniformed man with a loud silver whistle glued to his mouth. The cab driver eyed us through the rearview mirror.

"Where to?" he asked.

"A nearby hotel" was Stan's quick answer.

"Hotel?" he almost choked on the word. "Here? Not in the City?"

"Yeah," I said, pointing at the brown and gray cluster of old high-rise hotels just past the airport.

"Get out!" he demanded as the trunk popped open and the taxi's curbside door unlocked. "If you don't want to go to city then just get out."

The cabs behind us started honking as Stan and I picked our jaws off the floor then hoisted our luggage out of the cab's trunk. We stood in the middle of the road, bags in hand, wondering what to do.

"Cab?" asked the busy guard with the whistle, his hand waving for the next cab in line.

"Yeah," I said, pointing at our old cab slipping into traffic with another fare, "but that guy wouldn't take us to a hotel and told us to get out."

Tweet, tweet! his shrill whistle and outstretched right hand stopped one cab while he motioned for another with his left.

"No cab? Get off the island!" he demanded. We stepped back onto the curb, unsure what to do or where to go.

"Come on," Stan grunted. "We'll hoof it."

It took us nearly an hour of trudging through the grimy streets of Jamaica, New York to find the Airport Hilton. They had one room left with twin beds and we grabbed it, plopping our suitcases on the bed and picking up the phone in search of grub. The hotel restaurant had closed half an hour earlier, and the small white room fridge was empty.

As my eyes drooped to the flashing gray-blue of the television, Stan called me to the window.

"Check this shit out," he said.

Our room's view was of a curving elevated road that reminded me of a freeway on-ramp: cars zipped by at a frenzied pace. Parked on the shoulder of that busy road was a primer-colored Chevy Impala—the old kind from the 60s, with low, sleek fins and rounded taillights—shining its headlights onto a broken-down Cadillac. Two guys were busy with a car jack and tire lug, systematically stripping the Caddie of its wheels and whatever else they could manage to pry loose from under its open hood and trunk. Meanwhile, car after car—including several police and one fire truck—zipped past the crime scene as if it didn't exist. This was certainly more entertaining than late-night television. We pulled chairs to the window and watched for the half an hour it took them to gut the car, inspect their work, then rumble off in the old Impala.

"What the hell kind of place is this, anyway?" Stan mused.

It was definitely not Santa Maria, California.

After breakfast, followed by a late lunch, we rented a car and drove to Sea Cliff—an upscale community quite unlike Jamaica New York—and arrived at 176 Prospect Avenue right on time. Though neither Stan nor I had ever met HP, we'd heard plenty of stories. He was said to be demanding, dictatorial, mercurial, and sometimes nasty. None of that matched the Harry Pearson we met. A bit pudgy, of medium height, with a handsome cherubic face, he was a true gentleman: erudite and charming, with a twinkling eye and a laugh that shook the room.

But first things first, and for HP, the first thing was a good dinner. Manufacturers routinely wined and dined him at Sea Cliff's finest restaurants, but I think he knew that we could barely afford the plane tickets and rental car, let alone dinner for three. HP picked up the tab at Restaurant Zanghi, an upscale French place, and in the process introduced us to fine wine. In fact, the sommelier pulled out a special bottle for Harry, a 1952 Château Latour, which we shared. Then it was back to Prospect for our listening session.

The first time I'd stepped into Norm's house and seen his tri-amped Audio Research system with the 18-inch woofers and Janszen electrostats, I'd been floored by that temple to pure sound. But HP's system was from another planet altogether. The room itself wasn't all that large—long and rectangular, with a high ceiling. At the far end were four loudspeakers bigger than anything I'd ever seen. These were Infinity IRS-IIIs: 1.2 tons' worth of speaker rising from floor to ceiling. Facing us were two curving "wings" of Brazilian rosewood, each about four feet wide. Each speaker had 12 ribbon midrange drivers and 36 tweeters: 24 in front and 12 more at the back. Behind each wing was a massive woofer tower, taller and wider than I was, with six 12-inch woofers. Each tower was powered by a 1,500-watt amplifier. Along the sidewalls were row upon row of records, a turntable, and an impressive stack of electronics.

My hands began to shake. What chance did our little six-pack of English muffins—our phono preamplifier—have against all of this? It would be a gnat attacking Godzilla. We were doomed.

When the cloud of blue pot smoke had lifted, Harry put on a record: "The Look of Love," a song by Burt Bacharach and Hal David, from Bacharach's original score for the 1967 film *Casino Royale*. Holy moly. I'd heard the recording before, but never like this. Just like in Norm's listening room, I again felt as if I were listening through the lens of a microscope, every detail laid bare. I was instantly aware that the singer (Dusty Springfield) and Bacharach's orchestra had been recorded in entirely different environments. I could hear her breathing, and that she'd been recorded in a small isolation booth; I could also hear the ambience of the large studio in which the orchestra had been recorded. This odd experience of simultaneously hearing two distinctly separate sound fields that nonetheless worked satisfyingly together was another revelation: it told us just how much information was locked away in familiar recordings that Stan's and my systems couldn't reach. It wasn't as if, listening to this recording through another system, you wouldn't have heard everything: the orchestra, Springfield, the blat of horns. You would. You would with any system, even a tiny transistor radio. What was different about what we heard at HP's that evening was the totality of immersion in the sound—like being thrown into a swimming pool, or watching a 360° IMAX movie. We were surrounded and immersed. The rest of the world fell away.

Realizing that the wealth of information captured on recordings was far greater than I'd ever imagined excited me. Think of it this way. Rather than trying to focus on a single conversation at a noisy party in order to understand at least something being talked about that evening, it was like being able to hear, clearly and simultaneously, every conversation in the room—and not only understanding each one of them, but hearing parallels and contrasts and counterpoints in the different lines of argument and discussion, as well as the unique timbre and volume and enunciation and personality in the voice of each person speaking. It seemed impossible—yet I was hearing it. Not only could I hear the upper harmonics, the sibilance, the breathing of the players and singer—the beauty of the performance itself was so much greater.

Revealing all the underlying artifacts and studio tricks that go into making a recording might seem an undesirable thing—like a sharp lens revealing layers of makeup on an actress's face, where before we'd seen only a beautifully smooth complexion. Perhaps it would be better not to hear all the underlying flaws or techniques, just as learning how a magic trick is done ruins the illusion. That wasn't the case here. I wanted only to listen more and dig deeper, to open more ways into the secrets this recording held, to reveal its treasures of sound and the artistry of its creation. The ability of HP's system to remove the layers of sonic gauze obscuring these secrets helped me bridge some wide gaps: between me and the recording, between me and the musicians who made the recording, and between me and the music itself. I suddenly felt that I understood this music—this performance, the skills of the musicians, the effort it had taken to put it all together on a record—far better than I ever had. HP's system let me see into the musicians' efforts in ways I hadn't been aware were possible. It uncovered the clacking of clarinet keys, the squeaks of fingers on strings, and even the sounds of Bacharach's clothing and feet moving as he conducted the studio orchestra.

I'd attended studio recording sessions, where I'd been able to take in the entire experience: not only the sounds but the facial expressions of players and singers, the relative positions of the instruments, the vibe or feel of the music being made in that moment of that hour of that day—a feeling of immediacy. As I listened to "The Look of Love," HP's system helped me feel better connected to all of that.

Through recording after recording, we were transfixed. The title track of *Autobahn*, a 1974 release by the German electronic group Kraftwerk, is performed by a synthesizer, acoustic flute, violin, guitar, and piano; I'd played it many times on the radio, along with Iron Butterfly's "In-A-Gadda-Da-Vida." For me, "Autobahn" had always sounded boring: a strung-together riff of technobabble with a beat I paid little attention to. HP's system revealed it as the stuff of legend—an experience I still think about even today. The synth suddenly felt alive, as if it had acquired a body. It now possessed a timbre distinct and meaty, like the throaty tones of a tuba. Certainly, the removal of many layers of obscuring haze was a big part of it, but until this moment I'd been unaware that there even were layers of haze that I'd been listening through. Details I hadn't known to look for were suddenly obvious—such as the way the synth stood on its own, relative to the electronic drum and bass machines. On my earlier listens to this music, they'd seemed the same: unremarkable.

Locked away in every recording we played that night was an untold wealth of information and expression that Stan and I had never heard. It was exhausting, exhilarating, and just a bit depressing. During our entire visit we never even removed our phono preamplifier from its box, and we left with it under Stan's arm. We had come in the hopes of getting a rave review—to see if our $120 phono preamp competed with his multi-thousand dollar brands. We left knowing we were haplessly outgunned, and we both knew it from the first needle drop. What chutzpah we had to imagine our cheap box could compete with his handpicked state-of-the-art contenders.

Driving back to our hotel room that night, Stan and I said little to each other, but a crisis of confidence was brewing in my head. If we wanted to compete with the high-priced brands HP loved, what chance did budget electronics have? Was it even possible to produce low-cost stereo equipment in the same league as the expensive brands, with their unlimited component and engineering budgets? Was it even worth trying?

I parked the car and bid Stan goodnight. I needed some time alone. It was late, so only the hotel lobby was open. The night auditor, clacking away in a small office behind the front desk, paid no attention to me. I managed to find a quiet spot under a fading color poster of a happy couple lounging on a tropical beach, in front of a Hilton resort. The headline read "Serenity, seclusion, stunning cuisine." The ad offered all the trappings of a carefree life without worry or struggle — the promised rewards of successful people — but it also made me wonder. Was I still reaching for that elusive brass ring of overnight fortune? It had been slowly dawning on me that I might be trapped in an endless merry-go-round search for instant gratification: hoping that HP would proclaim us the winner, running Giorgio Moroder's studio, counting on Infinitizer vaulting me past Moog, and of course dreaming of fame as a big-time LA disc jockey. Maybe success didn't come as quickly as I had imagined. Could it be that long-term prosperity required years of effort with no miracle instant-on switch? Perhaps tonight's dip — a seemingly dead-end street with its insurmountable problems — was just part of our journey towards building a viable company that could stand the test of time. These were hard questions, but the more I thought about them, the more I began to realize this was just a temporary problem, one we could overcome with hard work. In fact, I was sure of it. Inside all those fancy high-priced stereo products were the same components we used: resistors, capacitors, transistors, tubes, wires, and connectors. Some were pricier than others, but we knew from months of work that it was clever design that mattered most. Yes, I reasoned, it must be possible to get within spittin' distance of the big boys, and Stan and I were just the mavericks to do it. We would continue to build products that people like us could afford to own.

By the time I took the elevator to our room and quietly slid under the covers, I was determined to spend the rest of my life on that very goal: bringing high-end audio to people like us.

CHAPTER 37

LIFE SEEMS TO WASH over us in waves: there's either nothing going on or everything. Terri and I got married in 1977, and in February 1979 she brought the first of our four sons, Lon, into the world. Sean arrived a year and a half later, in 1980, followed by Scott in 1982 and Rob in 1984. All four kids clumped together in a glorious whirlwind of activity that recentered our world.

By 1982 PS Audio had moved into bigger digs, leasing two bays in a modern cement tilt-up industrial building on Skyway Drive, within sight of AV-Alarm where we had started. The company had grown big enough to support our two families along with the handful of employees building the products, but just barely—we were hanging on by the slenderest of threads, risking imminent collapse at seemingly any moment. Paychecks were routinely late and sometimes bounced.

Eight years after we had started PS Audio, we still hadn't figured out the importance of making a big enough profit or how to manage the meager cash we had to work with. We had convinced ourselves the business was break-even if not slightly profitable, but we didn't have the accounting chops to comprehend the truth: PS Audio was leaking cash faster than we could top off its reservoir. Our monetary crisis had become a way of life, one that was taking its toll on the staff, our unpaid vendors, and worst of all, Stan and me. Without the business acumen to understand the root cause of our struggling business, we doggedly continued to patch the cash holes by expanding revenues with new products: products that weren't generating enough profit to fill our cash needs.

By this time we had six products: our phono preamplifier, two power amplifier models of differing wattage, a preamplifier, and an integrated amplifier (a combination power amplifier and preamplifier). This meant that, for the first time in our company's short history, the only things a PS Audio customer needed from other manufacturers were a pair of speakers and a turntable: we now made everything else required to make music. Everything, that is, except money. That was the one component we weren't yet making.

Although our sales increased dramatically—both because we had partnered with a handful of audio dealers and broadened our product line—we were only selling more and more units of marginally profitable products. Our accountant was telling us the business was fine and we were profitable. Our banker was telling us we hadn't got the cash to operate the business. I felt like pulling my hair out.

The problems with our self-funded business model were manifold. Parts and labor would have to be paid before finished products got into customers' hands and we received their cash. A typical cycle was about 120 days from parts purchase to receipt of payment from retailers, and we needed enough cash to keep our doors open during those four months. Banks wouldn't loan us money because we didn't have the cash flow to pay back the loan or the collateral assets to guarantee it; the only other source of cash was profit, and we weren't making enough of that.

By 1984, Stan and I had ten employees, PS Audio had crested a million dollars in annual revenues, and still—to cover payroll or parts costs—every few weeks we'd have to go without our own paychecks. And that wasn't the worst of it. Vendors increasingly had us on credit hold, which made it difficult to get the parts we needed to build the products to cover payroll and rent. It was the epitome of a vicious circle and it was taking its toll on the two of us.

Partners in business and life handle stress and crises in differing ways. At the beginning of our business, Stan and I found the strength to work through what seemed like impossible conditions because between the two of us we hadn't a pot to piss in. The insurmountable seemed more like a challenge than a threat to our livelihood since we had nothing to lose. Now, both families—ours of six and his of seven—depended on PS Audio to stay afloat, and after ten years the stresses and strains of our growing debt were tearing us apart. We began a downward spiral of arguments on how to run the company. Though we agreed that the way out of our financial mess was implementing changes to our products to increase profitability, we couldn't agree on the direction of those changes.

Stan was a minimalist who believed in axing any expense not directly related to the performance of a particular piece of equipment. In his view, scratching a customer's itch for a fancier chassis, better packaging, or shiny but unnecessary features was not only a waste of money but the root cause of our problems. He felt strongly that our cash problems could be remedied by reducing product build expenses: stripping off the unnecessary bling. I felt just the opposite. In my experience, our customers wanted bigger and better-looking chassis that matched the build and performance qualities of the circuits inside. I empathized with customers who found it hard to justify their product choice when the unit's outsides didn't match the quality of its insides. I thus proposed we charge more and give the customers what they were asking for.

This ever-widening disagreement over how to solve the battle between available cash and impending expenses became as deep and wide as the Grand Canyon. We began to drift apart, both personally and as business partners. Neither of us was much good at giving in or compromising once we'd taken a stand on something. In the end, we were just two Type-A bulls locked in heated battle. Since we were equal partners in PS Audio, we were at a stalemate. If we couldn't find consensus, we couldn't move forward — a bad situation in any business.

The stress of our basic disagreement, our meager profits, and our missed payrolls finally split us apart. Stan left PS Audio in the mid-1980s and moved to Eugene, Oregon, to form his own high-end audio company, Superphon. Terri and I purchased his half of the company by continuing his salary payments for two years after his departure, affording Stan and his family seed money to start their new lives.

PS Audio was ours now, but I found myself sad and empty. Our split felt like a divorce, and I blamed myself. Stan was my best friend. My partner. My mentor. We had raised our kids together: his five and our four. We had been through hellfire and brimstone to get the company started, but it just never seemed to get off the ground. This was all too familiar, a frustrating pattern of near successes ending in what felt like failure. Still, we had ten employees and our own family to support, not to mention several thousand customers that depended on us to help them keep their music systems playing.

It was now another make or break moment.

CHAPTER 38

WITH STAN GONE, it was up to Terri and me alone to make PS Audio work. At first it was liberating, but I soon felt weighed down by the extra chores, responsibilities, and challenges. I had followed my own advice of building better-looking products in larger, more attractive chassis that better matched the quality of the circuits inside. As I hoped, these were not only selling better than any products we had ever made but they also allowed us to charge more per unit, increasing our profitability. Our customer base was growing and our products were finding greater acceptance, yet we still had financial problems that kept me up at night, as I scrambled to pay vendors and meet payroll. My brightest ray of hope came from Terri who counseled me through much of the pain.

"We're on the right path. We'll be okay," she soothed. Strong, reassuring words that didn't quite match the occasional glimpse of worry on her face.

Convinced that fixing our financial problems through growth was the right path the company continued its expansion. Within a few years we had outgrown our two industrial bays on Santa Maria's Skyway Drive and begun the search for new and larger facilities. Meanwhile, Terri and I were looking to move our family out of Santa Maria, something I'd been promising her we'd do for years. She had always wanted to live in the university town of San Luis Obispo, but real estate prices in that community had skyrocketed beyond our means. Instead, we looked further north along Highway 101, up the Cuesta Grade and near the Carrizo Plain, in a small burg known as Atascadero: a Spanish word loosely adapted from the verb "atascar," which means to become stuck or hindered. It was a great little community that avoided the traffic and strip malls of San Luis and Santa Maria. We were able to afford a nice two-story, three-bedroom home on half an acre, off a quiet street: nothing fancy, but it was affordable and the four McGowan boys had room to run.

Atascadero is only 30 miles north of San Luis Obispo, so that is where we found our next headquarters for the company, in a new industrial development just west of the San Luis Obispo Airport. Now outfitted with three times the space of our older building and employing 18 full-time employees, our company felt like it should be a success, but the same old problems continued to plague us—worse now because of our size. We were making more profit but nowhere near enough to accumulate sufficient cash to self-fund that growth. I hadn't yet figured out the ups and downs of cash flow because I'd never bothered to learn enough about business and finance—I was still winging it. The cheapest accountant I could find was Trent, a scrawny man with black hair and eyes to match. Trent assured me we were profitable, and sure enough, each month our books would show a small profit. I thought that meant that, after paying all our bills, we'd have a small pile of cash left over—and even if there was no pile, at least we'd be able to pay our bills on time. But there was no pile of cash and we still couldn't cover our expenses, because that's not how business works. I had all the trappings of a real business—inventory, accounts payable, accounts receivable, and employees. What I didn't have was the knowledge of how to run it, or the sense to know I was in over my head. Truth be told, I was running scared. Deep inside me was that ever-present sense of doubt that I wasn't good enough, and the guilt of having already failed so many times.

I soon got a much-needed lesson in accounting from an unlikely source—Arnie Nudell, the founder of Infinity loudspeakers, a guy who'd done far crazier stuff than I had.

After that first visit to Sea Cliff, Harry Pearson and I had become good friends, often chatting on the phone. In one of those conversations, he asked what my reference loudspeakers were. I knew this was an important consideration—a few years before, at Norm's house, Stan and I had learned how important it was for audio designers to have access to loudspeakers revealing enough to let them hear minute differences in electronic amplification. The lack of such a reference meant that I had to spend many more hours of intense A/B testing to isolate and correct the tiniest details in our designs. Here's how all that works.

When the information stored on an LP has been converted to electrical signals and sent to the speakers, those signals rise and fall in time with

215

the music. In fact, they're close analogs of the music—the electrical impulses are similar in behavior, over time, to the sound waves that originally produced them, and into which they will eventually be again converted, or transduced. The very weak signal generated by the record player's cartridge is sent to the phono stage in the preamplifier to be magnified, then sent to the power amplifier to be magnified again, to make it powerful enough to move a loudspeaker's drive units in and out with enough speed and force to produce sound waves. In each of those drivers, the amplified signal powers a magnet that pushes and pulls a diaphragm—usually, a paper cone or a metal dome—which pressurizes and depressurizes the room's air in ways that are, again, a close analog of the electrical signal, which itself was an analog of the motions of the stylus in the groove, which ultimately were an analog of the waveforms of the sounds created by the original musicians and captured by the recording microphones. The air pressurized by the drivers hits our eardrums, our brains transduce those vibrations into electrical impulses, we experience those impulses as a mental phenomenon that we call sound—and we hear music.

Cone drivers are the norm in loudspeakers, but they're not perfect. The cones themselves are heavy, often made of paper, plastic, or even metal. They're good for reproducing low frequencies, but are too slow to accurately reproduce the higher sounds of violins, cymbals, and drums. The lighter the material, the more quickly and easily it can be moved back and forth to create sound waves—as in ribbon and planar drivers.

The planar drivers of my reference speakers, Magnepan Magneplanars, were tall, wide sheets of very thin plastic that looked like Japanese room dividers. They sounded good, but, in HP's opinion, not good enough to serve as my workshop references. Harry said I needed new speakers, and he thought the man to see about that was Arnie Nudell, president and founder of Infinity Systems, and the designer of HP's own reference system of mighty Infinity IRS-IIIs—the ones Stan and I had heard in Sea Cliff. HP arranged a meeting.

Arnie Nudell was a legend in our industry—not only for his revolutionary speaker designs, but for a never-ending fountain of wild escapades that made my own misadventures look tame. Like the time Arnie and

216

his business partner, Cary Christie, had drag-raced from Los Angeles to Las Vegas—Cary in a new De Tomaso Pantera, and Arnie in his Ferrari—at speeds exceeding 100 miles per hour, outstripping the Highway Patrol chasing them, only to be stopped by a police roadblock and a helicopter in their honor outside Barstow, California. They cooled their jets in jail. Or their nights in France, crawling back to hotel rooms after so many bottles of fine Bordeaux they couldn't remember what city they were in. Or designing (for military audio clubs) a best-selling series of loudspeakers, the SM models, that were thoroughly unmusical but could play at such high volumes that he demonstrated them not with music, but with a recording of a Boeing 747 passing overhead.

Arnie snubbed his nose at the hi-fi establishment, but wound up becoming both its poster-child savior and bad boy. In his earlier days he wore longish dark hair, a prominent mustache, bell-bottom jeans, and dark-rimmed glasses. By the time I met him he'd cut his hair, dressed in a smart, well-tailored suit that perfectly fit his short, muscular frame, and rarely showed up to work without a tie. He'd begun his career as a laser physicist at Litton Industries, helping to design guidance mechanisms for missiles—but his heart was in his garage, where in 1968 he built a type of speaker the world had never seen before. Called the Servo-Statik, it used a technology that would be adapted years later in servo-controlled powered subwoofers, with the delicacy and high-frequency extension of an electrostatic panel—a type of driver with even lower mass than my Magneplanars. The diaphragms of electrostats include no copper or magnets, instead relying on the motive force of static electricity. The speakers in Norm's system—the first to roll my socks down—were electrostats.

Arnie and his first partner in Infinity, John Ulrick, dragged this kludged prototype down to a Los Angeles audio dealer to compare it with other speakers. Before they knew it, orders were flooding in faster than they could build new units in Arnie's garage. Soon they were a real business, grabbing market share from the big boys of the time: Fisher, KLH, Jensen, Altec, Klipsch, JBL, Wharfedale—and Acoustic Research, which at that time made one of every two speakers sold.

By 1983, when I first met Arnie, Infinity Systems occupied a huge, intimidating building in Chatsworth, California, northwest of LA. Ferraris and Porsches were parked in the lot. I walked into the lobby and was stunned by the size of the operation. PS Audio was then housed in a 5,000-square-foot industrial building in San Luis Obispo; Infinity's plant was 20 times that size, with hundreds of busy workers making speakers and shoving completed units into semi-truck trailers filled to bursting. Here was a real and profitable high-end audio company, and I was about to meet and be shown around by its founder and chief designer, who would then treat me to dinner.

Infinity was big and intimidating and I was nervous as hell. I felt like a flea trying to impress a lion. I didn't know what to expect from this titan in the industry. Arnie Nudell could have been anything from a wild-eyed maniac, as some whispered him to be, to a stiff, businesslike ex-scientist, reserved and intimidating. He had some qualities of both. When Arnie walked into a room, the energy level changed—the room seemed to charge up, as if he'd rolled in on a Harley-Davidson, whaling on the throttle, attracting all attention, ready to mow you down if you couldn't keep up. At first, I could hardly catch my breath in his presence.

It was hard to have a lengthy conversation in that office. Every five or six minutes, his secretary or one of his many vice presidents would burst in with news, often of some problem that needed Arnie's immediate input. Infinity was then well on its way to becoming the largest loud-speaker company in the world—it achieved that status three years later, in 1986. Arnie had asked me to bring along PS Audio's financial records, to see if he could shed light on our troubles. Damn if he didn't explain in five minutes what no one had been able to make clear to me in five years. It turned out that our profits were all sitting there—just not in the form of cash. Instead, those profits had been invested in inventory, and in credit terms to our dealers. In order to have sufficient cash reserves to self-fund a company, he explained, either a lot more profit would have to be made or bank financing would need to be secured. PS Audio had neither.

After dinner, I tried to follow Arnie's brand-new Porsche 928 up Valley Circle Boulevard in my dilapidated VW Beetle, which would occasionally lose the ability to shift gears. Volkswagen had tried its hand at a hybrid transmission, using an electronic clutch that was activated when the driver's hand pulled the stick shift. It was fine when it worked, but it often didn't. As I followed Arnie through the entry gate of his home, an expensive place perched high atop brown, rolling California hills, my VW died just as I was crossing the threshold. A few minutes later, down came the gate atop my roof. It rose—then came down again, as if trying to beat my poor bug into submission. Arnie backed up the Porsche and helped me push the vee-dub out of harm's way. We got it moving again, but I was mortified. This couldn't be going any worse, but Arnie seemed not to care and beckoned me to follow him up the winding road to the top of the hill and his home overlooking the LA Basin.

Compared to our newly acquired three-bedroom house in the hot hills of Atascadero, Arnie's sprawling, single-story place was a mansion. Tall, arched, cathedral ceilings and large-paned windows opened onto the twinkling lights of the San Fernando Valley: it was a seat of power and opulence in the quiet of Woodland Hills, befitting a man of Arnie's position in the industry.

That evening, Arnie had invited over, for cocktails and music, some people he figured I'd be interested in meeting, among them a big-time cable manufacturer, a wise-cracking audio reviewer, and a brilliant engineer. The way Arnie referred to these industry heavyweights as "just some friends" was at first disarming then seconds later terrifying. I was being brought into the inner circle of the movers and shakers of consumer audio and I felt completely out of my element. Here I was, a bumbling bumpkin running a tiny, struggling enterprise they'd likely never heard of. Who was I to share a glass of wine and attempt intelligent conversation with these superstars? The great dinner Arnie and I had just shared together was turning into a nervous lump in my stomach.

"Let me show you the music room before everyone arrives," he said.

Arnie pushed open heavy double doors, and what I saw within took my breath away. At the far end were the IRS Vs, a prototype of a new version of the gargantuan speakers that had dominated HP's room: four columns of Brazilian rosewood, each 7.5 feet tall, standing a third of the way out into the room from the wall behind them, under an arched wood ceiling that looked like two angelic hands tented in prayer over those beautiful speakers. That the massive IRS Vs looked perfectly at home and in proportion will give you some idea of the size of that room.

To the right was a floor-to-ceiling wall of master tapes mysteriously collected from recording studios around the world. In front of those was a gorgeous Mark Levinson ML-5 two-track reel-to-reel tape recorder. Neat stacks of Audio Research tubed amplifiers—the same models as those I'd seen at Norm's and HP's—sat atop a long shelf also adorned with a turntable. Along the opposite wall was a floor-to-ceiling library of LPs.

The entire scene set me back on my heels. I'd expected a temple of sound, and this room did not disappoint. But it began to dawn on me that Arnie, Norm, HP, and a few other audiophiles I'd met were just the tip of an iceberg of obsessives of a type entirely new to me. I'd met hobbyists before: collectors of fine things, or those with personal wood shops for making furniture, or home auto shops complete with hydraulic lifts for custom-built cars. These audiophiles were different. More than just hobbyists, or hi-fi enthusiasts looking for better sound, they apparently constituted a small but worldwide community of people so passionate about how music was reproduced in their inner sanctums that they would not only spend thousands of dollars on equipment, but they'd commit entire sections of their homes to the art of sound reproduction—filling them with speakers, wires, glowing tubes, tape recorders, and exotic turntables, all in the service of music.

Until that moment at Arnie's, I'd never considered audiophiles to be part of a group, much less a community. Most of those I'd met seemed to be loners who rarely shared their passion with others. Perhaps they were afraid of ridicule or embarrassed by how much money they'd invested—it was hard to tell. But two things were clear to me: their passion for high-performance equipment, and the thrill each felt in building a system that was unique to himself and himself alone. None of the audiophiles that I knew bought an entire system's worth of components from a single manufacturer. Instead, they seemed driven to cobble together the best products made by disparate companies in a quest for the ultimate synergy, just so they could hear their music with as much clarity and realism as possible.

Arnie's guests soon arrived, and the cocktails began to flow. Fortunately, for me, the alcohol calmed my nerves at meeting these industry icons. One was Ken Kessler, a US-born audio reviewer now living in the UK. Kessler, whose prematurely receding hairline perfectly suits his impish grin, has always been the life of any party he's been invited to—racy jokes, stories, rumors, gossip, opinions on products, and political observations I rarely agree with.

Of great interest to me was someone else I knew of but had never met. Bascom King had gotten his degree in electrical engineering from Cal Poly in San Luis Obispo, less than a dozen miles from where PS Audio was then located. He'd designed the servo system for the IRS speakers, as well as the massive 1,500-watt power amplifiers that drove their woofer towers. Bascom was a bit of a legend to me. He often worked as a hired gun, brought in to fix a problem or design an entire product, without fanfare or public acknowledgment. He quietly worked in the shadows of a number of companies—Infinity, Conrad-Johnson, Harman Engineering, and Harman Motive (the car sound division of Harman)—and other firms that kept the relationship secret because they wanted the public to believe that their products were designed in-house. After Arnie's original partner, John Ulrick, had left Infinity, it was Bascom who took his place, helping with crossover designs, setting up a testing facility, and designing the legendary Infinity Hybrid class-A amplifier and FET preamp.

I'd expected a reserved, balding, pocket-protector-equipped egghead that I would have trouble even talking to. Bascom was nothing like that. Of slightly tallish build, he was skinny and somewhat bony. He had a full head of swept-back salt-and-pepper hair, setting off a lean, rugged face that bordered on gaunt, his high cheekbones holding up his ever-present wire-rimmed spectacles. His demeanor, too, was the opposite of what I'd expected. With his reputation for brilliance, I'd imagined he would talk way over my head. Instead, he was approachable and patient to a fault, something I really appreciated because I was feeling pretty self-conscious and inadequate around him that evening. I was a self-taught hack and Bascom was an educated seasoned pro, though he was always full of surprises. When Kessler passed a fat joint my way, I partook then tentatively offered it to Bascom figuring he'd turn it down—with all that education and professionalism and all. To my delight he took it, closed his eyes, and toked deeply on sweet cannabis.

But then there was Noel Lee, a Taiwanese-American who'd founded Monster Cable, a man I was afraid to talk to. Noel Lee was a legend in the industry and his company was a success by anyone's standards. Arnie had shared with me that Monster Cable was one of the most profitable companies in all of consumer electronics and that Lee not only ran every aspect of the business, including financial control, but was also responsible for the design and marketing of the products. Here was a man that was everything I was not: a success at business, marketing, product design, and making a profit.

Lee, with his round, always-grinning face and hair swept back from his broad forehead, was an intense man who then often worked 20-hour days. He'd fall asleep at his desk or computer for an hour or two, then be back at it. He believed in the quality of the wire he sold—its geometry, how the wires were twisted together, and the purity of its materials—but had far bigger aspirations than the tiny audiophile market. In 1979 Lee, who soon began calling himself Head Monster, had quit a steady job as a fusion design engineer at Lawrence Livermore National Laboratory, to take a gig playing drums in a rock'n'roll band, before deciding that his life would be about wire. "You could round up all the audiophiles in the world and throw them off the Santa Monica Pier," he told me over drinks that night at Arnie's, "and it wouldn't put a dent in my business. The bigger market is consumers."

Less than a decade after our conversation that evening in 1983, Monster Cable had grown its $20 million in highly profitable annual revenues to more than $100 million. By the early 2000s, Monster's revenues had nudged close to $500 million—and that was before the introduction of headphones. Noel allied himself with rock stars like Stevie Wonder, but he made his most profitable move in 2007, when he established a partnership with rap mogul Dr. Dre and Interscope

Records to design and manufacture the Beats Electronics line of head-phones called Beats by Dr. Dre. Revenues for the Beats brand in 2012 were estimated at an additional $500 million.

As the evening's festivities and conversation continued, I felt increasingly out of place in the midst of these successful industry giants and began to withdraw into my protective shell. I was embarrassed of my ongoing struggles and had nothing to talk about other than tales of our crumbling company. I hadn't even shared with Arnie that despite Terri's dire warnings I had dipped into the company's payroll withholding account to shore up our cash woes; nor had I told him of the resulting visit from an ominous Fed hiding behind a pair of impenetrable Foster Grants, demanding the government's money back or face a padlock on the front door.

At Arnie's home that night I got a glimpse of how people without the weight of the world on their shoulders acted. It was as if they didn't have a care. But for me, I could only feel my shoulders slump. I was envious of the people around me that evening, but clueless how to join their ranks.

CHAPTER 39

BY 1989, OUR FOUR SONS were all in grade school. We had a decent home, food on the table, 20 employees, and a ray of real hope. Arnie had not only helped me understand why we had no cash, but had also arranged a meeting with a new designer—Dr. Bob Odell—who would become an investor and our new partner in the company. Odell's injection of cash bought us time and a much-needed reprieve from the federal government's padlock as well as our vendor's threats to place us on COD. Arnie had explained the why—our cash was tied up in inventory and credit to our dealers—but not how to fix it. It didn't take long before we were right back in the same debt quagmire before Dr. Bob had joined the company.

Sooner or later, most entrepreneurs and garage startups run into the cash-flow wall, and in our case I was to blame. After struggling for years to become an experienced electronic designer, the skills required to run a business seemed almost secondary—something anyone could pick up in a matter of months. What's to know? How hard could it be compared to learning electronics? Hubris and ignorance make a dangerous cocktail.

Every time payroll rolled around, insomnia and an overwhelming gloom set in. I felt I was going nowhere fast, watching my life slip away as others around me, like Arnie Nudell, rocketed skyward. Would we remain trapped in an endless spiral of debt and crisis with no way to escape? I felt I couldn't keep doing this nail-biting dance every two weeks—something had to give. I was afraid it would be me.

If it hadn't been for my family—playing with my kids, piling into the station wagon for a picnic, and most of all hearing Terri urge me to put my worries aside and enjoy the moment with our family—I think I'd have just thrown in the towel. I remember one trip to the supermarket during this period—just the boys and me. Usually this would be fun—I'd push them along in the cart as they hung on for dear life and race up and down the aisles, making fun of weird-looking fruits, vegetables, and shoppers. This time, all I could do was worry about what we could and couldn't afford. I just wasn't having fun. My son Sean, a bright and gentle soul with far more insight than me, put his hand on mine and asked if I was okay. Even the boys could sense something was wrong with their pop. I'd arrived at the classic Midlife Crisis Event: my 40th birthday. I was halfway to 80. One foot in the grave. Already.

For that birthday, Terri — ever the bright spot in our lives — had come up with a surprise to cheer me up. We were all going to Hawaii — our first big vacation with the boys. My parents freaked out. On top of my depression and the state of the company, they knew we didn't have the money for this trip — especially when we'd told them that we were paying for it by taking out a second mortgage on our home. As far as they were concerned, this was lunacy. It was bad enough for them to listen to my complaints about constantly teetering on the edge of bankruptcy. Now we were borrowing money — against our house, no less — to spend it on … fun. My folks had grown up through the Great Depression, and had had to hold on to every penny. They thought our generation's spendthrift extravagance was at best irresponsible, and at worst flat-out insane.

Terri and I have always lived by a set of values different from those of our parents. We believed that memories of a life well spent were worth more than money in the bank. Those precious few years with our kids, before they grew up and left home, meant everything to us, even if we had to mortgage our home to enjoy them. We did it without batting an eye, and neither of us has ever regretted it. We may have never had much cash, but our savings account of fun memories is overflowing.

We six McGowans soon landed on the Big Island and set about enjoying ourselves: days on the beach, sightseeing at Kilauea Volcano, the Waipio Valley, Waimea, and Kona. It was refreshing and there were days and nights where I didn't think about the problems at home or the fact my life felt half over. But all good things must come to an end. Near the end of our trip, on the Kona side, we went on a long hike through a lush green jungle. As the volcanic peaks ahead vanished into the mist, a light, warm, gentle rain — the locals call it liquid sunshine — washed the air and brought us the scent of plumeria flowers. The boys had gone ahead of us on the otherwise deserted path, throwing rocks, picking up sticks, and laughing. Terri and I talked.

"We gotta make a change," I said. "I am sick and tired of being broke, always struggling, our family's future always in question. I don't know how we're going to do it, but I'd like to set a time limit of one year. We do what it takes to break this cycle—give it everything we have—and if, in a year, we're still like hamsters running on the same exercise wheel, we close up shop and do something else."

"Like what?' she asked.

"I haven't a clue," I said with my eyes glued to the ground. "All I know is this isn't working. We can't go through life like this. It's our only chance to break the cycle."

Intellectually, I knew it was the right choice. Emotionally, it was scary as hell.

It's easy to talk of change—like back at Pappy's restaurant in Santa Maria, when I'd asked Terri: "How much worse can it get?" before quitting my job and plunging us deeper into poverty. But this time I would not only be quitting our only source of income but potentially scuttling a decade and a half of work and a lifelong dream of building something great in the field of music. It was my biggest gamble yet, but one I believed would free us from the hopeless prospect of doing the same thing over and over for the rest of our lives, hoping for different results but afraid things would get only worse. If twenty years of hard work and commitment wasn't working, it seemed foolish to believe another twenty would be any different. I believed deep in my gut that drawing a line in the sand would give us permission to be open to new ideas and to try new things, to do whatever it took to keep from merely making that hamster wheel turn faster without ever being able to get off it. It was do or die—either we'd finally break through or fail miserably.

As Terri let my words sink in, the boys were working their way up the path, throwing every rock they could find. To the right of us a small stream bubbled and gurgled as it meandered through the undergrowth, feeding ferns and flowers that intoxicated the ether with a heavenly scent. The kids were laughing, carefree, and protected—their world sheltered by Terri and me. We followed close behind in silence. Hawaii's

226

thick, sweet air wrapped us in a comforting cloak as if everything were okay—as if the world outside our temporary bubble didn't exist. If we never left that lush garden path, it felt like the troubles of home would somehow just go away and fix themselves. For the moment it seemed as if they had. But soon we reached the walkway's end and I knew we had to turn around.

I looked into Terri's eyes for an answer. My darling Terri, I'm convinced, is the wisest human being on the planet. She can say more with a simple smile than most people can in sentence after sentence. Instead of speaking, she took my arm and called to the boys to follow us back. As we walked, the warm liquid sunshine and her hand on my arm washed away my angst.

CHAPTER 40

NOW THAT TERRI and I had drawn a line in the sand about PS Audio, we had given ourselves permission to place all options on the table, including selling the company—if the right opportunity arose. Within a month of our return from Hawaii, Arnie Nudell invited me to pitch Infinity System's owner, Dr. Sidney Harman, on acquiring our company and all its technologies. This seemed like a golden opportunity for PS Audio, its employees and customers. With the resources and muscle of Infinity's parent company Harman International behind us, we'd be on solid financial ground for the first time in company history. I spent weeks preparing a 50-page color presentation complete with financials, charts and graphs of our company's progress, and listed a wealth of innovations including what would have been the world's first optical audio interconnect cable—ideas and inventions that I believed would be of value to the Harman International group.

Infinity Systems had been sold in 1983 to Harman International Industries, a company headquartered in Connecticut and run by Sidney Harman (1918–2011), who would eventually own many of the world's major hi-fi brands: Crown, Infinity, JBL, Mark Levinson, Revel, and Soundcraft. Harman took his first job in 1940 with the David Bogen Company, then makers of PA systems, where he earned his engineering chops. In 1953, he and Bogen's chief engineer, Bernard Kardon, left to found their own company, Harman/Kardon, which in 1954 launched the world's first integrated hi-fi receiver, the Harman/Kardon Festival D1000.

By the mid-1980s, Sidney Harman's audio empire had already acquired many brands, including JBL and Infinity, and it felt natural to me that PS Audio might be in a position to join these esteemed and profitable brands.

We met at Harman International's 44-acre, seven-building campus in Northridge, California. Sidney Harman arrived by limousine, dressed in a perfectly tailored dark suit, white shirt, and red tie, his touch of gray elegantly coiffed as if there had never been a breeze. He was short but stood straight and tall, and quickly made it clear that he preferred to be addressed as Dr. Harman. His second-in-command, Don Esters, motioned for the group to sit in Dr. Harman's living-room -style conference area: two face-to-face white fabric couches—one for Esters, the other assigned to Nudell, separated at each end by a matching chair—one for Dr. Harman, the other for me which completed the rectangular seating arrangement. Without any fanfare or opening pleasantries he then delivered, to his audience of one—me—a lecture that lasted half an hour. It began by ceremonially tossing my beautiful 50-page presentation on the floor. He pointed out how small and insignificant PS Audio and its innovations were in the grand scheme of audio. "No," he said flatly, "PS Audio isn't worth my consideration."

The hairs on the back of my reddening neck bristled. Had he even read my presentation? Was he throwing away all my ideas and inventions that I believed deep in my soul would have furthered the art of high-end audio in the name of Harman International? Really? I was getting ready to tell him just exactly what I thought of his "consideration" when he almost offhandedly offered me the recently vacated position of Harman International's Director of Engineering.

"While I have no interest in PS Audio, I am interested in you. Why don't you join Harman as our director of engineering?"

I caught Arnie's eye. He was grinning from ear-to-ear. Holy crap. This was completely unexpected. So was his offer of a starting salary: $100,000 a year, plus a car, profit sharing, and stock options. At the time the most money I'd ever made in one year was $30,000: my two cars were old and questionable, and I didn't know what a stock option was. Harman's engineering and manufacturing facility, which I would be directing, was a 420,000-square-foot building that, at the time, was the largest single-story structure ever built in the San Fernando Valley. Compared to PS Audio's little 5,000-square-foot facility, the sheer size of the facility was almost as hard to get my head around as the fact that Sidney wanted to put me in charge of it. I didn't even have an engineering degree—I'd barely escaped high school with a diploma.

Whatever instantly regrettable things I'd been about to say flew out of my head. If I took this job, I'd have to abandon my own company, move my family into the smoggy rat race of Los Angeles, and answer to someone I'd already concluded was suffering from a Napoleon complex. After a moment's thought, I thanked Sidney for the opportunity but told him I had to decline. For me and my family, quality of life always trumped offers of grandeur and money. So, thanks to Arnie and the stiff brace of cold vodka he offered to calm my nerves after that meeting with Sidney, I headed back north to PS Audio, uncertain what would be next.

About a month after my meeting with Harman, Terri and I were given an opportunity to take the family on yet another vacation. This time to Colorado. A friend of mine at a local television station in San Luis Obispo offered us a week's stay at a five-star resort in Beaver Creek, Colorado, in exchange for a PS Audio power amp. We jumped on the chance.

With our station wagon loaded to the roofline, and Lon, Sean, Scott, and Rob strapped into their seats, we hit the highway. Driving along I-70, next to the Colorado River and through Glenwood Canyon, Eagle, and Vail, where the aspens had already turned their fall colors, was breathtaking—something none of us Californians had ever seen. Golds, reds, lime greens, and brilliant yellows painted the vast canvas of the Rocky Mountains with magnificent color. Clusters of aspens dotted the verdant groves of spruce, pine, and other evergreens, accented by the red of iron-rich soil. It was a wonderland. We stopped to throw rocks in the sparkling Colorado and marvel at the rapids, welters of frothing water cascading down the carved riverbed and tumbling over boulders bigger than our Ford. My youngest, Robbie, ever the adventurous one, nearly fell in the rapids attempting to throw a boulder half his weight. If it hadn't been for brother Sean's quick hand, he might have become fish food.

The cherry atop that sundae was Beaver Creek Resort. Our home for the week was a three-story, five-bedroom condo nestled among the green-covered peaks. It had a gourmet kitchen and two decks, but what most impressed me were the telephones in each of its five bathrooms.

This was opulence on a scale I'd never expected to enjoy. And just outside the master suite was the gentle rush of Beaver Creek itself, lulling us to sleep each night.

Our first day was filled with fun: riding the Centennial ski lift, watching the kids frolic in their first patch of snow, and a picnic lunch in the warm Colorado sun. When we returned to our five-bedroom mansion, there was a note from the front desk: a message from Harry Pearson of *The Absolute Sound*, asking me to call him immediately.

Harry told me that Arnie Nudell had left Infinity. He didn't know why or how, but it was a shock to him, and it soon became a shock to the entire industry. Arnie never shared his reasons for leaving with me, but I always suspected that Sidney Harman had fired him. After witnessing the two of them together in Sidney's office, and hearing Arnie repeatedly tell Sidney that he was "full of shit" and bark other insulting remarks, I figured that maybe Sidney had had enough. Arnie was running the most profitable division Harman owned at the time, and it was as big a surprise to me as it was to the rest of the industry. But whatever the reasons for his departure, Arnie was our friend, and he would need all the support he could get. After all, he'd founded Infinity in his garage and had spent the better part of 20 years building it into one of the best-known speaker companies in the world, with annual revenues approaching $70 million. Harry and I were sure that Arnie would be devastated.

As it turned out, Arnie was also in Beaver Creek, just a few hundred yards from where we were staying. He and his family, avid skiers all, had owned a condo there for years. I expected to find Arnie crushed and depressed—but he seemed fine. He smiled broadly, as if a massive weight had been lifted from his shoulders, and invited me in to look at a new tweeter. That, and a new company, was all he wanted to talk about. By the time Terri and I had packed up the station wagon and were headed back home, Arnie and I had agreed to start a speaker-building company together.

Over the next few months I traveled each weekend to Colorado, where Arnie and I plotted how to create our new company. We planned to call it the Rocky Mountain Speaker Company, or RMS. (We never ended up using the name.) When our plans were in place, I let the audio world know that PS Audio was for sale, and within a few weeks we had buyers: Randy Patton, formerly of Sumo Electronics, and Steve Jeffery, formerly of Harman International—both seasoned audio veterans.

I wish I could say that selling PS Audio was easy and the smartest thing I'd done up to that point. It didn't feel that way. The company was my baby, and I felt as if I was placing my child in the hands of people who didn't love her as I did. Still, I convinced myself that Randy and Steve would be great foster parents: they'd love and care for her, uphold her values, and continue her heritage of good customer relations. If I hadn't convinced myself that I believed that, I never could have let her go.

The day I signed the papers, I wept bitterly—not just because I was saying goodbye to Stan and my creation, but because I felt I'd failed. Dad was right—I couldn't make a go of it. In the end, I'd sold out my life's work and moved on. I hadn't yet proven a thing—not to Dad, not to Terri, not to myself. In my soul I knew it was the right path, the only one I could take and still have a fighting chance of making it, of honoring my pledge to myself to make a difference in the audio world. But at that point that conviction was still only a notion, an idea in my mind—and it was my mind that I'd come to question.

I remained on the board of PS Audio as a technical advisor, but my life was now in Colorado, excited by my new career: building loudspeakers with the legendary Arnie Nudell, and serving as his executive vice president. It would last eight years, and send me around the world tweaking systems for audiophiles. It would also teach me some hard lessons I should have learned at PS Audio but had not. Some people need to be hit on the head with a hammer before they get it. Others, like me, need to be hit more than once.

CHAPTER 41

BUILDING SPEAKERS IS NOTHING like building amplifiers, and I was both grateful and energized that we had one of the top speaker designers in the world to blaze the path ahead. Our new partnership was exciting, and, after many years of disappointment, we were finally living the dream. No more missed payrolls, no more worries about the federal government padlocking the doors. My family and I were living in Vail, Colorado, a picturesque European village-style ski town nestled in the green trees and red rocks of the Rocky Mountains. The kids were enrolled in their new school, Red Sandstone Elementary, with its playground directly across the street from one of the world's finest ski slopes, allowing Terri time to spend her days running the Genesis front office and handling our accounting. Suddenly, Terri and I together were making about four times my highest salary at PS Audio. We were a three-person team: Arnie, Terri, and I, ready to slay the world. Terri and I both pinched ourselves to make sure we weren't just imagining it all.

To fast-track the company, Arnie and I aligned ourselves with API, a Canadian speaker maker that owned multiple brands of its own, including Mirage and Sound Dynamics. The partnership was perfect: API would provide the funding and manufacture our designs in exchange for a 51 percent share in our company. We chose a name for our new company that we thought said it all: Genesis.

There are more different brands of loudspeakers than there are of any other type of audio component. Carving out a niche in so crowded a marketplace would be a challenge, but we had some advantages: two famous guys, a full production facility to build whatever we wanted, a new ribbon tweeter that measured among the best in the world, and speaker cabinets with a new shape that would not only stand out in any home but would also provide major sonic benefits. Instead of the classic rectangular box with cone drivers mounted on its front baffle, or the thin panels of ribbons or electrostats, Genesis speakers would be round, except for the flat front baffle: looked at from above, the speaker's cross-section had the shape of a capital D.

This round shape solved a perennial problem of rectangular speaker cabinets: flexure, or bending. Speaker designers want the sound to come only from the moving diaphragm of the drivers, not from the walls of the box. A driver mounted on the front baffle of a sealed box creates a lot of air pressure inside that box. The bigger the driver, the greater the pressure. This pressure makes the walls of the box move in undesirable ways—because the perfect enclosure would not flex at all—and that movement creates vibrations and sounds that are in no way part of the music itself. The ideal speaker enclosure would be made of the most rigid material possible—say, cement.

To solve this problem, manufacturers add extensive bracing inside their speaker cabinets. Often, in a high-performance loudspeaker, more than half the materials and weight of the cabinet are devoted to various types of internal bracing, so the results can be both heavy and expensive. And still, the cabinet will vibrate. Bracing only reduces flexure; it's hardly uniform in its effects, and it can never completely eliminate cabinet vibrations.

A round cabinet solves this problem without the need for bracing or exotic materials. The idea of a round shape adding a stability that's unattainable with shapes defined by straight lines and right angles goes back at least to the first millennium BC when the ancient Romans understood the power of the arch. The arch, or dome, is a compression form that uses the stresses of the structure to its advantage, rather than fighting against outside pressures with conventional brute strength, as builders of simple rectilinear speaker boxes must do. In fact, the arch form is strong enough to hold up long bridges and cathedral domes. Why not use it to eliminate unwanted vibrations in speaker cabinets? The round shape would maximize to infinity the number of angles at which sound is reflected within the speaker, thus obviating the distortions created by standing waves emphasizing some frequencies over others.

With our technology defined and API's production lines humming, we introduced Genesis Technology loudspeakers to the world in 1991. This was exciting not only to Arnie and me but to consumers and hi-fi dealers who, by this time, were already missing Infinity's signature speaker products. Shortly after Arnie's departure from Infinity, the company changed course from being a high-end loudspeaker manufacturer that coincidently made respectable consumer audio products to one that better matched Sidney Harman's vision of building a mass-market giant focused on car audio first and consumer audio second. Soon the big and exotic speakers Infinity had come to be known by faded into obscurity, replaced by legions of what Arnie called "shit boxes:" low-to medium-priced folded rectangular boxes that sounded like every one of their competitors. Only the iconic Infinity Mobius logo, with its sideways gold number eight that had stood for innovative, forward thinking in service of great musicality on the products it graced, remained of Infinity Systems.

Excited dealers, friends, and Arnie's former business associates from the Infinity days lined up to place their purchase orders for Genesis products. We were on a roll. With stars in our eyes and dreams of running a reimagined Infinity Systems rippling through our small company and the hi-fi world, we unveiled the Genesis line of loudspeakers.

There were three models of main speaker at launch, each proudly adorned with the moniker "Imaging Module" because of their unique ability to produce an almost perfect sonic image. First, there was the small, stand-mounted 2-way bookshelf with its ribbon tweeter and 5½-inch woofer, the IM 5200, followed by the IM 8200, a larger 2-way with an 8-inch woofer, and finally the largest, and our top of the line, the IM-8300. To cover the lowest notes of an orchestra or rock band, we also offered a round subwoofer called the Servo 12. Customers could use any of the three Imaging Modules as standalone speakers or couple them with a Servo 12 subwoofer for extraordinary sound. Each was an astoundingly good-sounding loudspeaker—by far the finest work of Arnie Nudell in the field of smaller home speakers.

There was one problem: regardless of how good round speakers sounded—even those crafted by the legendary Arnie Nudell—people weren't interested. They didn't fit customers' ideas of what a loudspeaker should look like. Selling our round speakers went from a slam dunk to a major debacle. Arnie's many retail contacts at first ordered scads of

Genesis speakers without a lot of questions or examination. Retailers trusted our word when we told them that customers were ready for a new look in home hi-fi and would eagerly embrace our models. Soon, retail audio chains—Atlanta's HiFi Buys, Minneapolis's Audio King, Seattle's Magnolia HiFi—were carrying our Genesis 5200, 8200, and 8300 models. But while the Genesis speakers were distinctive in appearance and excellent in sound, customers rarely took a pair home with them. Then came the calls from dealers, canceling purchase orders and asking if they could return their unsold inventory. Arnie and I spent many hours on the phone, calming retailers' unease that they'd be stuck with inventory they couldn't move.

One very depressing sales trip I made was to the headquarters of HiFi Buys, a chain run by Walter Liederman, to find out why sales of Genesis speakers were so slow. Walter, a toothpick-thin wiry fellow with seemingly boundless energy and encyclopedic knowledge of retail and audio, introduced me to his sales manager, Doc—a bright, jovial guy about my age, who treated me to a full dose of snark from his sales staff. "Well, if you'd included a foot pedal to open the top of this speaker," said Doc, pointing at the top of a pedestaled Genesis 8300, "it'd double nicely as a trash can." Ouch.

By the end of our first year we had managed to fill the showrooms and warehouses of quite a number of large retailers with Genesis loud-speakers, but customers were still not taking to the new shapes despite our assurances that the looks would grow on them. Reviewers praised our products to the high heavens and lamented that more customers couldn't see past their unconventional shapes to enjoy some of the best reproduced sound at anywhere near the price. But, try as we might, we struggled to stem the rising tide of returns from dealers, who didn't want to sit on unsold inventory.

Our visions of overnight success were fraying at the seams and our partners at API were getting nervous, hoping they had not bet on the wrong horse. All Arnie and I could do was try harder, make more phone calls, twist more arms, and attempt to convince an unwilling public that they were wrong in their feelings towards the IM Series aesthetic.

CHAPTER 42

WE KEPT FIGHTING, but our best efforts to sell our sonically superior round speakers were met with continued tepid acceptance or downright rejection. No matter how hard we tried, we couldn't force customers to like something they outright disliked. Neither Arnie nor I were willing to admit defeat and, like stubborn entrepreneurs, we rallied to solve the problem without throwing the baby out with the bathwater. We were determined that the sonic benefits of that round cabinet — the one feature we had based the entire company on — were genuine, and convinced ourselves that we had to keep the round speakers while assuaging customers' negative feelings towards the IM Series aesthetic.

Knowing that it was the unusual shape that customers didn't like, I proposed a half-round tube inside a standard rectangular speaker cabinet, with an interesting sloped front baffle. This, I thought, would offer the best of both worlds: the structural rigidity of the round enclosure, with the appearance of a stylish speaker. We hastily engineered a series of these hybrid models, called the Genre. The Genres began selling well, but it was too little too late — and we still had a ton of unsold Genesis inventory.

This was a particularly difficult period, and Arnie, Terri and I handled the stresses and strains differently. Arnie buried himself deeper in speaker design, working on a new and only partially round floor-standing speaker, the Genesis III. Terri passed all the rigors of training to become a weekend ski instructor at Beaver Creek. I chose a similar course to Terri's, although not as an instructor. In the early 1990s Vail was a locals' paradise, not the mega-wealthy resort complex it has since become. School kids from kindergarten through high school could get a full-season ski pass for $100, and their parents got great deals too. Powder days were often sick days for school kids and parents alike in Vail Valley, especially on weekdays, when the only route between Denver and the ski resort, Vail Pass, would be closed after a massive dump of light, fluffy, crystalline powder, leaving the entire resort open to a few stranded tourists and passels of fortunate locals. On those days, plowing through knee-deep fluff, we and our hooky-playing four sons—themselves now expert skiers—were the only moving objects breaking deep azure skies. Our backs were warmed by the unrelenting sun, and our music was the hoots, howls, and primal grunts of skiers playing in untracked powder in Vail's Back Bowls.

I wanted more. I'd learned of a program of volunteer mountain guides, sometimes referred to as Mountain Hosts, that the Vail ski resort company (then called Vail Associates) was experimenting with. Twenty or so expert skiers from the community would don ski resort company uniforms and ski-patrol radios, then traverse Vail's 5,289 acres of groomed and ungroomed snow, helping guests enjoy themselves. I applied for and was accepted into the Vail Mountain Hosts program, so I spent every Saturday leading mountain tours, helping visitors find that secret stash of powder, breaking up marital disputes when one spouse tried to teach the other how to ski, rescuing lost kids, teaching beginning skiers just enough to get somewhere safe, and radioing in the occasional injury to Ski Patrol. It was so rewarding that I eventually became a part-time employee of Vail Resorts: assistant supervisor of Mountain Hosts. For nearly 13 years of weekends, I was in charge of 40 mountain hosts. The work was intense enough that I couldn't think about audio, or about Genesis and its problems, and I was making a difference for a lot of people.

My ski job was also beneficial in other ways. Five days a week, I was the executive vice president of a high-end speaker-manufacturing company—a status very much like that of many of the guests who skied at Vail. On weekends, I was a lowly hourly employee of a ski resort. Those two very different sorts of positions gave me unique insight into customer service. By nature, I'm friendly and welcoming. I did well at the job of Ski Host, and I did well working with people interested in improving their high-end audio systems. And because of my humble beginnings as a dishwasher, cub reporter, wedding photographer, low-paid DJ, and Army grunt, I never differentiated among those I was kind and helpful to. As far as I was concerned, a waitress or factory worker was on equal ground with the CEO of a big company—I'd lived the lives of them all.

Riding the ski lifts as an employee was especially illuminating. If I joined a party of bigwigs on the quad chairlift while wearing my uniform, I was ignored as if I weren't there, even as the talk of mergers and acquisitions, marketing, customer relations, and business strategy went on around me. Forgetting the uniform I was wearing, I'd often join such conversations if I felt I had something relevant to add, only to get a dose of stink-eye. What the hell was a ski resort employee doing, trying to talk to paying guests about anything other than skiing? But if it was a non-work day and I was wearing my civilian ski jacket, my unsolicited comments were welcomed.

On those lifts I learned how it feels to be left out, ignored, and discriminated against solely because of my appearance. These people were my stereo customers, but they tended to be snobs. I decided on those lifts to make sure I would never be like that. To this day, someone who knows nothing of high-end audio is as welcome to me as someone who's been playing in the field for years. Often, I'll spend more time with the newbie or the doubting Thomas than with the cognoscenti—because of my experiences on the lifts.

After two years of struggle, Arnie and I gave up on round speakers. Sales had been bad—nearly 80 percent lower than we needed them to be. The only things that were moving with any volume were our Genre models, and that was hardly enough to keep the doors open. API was sitting on a warehouse full of unsold Genesis speakers and a tall stack of unpaid Genesis invoices. They demanded that we either sell the products for whatever we could get for them, to pay down what we owed, or buy out API's half of the company and part ways. API had its own growing pains—they were in the midst of selling the company to another Canadian speaker maker, Paradigm, and the last thing they needed was a big loss on their books. Arnie and I scrambled to find the nearly $750,000 we'd need to buy back their half of Genesis and its unsold inventory. We tapped every resource we could think of: banks, investors, and even bringing other partners into the business. Trouble was, it's hard to get funding for a losing operation. If we were to survive we'd have to get creative. And fast.

CHAPTER 43

TWO YEARS INTO OUR new company, my old feelings of insecurity still loomed in my mind's shadows, so I often retreated into my own little protective shell. I had been there more times than I cared to remember, and the whole experience felt like running in quicksand. We didn't have enough cash flow to cover the mounting invoices from our partner company, API. We couldn't move the mountain of inventory collecting dust in their warehouse. We were nearly six months in arrears, and with every visit I made to their Toronto headquarters I could see the look of growing alarm in Howard Heiber's eyes. Howard, the owner and CEO of API, had courted Arnie to join his growing company. To Howard, having one of the most famous speaker designers and successful company CEOs aligned in his stable of brands was a real feather in his cap, but now it was feeling more like a millstone around his neck.

To make matters worse, Howard's company was struggling too. Slow sales and a general economic slump following the partial economic collapse of the saving and loans industry in the United States had put a damper on the industry as a whole. API was still in the midst of negotiations to sell the company to Paradigm, but with Genesis still attached their negotiations were stalled. The pressure was on for us to buy out our partners and go our own way, no matter how we managed to get the money or what they had to do to wash their hands of the entire Genesis affair. Arnie, Terri, and I were running scared, and I imagined Howard and his company were as well.

Our rescue came in the form of an audio distributor based in Taiwan. Mr. Pu—or Pu, as he prefers to be called—was a full-bodied man of medium height, with a round face and gentle brown eyes. He imported loudspeakers and electronics into Taiwan or Hong Kong for resale in the burgeoning marketplace of mainland China, which seemed able to gobble up anything made in the US or the UK. Western brands of loudspeakers were hard for smaller Asian distributors to acquire; all the big names—Harman, Infinity, JBL, Klipsch, Polk, B&W,

Magneplanar—were already spoken for. Pu wanted to be the exclusive distributor of a prestigious American brand, and few of the available candidates were as well-known as Genesis—or, really, as Arnie Nudell. Pu was interested, and with the help and negotiating skills of Ben Chia, a good friend of mine and our Genesis distributor in Singapore, arrangements were made for Pu to purchase Genesis's entire inventory for $750,000 cash. This allowed us to regain full ownership of Genesis, thus releasing API from our partnership so that they could proceed with the sale of their company. Pu took delivery of hundreds of pairs of round Genesis speakers and sold them at a profit in mainland China. In exchange for the sale and cash, Pu became Genesis's exclusive distributor in Asia.

Finally, Arnie and I were able to return to our roots and build something we knew we could sell: an improved version of his four-column, 1.2-ton, 7.5-foot-tall Infinity IRS speaker system which by this time Infinity had discontinued. We would kickstart our new version of Genesis by building another version of what had set Infinity Systems on its path to become the largest and most respected brand of loudspeakers in the world. In a nod to our rebirth, we would call it the Genesis I.

CHAPTER 44

MY FIRST SLEDGEHAMMER-OVER-THE-HEAD moment in audio was when I walked into Norm Little's living room back in Santa Maria and came face-to-face with his temple of sound. That event helped launch my career in audio, but it was my visit to Harry Pearson's home to hear the mighty Infinity IRS that would forever change my life. Those seven-and-a-half-foot-tall sculptures of floor-to-ceiling midrange and tweeter columns, with their curved wings and twin woofer towers, were unlike anything I had even imagined possible in my wildest moments. From that first needle drop at HP's home as Dusty Springfield's breathless vocals on *Casino Royale's* "The Look of Love" started playing, I was hooked. There was no other speaker that could ever match the performance of what I had heard on that blustery pot-infused evening in Sea Cliff, New York. And now, nearly fifteen years later, me and Arnie Nudell, the designer of HP's Infinity Reference Standard, were about to try and rescue our fledgling company by building the next generation of that once-in-a-lifetime accomplishment. We would be starting from ground zero, with high hopes and a bright future in store for us if we could manage to get this version of Genesis right.

First, we'd need the all-important drivers to make our speaker. We had the Genesis ribbon tweeter, but we did not have a midrange driver — the sound-producing element that covers the frequency areas of 100Hz all the way up to 2kHz, essentially the lion's share of the sound made by the human voice and the majority of instruments in an orchestra. To build the best speaker in the world, we needed to start with the best drivers in the world. Our good friend Bob Carver, a short, fast-moving engineer who many affectionately call Captain Bob, for his signature blue captain's cap with a gold anchor on its crest, had somehow wound up buying a warehouse full of surplus neodymium magnets from the Boeing Company in Seattle, and was anxious to find a home for them. Carver and Arnie worked together to use those magnets in a new full-length midrange ribbon Carver would manufacture for us to use in the Genesis I. We arrayed 20 Genesis ribbon tweeters in a vertical column on the Genesis I's front baffle, and 10 more on the rear. Instead of replicating the IRS front baffle of veneered particleboard on which to mount the tweeter and midrange drivers, the Genesis version used machined Corian, an artificial stone of very high rigidity—and virtually no flexure. Where the IRS V had a flimsy base of molded fiberglass, the Genesis I's base would be a heavy block of cast porcelain.

The one feature of the IRS V we definitely wanted to keep was the swept-back wings needed to isolate the sound waves generated at the front of the speaker from the out-of-phase, rear-firing sound waves generated at the back. The Genesis I was a dipole speaker: it produced equal and opposite sound-pressure levels from both its front and its rear, but had no box or cabinet per se to contain those sound waves. Because its front and rear sound waves were out of phase—that is, the two sets of waves were simultaneously moving in opposite directions, one pushing air as the other pulled air—there had to be some sort of physical barrier to prevent the two sets of waves from canceling each other out when they met at the speaker's sides.

This was the function of the wings, originally designed by Infinity's Cary Christie to be built like airplane wings, with internal spars and ribs, an idea no doubt sparked by his years as an airline pilot. Inside each wing were thin wooden ribs, which formed compartments or pockets that we filled with sand, to deaden any resonances in the wings. Over these pockets would be laid and glued a quarter-inch sheet of medium-density fiberboard (MDF), and atop that a thin veneer of rosewood, capped on each side with a solid strip of Brazilian hardwood. And that was just the pair of midrange and tweeters. For the Genesis I's woofer towers we copied the design of six 12-inch woofers per tower, but there ended the similarity to the IRS V. In the Infinity speaker, all six woofers occupied a single common chamber, with a single motion sensor and a 1,500-watt power amplifier. In the Genesis I, each of the six woofers per speaker had its own sensor and high-powered amp.

Arnie and I were sure that all these contemplated changes and improvements to the original IRS would result in the most advanced speaker

244

systems in the world. But buying Genesis back from API had used up most of Pu's investment cash — there was little left over to keep the lights on, and we had no product to sell. Now that we'd committed our ideas to paper, it was time for us to scramble — to actually design the speaker and get it into production before we had no money at all.

Our first challenge was to get the cabinets built. Few woodworking facilities were capable of making speaker cabinets like the Genesis I's. Our limited production numbers — estimated to be two pairs per month — coupled with the cabinet's massive size, demanded expert veneer work and years of experience building the aircraft-like spar and rib construction for the sand-filled wings. That narrowed the field to one: Web Massey. Web Massey Inc had made cabinets for Infinity for years, including the original IRS series. Web Massey the man was a master craftsman, and a lifelong friend of Arnie's.

Web was a big man with short, wavy, unkempt reddish hair, a sunburned face full of freckles, and right index and middle fingers permanently stained nicotine-yellow from the four packs of Lucky Strikes he smoked each day. I met him at his woodworking facility, which he'd run for 30 years: four buildings on a quarter-acre in one of the seedier parts of Orange, California, a sleepy little bedroom community in Orange County, near Irvine Park and my hometown of Anaheim. Web's office was staffed by his daughter-in-law Kim, a bright, blonde young woman who seemed oblivious to the smoke-yellowed ceiling tiles, endless overflowing ashtrays, and constant blue haze from those Lucky Strikes.

Web's shop was a treasure. Unlike some of the fancier places I'd visited, with automated equipment run by computer numerical control (CNC), Web Massey was all skill and pride — handwork by artisans who knew and loved their craft. In the Veneer Building, as it was called, hundreds of flitches — paper-thin veneers of precious hardwoods — sat like vintage wines in floor-to-ceiling bins, with exotic labels: Padouk, Pau Ferro, Zebrawood, Gaboon Ebony, Honduras Mahogany, and Brazilian Kingwood. In the center of the veneer building were massive plates of curved steel resembling a commercial laundry's pants press. These were custom-built forms that used steam to heat and bend the flat surfaces of MDF and hardwood veneer, to then glue them around the wing-like structures of the original IRS III and V—and, soon, the Genesis I. Web's woodworking facility was what I imagined Antonio Stradivari's violin shop must have looked and felt like in 17th-century Cremona: more skill than machines.

As Web Massey built the first prototypes of the Genesis I, I had to design a servo amplifier with Bascom King for the woofer towers, find an industrial designer to turn the box of electronics that would power the woofers into a work of art, then find a subcontractor to build it. My first-choice industrial designer was David Barson, who'd been responsible for the looks of the impressive Mark Levinson line of amplifiers. Those tall, stately, black-and-silver structures of aluminum looked more like modernist buildings than amplifiers, a look both Arnie and I were enamored with. Contractual obligations to Levinson's parent company, Madrigal, meant that David had to decline, but he steered me in the right direction: toward Santa Barbara, California, and Neal Feay.

The Neal Feay Company is a complete metal-fabrication and finishing facility in Goleta, near the Santa Barbara airport. It's owned and run by Alex Rasmussen, a short, muscular, ridiculously handsome surfer with wavy black hair and an eager disposition. Rasmussen's amplifier designs, like Barson's, look like architecture, and in fact are inspired by the buildings of Frank Lloyd Wright, Louis Sullivan, and William Le Baron Jenney. We bonded immediately, and I hired Alex on the spot.

Genesis's new 12-channel power amplifier would be big. Its largest internal component was a massive toroidal transformer, a 30-pound donut of iron and copper 12 inches across and 6 inches high. Alex made the transformer the core of his design, and a few days later he sent me sketches of his vision. Instead of the conventional rectangular case with a thick, machined faceplate, Alex proposed a rounded façade, like Isozaki Arata's concert hall in Kyoto, Japan. The multiple flutings of the amplifier's curved front were made from flat, inch-wide, interlocking aluminum strips, in the way a series of flat windowpanes can approximate the shape of a building's curved wall. Instead of the standard audio-gear colors of black and silver, Alex proposed a blue-tinted gray for the curved front, and chunks of lightly sanded aluminum for the

246

top and bottom plates. The two side panels were actually large, ribbed heat sinks of extruded black aluminum. Arnie and I fell in love with the design at first sight.

With the cabinets and amplifier chassis in hand, there was one final piece of the Genesis I puzzle: coordinating all of these components into a workable process so they could be built. That job would fall to a good friend of mine, Jim Laib. Tall and freckled, with sandy-blond hair, Jim was a cowboy to the core. He loved horses and the countryside, and drove a Dually—a giant pickup truck with two wheels on each side of its rear axle. In many respects, Jim and I are polar opposites. I'm not religious; Jim is a devout Christian. I've never been a horse person; Jim wears only narrow-toed cowboy boots, and his ever-present jeans are secured with a thick round belt buckle. But the two of us felt an immediate bond, first through the craziness of our fathers. His was a hard-driving, chain-smoking tyrant who ran the family metal-fabrication business Jim was being groomed to own, and my own dad was an alcoholic, manic-depressive dreamer convinced that his son wouldn't make it out of the world free of chains and a prison uniform.

With our supply chain in order, we were now in an even tighter race to get the Genesis I designed and in production before our meager funds ran out. We were still in our upstairs office space in the Vail Professional Building, across the street from the slope-side Westin Hotel. The whole place measured less than 800 square feet, but when API was handling production, we didn't need more. Now, without them, we had to do everything. We hastily converted an unused conference area to a listening room by hanging a few acoustic diffusors on the walls and moving in the prototypes and measuring equipment. The building was intended for use as quiet professional offices, not the loud, often messy business of loudspeaker design, with raw cabinets and parts crammed into fancy elevators intended for the tenants' patients and clients. Worse than the crowded elevator was the noise generated by those massive woofer towers. Our landlord fielded complaints from our fellow tenants—an accountant, a dentist, a physician, a psychiatrist, and an office-supply dealer—who felt the rattle of those dozen 12-inch woofers pounding through our floor, so we tried to do all our bass testing after hours. In fact, when we tested the Genesis I's output at the very bottom of its range—16Hz, almost as deep as the biggest pipe organ's lowest note, C-1, or 8Hz—the rumble could be felt in the building's parking lot.

Our after-hours testing went on without incident until, one evening, I heard an incessant pounding. Thinking something was wrong with the woofers, I turned everything off. Then I heard it again—someone was pounding on the locked glass door between our office and the hall. It was Jackie, the psychiatrist, whose office was just below our listening room. She looked anxious—her right hand trembled, and in her left she held a box of tissues. She was crying.

"What in God's name are you doing up here?"

We'd had this conversation once before, at the checkout counter of the office-supply store; evidently, it hadn't registered. I explained it all again.

I pointed to the box of tissues. "Are you okay?"

"Oh, these? Sure. I was crying with one of my patients."

Jackie wanted to see what we were working on, so I walked her into the modified conference room.

"Jesus! Those are speakers?"

That was a standard reaction to the Genesis I. Until you're standing in front of four 7.5-foot-tall rosewood speaker columns in a not-very-large room, it's hard to imagine just how overwhelming they are. She seemed fascinated, and walked straight up to the curved wings to stroke their soft finish.

"Can I hear them?"

I had no idea whether or not her weeping patient was still waiting on her couch on the floor below, but I was happy to oblige. I cranked up the last ten minutes of Telarc's infamous recording of Tchaikovsky's *1812 Overture*, which has been the ruination of more than a few speaker systems. On the back of the album, this is printed:

> **WARNING!** The cannons of the Telarc Digital "1812" are recorded at a very high level. Lower levels are recommended for initial playback until a safe level can be determined for your equipment.

With the Genesis I or the Infinity IRS, no caution was necessary for loud playback of the multiple cannon shots. In fact, it was with the last few minutes of this recording that Arnie and Infinity had debuted the original IRS III at the Consumer Electronics Show in Chicago, back in June 1983. He'd played it at live levels from the master tape, courtesy of the man who'd engineered the recording: Jack Renner, a founder of Telarc. It was said that the line outside Infinity's demonstration room that year went a quarter of the way around the huge McCormick Convention Center.

As soon as Jackie heard the music, she settled into the center seat and closed her eyes, as if in a trance. With each cannon blast, she literally jumped. When it was over, she was again in tears, a not uncommon reaction.

Just watching her reaction alone was enough to convince me we had a winner on our hands. The Genesis Is were not only amazing sounding but they looked great as well. Everything was in place to launch our remade company. Our excitement was now at a fever pitch and we were both chomping at the bit to get these speakers into customers' hands.

CHAPTER 45

WITH OUR DESIGNS COMPLETED and our expectations high, life was looking pretty good, unless you looked closely: our financial clock was still ticking, our reserves of cash were running on mere fumes, and we hadn't anywhere to build our speakers. Divorced from our manufacturing partner, we now had to be our own manufacturer and distributor. Vail, Colorado, is not set up for speaker manufacture. It's a resort town of some 20,000 permanent residents and half a million visitors each year. We had trouble finding a production facility—until we stumbled on brothers Dale and Andy Larkin, owners of the optimistically named International Trade Center, in Minturn, Colorado.

Minturn, a small dot on the Colorado map one exit west of Vail, is two miles long and two streets wide, with fewer than 800 residents. Most of Minturn straddles Highway 24 on the south side or the Eagle River to the north. Named for Robert Browne Minturn, a long-ago vice-president of the Denver & Rio Grande Western Railroad, at the beginning of the 20th century Minturn was little more than a rest stop for weary train crews. It wasn't a whole lot more in the 1990s, when we took a tour of the Trade Center, which was next to the saloon and catty-cornered to Chili Willy's, a Tex-Mex restaurant. Dale and Andy Larkin had bought the nearly 100-year-old building as a hopeful investment, but it was apparently costing them more to keep it open than it was generating. Dale, the older brother, seemed ready to agree to just about any proposal that would pay them some rent. When we asked if the building was zoned for manufacturing, he winked. "Sure. It's Minturn."

The basement of the Trade Center was a dank, musty, cement catacomb carved out of the Eagle River's riverbed. The river was constantly trying to reclaim its land, oozing out of every crack in the old walls and nourishing the roots that sprouted through the floors. On the lowest level, a gurgling sump pump labored 24 hours a day to return the water to the Eagle. The few lights in the basement dimly revealed turn-of-the-century iron plumbing. Electrical wires haphazardly strung along the ceiling would have to suffice for factory illumination and powering our tools. But as disheartening as the basement looked, it had one redeeming value: an old coal chute just big enough for the grand exit of a pair of finished Genesis I towers. The top floor, too, was acceptable, if just barely—old, bouncing wooden floors that had sunk toward the river gave me vertigo every time I walked across them. But the Trade Center had charm, low rent, a deck facing the Eagle—and landlords willing to turn a blind eye to zoning laws. It was perfect.

A year after we left API the Genesis Is were ready to build, but we'd run out of cash—in fact, we were limping along on money borrowed from Arnie's dwindling retirement account. To survive we'd have to start selling a speaker we'd not yet produced, built with parts we didn't have the cash to buy. In a scene reminiscent of PS Audio's beginnings, we began selling vaporware in the hopes of getting pre-order cash. I remember one gorgeous, sunny, blue-sky Colorado day, sitting on my office deck as fresh snowmelt engorged the Eagle, not ten feet away. The roar of the river at its peak was loud, broken only by the occasional hoots and hollers of kayakers fighting for their lives in the rapids right outside my deck. I was on the phone with a potential distributor in Dubai, and clearly remember the feeling of wonder. There I was on that sunny deck, mere feet from torrents of white water close enough to occasionally wet me, pitching this guy in Dubai about sending us money to buy a pair of Genesis Is that did not yet exist. At one point, he interrupted my spiel: "What's all that noise?" He sent us the money for a single pair, but it was not enough to begin production. Pu had placed orders that would be paid for upon shipping, but that wasn't going to happen without parts. Then came our first big break. Arnie's best friend Mike Kay, of New York City's prestigious Lyric HiFi, preordered ten pairs of Genesis Is and paid for them in advance. That, and the Dubai funds, were just enough to get the ball rolling, so within three months we began delivering the massive speakers: a pair to Dubai, a pair to Mr. Pu in Taiwan, and more to Lyric HiFi's Lexington Avenue show-room and warehouse. Mike cleared out the biggest sound room and installed a pair of Genesis Is as his premier high-end speaker model. Word of them quickly spread, and soon Lyric had run through its stock and had us back-ordered. Thanks to Mike, we were cranking out one pair of Genesises a week, at $70,000 retail each.

Buoyed by our success with these big beasts, we quickly designed a series of scaled-down versions: the Genesis II, followed by the Genesis III and, eventually, the Genesis V. We did well in the US and Pu took a steady trickle of product in Asia too. We were growing, and growing fast— something we had only dreamed about when we first started Genesis, but now it was real. Customers loved our products and wanted more. It was exciting and energizing. I could almost see that gleaming brass ring I had lusted after for so many years. There, its golden glow was just beyond that next horizon. Sure, there were mounting cash problems—there always are when a company self-funds its growth. But this time it would be different. Emboldened by the success of our speaker models, Arnie and I were pumped, and we marched forward to open up the rest of the world.

CHAPTER 46

MY KNOWLEDGE OF the audio market outside the United States was limited—PS Audio had always been primarily a domestic brand. We had a few foreign distributors and dealers, but effectively selling products overseas had always been a mystery to me. Not so to Arnie—he'd sold Infinity speakers all over the world. This was crucial for a company that wanted to grow; exports traditionally account for up to 40 percent of the sales of US audio brands that seek a worldwide market.

We began to build the Genesis brand outside the US with the help of Mr. Pu and distributors we met at electronics-industry trade shows, such as the Consumer Electronics Show (CES)—which back then was held every six months, alternating between Chicago in June and Las Vegas in January. This worked, up to a point. But developing a worldwide market is something that must be done person-to-person, face-to-face, especially at consumer audio shows. These big annual events were held in hotels and conference centers, their rooms filled not with beds and dressers but electronics and speakers, and halls filled not with suitcases and travelers but with audiophiles and music lovers eagerly in search of the holy grail: reproduced sound that mirrors live performances.

My first trip overseas for Genesis was a month-long jaunt through the Far East to attend multiple consumer shows, set up Genesis I systems for the customers who'd bought them, visit the few dealers we had, and interview potential new dealers. I began in Australia—or Oz, as its inhabitants call it—a place where I envisioned snakes, kangaroos, brawling drunken men, and vast, deadly deserts. I got these uninviting images mostly from the same source many Americans rely on for their knowledge of the world: the movies, especially the Australian film *Crocodile Dundee*, in which Paul Hogan portrays the weathered main character, Mick Dundee. Australia does, in fact, have all of those things, but it's a lot more. Its immensity supports a wide variety of landscapes, from tropical rainforests in the northeast to a ring of mountain ranges surrounding one of the world's largest deserts.

Despite my stereotypical images of Australia, I didn't actually expect to see snakes, koalas, or distant landscapes on this first leg of my journey. Instead, I would stick to the nation's coastal cities, which looked like so many other prosperous enclaves I'd visited. But to go Down Under, I first had to travel the great, empty expanse of the Pacific Ocean.

In the early 1990s, the only way out of Denver by air was via Stapleton Airport, an aging facility near the center of downtown — a two-hour drive from my home in Vail on a good day.

I awoke on the morning of my departure and, for a moment, couldn't figure out who'd snuck in during the night and covered our bedroom windows with white sheets. As sleep drained from my head, I saw that we were at the tail end of a blizzard: two-foot-high drifts of white fluff blocked our front door. I pulled my knit ski cap over my ears, cinched my parka's hood, grasped a snow shovel, and began clearing the Driveway from Hell.

Our home in Eagle-Vail, a small bedroom community outside the entrance to the posh ski resort of Beaver Creek, was built against a steep hill accessed by an even steeper driveway. On days when there weren't multiple feet of snow to contend with, my all-wheel-drive Mazda minivan, if piloted quickly and deftly, could just make it to the top. My oldest son, 16-year-old Lon, wasn't so lucky. He couldn't afford an all-wheel drive vehicle, and if he wanted to park in front of the house, it required planning, courage, speed, and luck. Idling his car down at street level, he would angle his front wheels just so, gun the accelerator, then make a headlong dash up the driveway while keeping the front tires in the dirt border, in hopes that at least one wheel might gain enough traction to let him lope and stutter up the driveway.

Mostly Lon was unlucky and slid back down to the street sideways, to his brothers' jeers and shouts. But if he did make it to the top, getting back down that driveway again was even harder. More often than not, he wound up at the bottom sideways.

My packed bags were in the Mazda, and already I was freezing in the flimsy dress slacks and fancy shoes I'd wear in Australia, where it was summer. Luckily, I made it down the driveway in some semblance of a straight line and waved goodbye to Terri. It would be a month before

I returned, and already I missed her and the boys, but at that moment my mind was focused more on getting to Denver in anything less than the five hours I had before my flight to Los Angeles was scheduled to take off.

Flying from Denver to Oz is not for the faint of heart. After the two-hour flight from Denver to LA and two more hours waiting at LAX, my flight to Sydney took just under 21 hours. Up to this point, the longest flight I'd ever taken was between Europe and the US—not more than nine or ten hours. The first half of an LA-to-Sydney jaunt is tolerable if you sleep, read, get up, and walk around a lot. The second half is torture. You've read the books you brought. You've scrunched in the cramped seat, fighting for your share of the armrest, unsure how much territory is yours to claim, or how much to pity the poor passenger in the middle seat. You're hoping not to hit the bathroom again, because you've already been repulsed by the overflowing paper-towel bin and the smells left by your 350 fellow passengers. Then there's the food. Breakfast, your third meal—with eight more hours still to go—consists of cellophane-wrapped pastries, a cup of applesauce like the ones you got in kindergarten, and a plastic cup of a watery excuse for orange juice. Your reward at the end of the long flight is to be herded like cattle into long queues of passengers as grumpy and tired as yourself, shuffling toward the customs and immigration desks, before being released into the waning sunshine of a day you've missed altogether.

But grumpy or not, I arrived. Sydney reminded me very much of San Francisco: hilly, and cooled by moist, salty sea breezes wafting off Sydney Harbor. Everyone wants to see the Sydney Opera House, and I was no exception. It sits on Bennelong Point, a narrow strip of land—in fact, a former tidal island—that juts out into the blue harbor. The small leaflet I'd picked up at the hotel told me something of the Point's history. Formerly known as Limeburners' Point, the rocks of the beach had been layered deep with hundreds of years' worth of the shells of oysters shucked by Indigenous Australians over the millennia. The convicts who made up Australia's first generations of European settlers burned these shells to make lime, from which cement was made for the building of Sydney. In the early 1970s, engineers elongated and built up

Bennelong Point to erect on it one of the architectural treasures of the world. The Sydney Opera House's huge white tents of precast cement look like white nun's habits, or billowing sails, pointing toward the harbor.

Thanks to jet lag, my first few days in Sydney I rose at 4 am, then walked the rolling city streets still slick with dew, scattering hundreds of pigeons that were scrounging for food. In the afternoon I'd spend time with Genesis's newest dealer, Seto, a gentle Filipino who owned Audio Excellence, a lavish high-end shop in the Inner West Sydney suburb of Drummoyne. As I recall, Seto's shop was upstairs, in an upscale residential area. Its three listening rooms overlooked the Parramatta River on one side, and the peninsula between Iron Cove and Five Dock Bay on the other. I'd never seen an audio dealer's showroom with such views. Customers could enjoy some of the best waterfront panoramas of Sydney Harbor and the Opera House—reasons enough for Seto to rarely lower the lights or close the curtains during a listening session. The shop's staff needed training on the new Genesis Is that I helped set up. Seto's original pair had been sold to a man in Perth, in Western Australia, where the climate is dry and the land bereft of greenery. This was to be my first customer visit.

Perth itself is a gleaming, modern, seaside metropolis. Its nearly two million inhabitants hug the sandy shores of the Swan Coastal Plain, a narrow strip of land between the vast Indian Ocean to the west and a range of low mountains, the Darling Scarp, to the east. Fresh from the airport, I was met by my host Winn, a pleasant fellow of medium build with short-cropped hair and a thick Oz accent. Soon we were motoring northeast toward Winn's home along a lonely two-lane highway.

I'd begun to get a better sense of Australia's vastness on the five-hour flight west from Sydney, as I watched the Outback unfold endlessly below. But viewing the great emptiness of the Australian interior from a passenger jet, drink in hand, has nothing to do with being down there on the ground. Winn's SUV was outfitted with a miniature version of a locomotive's cowcatcher, but I saw no cows anywhere. As far as I could see spread an endless expanse of pale green shrubs and arid red dirt. An hour into our drive we passed the Morangup Nature Reserve, a desolate stretch of brown, cracked soil with scatterings of parched looking gray-green scrub brush and I saw my first family of kangaroos, which explained the thing protecting the front of his SUV: a 'roo bar.

These far outskirts of Perth reminded me of California but were far more desolate. In the distance I could see lines of power poles struggling to stand straight. Joining the leaning poles was a single black cable, attached to each pole with a brown ceramic insulator. I'd read about this unique power grid, which Australians call Single-Wire Earth Return (SWER). In the US and Europe, we use a two-wire AC system that's isolated from the ground by utility poles. In this rural Australian electric system, the earth itself is used as the return path for the current, which means that only a single wire is needed, thus reducing costs. Single-wire power, while workable, can be problematic in areas where two SWER grids meet. If safety standards aren't maintained (as they often weren't, in the Outback), an unsuspecting quadruped could find itself converted to charcoal if its hind legs found purchase on one side of the grid's dividing line and its front legs touched the other side.

An hour's travel passed as we talked of stereos and got to know each other. Then, as the road veered south, we left the highway, rattled up a washboard road to a small rise, then got out of the car. Below us was Winn's estate—100 acres of low scrub in a dry riverbed whose waters, forced underground by the relentless sun, still fed a swale of green in a sea of brown bordered by low, rolling hills. Winn lived in a sprawling, one-story wooden house of beige and white with a green roof, surrounded by the red of two flagstone patios: one in the front, near the entrance, and the other to the rear, facing south. The property was overseen by a friendly yellow Lab that pranced with joy as we left the car.

Winn had brought me here because he had a bass problem with his new Genesis Is, bought from Seto's Audio Excellence. A 27-hour flight from Denver via LA to Sydney, then a five-hour flight to Perth, then a three-hour drive through the Australian Outback, might sound over the top for a service call to fine-tune a customer's speakers—but not for someone who'd just invested $70,000 in 1990 dollars ($118,000 today) in speakers that didn't sound right.

Word of mouth—good word of mouth—was our best chance for success in the small community of audiophiles worldwide who were interested in the highest of the high end. Dealers who sold Genesis Is were charged with ensuring that each speaker system was set up properly, and that the customer was excited and thrilled. We expected dealers to offer free service and setup for as many hours and trips as it took to make the customer happy. But because none of the few dealers who'd signed on in those early days actually knew how to set up a pair of Genesises, it was my job to make sure both dealer and customer were taken care of.

By definition, audiophiles are obsessive about sound, and Winn was no exception. His listening space was a dedicated room on the south side of his house. When I walked in, the sound of my voice and a few hand claps sounded all right. The room's dimensions, too, were reasonable: long and narrow, maybe 20 feet long by 15 feet wide, with a 10-foot-high ceiling. The room was decent, but the speakers' positions were not. It didn't take much listening for me to know that the bass was overwhelming everything else and would need taming.

Each Genesis I system included a standalone multichannel power amplifier for the servo-controlled woofer system. Incorporated in that amplifier was an extensive electronic crossover that customers could use to adjust how high in frequency and how loud in volume the woofers would be allowed to go. I did my best to adjust the available parameters with the crossover's remote control, but with only minimal success. It was obvious that the woofer towers would need to be moved—but each of those massive, 7.5-foot-tall rosewood towers weighed in excess of 350 pounds.

Moving a Genesis I tower very far without the aid of a hand truck was not only difficult—it was dangerous. With two people simultaneously bear-hugging one tower, it was possible to walk it some distance—as long as the tower didn't tip too far from the vertical. I'd once attempted to walk a tower across the room by myself, but had managed to tilt it too far. It carved a chunk of drywall out of one wall of the International Trade Center, smashed a $3,000 C.E.C. CD transport, and would have flattened me had I not been able to scramble out of the way. Standard practice with the bass towers, as described in our owner's manual, was to place them just outside and behind the midrange-and-tweeter wings, as the dealer had done in Winn's room. But the woofer towers hit just the right room resonances to create a major bass peak at about 50Hz, which is just above a double bass's low E — and was, apparently, a very popular frequency among the recordings in Winn's library. Every time that note occurred, it seemed as if all the air in the room became that note — our heads vibrated as if they were inside a bass drum as someone pounded it hard.

To reduce this unwanted peak, we carefully but laboriously walked the woofer towers toward the center of the room, where the amplitudes of bass frequencies were lowest. This is because the room's walls act like reflectors bunching waves together and forming louder waves: the farther away from the walls, the less exaggerated the peak. Finally, with the towers closer to the center of the room, that 50Hz note was much diminished, and in better proportion with the rest of the audioband. Happy at last, we mopped our brows.

Winn and I spent the next few hours enjoying his system by playing favorites; I'd brought along a handful of reference CDs, and his racks of LPs lined the walls. Soon it was late — he'd have to drive me back to Perth for a few hours' sleep before I caught an early-morning flight. But first he insisted that, after our long day of travel and work, we enjoy a moment of rest and reflection outdoors, in the quiet of his spread.

Winn's estate had once been a sheep station, but there wasn't a sheep to be seen as I sat on his south patio. Instead, I gazed at land so empty that the distant horizon was lost in the hazy blur of heat-distorted air. A cold Foster's Lager and the patio's canopy were the only things between us and the fading heat and light of the westering sun, as it painted red this relentless stretch of scrub, sand, and dirt. We talked of stereos, of music, and of the great scheme of things — the sorts of things one thinks about in the crushing silence of endless lands at sunset. Another Foster's later, a sheet of stars thick as clouds rippled across the night sky. From the still-warm earth rose a chorus of crickets accompanied by the cries of dingoes, and the sounds of small animals scurrying for safety from nocturnal predators. As his yellow Labrador inched closer to me, Winn asked me where I was off to tomorrow. The truth was that I hadn't thought about tomorrow. For that moment, in the stillness of time, it seemed this was all there was in the world. Genesis, speakers, and amplifiers all seemed distant and contrived compared to nature's symphony unfolding for me.

Tomorrow could wait.

CHAPTER 47

As THE PLANE'S TIRES hit the runway and I began filling out the entry form I had just been given, I saw the warning printed across it in big, bold, red letters: "drug trafficking in Singapore is a capital offense punishable by hanging." What kind of country had I just landed in? I hadn't brought along any pot or other drugs, but suddenly I was afraid. Images popped into my head of machine-gun-toting police on every street corner.

Winn had told me that Singapore was nothing like the emptiness surrounding his estate in the Australian Outback—that the city-state, just one-fifth the size of New York's Long Island, was a crowded forest of tall buildings ringed by the sea, each building trying to outdo the others in architectural design. I knew that Singapore had hardline police tactics, public whippings, and hangings, but not much else about it. My impression of the country's conservatism had recently been reinforced when Singaporean officials refused entry to a fellow audio manufacturer, the eccentric Michael Green of RoomTune, who looked very much like a modern-day Jesus Christ. His crime had been his longish hair.

Between 1994 and 1998, Singapore had the world's highest rate of executions per capita. In 1994, the year of my visit, there were 76 hangings in the Changi Prison Complex: 21 for murder, 54 for drug trafficking, and one for possession of a firearm. The following year, whippings—or, as the Singaporeans call them, canings—made world headlines when Michael Fay, an 18-year-old American, was whacked six times with the whip for doing what 18-year-old males often do: a bit of vandalism and mischief.

I was nervous as I deplaned, and kept an eye out for signs of official aggression or anyone who looked like police. But at the airport, and even on street corners in the city, there were none to be found. I couldn't believe this was the country I'd read about. Instead of being stiff and rule-bound, Singapore reminded me more of laid-back Hawaii. Palm trees lined streets as clean as Disneyland. Instead of being uptight and wary of strangers, Singaporeans seemed to be chilled out, all smiles. My preconceptions aside, it seemed a paradise populated by the gentlest people I'd ever met.

Our distributor, Ben Chia—who'd introduced me to Mr. Pu and arranged for the purchase of our stock of unsold round Genesis speakers—had picked me up at Changi Airport. Our first stop was a seafood restaurant along the East Coast Parkway, aka the ECP, facing Changi Bay. We ate pepper crabs—or, as the locals call them, Chile Crabs: whole mud crabs fried in a wok and served in a spicy tomato-chile sauce that Singaporeans enjoy with a cold beer on open-air patios. Singapore's warm tropic breezes, lush plant life, and sparkling blue bays were a stark contrast to the endless dry-scrub plains of the Australian Outback.

The first of the two stops on my fixit tour of Singapore would be easy. A physician, who lived in a modest neighborhood with his wife and children, had bought a pair of our smallest and most popular speaker, the Genesis V: a compact, floor-standing model with a built-in powered subwoofer. Their white colonial-style home, with wooden floors and stucco walls, was nothing special, but it was tastefully decorated, with only a few tchotchkes on tables and fresh flowers in the dining room. The whole family was there to greet me, including their two tall teenagers, a boy and a girl.

Surprisingly, the doctor's Genesis Vs were set up as the centerpiece of the living room. In most American audio systems, the speakers are placed against a wall, or in the corners, or to either side of a fireplace—or even hidden, as if they were embarrassments. But here the furniture had been arranged around the speakers, which were proudly displayed away from the wall behind them, about a third of the way into the room. I was pleased to see our speakers given pride of place, but right away, I was concerned about the setup.

With the family sitting in rapt attention on a sofa behind us, the good doctor offered me the sweet spot—the central position on a couch wide enough for three, and the classic seat of honor among audiophiles the world over. He played a few cuts, all classical. The system sounded all right to me, if a bit edgy in the high frequencies. Then I saw why; the speakers were toed-in too far—angled to point directly at the sweet spot, a mistake commonly made by those new to setting up speakers. Too much direct sound from the tweeters — the drivers that reproduce the highest frequencies, the sounds of cymbals, triangles, piccolos, snare drums, and the upper harmonics of stringed instruments — was being fired directly at the ears of anyone who sat in that central position. While years ago this may have been a good idea, it's usually not optimal with modern, well-designed speakers. Designers like Arnie Nudell and others spend a great deal of time and effort maximizing a speaker's off-axis response so that it produces good sound even when its tweeters and other drivers aren't pointed straight at the listener's ears — and so it will have a better chance of sounding good to those not seated in the sweet spot.

Like many audiophiles, myself included, the doctor was a serious fan of classical music, and his ears had been well-trained at the concerts he attended almost weekly. To his ear, he told me, stringed instruments just didn't sound right through his new Genesis Vs — they were too strident in the highs, sounding more like electronic than acoustic instruments. He complained that his enjoyment of chamber music had been diminished by these speakers: the beauty of the sounds of gut strings, wooden-cased pianos, and small-bore woodwinds seemed to have been replaced by the cold sound of loud, bright, resonant steel. To demonstrate the difference, he did something I'd never seen a customer do, before or since. He beckoned his daughter over, and she stood between the two Genesis Vs and played her violin.

It had all been well-planned; the girl played the same solo passage from Beethoven's violin concerto that we'd just listened to on a recording. Of course, it didn't sound the same. It couldn't — the recording was made in a very different room, with microphones positioned to pick up not only the soloist but the entire orchestra. But as I listened, I suddenly realized what he wanted me to hear. His daughter's violin sounded full and rich, the recorded violin squeakier. It wasn't that the violin on the recording produced more upper-treble energy, but that there was less lower-frequency sound, as if the instrument itself were smaller. In contrast, the girl's instrument sounded more like a viola.

The fix was easy; we brought his system a lot closer to the quality of live sound than he'd imagined possible by reducing the toe-in angle.

263

Having the speakers fire more or less straight ahead reduced the brightness of the strings and amplified the separate, scraping sound of the bow drawn across them—the two sounds were now distinct, as we'd just heard when his daughter was standing there before us and playing. I also reduced the distance between the left and right speakers, which better coupled the midbass to the woofer for a fuller sound, and gave a better sense of the instrument as a three-dimensional physical object generating sounds. My last tweak was to adjust some of the controls on the built-in subwoofer so that notes in the bass region sounded more natural.

One tendency I've noticed in my travels is that people want the bass to be louder and higher in frequency than it is in natural sound. As I'd learned from Harry Pearson years before, the role of a subwoofer like the one built into the Genesis V is to supplement the output of the smaller woofer or midbass driver; ideally, the result sounds like a single driver producing sound waves across the entire range of human hearing, and thus comes closer to the sound of actual musicians making music right there in the room. In the best systems I've heard, the main speakers sound as if there's no subwoofer at all—instead, it's as if they go all the way to the bottom of the low-bass range without compromise or strain, and the music sounds entirely natural.

Our work there was done. Ben and I ate a late lunch before driving on to the next customer's house—and to a bigger problem. Unlike the doctor's modest home, the next system was installed in the residence of a huge estate hidden behind high fences and accessible only through a guarded gate. Singapore has some of the highest-priced real estate in the world, and this park-like estate near downtown Singapore must have been costly beyond imagination. We motored past rolling grassy knolls, beds of flowers, bending palm trees, and the far-reaching spray of fountains to the mansion that all this landscaping surrounded. The owner was a government official high in the administration of Prime Minister Lee Kuan Yew. His actual position was very hush-hush; I have no idea whose estate we visited that day, but I'm pretty certain that if I did, it would still be better, almost 30 years later, not to say.

We weren't here to meet the official himself; our customer was his thirty-something, unemployed son, whose only passion seemed to be high-end audio — a fact that, apparently, his father hated. This was why the 1.2 tons of Genesis I his son had bought had been relegated to a bedroom of only 250 square feet at the end of the mansion's west wing, as far from Dad as possible. The sound of the Genesis Is in that room was unbearable — bass overpowered everything. The problem was that the sound waves of bass frequencies are so long. Because high frequencies have very short wavelengths, typically measured in inches or their fractions, changing the positions of the tweeters that produce them by as little as an inch or two can make a big difference in the sound. But the sound waves of the low frequencies reproduced by woofers can be 20 or more feet long — far longer than any dimension of this young man's bedroom. For these speakers, this room was ridiculously small. He'd tried to solve the problem with a device called a multiband graphic equalizer, in this case an Audio Palette. Essentially, a graphic equalizer is a far more complex version of the simple bass and treble tone controls once common on receivers and integrated amplifiers. The difference is that, with an equalizer, the levels of far narrower ranges of treble, midrange, and bass frequencies can be independently adjusted, for more accurate fine tuning.

Using the Audio Palette and a combination of volume adjustments and repositioning — bringing the massive bass columns closer together in the center of the room, as I had in Australia — we tweaked it enough to at least sound a bit better. The young man was thrilled. I hadn't the heart or the balls to tell him he'd have been much happier with a pair of our smaller Genesis Vs, like those owned by the doctor we'd just visited. Ben knew me well enough to give me a dirty look when he saw my resolve to keep my mouth shut starting to crumble. This guy really wanted the prestige of owning the world's biggest, most expensive speakers, and it was a big sale for Ben. Who was I to pull the rug out from under both of them, even if it was the right thing to do?

Dinner that evening was at an upstairs eatery overlooking the Singapore River. The night was pleasantly warm and humid with the hint of an offshore breeze. My trepidations of Singapore as a repressive society with armed guards at every corner had long ago melted into nothingness. This country and its people made me feel at home. Over cold beers and another round of wok-fried Chile Crabs, Ben and I built upon our trust and friendship developed in small chunks at CES. Sitting face-to-face with Ben in his own country gave me an entirely new perspective I could not have gotten any other way. I ate the food, breathed the air, heard the sounds, rode the subways, and mingled with the people of Singapore. I visited The Adelphi Center, a multi-story shopping center dedicated to selling high-end audio. And I could picture, for the first time in my audio career, what aspects of our products these people liked and didn't like by their subtle cues: a facial expression, the way their hand gently caressed the rosewood veneer, a twitch from the whack of a bass drum or a gentle sigh as the music faded. I could see it in their eyes, I could sense it in their expressions.

As Ben and I said goodnight to each other with a handshake and then a warm hug, I knew Arnie was right. Learning a country's culture firsthand, developing trust between people, was the path to our success.

CHAPTER 48

I AWOKE EARLY the next morning excited for the next round of travel and the opportunity to immerse myself in yet another culture. This wasn't like traveling within America where subtle differences define each state. The contrast between Georgia and California pale next to the contradictions separating Australia and Singapore—and now I was on to another entirely divergent society, this time to Taiwan, an island almost precisely 50 times the size of Singapore.

In the mid-1990s, Singapore was quiet, clean, laid-back, and highbrow. Taiwan was more like the Wild West. The polluted streets of the capital city, Taipei, were congested streams of motorcycles and scooters—often, I saw an entire family crammed onto a single motorbike, zigzagging in and out of traffic amid honking horns and oppressive humidity. Open-air markets displayed animal carcasses hung by their feet in the broiling sun, and everywhere was a multifarious roar of sounds, sights, smells, and exhaust. I did my best to immerse myself in the culture by walking a few blocks from my hotel, but Taipei's sensory overload made even short excursions challenging. The smells of its shanty town markets and passels of street food vendors, coupled with overflowing trash bins, dogs, cats, and rats running rampant, and mosquito-infested pools of standing water from the recent rains, conspired to overwhelm my senses. I had to steel myself just to feel marginally comfortable outside my hotel room. Fortunately, Taiwan's people were its saving grace. Wonderful, warm, and constantly bustling with energy, the citizens of this cacophonous symphony of noise and pollution seemed both oblivious to its chaos and welcoming to its newcomers.

Taiwan's culture was the polar opposite of Singapore and felt as if from another planet compared to Australia, but I was here to help Mr. Pu with one of his customers, not to sightsee. Pu's customer lived in Tainan, Taiwan's oldest city situated at the south end of the island, a two-and-a-half-hour flight from Taipei. It was late afternoon when Pu and I arrived, our commercial aircraft landing at what looked like a military airfield, replete with fighter jets at the ready. Parts of this flat metropolis were minimalist in style and looked very Japanese, but the area of Tainan we stayed in had buzzing motorbikes, trucks filled with live pigs, belching factories and other sources of pollution, and row after row of tall, cement apartment buildings with thousands of windows, many filled with laundry hung out to dry.

Pu's customer owned a factory that, every day, produced millions of screws of all sizes. He was gruff—during dinner at a crowded and noisy seafood restaurant, festooned with saltwater tanks of fish waiting to be selected as dinner, food and spittle erupted from his mouth at regular intervals. His skin was dark and his receding hairline darker still. Small tufts of black hair sprouted from just above his ears to meet in a narrow strip of wispy tresses that broke the glistening scalp carving up from his permanently creased forehead. I couldn't tell much from his facial expressions because his eyes were permanently hidden behind big aviator-style sunglasses perched high atop the bony arch of his broad nose. Only the periodic rise of his eyebrows or the pursing of his thin lips, or the occasional smile, gave a clue to his disposition. He talked to Pu but never spoke directly to me, only gesturing in my direction. Our customer lived on the 11th floor of one of those nondescript cement apartment blocks; directly below him, his sound system occupied the entire tenth floor, accessible only via a low-ceilinged private elevator with key access. Inside that cavernous, 1,000-square-foot space, a single couch faced his enormous Genesis Is, which sat at the center of the room, an island of speaker rising from a sea of polished cement. How Pu had gotten those 7.5-foot-tall beasts up into this loft was a mystery.

A handmade, silk, single area rug covered the floor between speakers and couch; behind the couch, LPs and CDs were piled high. A lone turntable sat directly in front of the couch, and it was an impressive sight. Many audiophiles spend small fortunes on their turntables; I'd guess that this turntable alone had cost our client $50,000 in mid-1990s dollars, with another few thousand spent on the Souther SLA-3 Triquartz linear-tracking tonearm and Clearaudio Veritas moving-coil phono cartridge, and many more thousands on the exotic electronics from German company MBL. I knew turntables and vinyl, but by 1992

I no longer listened to LPs, instead preferring the greater dynamic range and sound quality of digital recordings. Still, I understood the appeal of vinyl to many audiophiles—and this gentleman was at the top of that heap.

Surrounding this system, in the middle of the room, was a forest of what looked like cloth-covered beige barrels of various heights. These were TubeTraps, designed and made by Acoustic Sciences Corp. to absorb unwanted resonances created by the interaction of the speakers and the room. His system sounded pretty good, but the sound was muddled—all mush, no articulation. Fast passages became blurs. Voices and instruments weren't independently audible, as they are in close-miked recordings or in the first few rows of a concert hall; instead, they drowned in a sea of confusing reverberations heard from many home music systems that haven't been properly set up. The fact is, when you're hearing a live concert in a hall, it's rare that you sit close enough to the performers to hear the separation of instruments I'm talking about. However, with the advent of excellent recordings and systems, listeners are vicariously treated to a first-or second-row seat—or even get to stand on the podium next to the conductor. Just as a televised football or baseball game gives you a far more intimate view of what goes on in the field than you could ever have in the stands, modern recordings made with onstage microphones can provide instrumental separation that's better than live.

Pu had done a good basic job of speaker setup, as far as I could tell, but he and I suspected that the problem was the forest of TubeTraps—which, apparently, had been installed in defiance of Pu's advice. After all, a pair of speakers of the size and authority of the Genesis Is will tend to dominate any room of decent proportions. Set up even close to correctly, the 1.2 tons of speaker would be hampered only by factors outside their influence, such as the room and its furnishings and/or acoustical treatments. Pu told me that he'd tried to remove the expensive tweaks from the room, but the client wouldn't listen, preferring to wait for the arrival of the expert, the Genesis authority. Me.

The task was a monumental one, so I was grateful we weren't rushed. If the customer hadn't been present, I would have begun by removing

269

every TubeTrap and starting from scratch. But I saw the panic in his eyes when I started carting them off—it was clear that he'd never accept a wholesale TubeTrapectomy. I soon saw why. The Traps weren't in orderly, symmetrical rows, but in odd places and groupings, as if each had been hand-placed by the customer. Of course, they were. He'd spent countless hours positioning them for the best sound—a process that I knew, from personal experience, can take days or even weeks of hard, exhausting work. Clearly, dismissing and undoing all his effort would have been taken as an insult—the last thing I wanted to do, regardless of how much easier it would make my job. I'd been to this party before. To assuage his fears I used masking tape to mark where each trap had been placed, making it easy to return them if need be.

Through trial and error, I began to notice what worked and what didn't. Stacking Traps on top of each other, I built tall towers that stood maybe six feet behind the speakers: one each behind the left and right speakers, and a third between them. Three hours later, the sound had come alive. Voices and instruments were freed from their shackles, partly because I'd removed enough TubeTraps that I could now tune the speakers' positions even more finely than Pu had managed.

To see how we'd done we played an audiophile favorite, a recording released by Reference Recordings: John Rutter's *Requiem*, sung by a soprano soloist and the 300 voices of the Turtle Creek Chorale and the Women's Chorus of Dallas, accompanied by harp, cello, winds, timpani, percussion, and pipe organ, all conducted by Timothy Seelig and recorded in Dallas's Meyerson Symphony Center. The magic of this performance is the sheer majesty of its sound.

The *Requiem* begins very quietly—we heard the squeak of Seelig's movement, and a lone cello. Subtly at first, the organ laid the foundation: its low A pedal purred like a contented feline the size of a dinosaur, and we began to get a sense of the Meyerson's vastness. Then, far back in the hall and right of center, as the solo soprano sang a melodic line, her voice reverberating off the walls gave an even greater sense of the space. Quietly at first, then almost overwhelmingly, all 300 voices joined in—we were flabbergasted that the sound could be so big and so loud, even as we could "see" tier after tier of choristers rising toward the rear

270

of the soundstage. Suddenly, we realized that the aural image of this vast chorus was extending far beyond the speakers' outer edges, to fill the space beyond and behind them. The depth of sound was extraordinary, and we sensed that the stage must be 50 feet deep—deeper even than the large room we sat in. And just when we thought it had reached the maximum sound level, the pipe organ rumbled in underneath the hundreds of voices and we were almost frightened, taken completely by surprise by an auditory experience only a few people have been lucky enough to hear: those who made the recording, and those with sound systems like that one in Tainan, Taiwan.

The music, the new sound of this system, had mesmerized the three of us. We could barely breathe, and no one spoke. Words could not express the sort of audible power that grabs hold and utterly dominates a listening space and your very soul, when, to your astonishment, you seem transported to the very time and place it was recorded—or as close to that time and place as you'll ever be. As the music soared and the organ's lowest pedal notes shuddered, the listening room of Pu's client—his building's entire tenth floor—seemed lifted into the heavens. Our pant legs flapped, and I don't mean figuratively. They flapped as if in a wind—which of course is exactly what's happening: a wind of sound waves.

That evening I had to return to Taipei, to catch my flight to the Philippines early the next morning. But Pu and I had stayed so long in Tainan, listening to and tweaking our client's system, that I missed the last plane out. Pu told me not to worry, and put me on a bus headed for the capital.

"You take bus," said Pu. "Good ride. Last bus tonight. You get sleep."

The trip would take eight hours, he said, but at least I'd have time to get to the hotel, pick up my stuff, and catch the plane to Manila. He left me alone in the station with an expectation of a reclining seat and a few hours of sleep. But, when the bus rolled up to the curb I soon learned Pu's idea of a good ride was quite different than my own. This last bus to Taipei was like the one I'd taken to school as a kid, only worse. A lot worse. It rumbled and belched foul-smelling exhaust fumes and the driver reminded me of a serial killer: he bared his teeth through

271

snarling lips as I handed him my ticket, his black eyes glued to mine. Instead of the expected reclining upholstered seats, there were instead fixed bench seats, with a rounded steel bar for a headrest. It was packed with workers, crying children, wire baskets full of chickens, and an old man carrying two small dogs in a cage. I was the only Westerner. In the dilapidated faded green cracked vinyl seat next to me was a snoring, 300-pound man with a scraggly goatee that moved up and down with each inhalation, and flapped against the folds of his chest with each exhalation. He stank of BO, which didn't improve over the next eight hours. Dammit, Pu.

We pulled out onto the highway, and soon I knew it would be a long night. The driver operated the gas pedal the way my mother used to: on and off. Instead of holding the pedal down steadily, he would accelerate until the bus was going too fast, then lift his foot until it was going too slow, then pedal to the metal again, then off—an endless lurching of fast and slow, fast and slow. The highway had been built long ago, in cement sections without expansion joints. Where each pair of blocks met, their ends had lifted, forming between them a shallow cup just shorter than the bus. Mile after mile the bus see-sawed, front wheels rising as the rear wheels dipped, then the reverse. This, in combination with the driver's lurching pedaling, made my head constantly bang against the bare steel headrest. To add to my discomfort the passengers in the rear of the lurching bus had opened their windows for what I assumed was fresh air in the warm Taiwan night. Instead, the vehicle's acrid diesel exhaust filled the cabin in choking, eye watering fumes and a nauseating stench. If those weren't bad enough, there was still the serial killer to contend with. Every few minutes his beady black orbs met mine in his rearview mirror. When we locked eyes it meant his were not on the road, and that made me nervous. I tried to ignore him but every time I stole a glance he seemed fixated on me. Sleep was impossible.

Four hours into this trip, I had to pee. Trying to establish my own tottering rhythm to counteract the seesawing of the bus, I passed more snoring passengers—how could they sleep?—on my way to the single bathroom at the rear. Inside, it was cave-dark, and I could barely make out the toilet: an open pit to stand or squat over. A man needs a steady stance and good aim to pee: hard to do in a rocking bus in pitch dark.

I was doing my best when I realized that something cold, wet, and slimy was wriggling down the back of my shirt. It must have fallen off the ceiling. Panicked, I grabbed the thing and flung it into the toilet. It left my hand slimy and cold. As I opened the door to escape, enough light entered that I could see, crawling on the ceiling, the biggest, blackest, wettest, evilest-looking colony of water bugs. I lifted my hand to cover my mouth, already opened wide in horror, but realized just in time that I'd be smearing my lips with bug slime — and no way was I going to try to rinse it off in that filthy little sink. Then the bus hit a bump and I was nearly thrown back into the toilet. I held on to the little door handle for dear life until the bus smoothed out. I smeared the goo on my pants, gritted my teeth, and careened back down the crowded aisle, stepping over the caged animals, avoiding stumbling over outstretched feet, before sliding in next to my snoring seat-mate. I settled in for another four hours of hell, only to meet again the eyes of the serial killer driving the bus.

It would be a long night.

CHAPTER 49

BY THE TIME THE BEADY-EYED DRIVER let me out of his bus, it was 2 AM: I was bone-tired, soul-shaken, and completely disoriented. All I could think about was getting back to my hotel room to sleep. I managed to flag down a passing cab and hire the serial killer's brother-in-law to drive me to my hotel. An hour later, I finally collapsed on the bed in a crumpled heap, desperate for a few winks of sleep. My flight to Manila was taking off in less than six hours and I would need to leave for the airport in less than three. Confident that the reassuring desk clerk had understood my request for a 6 AM wakeup call, I floated off to sleep: luscious, delicious, renewing sleep.

Bam, bam, bam!

What seemed like an instant later, I was awakened by an incessant pounding and realized the only way to make it stop was to open the door. It was the desk clerk and he looked worried.

"You no answer phone," he said apologetically.

I fumbled for the light switch and soon discovered the problem: the phone's receiver lay upright like a dying cockroach. Shit. I must have knocked it off its cradle when I flopped onto the bed and passed out.

"You wake now?" he asked, then bowed ever so slightly, before tiptoeing down the quiet hall.

It was 7 AM and I was already late. By the time I shoved my belongings into my suitcase, paid my bill, and got into the taxi it was 7:30. The airport was easily an hour's drive in light traffic, and my flight left at 9 AM.

"How long to the airport?" I asked, thankful this cab driver spoke a bit of English.

"Long time now. Lots traffic." He looked at his wristwatch, glanced up at the unmoving lines of cars on the freeway we were trying to merge with, and predicted two hours if we were lucky. Dammit. I had had enough of Taiwan: the massive pollution, the crowded streets, the families crammed onto scooters, the rows of naked dead chickens hanging feet-first from food carts (with swarms of flies to keep them company), and most of all the chaos that seemed commonplace. The Manila I'd read about in the airplane's travel magazine — swaying palms, clean white beaches, and laid-back lifestyle — seemed like heaven compared to this Wild West mélange. I could not imagine another night in Taiwan.

"I'll give you $100 US to get me to the airport in 30 minutes," I said, holding up a crisp Ben Franklin to his rearview mirror.

The driver's grizzled, weathered face split into a broad grin featuring his two missing front teeth. Immediately he whipped the steering wheel hard to the right and pointed the taxi straight down the dirt hill of the on-ramp we had been inching forward on. I held on for dear life as an explosion of dust covered the taxi and uprooted plants flew past our window, like snow out of a blower. Holy crap! Left turn; right turn, slam on the brakes; put it in reverse; blow the horn. Now we were heading the wrong way down a side street, the taxi's insistent horn warning oncoming traffic to move over — they did not, so on to the sidewalk we went, scattering pedestrians. Sharp turns to the left down a side street, then to the right, and accelerating ahead — the horn's blare constant — again up the sidewalk, flying past rows of parked cars like pickets in a fence. I fumbled to find a seat belt. Now we were roaring down the freeway's emergency lane, then along the road's shoulder: one side of the car in the dirt, the other plowing furiously through raised yellow reflectors. This guy was nuts.

The ride was a combination action film and roller coaster that could have easily gotten us both killed. But then, suddenly, I could see planes landing in the distance. We were close but apparently on the wrong road. A jarring right turn again pointed the nose of the car straight down and we careened at a wicked angle along the embankment. The taxi jumped and bumped before bouncing onto a side street — then along the sidewalk to avoid a row of parked scooters and up yet another freeway embankment, before bursting onto the crowded entrance-way to the airport, where we mercifully force-merged into the slowly moving traffic. My heart pounded so hard I thought I might pass out, but then I realized it was my death grip on the car's suicide handles that was making me light-headed. He had made it to the airport in under 30 minutes — no doubt some sort of record. It was the best $100 investment

I have ever made, especially since he didn't kill us in the process. Soon, I would be leaving this crazy place and headed for the warm calm of the Philippines and the quiet of Manila.

The plane asserted itself through the gray polluted skies of Taiwan and arched into the clear blue sky. I leaned my seat back and closed my eyes. The whole way there, all I could dream about was the Pacific's calming blue and the swaying of gentle palm trees in the warm winds of Manila.

On my trip from the airport in the hotel's classy white Mercedes I rolled down the car's window to take this latest destination in. Manila looked to be everything I had hoped for: pristine beaches, emerald-green and turquoise-blue waters lapping the roadway's edges, and yes, palm trees swaying in the warm, fragrant breezes.

I'd come to Manila in response to an urgent plea from the only customer we had in the Philippines. His name was Victor, and he was wealthy by anyone's standards. His driver picked me up at my hotel the next morning in a black Mercedes with two small flags fluttering on the hood: an American flag on the left, and the blue, red, and yellow of the Philippines on the right. We drove through the modern cement, steel, and glass of the city, whizzing past curious patches of poverty that hadn't made it into the travel magazine. Small glimpses of ramshackle clusters of homes squatting between sparkling glass buildings came into view, then suddenly seemed to disappear behind a wall that blocked our view. Odd. I had read that there was quite an economic gap between the ultra-rich and the ultra-poor in this island nation. In fact, it was difficult to pick up a newspaper about Manila without reading the tales of former First Lady Imelda Marcos and her thousand pairs of shoes.

But I was here on business: Victor had bought one of our Genesis I speakers, and that kind of investment warranted personal service. As we entered through the gate in the tall masonry walls surrounding his several-acre compound, which overflowed with bright flowers, ferns, and manicured lawns bordering tropical lushness, I felt like a visiting dignitary. Victor's home was a white mansion in the old plantation style: tall columns supporting and enclosing a high front porch, with the sharp lines and stone-and-plaster work of traditional Spanish architecture.

276

As I stepped out onto the cobblestone drive, he greeted me personally, wearing a flowered Hawaiian shirt and white pants with turned-up cuffs, a gold chain around his neck that seemed heavy enough to cause him discomfort. He wasn't a big man, though his midsection hadn't missed the growth curve. His eyes were a gentle brown that matched what little hair remained atop his head. Offered "a spot of gin," I took the tonic water instead, sipping it during a quick tour of his palace: terra-cotta floors, white plaster walls two stories tall, and a grand staircase spiraling upstairs. In one room, hanging from the center of a white dome, was the largest chandelier I'd ever seen.

My time there was short—I had to catch another flight later that afternoon. Victor was disappointed that we wouldn't be enjoying a meal together, but he led the way to the Music Room, which I assumed would be in one of the mansion's wings. Instead, we made our way through double shuttered doors, across an outdoor patio and then a lawn, to a standalone building—a miniature copy of his mansion, complete with a two-story portico, its roof supported by tall, fluted columns.

Inside was more opulence, this time entirely in the service of high-end audio. The Music Room couldn't have been smaller than 1,000 square feet—a single rectangular room with arched 20-foot ceilings and near-perfect acoustics. I can almost always tell if a room will make a good home for a stereo system by the way my voice and footfalls sound. The perfect music room isn't acoustically dead—or, by contrast, extremely loud and "alive." Instead, when you speak, walk, or clap your hands in an acoustically correct room, there is a naturalness that just seems right. It should be obvious that you're neither outside, with no reflected sound, or inside a tiny reverberant bathroom or closet. Test out the naturalness in your own home or somewhere else you're comfortable by speaking a word aloud and listening to the results, which should not substantially add or subtract from your voice. Most furnished living rooms are pretty good for sound quality and don't echo like some of today's restaurants, which amplify conversations to the point of unintelligibility.

Victor's magnificent temple of sound had perfect acoustical dimensions—a well-known ratio that's easily calculated. Though acousticians endlessly quibble over the perfect room dimensions, the most successful ones seem

277

to be based on the Golden Ratio or Golden Section, a number found by dividing a line into two parts so that the longer part, when divided by the smaller part, is also equal to the whole length divided by the longer part. If you know one dimension of a room, you can easily calculate the remaining two with the formula embodied in the Golden Ratio. It is thought to have been first discovered and formalized by the ancient Greeks—the proportions of the Parthenon, in Athens, conform to it.

Victor's listening room—his listening building—was beautifully built and well-treated. Its proportions felt comfortable, something that most of us unconsciously feel when in a space whose dimensions approximate the Golden Ratio. The minimal room treatments consisted of a series of diffuser panels—wall-mounted boxes filled with varying depths of vertical wooden slats stacked in a horizontal row, made of a tasteful dark wood and placed sparingly along the wall behind the listener, blending nicely into the wall's dark beige. The furniture was elegant, not overblown, as in some listening rooms I've seen, which seem to have been designed to impress the first-time visitor. This room had three chairs exactly one-third of the way into the room from the wall behind them. The backs of the chairs were no higher than a seated adult's shoulder blades, so as not to bounce sound back toward the listener's ears, and the central chair was in the sweet spot. In front of the center seat was a low coffee table, where rested a single remote control. A third of the way out into the room from the far wall, on thick, white, wall-to-wall carpet, stood a gorgeous pair of our big Genesis Is, their dark rosewood veneer gleaming from a recent cleaning. Between the speakers and listening seats spread a handwoven area rug of deep, elegant red. It was a perfect audio room, tastefully set up and appointed.

Audiophile protocol demands that the host first play a few favorite tracks, to give visitors an idea of the system's capabilities and to adjust to the sound of the system and room. Visitors are then offered a chance to play their own choices. No one arrives at such a session without bringing along some LPs or CDs—or, nowadays, a thumb drive or other storage device. I pulled out my collection of favorite reference recordings. I've listened to these recordings so many times through so many different systems that I know every second of each one, especially what I should be hearing in particularly difficult passages. In this set, these included the low organ notes, explosive percussion, and loudly blatting brass of *Pomp & Pipes! Powerful Music for Organ, Winds, Brass & Percussion*, with organist Paul Riedo, and Frederick Fennell conducting the Dallas Wind Symphony (CD, Reference Recordings RR-58CD), as well as the delicate voice of Ana Caram on her album *Rio After Dark* (CD, Chesky JD 28), in particular "Meditation," which pairs Caram's whispering with the guitar stylings of Antônio Carlos Jobim. Systems capable of effortless reproduction of the loud and aggressive as well as the soft and detailed are rare; the Genesis Is, properly amplified and set up, were superb at both tasks.

Victor put on a CD: *Cantate Domino*—Torsten Nilsson conducting Oscar's Motet Choir in an album of Christmas music (CD, Proprius-AudioSource 7762). My favorite track, "Cantique de Noël" ("Christmas Song"), a version of "O Holy Night" sung in Swedish, is a soaring choral performance with pipe organ, recorded in 1976 by Bertil Alving in Oscar's Church, in Stockholm. This is a tough recording to reproduce properly because of the many voices and the large space the system is trying to recreate, and Victor's confident smile told me that he knew it well.

I'd expected to hear good sound but also assumed it would be problematic. After all, I'd been called here to make things better. But from the first organ notes to the final crescendo, I was gobsmacked by what I heard. Indeed, the room was perfect, the electronics were just right, and the interconnects and cables couldn't have been better. With the lights nearly out, I closed my eyes and seemed to be transported to Oscar's Church—a massive, three-aisle Gothic cathedral that can hold 1,200 people, has a tower 260 feet tall, and features one of the largest pipe organs in Europe, boasting 5,200 pipes. There was a ruffle of air on my back—the physically palpable sound of the deepest, largest notes of that massive pipe organ. Gruff and rumbling, it nearly lifted me off my seat. Then, as if heaven-directed, my soul was soothed by the delicate, honeyed voice of a soprano. My eyes were shut, but by sound alone I could picture the 260-foot-tall ceiling of stone arches and the 33 stained-glass windows of the Oscarskyrkan. The reverberant voices of the Oscar's Motet Choir energized every square inch of the vast space. I felt the hair on my arms rise.

This wasn't like the pale imitations of virtual reality or even a modern 3-D movie. It was immersive in a way that let me fully—and joyfully—suspend my disbelief. It felt real. I was spellbound and unwilling to let go of the total immersion—the feeling that I was there, in that church, my body, heart, and soul taken over by the music.

When the last reverberation died away, and we were left with only the hiss of the original tape recording, Victor turned to me and grinned. He could see from my expression that he'd led me up Mount Audiophile, and that now we stood together at the summit, looking out at all the lesser peaks below us. I've met few audiophiles who've attained this height of audio nirvana. I asked him why I was there.

"I just wanted you to appreciate the work you and Arnie have done."

So that was it. There was nothing to fix—no sound to improve, no equipment choices to suggest. Nothing to do but revel in the best reproduced sound I'd ever heard. I'd been invited to this man's home so that I could appreciate—and so that Victor could show his appreciation for—what Arnie and I had created: the best loudspeaker system we knew how to build. Victor knew it was a stretch to have asked me to fly thousands of miles to hear this system for no reason other than listening. But I was happy to be there and proud of our accomplishment. A few hours of music later, it was time to go and we said our goodbyes with promises to connect again.

The same driver in the same black Mercedes picked me up at Victor's house again, and apologized profusely for the route we were about to take. Turns out that construction along the roadway would force us to take a detour through some of the seedier parts of Manila. To be honest, I was only half-listening to what he was going on about: I was still hungover from the wonderful experience of listening to Victor's magnificent system. At some point we crossed a rickety bridge over murky waters filled with mounds of trash, then stopped at a red light. Suddenly, the car was surrounded. Women in shawls and tattered dresses pounded on the window, begging for food. Dirty children with snot-streaked faces, blotched skin, and tousled hair stiff from sleeping on the streets clamored for attention, beating on the windows with one hand and using the other to mime the motion of eating. I dug into my pockets, then rolled down the window to hand out the few dollars in my possession. The driver, alarmed, yelled at me to stop, but I ignored him and gave them all the cash I had. What else would anyone do? These people were desperately hungry.

The people shoved harder, demanding more money, and the car began to rock. As I realized what I'd done, I panicked and tried to close the window, but I couldn't. Arms reached inside, hands outstretched for more. The car bounced—someone had jumped up onto the trunk, while others tried to climb onto the roof. If we'd been rocked much harder, the car could easily have tipped over. The driver yelled something and started blasting the horn. It was loud, and most of them backed far enough away that he could begin to creep forward. As the car gathered speed, I closed the window. The driver swerved right and left, frightening people back into the crowd. Finally, they moved far enough out of the way and we escaped.

I hadn't known such poverty existed—here were pain, hunger, and suffering on a scale unimaginable to a middle-class kid from California, and in stark contrast with the opulence of Victor's home. If these were the consequences of a society built on the principle of "every man for himself," without benefit of a social safety net, I knew it was wrong.

As the plane rose from the runway, I saw this nation of thousands of islands in a different light. I couldn't understand how the Philippines' wealthy few could sleep at night, knowing the plight of their fellow citizens. I had come to the Philippines with high hopes of escaping the Wild West chaos of Taiwan and relaxing in a bit of tropical island splendor. What I saw horrified me: a handful of wealthy people hiding unthinkable poverty behind cement walls and tall buildings. Certainly there had been poor people in Taiwan—entire families on scooters or bikes—but at least they weren't sleeping and dying on the streets. Even in later years, when I traveled to the poorest parts of India, I saw nothing like the desperation I'd seen in the eyes of those Filipino women, men, and children, as I stared back at them through the tinted windows of Victor's black Mercedes.

CHAPTER 50

IN THE EARLY 1990S the two biggest overseas markets for high-end audio products were Japan and Hong Kong. These two Asian giants often represented half the sales volume of an audio company's entire overseas market. Genesis products were doing well in Hong Kong but almost nonexistent in Japan—a problem not uncommon for American high-end audio companies. At issue was not whether the Japanese wanted our products or not—they were just difficult to get into the country.

Japanese audiophiles covet American high-end with an almost reverential passion. Millions upon millions of yen are invested yearly in just about anything and everything they could manage to get their hands on: JBL, Infinity, Altec, Audio Research, and McIntosh in particular. In the early days of hi-fi most of these products had to be purchased outside Japan and brought into the country by private individuals, because outside manufacturers had limited access into the marketplace. Companies trying to import goods in Japan ran into an impenetrable wall from a hierarchal trade system known as the Keiretsu, by which large blocks of the Japanese economy were controlled by trading companies. For most of the 20th century and continuing still into the 21st, gaining access into the Japanese market required specially connected distributors within Japan to get the products to market.

Our distributor was Yasua Nakanishi, a gentle Japanese man with big wire rim glasses in front of his compassionate brown eyes, silver-streaked tufted hair that swept back from his broad forehead, and a delicate mouth that always seemed to be on the verge of a smile. Yasua was known as The Godfather of the Japanese audio market and his organization had single-handedly managed to build Infinity into one of the best-selling brands in all of Japan. Yasua and Arnie were tightly knit friends—thick as thieves, as they would joke at cocktail parties. Yasua was still running Infinity Japan, but out of friendship and loyalty to Arnie he had agreed to do what he could to muscle Genesis speakers into the country. We had yet to ship a pair into Japan. It would be up to me to win Yasua over to our brand. I had every intention of doing whatever I could to impress this audio legend, and hopefully score some points for the Genesis team.

I had never been to Japan before and hoped to get a bird's eye view of the country from the airplane but low-hanging clouds and an offshore approach into Tokyo's Narita Airport didn't offer much. Just stepping off the jetway into Narita's modern terminal was a stark contrast to Manila. Everything here was precision neat, almost German in its orderly manner, but distinctly Asian: brightly colored takeout foods behind a glass walled shop, ornately decorated gift shops with yellow fabric fronts trimmed in red lacquered wood, bookstores with colorful Japanese lettered books neatly stacked in perfect rows, and shopkeepers standing at polite attention to help with customer questions. I had met Yasua at the Vegas Consumer Electronics Show on numerous occasions but never on his home turf. He, and one of his assistants introduced to me as simply Ken, were right on time and walked me to their waiting car.

I had expected the trip from Narita into Tokyo would take us past iconic villages and temples with their ornamented columns supporting curved rooflines — tips pointing skyward — and everywhere reflective pools encircled by neatly flowered gardens. Instead there were only row upon row of crowded housing with blue or gray tile roofs broken on occasion by a green expanse of a small rice field.

Our conversation centered at first around the countryside but soon turned to stereos and then the inevitable, dinner. Yasua, ever polite and respectful to a fault, cautiously asked if I ate sushi or would prefer something less challenging — perhaps a hamburger? The last thing I wanted to do was act like an ignorant outsider, and I figured the quickest way to earn Yasua's respect would be to go where he goes and eat what he eats. I professed my love for sushi, bragging that I could eat anything a Japanese sushi bar could put in front of me. A classic Paul McGowan cocktail of hubris and bullshit.

Before this first visit to Japan, my entire experience of Japanese food consisted of the occasional California roll, an American invention

283

unknown in Japan, and sunomono, a light dish of pickled cucumber sprinkled with sesame seeds and laced with bits of crab. Yasua, a far wiser and more seasoned professional than me, sensed a challenge and took me up on it by arranging for us to dine at a tiny, exclusive sushi bar with only ten seats. We were greeted by the owner and his wife, who were also our sushi chef and hostess. Three of Yasua's dealers met us there, effectively filling all the available seats. The restaurant's front door was locked and a "closed" sign placed in the window.

I was as nervous as a cornered cat. Sitting at that tiny sushi bar surrounded by lifelong experts in the art of eating this Japanese delicacy, it wouldn't be long before my boastful ruse—that I was an experienced connoisseur of the tasty fish and rice delicacies—would be laid bare for ridicule. I couldn't let on that I was completely out of my element, not if I was to uphold the charade. I determined to show no surprise, no admission of ignorance, and certainly no squeamishness. The challenge was on, and the fate of Genesis in Japan hung in the balance.

My first surprise was a pleasant one. Instead of quaffing the slender white porcelain carafes of hot sake I was accustomed to, my potential partners drank sake cold, from a wooden box, with a pinch of salt on one corner. It was delicious, and it went down smoothly as the first round of food: mackerel. This was sashimi—fish sans rice—which I'd never eaten. At least I had the art of chopsticks down and didn't look entirely silly. I picked up the flaky white meat, a small dark vein through its center, and drenched it in soy sauce laced with wasabi, a pungent Japanese mustard similar to horseradish. As I chewed, I could see that everyone was staring down at the table. Yasua shook his head slightly, so as not to embarrass me, and leaned toward me. "It's not ketchup," he whispered. "Not for the fish." He pointed at the soy sauce. My first faux pas. Apparently, the soy sauce and wasabi mixture was only used for the sushi rice, never with sashimi alone. Strike one.

Many more small plates of fish came our way, most unknown to me but edible—until the odori ebi: live shrimp, still wiggling, to be dunked in some kind of liquor and popped in the mouth. Emboldened by the many boxes of sake I'd drunk, I swallowed the wiggling creatures

284

whole, to the delight of all. It was damned hard to act nonchalant as each shrimp slithered down my throat on its way to the acid bath of my stomach, but I had a job to do. I wasn't going to be deterred by the likes of a shrimp, though I hoped that was the extent of the challenging courses. Then came an orange goo, uni: raw sea urchin wrapped in black nori seaweed. The uni was too big to swallow whole. Chewing that sweet, sticky, somewhat gag-inducing concoction of sickly library paste, I was sorry I'd ever boasted of being able to eat sushi like a native Japanese. Surely they couldn't come up with even more disgusting food, but it turned out they were just getting revved up. Deep-fried shrimp heads—brains, antenna and all—were next, followed by crunchy fish spines. The little shards of crunchy bone stuck in my throat and it was all I could do not to gag.

Yasua slapped my back and told me that now I was almost Japanese—but I would have to endure one final rite of passage. Oh God, I thought. There's more? My stomach had long ago waved the white flag of surrender but several trips to the toilet hadn't helped me excavate its contents, and I began to sweat from an almost constant nausea welling up inside my gut. I had to soldier on. The Genesis honor was at stake. One more, he had said, just one more trial before a truce could be declared and I could uphold my honor. That rite was natto: stinky, fermented soybeans swimming in what looked like snot. I didn't think I could do it. No, in fact there was no way I could put that rot-smelling abomination in my mouth, let alone feel it slithering down my throat. I picked at the mucus with my chopsticks, pulling long sticky threads of the translucent gelatinous goo from the bowl of sludge, and then watched them spiral back into the muck. All eyes were upon me. The chef and his wife, the three dealers, and Yasua all held their collective breath and waited for me to take the plunge. There was no escape. Dammit! Me and my big mouth again. Biting my lower lip, I plunged the chopsticks deep into the gray ooze and pulled from it a helping of gleaming slime. I bent closer to the bowl and sucked it into my mouth like long spaghetti noodles. Before my taste buds could even respond, my nose revolted. The smell was overwhelming and I nearly hurled, but somehow I managed to

285

choke down one mouthful. To my surprise, everyone at the table and the two hosts behind the counter clapped. Yasua turned to me, grinning broadly. "You're Japanese now."

I rolled around with my stomach in a knot that night. I was so full I had to lie flat on my back, bracing for each awful rumble that passed through me like an earthquake. I was miserable, and in the blackness of that hotel room, I promised myself over and over again: "I will stop bullshitting people." It was a habit I knew would be hard to break, but that night's anguish was hopefully enough to make a dent.

After I finished my work—introducing Genesis speakers to the Japanese press and Yasua's top ten dealers—and paid a visit to the Tokyo high-end audio show, I was feeling pretty confident I'd made some progress towards getting Genesis speakers into the Japanese market. It was always going to be a slow process: first samples, then a small trial order, and if we were lucky, a steady stream of business after five to ten years of hard work. This was a great first step. Yasua had given me a firm handshake-promise that he would give us a PO for samples of the entire line of products, and that was exactly what I had hoped to accomplish. Now, it was time for Hong Kong, a much stronger market that Mr. Pu had already helped us develop.

286

CHAPTER 51

I BOARDED A CATHAY PACIFIC 747 bound for Hong Kong, thankful for a business-class seat on the upper deck, and was surprised and delighted to find myself sitting next to Steven Taylor, president of Acoustic Energy Loudspeakers, a British company. We'd both attended the audio show, so we had plenty to talk about as the giant silver bird lifted into Japan's cloudless skies and we began our 5-hour oceanic traverse to Hong Kong's Kai Tak Airport. AE speakers were distributed by a different importer than Yasua and Steven helped expand my knowledge of how products are distributed in the closed economy of Japan.

Soon our conversation turned from stereos to travel. I had never been to Hong Kong and was excited for the chance to visit this storied amalgam of British and Chinese culture. Steven, an experienced traveler, was excited for me to see the country, and made multiple recommendations of the sights I should visit: Victoria Harbor, the Star Ferry, The Peak tramway, the Big Buddha on Lantau Island, and a bevy of restaurant suggestions I scribbled into my notebook. He also said I should get prepared for our upcoming landing at Hong Kong's Kai Tak Airport, which he described as one of the most terrifying approaches in all his travels. Apparently, on landing, the plane had to slide sideways in a sharp right turn so steep passengers on the right side of the aircraft were treated to a front row seat view of rooftop laundry fluttering in the breeze, just before the plane righted itself and dropped suddenly onto the runway in a maneuver known as the Kai Tak Heart Attack. Steven was nervous enough of the landing that he often closed his window shade and white knuckled his seat. I, on the other hand, was stoked to hear about this upcoming adventure. I love planes and flying and pumped Steven for all the information I could.

After we reached cruising altitude for the journey to Hong Kong, the cockpit door was left wide open. From my aisle seat I kept leaning out to peer into the cockpit, fascinated by the dials and displays. I love electronics, their flashing lights and switches and noises, and the cockpit of a Boeing 747 is full of all that and more. The pilot had walked past us down the aisle, and now, as he strolled back to the cockpit, he was chatting with the passengers. A tall, bald Brit in a crisp white shirt, tie, and captain's bars, he looked precisely like Patrick Stewart as Jean-Luc Picard, captain of the Enterprise NCC-1701-D in *Star Trek: The Next Generation*. Steven was reading a magazine when the captain reached our row.

"How are you gentlemen doing?" He even sounded like Picard.

"Great, and yourself?"

He was fine, he said. I had an idea. "May I ask a favor?"

"Sure. What can I do for you?"

"I've always wondered what it would be like to be in the cockpit of a 747 on landing. Is there any chance you'd let me watch you land this thing in Hong Kong?"

The captain furrowed his brows, sized me up from top to bottom, and said nothing for a while. Then, he ventured: "Are you a pilot?"

No, of course not, but that never stopped me before.

"No, not officially, but I've been in the cockpits of plenty of small planes."

I diverted my eyes from his piercing blue daggers, panicked he'd discover I was making that up. Wasn't it only a few nights ago I had promised myself I'd stop bullshitting people?

Apparently, Steven had been listening. He slammed the magazine into his lap and stared up at the captain with big, pleading, puppy dog eyes.

"I suppose your friend here wants to watch as well?" Our captain was a kind and generous man.

Steven evidently couldn't speak. He nodded his head violently, but I couldn't tell if he was just scared shitless of the landing and figured he'd be better off up front or just didn't want to be left alone.

"Okay. I'll have the flight attendant come for you two about an hour before we land."

The captain turned, entered the cockpit, and the door shut behind him.

"I thought you were scared of this landing," I said.

"I am," he said. "But I'll bet it's a lot less scary when you can see where you're going rather than hanging on for dear life back here."

I had never been in the cockpit of a plane before, but his logic seemed to make sense.

The next few hours were torture. I tried to close my eyes and sleep, but I was worried he'd forget, or that the attendant wouldn't know it was us the captain meant. I was so excited I was afraid to leave my seat, even to go to the bathroom. I would not miss this.

"Mr. McGowan? Mr. Taylor?" It was the gentle voice of the flight attendant. "The captain would like to see you both. Please follow me."

This never happens in real life, and it was happening. To us. Right now. Steven and I bolted up—and sat right back down again, hard. We'd forgotten to unbuckle our seat belts. I sure hoped he didn't ask me any piloting questions to verify my story.

There were four seats in the cockpit: two facing the windshield, for the pilot and copilot; and behind and to the sides of those, two others. The captain rose to greet us—the immense jet, apparently on autopilot, just kept humming along with the copilot tending to its dials, meters, screens, knobs and controls.

"I need to give you two a safety briefing before we land," said the captain. "It's different than a small plane." He looked straight at me. "The thing you have to know about this cockpit is that, in the case of an emergency, we do not follow the passengers out the exits. If something happens, you're much better off as a passenger than being here in the cockpit. Are you both okay with this?"

Steven and I had no idea what he was talking about, but we eagerly agreed. We were sure that, in the hands of our own personal Jean-Luc Picard, we weren't going to die in that plane. He was about as confident and in-charge a person as I have ever met. Whatever he wanted us to do would be just fine.

"Take a look over here, behind us. See those reels?" There, behind glass, were coils of what looked like fire hose. "In case of an emergency, these reels are how we get out of the plane."

That sounded wacky. Passengers in the back of the plane jumped out of doors and emergency exits, sliding down big inflated slides. All that made sense. We were going to grab a fire hose and launch ourselves out of…where, exactly? Visions of the Keystone Kops entered my head.

"Take a look at the handles above each window. You are going to have to grab on to this handle, and swing your legs up, and kick the windows out. Then you'll grab this hose and eject yourself out of the cockpit to safety."

This was not what I'd expected. Squeeze through those tiny windows holding one end of a fire hose, then jump from, what, the equivalent of the top floor of a five-story building?

Steven and I were handed headsets like the pilots wore. "Who gets the main seat?" Jean-Luc looked right at me. I had no idea what this meant, but it had been my idea and I'd asked first, so it was going to be me. Turned out the main seat was an electric affair that slid out silently to take up a position precisely between, behind, and above the two pilots. I think it must have been an observation seat for a flight inspector—from it, I could see everything the pilots were doing with amazing clarity, as well as everything through the windshield. It was the best seat in the house. Steven's seat was at the same level, directly behind and above the captain—to see anything, he had to look over Jean-Luc's left shoulder. I felt I was sitting on the bridge of the Enterprise with the real Picard, my two trusty pilots at conn and ops, waiting for my next command.

At that moment, we were no longer passengers. We were in the cockpit of the world's largest passenger airplane, a mighty Boeing 747-400, sitting right behind the captain. For a while, we chatted and asked questions about the plane. Then the captain looked at us seriously.

"When we start the landing sequence, I need both of you to sit quietly and just watch. This is a very difficult landing, and it takes all the concentration I have to manage it. We are going to Runway 13—"

Oh, no. I couldn't believe it. It had to be Runway 13. Perfect.

"—which requires us to essentially fly straight into the mountain, right behind Kowloon, and then make a sharp right turn and land the plane."

As we approached the mountain, I could see the back of the captain's head. Sweat was beading up on his neck and pate, glistening in the darkened cabin as he switched off the autopilot and took over the controls. Sweat? It didn't seem like something a confident pilot would be doing while landing this beast safely in Hong Kong. I mean, you don't sweat when everything's okay. The hairs on my arms stood to attention and

290

I joined Picard in a perspiration battle. What had I gotten us into? I glanced over at Steven, who was visibly shaken. He looked back at me with an expression I imagined he shared with a first-time parachutist who'd changed his mind but realized it was too late. There was no turning back now.

The copilot called out the altitude every few seconds, calmly at first, then with greater frequency as the ground loomed closer. The plane continued its descent, and now we were low—really low, only several thousand feet in the air. The captain gripped the stick—it was a wheel—with both hands as the copilot adjusted the four engines, then extended and lowered the flaps to slow the plane enough to land while still keeping it in the air. The ground rushed up, the mountain loomed, and soon we saw our target. Right in front of us was a checkerboard pattern—a massive chunk of painted cement—embedded in the side of the hill behind the city of Kowloon. We were aiming straight for that checkerboard square. Insanity, it seemed. The mountain ahead looked the size of Everest from where I sat. An impenetrable wall. And now we were so low that it was clear no one could change his mind about whether or not to land. We were committed. The sweating captain gripped the stick with white knuckles, the copilot rapidly calling out our altitude as we dropped below 1,000 feet. There was a distressing urgency to his voice that was scaring the living shit out of me. Steven's eyes were squeezed shut. Then the pilot suddenly advanced the throttles, accelerating straight in to that mountain, and kicked the aileron pedals with his right foot to slew the rear of the plane around and make the sharp right turn. Holy crap! We were sideways and falling. I hung on, unable to speak.

"Clang, clang, clang…" yelled some incessant gong. "Warning…" demanded the mechanical voice.

"Shut it off!" ordered Picard without pulling his eyes from the windshield. His bloodless hands clenched the wheel, sweat still pouring down his neck. The copilot's fingers were already on the switch.

What the hell was that alarm? I glanced over at Steven; his face was deathly white, his eyes now wide as dinner plates. I honestly wondered if I'd pissed my pants. Was the wing about to scrape off the tops of those buildings? Our own speeding five-story building was tilted on edge at 250 MPH, as if it was going to spill us onto the rooftops of Hong Kong, which looked to be mere feet from the plane's wingtip. I could see laundry fluttering in the breeze: T-shirts, underpants, pajamas, a flowered kimono, even diapers. We were close enough that I could have grabbed a handful of clothes. I wondered if the crash crews would tell my family they found me in the cockpit, and what Terri might think. Would she wonder what I had been doing in the cockpit? Question whether I had a hand in the plane's demise? Honest to God, I had never been so frightened and helpless in all my life. What had I been thinking?

As quickly as we had made that terrifying turn, the plane righted, its nose pointed straight towards the airport below. Damn. This was it. Then, calmly, as if there were nothing wrong, Picard aligned the plane's attitude for touchdown, hauled back on the throttles, pulled its nose up, and set down that five-story beast as if laying a baby on a pillow. We'd landed. Reverse thrusters, brakes—and then the slow taxiing in a queue of other planes, calmly waiting our turn to roll up to our terminal gate. I don't think I have ever been so happy to be safe on the ground. We thanked the captain and his first mate, and were the last passengers off the giant aircraft.

Steven and I walked off the plane in stunned silence—both still in shock, as if hungover from that terrifying experience. Dazed, we shuffled along with the other travelers, who probably thought no more about their flight than any other passenger. Just another seat on an airplane. But we knew. We were there when the alarms went off. We were there to witness the rivers of sweat pouring off Picard as he somehow managed to land safely. We saw it all and we knew what seemingly no one else in the terminal knew: just how lucky we were to be on the ground. When we'd made it past immigration, we stopped, put down our carry-ons, and gave each other a big hug. Safe.

292

CHAPTER 52

I WAS EXCITED to be in Hong Kong, a city I'd only read about in travel magazines but had never been to: a Chinese culture organized into the Brits' version of civility. HK, as the locals call it, is a collection of 261 loosely connected islands in the South China Sea, bordering mainland China. The city of Hong Kong is named after the second-largest of its islands, known to locals as Central. Lining the northern coast of Hong Kong Island are hundreds of stunning architectural masterpieces, 600 of which soar more than 350 feet into the humid air. The first time I saw them in person, they were dazzlingly reflected in the early-morning calm of Victoria Harbor, which separates the mainland's Kowloon Peninsula to the north, from Lantau Island to the east, Taiwan to the distant west, and, far to the south, Indonesia.

This first visit was in the early 1990s, when Britain still governed Hong Kong—it would be nearly five years before the colony was returned to Chinese jurisdiction. Evidence of the mix of British and Chinese cultures was everywhere, but perhaps nowhere more than where I was staying, in the Marco Polo Hotel, and their buffet breakfast. It was an interesting amalgam: the formal setting and the coffee, toast, eggs, beans, bacon, sausage, tomatoes, and mushrooms were all undeniably British; the dumplings, congee, rice, pork buns, steamed whole fish, miso, and wok-fried vegetables were decidedly Asian.

Fueled up that Sunday morning, my mission was one of exploration. I had allotted myself an entire day to get a feel for this, the wealthiest first-world nation in all of Asia and the biggest hi-fi market on this side of the world. I headed through the hotel's revolving glass door, leaving behind the building's air-conditioned cold for the humid warmth outside, and began jogging along busy Canton Road. The traffic along Canton was a river of cars, bikes, and small trucks running between rows of shops: on one side were such upscale names as Gucci, Prada, Coach, and Dolce & Gabbana; on the other were The Body Shop, New Korean Barbecue, Taiwan Beef and Noodle, massage parlors, and discount luggage stores. I was headed for Steven's suggestion of Kowloon Park, a local delight that few tourists seemed to know about. The park's grassy hills overlook the glittering emerald green of Victoria Harbor, while its narrow paths wind through hundreds of flowering trees and bushes, their sweet scents attracting buzzing insects busy with the day's harvest.

I ended the first leg of my jog at the top of the highest hill, where there was a tall, round aviary with a pointed metal top like a circus tent. The birds were just awaking, cooing and squawking as tree squirrels cleaned up the seeds and shells the birds had missed. Just in front of the cage, I caught my breath on a park bench with a sweeping view of Hong Kong Island, its tallest buildings rising like crystal stalagmites from the concrete apron of bridges and roads. Once rested, I jogged past T'ai chi practitioners waving ceremonial swords, as well as rows of elderly people sitting on the grass in lotus position, eyes closed in meditation.

After my morning run and shower, while sipping coffee in my 14th-floor hotel room, I watched the constant crisscrossing of what looked like old steam-powered river boats plying Victoria Harbor, the narrow waterway separating Kowloon from Hong Kong Island. These were part of the Star Ferry Line originally built in the 1920s as the only means of travel before new tunnels and bridges made them obsolete. Today, they were more history than a necessary means of travel—still, I couldn't resist trying one out. The Tsim Sha Tsui Ferry Terminal was right outside the hotel door. I climbed 24 crumbling cement steps to board the ferry's second level, then paid 50¢ to a bored-looking man sitting in a small vestibule. He pointed me up the ramp to the waiting area.

The strong smell of salt and sea floated through the permanently open windows overlooking Victoria Harbor. Long wooden benches, thick with years of yellow-green paint, lined the rounded walls. The boarding bell rang, and twin metal barriers scissored open like the starting gate at a horse race. Keeping the crowd headed in the right direction was another bored-looking Chinese man in a blue sailor suit, with white stripes and matching blue bibs front and back, like Donald Duck's costume.

The throng pushed across the gangplank onto the Celestial Star, an old double-decked ferry that looked like an oversized version of Bogart's African Queen: green on the first deck, white on the second, with rows of life preservers that looked more like candy than like anything I'd trust with my life. Sticking out of its top amidships was an oval smokestack with a black star on each side, and crowding the lower deck were two rows of long benches with backrests that were reversible, depending on the direction of travel.

Dockhands threw the mooring hawsers to the onboard crew, and the Celestial Star began chugging across Victoria Harbor to Central Hong Kong. As we began our five-minute voyage across the harbor, Hong Kong's warm, moist air ruffled my hair, and I inhaled the sweet smells of ocean and incense that seemed to come from everywhere. The smokestack rising through the middle of the Celestial Star was a relic of the days when she was a true steamship, before being updated with diesel engines. Attached to the lower part of the stack was a brass plate stating that the ship had been built in 1956 by the Hong Kong & Whampoa Shipyard. I was thrilled to be plowing through the harbor in this real piece of history.

My five minutes' plying of Victoria Harbor's waters left me ready to explore Central. From the ferry terminal, the city seemed connected by a series of elevated walkways that spanned the busy lanes of traffic below. I walked this warren of twisting cement paths and stairs until a sea of women suddenly began gathering on the walkways, stairs, and tree-lined open areas, like birds crowding a ripe fruit tree. They were all dark-haired Asian women, and most wore gaily colored flowered blouses. I later learned that they were some of Hong Kong's hundreds of thousands of Indonesian and Filipino maids and servants on their ritual Sunday lunch break—live-in "helpers," as they're called, who had immigrated to Hong Kong with the understanding that they would work 24 hours a day, six days a week, caring for the homes and families of their wealthy employers. HK's government regulations demand that these helpers get 12 consecutive hours of free time each Sunday. Since the women make little money and send most of it home to their families—families like those starving people I had seen out the window of Victor's black Mercedes—they gather in Hong Kong's train stations, walkways, parks, or outside public buildings to enjoy time together: laughing, eating picnic lunches, playing cards, styling each other's hair,

295

and generally smiling a lot, something many would not be doing in their own poverty-stricken homes.

After a lunch of noodles in a tiny shop where no one spoke English, I headed back to the Marco Polo to catch up on work. I was tired of the constant dinners and glad-handing required of the traveling sales-man and fix-it guy I'd become, and that Sunday evening was one of the few I would have just for me. I planned to treat myself to a bottle of good red wine and a fancy lobster dinner, and the hotel concierge suggested that the best in the city could be found back on Central, in a restaurant high atop the Mandarin Oriental Hotel. It seemed just the ticket. I put on nice shoes and slacks, ironed an already-worn short-sleeved shirt so that it looked new again, and took the Star Ferry back to Central. Evenings in Hong Kong are magical: warm, but just blustery enough to keep the heat and humidity in check. I gripped the cool of the Celestial Star's handrail as she motored across the now-black harbor toward the lights of Central, the cityscape's reflection twinkling in the mirror-calm waters.

The Mandarin Oriental was the fanciest hotel I'd ever seen. The staff wore old-style Asian garb: small, fez-like hats, and buttoned, high-necked collars like those seen in old Charlie Chan movies. I took the elevator to the 27th floor and marveled at the restaurant's panoramic views of the city. The more than 5,000 high-rise buildings on the Kowloon side were lit up like Times Square. Breathtaking.

The maître d' approached me, a concerned expression on his face. He looked British, but his accent gave him away as Australian or South African. "Good evening, sir. Do you plan to join us this evening for dinner?"

"Yup." I inhaled the rich aromas from the kitchen and closed my eyes in the pleasure of anticipation. "I have a reservation for 7 pm."

He looked pained. "Have you a coat? Gentlemen are required to wear coats for the evening meal."

A coat? A suit coat? Not only had I not brought a suit coat, I don't think I even owned one.

"Suit coats are required."

296

Indeed, one look around the place and I could see women in evening gowns and men in dark suits. This was High End Hong Kong at its finest. If I was going to eat there, it would clearly be in a suit.

"I can suggest the bar downstairs, sir. They do not have the same dress code."

I would not be deterred. The thought of that lobster dinner had captivated me.

Perhaps my old hick routine would work, if applied gently. It was worth a try.

"I'm sorry. I'm from out of town and didn't know the rules. Can you make an exception for tonight? Maybe put me in a faraway corner of the restaurant? I promise to eat quickly and be on my way."

He was not swayed. "Might I suggest a house coat?"

To me, a housecoat was something my mom wore on Sunday mornings. When I cocked my head inquisitively, he walked me to a small closet tucked away in one corner, and pulled from it a dark suit coat. I'm not sure who this coat fit—maybe Hulk Hogan—but it wasn't me. The sleeves hung over my fingers. The pads extended a few inches past my shoulders. I'm sure I looked like something between an idiot and a kid trying on his father's suit. But it was the only coat in the closet.

My eyes pleaded with him at the ridiculousness of my image but he was unwavering and so I just shrugged. "That's ... fine."

"Excellent, sir." His nose rose high in the air, beckoning me to follow him to a tiny table in a far corner, where the lights were dim and the guests few.

But dinner was excellent. I capped it off with a glass of port, along with a fat cigar the waiter offered me from a box of hand-rolled Cuban delights—impossible to get back in the US. As a show of defiance I left the house coat on the back of my chair and paraded past the maître d', cigar clamped in my teeth Winston Churchill style, my short-sleeved shirt proudly proclaiming my freedom from the stiffness of this British dress code.

It felt good. I was ready for tomorrow's mission: China awaited.

CHAPTER 53

I KNEW FROM THAT first trip to Hong Kong that it was the modern financial capital of Asia. What I didn't understand was that, not more than a 40-minute subway ride away, in the city of Shenzhen, there was a very different Asia.

I was here to meet Mr. Pu and get a feel for this burgeoning market, because Pu predicted that China would someday be one of the world's largest marketplaces for high-end audio. Today his idea certainly seemed prescient, but back then the majority of speakers China purchased were what Arnie and I referred to as "shit boxes": mass-market big, loud, many-woofered, speaker cabinets that razzle-dazzled the listener. Only a very few among the nation had ventured outside China enough to have even heard of high-end audio. I was here to meet with some of those leading-edge dealers and perhaps even a few of the audiophiles themselves. Call it an exploratory mission.

The border crossing between the People's Republic and the New Territories—the part of Hong Kong that's on the Chinese mainland—was as clean, neat, and orderly as one might expect after more than a century of British rule. After I'd passed through immigration, I walked across a long, enclosed bridge over the Sham Chun River, which divides the two regions. Crossing that bridge seemed to take me 30 years in the past. There, luggage that on the HK side had already been carefully x-rayed and inspected went through a conveyor-belt system into an x-ray machine that looked as if it might have worked at one time, but certainly didn't now. Neither did the darkened video monitor in front of the sleeping inspector, as bags tumbled into a heap at the end of the belt. A border guard so skinny that his shirt and tie flopped around his neck had me fill out some incomprehensible papers, then demanded $100 US in cash for my visa. He stamped my passport and shooed me away.

Outside was something quite different from Hong Kong's orderly parade of taxis and Mercedes-Benzes: filling the busy streets and traveling in all directions was a chaos of new and old cars, tractors, bicycles, motorcycles, and human-drawn rickshaws. On first glance I was reminded of Taiwan, but this was even more third-world—something quite unexpected. I struggled to adjust to the mix of the loud blare of horns, the smells of chicken and pork frying in open carts, the exhaust fumes of rumbling diesels belching blue poison onto my pant legs, the thick gray of humid, polluted air burning my eyes, and the outstretched hands of a one-legged beggar desperate for food.

Down the main road came a rickety tractor, limping and swerving—one tall rear tire was flat. It hauled a wooden pen the size of an automobile, stuffed full of pink, hopeless-looking hogs, their eyes hidden behind the boards, their snouts forced through the gaps between. As this wheeled and clacking hog pen slowly lumbered past, circling it and crossing its path before and behind were small noisy scooters, green-and-yellow taxis, white Isuzu freight trucks driven by men in sweat-soaked sleeveless T-shirts, bicycles with front and rear baskets overflowing with anything and everything, and honking, dilapidated Toyotas. Everywhere, faces were hidden behind white or blue surgical masks, to keep out the choking dust and pollution. It occurred to me that I wasn't watching some frantic exodus or emergency—this happened every day. The Wild West rough and tumble of Taiwan had once been my benchmark of utterly foreign places. Now China made downtown Taipei look like New York's Central Park.

I had no idea where to go or what to do. My only instructions had been to wait for Mr. Pu outside the train station, located within walking distance of the border, which I did for nearly an hour before a taxi honked and flashed its lights. It was Pu, waving. We were late, he told me. Off we sped to a dealer's showroom, Pu talking loudly in Chinese on his black Motorola flip phone, its antenna pulled all the way out and occasionally getting tangled in the taxi's side grab handles.

The dealer we wanted to visit lived several hours outside of Shenzhen. I closed my eyes for a bit of rest until we arrived. When we finally got to the dealer I was surprised. Instead of an upscale front entrance with speakers and equipment on display and separate sound rooms in the back, as at all the high-end retail dealers I'd seen so far, this place was little more than a single room—it couldn't have been more than a few hundred square feet—crammed with more loudspeakers than I'd ever imagined could simultaneously occupy so small a space. Nearly blocking the front door was a small couch that faced this forest of speakers, which were arranged in a semicircle on three rising tiers, like seats in a raked theater. Atop every speaker was a small sign in Chinese; eventually, I figured out that customers would just call out the number of the speaker pair they wanted to listen to. In the States and everywhere else I'd visited, dealers took great care to properly set up speakers in their showrooms so that customers could hear them at their best. This was the opposite. I couldn't imagine how anyone could make a purchase decision based on sound quality in this jumble of boxes. For one thing, this entire setup flew in the face of all the hard work Arnie and I did adjusting one pair of stereo speakers in a customer's home for audio perfection, let alone 20 pairs arranged in tiers like singers in a chorus.

I heard Pu's raised voice from the next room. Through a small window I could see him in the dealer's office, alternately pounding his fist into his open palm and pointing at the dealer as he kept yelling. I figured this must have been Pu's way of collecting money or demanding more sales. That evening, after we'd left the dealer and gone out for dinner, I learned it was the former.

When our cab arrived at the restaurant, a burly man holding a menacing-looking metal baton used his other hand to open the cab's door. Pu informed me that in this city, the club was needed to keep unsavory types from entering the restaurant—a bit different from the "no shirt, no shoes, no service" signs I was used to in the States. Dinner that evening was with the dealer we'd visited that afternoon, as well as two others new to me. Either the dealer had paid up, or he and Pu had come to some sort of agreement. There were no more harsh words; at the dinner table, all was grins and laughter.

Food in China was always problematic for me because so much of it included meat—pork, chicken, beef, ducks, dog, and God knows what else. And at that stage of my life, the only meat I ate was fish (now I don't even eat that). Fortunately for my tender stomach, I was able to opt out of the plates of crispy fried duck feet, pig ears, pig feet, and other delicacies by reminding them that I was a pescatarian. Besides, after my sushi debacle in Japan I was being as cautious and reserved about any boasting or eating challenges as I could possibly manage.

"Why you not eat meat? Pig good for you. Tasty!" taunted Pu.

My avoidance of meat was a constant vexation to Pu, whose delight in eating anything and everything was vigorous, to say the least. I'd told him I had concerns about my health and about animal rights, but he could never quite wrap his head around that. It was clear that evening that Pu had told the others of my dietary habits—every time he challenged me to eat a meat dish and I refused, they seemed to have a good laugh at my expense. I didn't mind. I knew that most people found vegetarians strange, and it was all in good fun. But Pu seemed determined to trap me into eating something I didn't want. To him it was a game, a challenge, and he was determined to win. I, on the other hand, was determined not to play. Once burned, I sure didn't want to go through that again, especially not here in China. Japan is very first-world in their food supply and sanitation requirements. In this part of China, though, I felt about as squeamish as I had ever been. The restaurant seemed to have no worries about the buzzing flies, scraps of food littering the floor, packs of stray dogs lurking in the shadows in the hopes of a few morsels of food, unwashed hands, and less than sanitary conditions.

"What about snake?"

"No." Clearly, a snake was an animal. I still stood on solid ground. There was no way Pu was going to trap me in his snare.

"Fish?"

"Sure."

I felt almost safe eating fish. This restaurant had a big saltwater tank in which fish dinners swam, waiting for diners to choose them. That seemed fresh enough, but the idea of choosing which fish would die for my sake freaked me out. It's one thing to pick out a prepacked fish or slab of meat in the supermarket's meat section, and quite another to actually see the animal alive just before its demise. In fact, I remember the first time one of my four sons made the connection between packaged meat and the real animal.

"Hey Dad," said my youngest, Rob, picking up a pack of chicken breasts in the meat department. Rob was just learning to read that year. "The 'chicken' on this pack of meat is spelled the same as the chickens they brought to our class. That's funny."

"That's because they are the same, buddy." I don't think Rob touched another piece of cooked chicken for quite some time after that revelation, though in the end, the fried and breaded chunks of meat known as chicken nuggets got the better of him.

I was hoping we could skip the part of choosing which creature was to become dinner and head right for the vegetables, rice, and noodles, but Pu was determined.

"Sea snake?"

I wanted nothing to do with snakes, regardless of where they came from. But by now there'd been too much laughter at my expense. I had my pride.

"Sure. Sea snake. It's okay," I said bravely.

Or stupidly. No sooner had the words left my tongue than the memory of that sushi night, where I rolled in agony, came rushing back. But it was too late: the die had been cast. Soon, a waiter approached with a bucket of sloshing sea water. Pu directed him to me, and the waiter held up the bucket for my inspection. Sure enough, staring back at me was a damned snake, complete with beady black eyes and fangs, which it bared, looking ready to strike. Pu was definitely getting the best of me with this one.

Again I tried to be brave, now realizing Pu had me by the short hairs. "Okay ..." I said weakly. The waiter left with the bucket and soon returned with the snake, now cooked and coiled around a whole pineapple. Between its jaws was a red cherry.

Pu smiled. "For you. Eat!"

Our three guests stared at me, their faces not betraying the slightest hint of a smile or an expression. It was like the distant stare of onlookers at an auto accident: riveted, unsure what to expect. I picked at the snake, pulling off a chunk of meat that seemed mostly vertebrae. A small flake of white flesh stuck to one chopstick, and I looked back up at the guests.

Pu was nodding his head "Yes," while the others gripped the edge of the table. The memory of the crowd waiting for me to take a bite of that snotty-nato slime in the Japanese restaurant came rushing back. No backing out now.

It didn't taste quite like chicken — more like tuna, but greasy. A piece of black snakeskin still clinging to the meat draped my lower lip. I closed my eyes and sucked it in, slimy skin and meat, and swallowed the whole clump before reaching for my water glass to wash it down. That bite was all that was needed to preserve my honor — the others quickly devoured what was left, along with half the pineapple, before the waiter removed the plate still replete with the ghastly remains of snake spine wrapped around what remained of the pineapple. Dinner was almost over but I wasn't yet done.

Traditionally, in China, fruit and tea are served at the end of a meal, but I just couldn't let Pu's challenge go. They'd had their fun at my expense. Now it was my turn. Hoping to gain the upper hand, I asked Pu if he might join me in some wine. I knew he didn't drink, and I suspected the others didn't either. Pu shook his head, and I struck.

"You made me eat that damned snake," I said. "Now it's time for me, your guest, to enjoy some of my own pleasures with my new friends." I pointed to the dealers.

Pu's eyes narrowed as he sensed my plan and I could almost see his mind spinning with possible defenses to this counter challenge. His mouth tightened into a knowing smile and he reluctantly ordered a round of drinks. Now I had him. He was mine. My plan was simple. We'd *kanpai* the drinks: each man had to down his entire beverage in a single gulp and then refill the glass, something I knew Pu would not be happy doing. I intended to repeat this until I saw a look of defeat on his face. I watched his every move, studying his face for the tiniest of clues he might have something up his sleeve, but I sensed nothing. I had the upper hand in this fight and he was trapped. There might be other battles to be fought in the future, but this one was mine. Victory was near. As I raised the glass of colorless liquid in a toast, I caught a whiff of the foulest stench I'd ever smelled — a cross between turpentine and puke, which was what I suddenly felt like doing. If I had thought the open-sewer smell of the nato was bad, this was off the charts awful. With a big, shit-eating grin, Pu emptied his glass. So did the others, before returning their fascinated gaze back at me in anticipation of my suffering. No! How had he done this? How could he have turned the tables yet again and gotten the best of me? Would there never be a winning hand I could play with Pu? Dammit. I was committed. Careful not to smell the stuff again, I slugged it down and nearly gagged as it burned and tossed my stomach in a knot.

"What the hell was that?"

"Wine." Pu smirked. He had won again.

"That's not like any wine I've ever tasted. Show me the bottle."

There was no bottle. We rose from the table. Pu led me into the bar and pointed to a big, multi-gallon glass jar like the ones seen in some American bars, full of pickles or pickled eggs. This one was filled with what looked like the same clear liquid we'd just drunk, and floating on the surface were dozens of dead, flattened lizards. As I realized what I'd just drunk—lizard blood wine—my stomach waved the white flag and it was all I could do not to hurl on the spot. Pu had gotten the best of me again. I could have left the battle in his favor at the sea snake and been done with the whole affair, but no. I had to try and get the upper hand with Pu and lost. Now his victory was even sweeter, with my defeat complete.

I hadn't succeeded at getting Pu back for his food taunts that night, but at least I had a decent night's sleep in my cozy Hong Kong hotel room to look forward to, and later that afternoon I would wing my way home again. If I wanted to win at my silly game of besting Pu I'd wait until he was on my own turf to strike. In Colorado there was always the possibility of springing Rocky Mountain Oysters on Pu: deep fried bull's balls. I realized trying to beat a master at his game while in his realm was foolhardy at best. Time to put it to bed, as well as myself. I would make sure breakfast the next morning was the British version, just to reset my food clock from Pu's snake assault.

Then everything started to go wrong with my return plans. Between

304

the sea snake and the lizard-blood wine, the night had slipped away, and it was now past 10 pm.

"No train now," said Pu. His eyebrows rose in concern when I asked him about getting back to the train station. Oh crap. This all had a familiar ring to it. The last time we overstayed our welcome was in Tainan and Pu put me on the bus ride from hell. This wasn't going to plan. I hadn't packed a bag because I hadn't planned on spending the night in this faraway province of China. Not only did I have no change of clothes or a place to stay, I had a full day's worth of appointments scheduled for HK tomorrow, followed by an afternoon's flight home.

"No problem," said Pu. "You take ferry home first thing in morning. It land at nine. You okay."

I wasn't okay. Pu and his buddies were heading to the clubs and Lord knew what else. I've never been much of a nightlife person, preferring the quiet of a hotel room or maybe an evening spent with friends and a few glasses of wine. Bars, strip joints, massage parlors, whatever it is other people do when they're away from home—doesn't attract me. And I was tired—catching up on work and sleep sounded good.

Pu said he knew what to do, and flipped open his phone. A few hasty calls later, a rickety red and yellow Toyota taxi cab pulled up in front of us, the passenger door popped open seemingly of its own accord. The strong smell of stale cigarette smoke wafted out of the rear passenger compartment.

Pu sidled up next to me and said in a quiet voice: "You put wallet and passport in front pocket. You okay. No sleep until hotel." His eyes and head beckoned knowingly towards the cab driver as if I was supposed to understand what this meant.

"What?" I asked. "What do you mean? What's wrong with this guy?"

"No, no, no," Pu laughed and pushed my head down so as not to bump it on the car's frame as he coaxed me into the back seat. "You okay. Just be careful."

Careful? Careful of what? But it was too late for questions. I was packed into the rear seat of the cab with only my briefcase and Pu's instructions for the next morning. He'd paid the driver to take me to a

305

hotel very near the Fu Yong Ferry Terminal, next to Shenzhen Airport. Pu knew I had no local currency—he'd generously prepaid for the hotel, and even for an early-morning cab ride to the terminal, also prearranged.

This all was way too similar to that bus ride in Taiwan with the serial killer. At least on that bus I wasn't the only passenger. This time around, I found myself alone and locked in the back of some stranger's vehicle heading to God knows where with instructions from Pu to watch my wallet and passport.

"You be okay," he assured me.

Off we sped into the night and the welter of honking horns, bicycles, and tractors that zigzagged through the crowded streets. My driver spoke no English. I spoke no Chinese.

Soon we'd left the faraway province and were on a dark highway heading for parts unknown. Pu had done it again. He got me twice at dinner and now this was to be my dessert. A lonely cab ride in a rattle trap smoke-filled car in the middle of nowhere.

"Eeeh, eeh, eeeh!" The sharp tension-filled violin attacks from Hitchcock's slasher film *Psycho* resonated in my head. I struggled to position myself as low in the seat as I could without losing sight of the rearview mirror. I'd noticed the driver watching my every move in that mirror, in the same way the bus-driving serial killer had. Each time our eyes met, the taxi driver's upper lip curled to expose a missing front tooth. It wasn't a Norman Bates look, but it still creeped me out. I glimpsed small gulps of the driver's face through the mirror. His hair was the color of his intense eyes, jet black, and greased back in a tight bun, ending in a short ponytail that mashed against the car's tattered head rest with every passing bump in the road. His heavily pockmarked face was decorated with a black stubble just above his narrow chin and there was the hint of a mustache vying for purchase just below his meaty nose. Was he trying to smile when he bared that single tooth? I couldn't tell if it was a nervous tic or some sort of threatening move. After each stare at the back seat he'd mutter something and return his gaze to the nearly empty highway before lighting another smoke. There were no streetlights and the darkness felt as if it were closing in like a death shroud. Only the red glow from his cigarette illuminated his face.

I had no idea what was happening, or even if something was happening. All I knew was that I was headed ever deeper into a country utterly foreign to me, driven by a strange man who kept his eyes glued on me. I had no cell phone, a rarity back then that worked only in the country where you paid your bill. What would I do if he pulled off the road and demanded my wallet or, worse, my passport? Pu had said to watch my passport and I'd read an article about the burgeoning black market in China for US passports. I'd also read an article about a black market in human organs. There were no police to be seen and even if there were, it was highly unlikely they spoke English. Few here did.

I searched every inch of the passenger compartment for a way out. The doors were locked and only the driver could release those door locks. Why had Pu warned me to watch myself and the few possessions I had? I trusted Pu, and while he had already sent me on a crazy ride in Taiwan and tortured me at dinner, I didn't believe for a moment he would knowingly put me in harm's way. No, he wouldn't do that. He was my friend. But then maybe cabs were all a bit shaky in this part of the world and he was just watching out for me. Yes, perhaps that was it. A rough neighborhood. The guard outside the restaurant wielded a club to keep unsavory types away so, clearly, that was not the town of Mayberry. Not good. I was on my own with a cautious reminder from my friend to be on my guard. I began to plan my escape.

Plan A depended on the driver reaching into the back seat for my belongings. In this cab there was no barrier like one might find in its New York City counterpart. I would hand him my wallet and briefcase, and hope he'd then just throw me out of the cab without asking for my passport. I'd fumble my way out of China from there. Somehow.

Plan B would go into effect if he wanted my passport, or got out and came around to open a rear door. If he demanded my passport, I'd refuse, leap into the front seat, and either take his cab or hightail it out the door. I hoped.

Meanwhile, my hands were wet with sweat, my stomach heavy with lead, the road seemed to be taking us into ever darker, more remote country, and his lip curled higher, that missing tooth more obvious now than ever. The driver mumbled something unintelligible and pulled off the road. Oh crap. This was it.

Banjos played in my head as they did in the movie *Deliverance*. My worst nightmare. Plan A or Plan B? The little car trundled off the pavement and onto a small turnout tucked down a short incline. It was pitch black outside and we seemed the only car on the road.

"What's wrong?" I asked as he turned off the engine and the air conditioning stopped.

His cold black eyes looked me over in the rearview mirror, but he said nothing and then rolled down his window.

"Are we okay?" I said, trying my own windows, which seemed locked.

Still nothing. This time my question didn't even warrant a set of cold eyes. The windows didn't work so I checked the doors again and could see in the dim illumination of the taxi's dome light that the locks were still engaged. I was trapped. Really trapped.

He cleared his throat and gagged up a wad of mucus before spitting it out the window, then lit another cigarette. He seemed intent on some papers in the front seat.

My hand gripped the plastic handle of my briefcase. It'd be a good weapon across his head if the occasion warranted it. He wasn't that big of a man. Small, actually, but wiry. It was hard to tell about people's strength. It's usually driven by their determination to get what they want, but I had no clue what this man wanted. At that very moment it didn't seem to matter. It was just the two of us on a dark night in the middle of nowhere, China. The cabin lit up with the lights of a passing truck that shook the car as it rumbled past, then it was quiet again. My driver seemed more concerned about the papers than me. Perhaps we were lost. This was, after all, before the advent of Google Maps or even Google itself. Hell, this was before anyone I knew had even heard of the World Wide Web.

The man mumbled something in Chinese, lit yet another cigarette, cranked over the engine, pushed in the clutch, and crawled back onto the lonely highway, and we motored along as if nothing had happened. I was sweating, and my hand was still shaking, but my blood pressure lowered. Then, as we crested a small rise, as if in a scene of redemption, I saw lights. In the distance was what appeared to be the airport, a twinkling shard of civilization in a sea of black unknown.

We pulled in front of a dilapidated three-story building of cement block, with a flickering neon sign in red-and-green Chinese characters. There were no other buildings around. I stepped out and saw moths circled the blinking lights. The driver pointed at his watch, then at the hotel's front door—I took this to mean that he'd pick me up early the next morning. He flicked the glowing butt of his cigarette out the window and drove off, leaving me standing alone with nothing more than my briefcase and the last embers of that smoke. Where the hell was I? This really felt like the Bates Motel.

I entered and found myself in a dark room with what looked like a front counter. This was definitely not the Ritz-Carlton. I heard something rattle behind the counter and leaned over to check it out. There sat a short, plump man in a sweat-soaked, sleeveless T-shirt, his head down on his folded arms, asleep. He didn't look anything like Norman Bates, so I cleared my throat loudly enough to wake him.

His bloodshot eyes opened wide, then narrowed. Definitely not Norman Bates. He put out one hand. I pulled a credit card from my wallet, but he scowled and stuck out his hand again. My passport? Indeed. He wrote something down, gave me back my passport and a key, laid his head down, and went back to sleep.

Fortunately, written on the key was something I could understand: "4." I stumbled up dark stairs reeking of disinfectant and unlocked door Number Four. Inside the room, which couldn't have measured more than 50 feet square, the only source of light was a flickering yellow fluorescent bulb above the door. On the right, hard against the wall, was a single bed covered with a gray, dingy sheet. At its head was a striped pillow—no pillowcase. Folded at the foot of the bed was a faded blanket the color of canned peas. In the far left corner were a washstand and, unfettered by walls or even a stall, a toilet. I drew aside what looked like window curtains, but behind them was only more wall.

I looked at my watch: 11 pm. Tomorrow's ferry was scheduled to sail at 6 am, and I'd need to be there by five. I set my fold-up alarm clock—a gift from my son Sean—for 4 am and put it on the floor, next to the bed. I'd already promised myself that I wouldn't use that toilet for anything other than pee or crawl under that green blanket, even with my clothes on. I was afraid to lay my head on the pillow, but the grimy sheet over the mattress didn't look much better. I switched off the light and lay down.

The room was utterly dark—the only source of light was the faint green glow of my alarm clock's dial. I closed my eyes and tried to sleep, focusing on the tick-tock of the clock, but soon it was interrupted by a chorus of scratching noises from the far side of the room: chh-chhh-chh. I sat upright, flicked on the light, and the noise stopped. All was dead quiet again, save for my ticking clock. I switched the light off. This damned place was haunted. I knew it.

As my breathing slowed, the scratching returned. What the hell? A captive's desperate nail scratching to escape their prison? If memory served correctly, Norman Bates wasn't interested in imprisoning people, just slashing them. It sounded as if it were coming from below the floor. The yellow flicker of the fluorescent again silenced the noise.

I decided to try something different. I held the dial of my clock up to the room light, to recharge its phosphorescence, then set down the clock at the far end of the room and once more switched off the light. As I stared into inky black until my eyes adjusted, the scratching came again.

"Hello?" I said meekly into the darkness.

The scratching stopped at the sound of my voice but then continued in earnest. Sleep was now the last thing on my mind. Clearly, I was not alone.

Quietly, I sat up and peered at the clock. Silhouetted against its faint green glow I could see a caravan of dark objects passing back and forth. I swung my legs over the side of the bed and, on my knees, crawled closer to the light. These creeping things had antennae, and seemed suddenly alert to my presence. I turned on the light to see hundreds of cockroaches fleeing across the floor. They were everywhere, waiting for the darkness that set them free. But these were no ordinary cockroaches. No, these Chinese beasts were easily twice the size of the biggest, nastiest, cockroaches I'd ever seen. Bigger still than the monsters Georgia had to offer. They were enormous and powerful, looking as if they might have been holdovers from a Japanese sci-fi movie where radiation poisoning had mutated them like Godzilla. The only thing keeping them from me seemed to be the room light, but that could easily change as they became acclimated to my presence. What did they want? Surely it was food. Or me.

I couldn't sleep thinking about the army of clicking, clacking monstrous beetles that might soon invade my bed. To make matters worse, our family physician and the kids' godfather, Stu Weiss, worried for my health on this first overseas trip, had warned me about contact with cockroaches. Turns out they are natural carriers of pathogens like typhoid, polio, and dysentery. The prospect of spending my 13-hour flight home locked in the airplane bathroom, sweating out a bout of dysentery, had little appeal.

I tried closing my eyes and dreaming about something other than invaders, but just before sleep I would wake up from the same nightmare of being covered in black, wiggly cockroaches, nibbling on my clothes, smothering my face, releasing their pathogens, and procreating in my hair. I tried over and over again to catch a few winks, but the effort was useless. I would have to remain awake and vigilant until the dawn's early light.

CHAPTER 54

MORNING COULDN'T COME soon enough, and though it took its time, it eventually did arrive. I stood in front of the hotel in the cool of the morning, hoping the weird taxi driver would actually show up. Sure enough, at 5 AM he arrived, rolled down his window, motioned with his thumb for me to get in the back, and curled the right half of his upper lip, exposing that missing tooth. I do believe he was trying to smile.

Fu Yong Ferry Terminal is at the end of a long cul-de-sac within view of Shenzhen Airport, and at 5:30 that morning the nondescript, single-story building of gray cement looked deserted. The driver let me out and drove away. As I watched his red taillights disappear in the morning's gray light, I realized that my last chance of transportation was gone. I was on my own with no luggage, no language, and only $20 in cash and a few credit cards. I hoped the ferry people took American credit cards.

I could smell the salt sea air and hear the quiet bickering of seagulls in the early-morning gray. Inside the terminal there was not a soul to be seen, which seemed odd—the ferry to Hong Kong was scheduled to leave in half an hour. To my right were three glass office windows, and set up inside each one was a marquee of green felt, its rows of grooves filled with Chinese characters on white plastic pushpins. I cupped my hands around my eyes and peered through one window. Inside the dark ticket office was a single unoccupied barstool—nothing and no one else.

Behind me I heard a hacking cough. I went around a corner, toward what looked like the gangway to the ferry, and saw an old man curled up on the floor, his head laid directly on the cold slabs, back against the wall, and feet curled under his coat for warmth. To his left, on a tripod easel, was a sign in English and Chinese: "Typhoon warning. ferry closed."

Well wasn't that just the icing atop the cake? All I had gone through to arrive on time at this miserable ferry station and it was closed. I had no idea what to do. I had no cell phone, I didn't speak the language, and even if I did, there seemed to be no one around to speak it to. Nor was there a telephone in sight. The nearest suggestion of civilization was Shenzhen Airport: close enough to see through the morning fog, but easily an hour's hike through unknown territory, and no guarantee of what might or might not happen when I got there. Other than the likelihood of more humans, I wasn't sure what the airport could offer that the ferry terminal didn't. Did they even have a commuter flight to neighboring Hong Kong?

My flight back to the States left Kai Tak Airport later that afternoon, and before that I had to get my luggage, still waiting for me in the Marco Polo Hotel several hours away by car—and days away on foot. Possibilities flitted through my mind so quickly that I realized I was beginning to panic. Hoof it down the quarter-mile of road separating me from the highway and hitchhike to Hong Kong? Walk the several miles to the airport and hope for the best? Curl up on the floor like this poor coughing man in the hall and wait for the typhoon to pass? No option seemed good.

I decided to explore the terminal. Maybe I could find a dockhand in the back, near the water—or maybe another unlucky traveler would arrive to discover the ferry closed, and I could…we could…well, I didn't know what. Soon I again stood at the terminal entrance, just as the sun rose above the distant black rolling hills to the east. It would be another hot day. To my right, hazy in the distance, was the airport; to my left, signs pointed toward the back of the terminal. I followed them and found three parked cars—and just past them, in a darkened alley, three men clustered around a small portable table. Two seemed engaged in a thoughtful game of backgammon; the third watched and smoked a cigarette. As I approached, all three stopped what they were doing and looked up.

"Do any of you speak English?"

The backgammon players shook their heads and returned to their game. The smoker took a long drag and exhaled a cloud of smoke. "I. A little." He was of average height and shaped like a string bean, his black hair pulled tight into a short ponytail.

"I need to get to Hong Kong."

He cocked his head inquisitively.

"Hong. Kong." I spoke more slowly, and a little louder. I don't know why most people's first reaction to not being understood is to speak louder, as if the person being spoken to might have a hearing problem, but I was no different. Slower is good; louder is an insult.

"No Hong Kong. Typhoon."

I pointed at my chest. "Me. Hong Kong." I pulled out my wallet and dangled before him the only cash my wallet contained: a US $20 bill. As all three pairs of eyes fixed first on the bill, and then on me, it occurred to me that this might not have been the smartest move I'd ever made. Alone in a dark alley with three strangers, a stupid American opens his wallet and starts waving cash around. I returned the wallet to my pocket, held out the twenty, and backed up slightly. The smoker took a final drag, crushed the butt under one sandal, and stepped toward me.

"Shenzhen." He swept one arm from my general direction toward one of the cars.

"Hong Kong," I repeated.

He shook his head and pointed again to the car. "Shenzhen."

What the hell. By now it was clear that anywhere was better than the terminal, and he didn't seem all that threatening—kind of skinny, and maybe 20 years older than I was. If push came to shove, I thought I could hold my own. Then again, maybe he was some sort of martial arts master who'd drive me out to the sticks, beat me up, and rob me. But while caution is always a good idea, something told me my driver was okay. His eyes never seemed to open wider than cracks, but from what I could see, they were gentle. I got into the passenger seat.

Soon we were motoring along the highway, the driver zigzagging among the occasional Mercedes, BMW, or Lexus, the many trucks filled with pigs, and one truck that left a white trail of chicken feathers, as the wind cleaned out dozens of cages in which squawked hundreds of alarmed-looking birds.

We didn't share enough language to speak, but I could tell from his old Toyota's sparse interior that my driver wasn't wealthy. Thin red curtains weighted at their bottoms with rows of white beads covered the two rear-door windows. The seats were covered in thick, clear plastic yellowed with age and sun, and on his dash sat a fat plastic Buddha. Dangling

314

from the rearview mirror on a gossamer red string was a small crystal sphere that swayed and sparkled in the sun. When we jerked to a stop in traffic, it just missed the head of the Buddha.

We'd been on the road for more than an hour, but my worries about this man eased as we headed back into civilization and away from the rural roughness of Fu Yong. Soon we were deep in Shenzhen, which like Las Vegas never seems to sleep. Bicycles flooded the sidewalks and streets. Directly ahead of us was a motorcycle bearing a helmeted rider and two cages filled with what looked like dozens of cocker spaniels. I knew their fate. The day before, when we were passed by a similar transport of fluffy yellow dogs, Pu had explained in one word: "Dinner."

The driver flashed his right blinker, and we turned up a ramp to the front of a long, tall, glass-fronted building with gray cement columns and a row of flags I didn't recognize. People streamed in and out. It was Shenzhen Railway Station—now I understood what he'd meant when he'd said "Shenzhen." From here I could get a train to Hong Kong. Life would be good again.

He pulled up to the curb and stopped. He'd driven a total stranger for nearly an hour and a half to get to the station, and now he'd have to make the return trip to his friends and their game. I wished I had a crisp $100 bill to give him, but all I had to pay for three hours of his time and a tankful of gas were a $20 bill and my business card. I doubted he had the means to contact me, but giving him my card at least made me feel a bit less guilty.

He refused the money. Thinking he hadn't understood, I placed the bill on the seat next to him. He picked it up and gave it back to me with a big smile. Then he lowered his eyes and folded his hands, his fingertips touching his nose in that beautiful Asian gesture of thanks. I fumbled as I repeated the gesture back to him and lowered my own eyes, the twenty still pressed between my palms. As he pulled away from the curb, I waved, but he didn't wave back. I watched his car descend the ramp, to be swallowed again into the endless *mêlée* of Shenzhen traffic.

That afternoon, as I sat in the terminal of Kai Tak Airport with my fancy Western luggage, all my appointments canceled, apologies made, waiting to board the shiny new Boeing 747 that would take me back to

San Francisco and then on to Denver, all I could think of was the man who'd driven me to Shenzhen Railway Station. That may have been the kindest thing anyone has ever done for me, and I wish I could reach out and touch his gentle soul one more time.

He changed my life that day. I'd been scared to death of being stranded in a strange land full of strange people, but his act of unselfish kindness helped me realize that we are all in this together, and that the most rewarding things we can do—the things that enrich the lives of those around us, and our own lives at the same time—are acts of kindness with no thought of return. I decided that I would teach what I could, and write, to share what knowledge I have—to bring love, not hate, to the world; to sidestep negative energy and focus on the positive.

My first business trip abroad was a rite of passage that, nearly 30 years later, I'm still grateful for. If I had the chance to do it over, I wouldn't change a thing.

CHAPTER 55

OVER THE NEXT FEW YEARS I traveled often to Europe and Asia for Genesis, honing my skills in setting up loudspeakers and learning the ropes of international distribution, the importance of face-to-face meetings, and the power of personal relationships. What brought me the greatest joy was being in a position to improve the listening lives of this international community of audiophiles — to be counted among them and accepted, even welcomed, into the group.

But despite the hard work and years of struggle, Genesis never really hit its stride. Arnie Nudell and I were undercapitalized from the beginning. Pu's money had been only enough to extricate us from API and buy our shares back, so we limped along, with too little profit and too much overhead for a company as small as ours. We'd made the first of many classic mistakes companies fall prey to: we tried to grow in a hurry by investing more money than we should have in marketing, warehouse inventory levels, our own executive salaries, the purchase of a new building, and travel.

Soon, fingers were pointing in all directions — none of us wanted to take the blame for the lack of profits and cash — and going to work soon became a chore. Even my weekend ski job wasn't helping. So, seven years after starting Genesis with my buddy Arnie, I decided it was best for all concerned if I moved on. I wanted to get back to my first love, electronics, and in 1997, Arnie and I parted ways. Arnie kept Genesis, and I started over. As always, Terri was there through it all, encouraging me to take the plunge and make the choice for our family. She and Arnie had long ago disagreed over the way he wanted the business run and a year earlier she had left her job managing the office and the company's accounting.

My exit from Genesis was not an easy transition. There were lots of hard feelings between me and Arnie. We were angry with each other, each laying blame on the other for the collapse of the company, and the pain of separation cut deep. We did not speak to each other again for five years.

Just before I left Genesis, Dad died. His years of smoking tobacco had given him emphysema, a withering disease that slowly starves organs of oxygen—a terrible way to go. Mom died soon after. Her health, too, had been destroyed by years of smoking. My father had struggled with many personal limitations in his life, but for him perhaps the hardest thing was praising others or sharing his warmth with them—particularly me. He did live long enough to see me succeed and be able to take care of my family, and though he never told me so, I like to think that it brought him some measure of pride. Still, it would be years more before I would forgive him and begin to understand his generation and the way they felt toward their children.

My father's generation believed in the adage "spare the rod and spoil the child." Too much praise, it was feared, would swell a child's head. They believed it to be in their children's best interest to keep them in their place, to make sure they never got cocksure or enjoyed themselves too much—pleasure was a sure path to the Devil. I wish I'd understood all that earlier. If I had, I might have been able to forgive my father and remove the lifetime of blame I had mentally heaped on him before he died. Like all of us, he was the product of a world he didn't create and a life that he struggled to control. I blamed him for being who he was, instead of blaming the world that he had known and that had made him. I should have known better—long before, I'd figured out that my father was a fraud in the ways we are all frauds, in the ways that I'm a fraud. In his novel *East of Eden*, John Steinbeck said it far better than I can:

> When a child first catches adults out—when it first walks into his grave little head that adults do not have divine intelligence, that their judgments are not always wise, their thinking true, their sentences just—his world falls into panic desolation. The gods are fallen and all safety gone. And there is one sure thing about the fall of gods: they do not fall a little; they crash and shatter or sink deeply into green muck. It is a tedious job to build them up again; they never quite shine. And the child's

318

world is never quite whole again. It is an aching kind of growing.

When I got the call from my younger sister Bobbi that Dad had died, I wanted only to be alone. I drove into the hills above a stretch of I-70 near Wolcott, Colorado, parked the car on a steep incline hidden from the world, and wept — as I'd wept years before, on the dunes, when Infinitizer died, and again when I sold PS Audio. But this was a different kind of mourning, and at first it frightened me. It seemed so selfish: my tears were less for my father than for myself. Now I was the next in line to die, and that frightened me even more. We all "know" we're going to die, but none of us actually believes it. It's something that happens to other people. But now death had come very close to me, and I was shaken. It wasn't until a few years later that I could allow myself to believe that Dad might have been proud of me, although I'd come to peace with the knowledge that, even if he was, he could never have told me.

Our childhood years remain formative, well into adulthood. As parents, we're handed our babies without benefit of an instruction manual, relying instead on convention, the advice of friends, and our own well-intentioned parents. Yet conventions and advice aside, I'm convinced that every parent struggles with how much love and attention to offer his or her child, and how to balance that with guidance, denial, and punishment. On the one hand, we understand that children, unlike, say, young birds, need many years before they can survive on their own. In nurturing and protecting them, I think we can justify almost any behavior except the outward expression of love. It's hard to think of love as a protective measure — we're often alarmed that too much of it, too much coddling, will weaken our children and make them soft, incapable adults. That's certainly what my father believed, anyway.

Like so many of us, I've been both a child of parents and a parent of children. For whatever it may be worth, my experience has taught me that there cannot be too much love for and attention to children. The dreaded "spoiled brat" isn't the result of too much love and attention, but of too little trust and guidance. By guidance, I don't mean punishment — it's easy to confuse the two. I don't believe that Terri and I ever punished

319

one of our children for anything. We drew boundary lines, and made clear the consequences of stepping over them—but whippings, beatings, slaps, deprivations, or any sort of isolation longer than 60 seconds were not among them. Instead, we rewarded good behavior, and pointed out the consequences of bad.

In the families Terri and I grew up in, punishment for wrongdoing was more important than rewarding honesty. We wanted our own kids to respect the truth, but it seemed illogical to us to punish them for lying if eventually they did tell us the truth. Hence the McGowan Rule: "Tell the truth, and there will be no punishment for crimes committed, no matter how heinous."

When he was six years old our son Scott sprayed a streak of red paint down the white side of my brand-new Ford Thunderbird. As soon as he realized the damage he'd caused, and how angry I'd be, he ran. Then he remembered the Rule. Scott believed his parents' word, gathered his courage, and told Terri what he'd done. A quick application of paint thinner repaired the damage. Scott was assigned some chores in the family paint shed for what he'd done, but we never punished him. Today, Scott is in line to run PS Audio. A finer, more responsible, and more loving young man cannot be found.

I've seen some people treat their pets better than they do their children. I'd have to place my father in that category, if for no other reason than my painful memories of lying face-down on the bed, butt bared, paralyzed by the sound of his belt slithering from his pant loops. Terri and I are both committed to breaking the abusive pattern of arbitrary punishment—of the once-punished becoming the next generation of punishers, and on and on—by lavishing love and attention on our sons, our grandchildren, our relatives, and on the community we revere as extended family: our customers, employees, and vendors.

Now, in what seemed like our hundredth time at bat, it was just Terri and me on our own again, our four sons excited to see what new course we'd take to support our family. As has happened so many times in our life, when we choose to move toward change, things—life, the universe, call it what you will—seemed to accommodate us. No sooner had we decided to leave Genesis Technologies than we learned that the partners who'd bought PS Audio from us seven years before, Randy Patton and Steve Jeffery, had just gone through a rather heated business divorce. PS Audio soon collapsed, and eventually it went bankrupt.

So in 1997, for the princely sum of $1, Terri and I repurchased the brand name PS Audio from Steve and relaunched the company on a shoestring. That is hardly an exaggeration. We needed $150,000 in cash to get PS Audio back on its feet, and we didn't have it. Terri and I discussed getting a second mortgage on the house, but I was now unemployed—no bank would touch us.

Following the near collapse of the US banking system in the mid-1990s, the economy had bounced back, and credit card companies were hungry for business. Our mailbox was constantly filled with offers of "free cash," zero-interest credit cards, and lines of instant credit, all to be had for a signature. I knew that in those early days of computer technology, before online banking, banks still used paper files and ledgers. A bank's right hand thus didn't know what its left hand was doing. Over the next few months we collected 30 or so credit card offers, filled them out, then mailed them in all at once. Before the banks had figured it out, we'd amassed more than $150,000 in unsecured credit—about $150,000 more than any bank was willing to lend us.

Money in our pockets and spirits renewed, our next challenge was to figure out what the new PS Audio's first product would be and how we would sell it. Terri and I and our four boys, now aged 12 to 17, were living on borrowed money and borrowed time. Needless to say, the pressure to reestablish PS Audio in the marketplace and earn a profit—fast—was intense.

The safest, most obvious course would have been to relaunch the products and models that PS Audio was already famous for: power amps, preamps, and DACs.

But...

CHAPTER 56

WHEN WE RELAUNCHED PS Audio in 1997, it had been seven years since I'd left the company to build speakers. Much had changed in the interim. For one thing, by 1988 CDs had overtaken LPs in sales, though most audiophiles still clung to their turntables and collections of vinyl, unwilling to make the switch, and for good reason: early digital audio sounded awful.

Sony and Philips had jointly developed the Compact Disc (CD) format, which was commercially launched in Japan in 1982, and in Europe and the US in 1983. It wasn't long before all the major record labels were releasing their new music only on CD. Record labels were happy to leave the LP behind because quality control was so much more difficult to maintain with LPs, and because it was expensive to design, produce, and distribute dual inventories of everything. So, they were glad to leave the expensive production of vinyl to history—and by 1990, vinyl seemed nearly finished as a consumer audio format. But the high-end audio community was soon in a tizzy over the poor sound quality of CDs. Sony's original marketing slogan for the Compact Disc: "Perfect Sound Forever," was salt in the wounds of many audiophiles, who'd seen a fragile, inconvenient, but dependably good-sounding playback format replaced by a far more convenient but worse-sounding one. The oft quoted chestnut "convenience trumps quality" might fit in well.

For most of us in the high-end world, the problems of the CD began with the format's launch. Expectations for "perfect sound" were high, even among those in love with vinyl. The promise of digital's great sound was intoxicating: increased dynamic range, lower distortion, no ticks or pops, and no surface noise at all. The one quality of CDs that no one questioned at first was the format's measured performance, in which CDs were claimed to be superior in every way. But in terms of sound quality—which is not directly measurable but which is, ultimately, the most important thing—early digital recordings and early CD players sounded harsh and bright compared to the lush musicality possible with the far more mature technology of vinyl. Listening to music that had been recorded and/or played back digitally often brought on exhausting listening fatigue after only a few minutes.

Today these problems have largely been addressed, but in the early 1980s they were audible in all but a few recordings, those in which artists and mastering engineers had paid extra attention to sound quality. One such recording, Dire Straits' 1985 *Brothers in Arms*, was one of the first rock albums released on CD and became the British band's biggest: it sold more than 25 million copies worldwide, nine million in the US alone. In the UK, it was the biggest-selling album of the 1980s. It was also the first album to sell a million copies on CD. *Brothers in Arms* was recorded on a new type of machine: a Sony 24-track digital audio recorder. Once recorded, the files were downmixed to two-track stereo, then transferred to CD after running through as many as 20 Neve Modules (a type of analog preamplifier and equalizer) in a row, to reduce what Dire Straits' Mark Knopfler and recording engineer Neil Dorfsman referred to as "digital harshness." Passing through so many analog "helpers" sweetened digital's hard sound—each successive Neve reshaped the sound by gently rolling off the ultrasonic frequencies. In the end, *Brothers in Arms* won three Grammy awards for recording excellence. But the album's good sound was an anomaly among early digital recordings.

Many of the sonic problems ascribed to the CD were not its fault, but were the products of mastering and recording engineers used to working in analog, many of whom were unfamiliar with digital's quirks and requirements. For example, overmodulation—driving up a recording's loudness level into the red zone of a VU meter—is an acceptable practice in analog recording, but in digital recording it results in a nasty sound like the sharp crack of a shattered walnut shell. Afraid to violate such absolute technical limitations but still wanting maximum volume, over-cautious mastering engineers used hard audio limiters to compress the sound's dynamic range: the range of sounds on a recording, from softest to loudest. The result was a homogenization of volume levels—in pop and rock music, a continuous relentless assault at more or less the same volume level throughout a recording, rather than preserving the full range of the loudest to the softest sounds, and the sounds of any and every relative volume level in between. Composers and musicians have used these ranges for millennia to create tension and release, drama and variety.

Some critics of digital music were so disappointed and offended by what they considered to be a sonic outrage that they formed committees to have the CD outlawed. One of the most memorable and vocal of these critics was Dr. John Diamond, a Fellow of the Royal Australian and New Zealand College of Psychiatry. In several lectures and demonstrations at the 1977 Conference of the International College of Applied Kinesiology, Diamond used muscle testing to demonstrate that digital audio recordings weakened the muscles of subjects exposed to it. On the basis of these findings, Dr. Diamond campaigned to ban digital recordings as a public health hazard.

Other factions of the high-end audio industry, including me, hadn't given up on the promise of digital and were determined to see it succeed. I wanted to work on the frontiers of digital audio: I felt that digital could ultimately exceed the sound quality of the best vinyl playback, though I knew it had a long way to go. But perfecting any new technology takes time, and that wasn't something we had a lot of. We still had a company to rebuild, and all Terri and I had to build with was $150,000 borrowed on very short terms.

I'd been toying with a new idea that excited me at least as much as digital did. Instead of building another line of audio playback components, as PS Audio had in the past, I felt that our chances of success would increase if I could come up with a brand-new product category—something that by definition would have no competition, at least at first. What I had in mind would not amplify or control musical signals, but would be applied to something far more basic: the AC power from a house's wall outlets.

Since the earliest days of PS Audio, I'd recognized that an audio component's sound quality was affected by the quality of power fed to it. At first this had seemed counter intuitive; after all, few other electronic products in my life seemed to care about the quality of their power.

324

My vacuum cleaner, kitchen mixer, and living-room light bulbs—even my original Kenwood integrated amplifier—seemed to perform the same, regardless of what they were plugged into. A wall socket was a wall socket, and it worked. That had changed one day in 1978, when Stan Warren called me into PS Audio's listening room for an A/B test.

As was our custom, Stan told me nothing about the comparison he was about to run. He played a track we had routinely used as reference material. Then he changed something, somewhere in the system, and played the track again. It sounded remarkably different. The sound no longer seemed trapped between the left and right speakers—it had grown in size and openness, as if the music had been under a blanket that now had been thrown off, letting the sound breathe and expand. Bass notes seemed to go deeper, and I noticed, for the first time, the initiating plucks of the electric bassist's fingers on the strings. Was it a new circuit? Some crazy tweak that we could include in one of our pending designs? Nope. What Stan had just demonstrated for me was the difference in sound made possible by switching from a smaller to a larger power transformer.

All consumer electronics that are plugged into a wall socket are isolated from a direct connection to the house's AC power supply by an internal power transformer that transfers the power magnetically. This assemblage of iron and copper serves two purposes: it keeps us safe from electrocution, and it changes—transforms—the wall current to the voltage that the particular component has been designed to be powered by. Because transformers are heavy and expensive, manufacturers try to make them no bigger or better than is required to do the job. Until Stan's moment of discovery, PS Audio had been no different: our transformers were just big enough to power our products without strain. Now he'd demonstrated to me that simply using a bigger transformer could greatly improve the sound.

Was there some way I could use that knowledge to design a component that would improve the sound quality of any component connected to it? If so, that would indeed be an interesting and attractive new product. I couldn't increase the size of the transformers already built into other manufacturers' gear, but maybe I could change and condition the power itself, before it even reached those components, in the hopes of having the same impact.

Today, power conditioners are a dime a dozen — everything from Walmart surge protectors and computer power-backup boxes to sophisticated models costing many thousands of dollars, used by laboratories and audiophiles. But in 1997 there was almost nothing designed for high-end audio gear. That vacuum looked to me like an opportunity — I could start at the very beginning of the equipment chain, design and build a new box that would regenerate AC power, and market and sell it to audiophiles. The idea sounded exciting.

I knew that the big problem with the AC power supply is that it's simultaneously shared by many users, both domestic and industrial. This is why the level of available voltage in your house changes throughout the day as you and your neighbors turn on and off your washing machines, heaters, air-conditioners, lights, computers, and TVs — each one of these devices, when in use, reduces the fixed supply of power and distorts what started out as a pure source of power being shared by all. This isn't something most of us care or even think about, because we almost never notice it — we can't tell if our lights are slightly dimmer than they were an hour ago, or if the blender is running a little slower or faster than it did yesterday. But a sensitive high-end audio system can reveal such differences in voltage level and AC sinewave purity clearly enough that music lovers who care deeply about sound quality can hear them, and know that these fluctuations are keeping them from hearing all that's on the recording. What was needed, I thought, was a way to regulate and remove the impurities of the home's power by regenerating it, thus smoothing out its irregularities by sending a steadier voltage stream on to the audio system.

Within a few months, I'd built and tested a prototype. Miraculously, it worked: any audio component plugged into my electronic AC generator sounded remarkably better than when that same component was plugged directly into the wall. By regulating the power and removing the distortion in the AC sinewave, my regenerator kept the rising and falling AC signals pure and the driving force of the AC stronger. Engineers refer to this as a lowering of impedance, as in Stan's original idea of using bigger than necessary transformers. I now had a prototype of an audio component of a breed that no other high-end audio company was making: the AC power regenerator. Two good friends—Mark Schifter and Peter Rudy—simultaneously suggested calling it the Power Plant.

I was excited to have completed the prototype and proof of concept piece, but I also realized that marketing a new type of product presented a problem: neither audiophiles nor engineers were thinking they needed better power. As far as they were concerned, the power in their homes was just fine. Why would they spend time and money fixing something that wasn't broken in the first place? This complication reminded me of a time before filtered water. When I was growing up there was no such thing as bottled or filtered water. We drank what came out of the tap without so much as a thought about taste or purity. Sure, had I been asked if the water out of a garden hose tasted different than that out of the kitchen tap the answer would be easy. Yes. But back then we didn't think about water's taste any more than we worried about how our music sounded. Over time, things change. I now had a reverse osmosis water filter to improve taste and keep out harmful chemicals, and I was extremely sensitive to how my reproduced music sounded.

I knew AC power was problematic, but few others did. I had a solution in search of a problem. In fact, the situation was worse than simple ignorance. There was downright disbelief. Once I began sharing my thoughts on the benefits of clean, regulated, AC power with my fellow engineers, their looks went from simple eyebrow lifting to outright laughter. They'd learned plenty about what makes things work, examining problems from a scientific perspective, and understanding the world around them in terms they could measure—experimental procedures and results that they could document for others to refute or, hopefully, duplicate. That's all well and good for measuring electrical impulses, or the frequencies and pressure levels of air in motion—sound waves—but it can't address how the electrical impulses created by the nerve endings in our inner ears, in response to sound waves striking the eardrum, are processed by the brain and transformed into the entirely mental phenomenon that we perceive as sound.

327

Microphones, which recordists and engineers use to capture sound waves, are electronic equivalents of human ears. My audio engineer friends and I agree on that point. Where our views of sound diverge is when we enter the little-known field of perceptual hearing. Perceptual hearing utilizes not just our ears, but our brains and imaginations as well. When we hear sounds, and music in particular, we form a mental image of those sounds and their presentation in live acoustic space. Audiophiles refer to this image as a soundstage, but it goes deeper than that. Close your eyes at this very moment and just listen. Even if you're in a quiet place, as you focus on what sounds there are around you, an image of the space you are in forms.

As I write this in my home office, in a spare basement room, I too pause to listen. An image forms of my office. Beyond its south wall is the furnace — through the drywall and studs I can hear the flame of the hot-water heater. There's the clack-clack of my two-finger typing, the clicking of the keyboard, the sound of water running through pipes in the ceiling, and a squirrel outside my window creeping through the snow. Behind me I can just make out the sounds of Terri in the kitchen upstairs. These mental images tell me about the space I'm in, in the same way a musical soundstage is recreated by a highly resolving two-channel audio system. It's formed not by the equipment — the only thing the gear itself can do is set air molecules in motion — but by my perceptual hearing mechanism of ear, brain, experience, and memory.

Science has yet to figure out how to accurately measure or quantify how this complex system of hearing works, let alone determine all that it can hear (though great progress has been made in the field in the last few years). It's an area of serious contention among subjectivists and objectivists. Basically, objectivists believe that only those aspects of sound that can be measured quantitatively should be considered in the design, manufacture, and evaluation of audio equipment and recordings. Subjectivists believe that such measurements, while useful and even crucial in audio engineering and recording, and in designing audio gear, cannot measure every nuance and subtlety the human ear can detect, and thus are ultimately less important than what the human ear actually hears.

328

In short, the objectivist believes that if an audio component measures well, then it must, by definition, sound good. To a subjectivist, a component that sounds bad still sounds bad, regardless of how impressive its measured performance may be. Basically, the two sides find themselves arguing at cross purposes because of a misunderstanding that neither side is fully aware of and that thus goes unacknowledged: the human ear-brain can't measure because it doesn't quantify, and that measuring devices can't hear because they have neither brains nor minds. In philosophy, this is called a category error, which Wikipedia defines as an error "in which things belonging to a particular category are presented as if they belong to a different category, or, alternatively, a property is ascribed to a thing that could not possibly have that property."

I understood that cleaner, less voltage-restricted AC power helps audio gear perform best. It's like cooking—the better the ingredients, the better the taste. But, how was I going to get that idea across to consumers who had never heard of such a concept? And more importantly, should we even take the gamble? It would be risky to put all our eggs in this one basket: up there with my other leaps of faith that so far hadn't worked out too well.

CHAPTER 57

I STRUGGLED WITH how to convey this idea in a marketplace unfamiliar with such concepts. I did, however, have allies: the same ones that had gotten PS Audio launched in the first place, my fellow audiophiles. Those of us who get excited about hearing recordings in higher fidelity seem willing, even anxious, to try new ideas, new products, and new concepts. The few audiophiles for whom I demonstrated my first Power Plant prototypes were easily convinced of its merits and encouraged me to go forward. Their excitement was infectious but still there was a lot at stake. Terri and I endlessly debated the merits versus risks of launching with a new and unproven product category, but we kept circling back to the same conclusion. Launching the company with a device that made everyone's stereo system a better performer was a safer path than entering an already crowded field with remakes of our old products. It was what Stan and I had done with the phono preamp when we launched PS Audio 33 years earlier: offered the world a new concept piece applicable to everyone's stereo. So, one quiet evening after the boys were tucked in bed, following an epic blue-sky day of deep powder skiing in Vail's Back Bowls, Terri and I opened a bottle of champagne to celebrate our decision. We'd relaunch PS Audio with a brand-new category of audio product, the Power Plant. It felt good to have a direction and I couldn't wait to get started in earnest. But first we needed an actual product to sell, and a functioning company to produce and sell it.

This time around, Terri and I wanted to keep PS Audio small: no employees and no partners. It would be family owned and run. Terri would manage the finances and administration the way she wanted while I handled design, manufacturing, marketing, and sales. We would outsource to contractors whatever we couldn't or didn't want to handle ourselves. To that end I convinced my old buddy Rick Cullen, PS Audio's former production manager, to quit his job and start his own company to build Power Plants. This was a big leap of faith for Rick—at this point, I still had only a prototype. I also consulted with an engineer I'd worked with at Genesis, Bob Stadtherr, who agreed to help me develop my cobbled-together prototype into a manufacturable product. To house the Power Plant, my old buddy at the Neal Feay Company, Alex Rasmussen, sculpted a wild-looking case with curved aluminum sides that evoked the shape of a sinewave. Before long, we were ready to hit the streets with our first model, the P300 Power Plant: a silver-and-black metal sculpture 8 inches wide, 4½ inches tall, and 18 inches deep. Its sweeping curves broke with the then-universal tradition of housing audio products in rectilinear boxes of black or silver.

Our setup was idyllic: skiing on weekends, answering phones and mail on weekdays. I'd kept my part-time job as assistant manager of Vail's guest-services program, managing 20 Mountain Hosts a day, skiing around Vail Mountain, radioing ski patrol about the occasional accident, and leading tours of the mountain. Terri had also kept her job as a part-time ski instructor at Beaver Creek ski resort. One of my fondest memories of that time was barreling down a ski run, a mountain-tour group following close behind, when my cell phone rang: a customer-service call for PS Audio. I pulled up next to the woods to take the call, and answered the customer's questions as skiers schussed down the slope next to me and the ten or so skiers in the tour group waited uphill. Soon we were on our way again, skiing down Vail's white-powder slopes, warmed by the bright sun in the clear blue sky.

Starting up a company that was brand new in everything but name, while introducing a product based on a concept entirely new to its target market, was not easy. At first, the Power Plant met with considerable skepticism because audiophiles distrusted what they considered snake oil: wild unsubstantiated marketing claims with little to no basis in science or even performance. Their distrust of wild pseudo-science claims was not too far off the mark. By the end of the 1990s, Noel Lee's firm Monster Cable had grown significantly, and where there's big market growth, there's always a fringe element along for the ride. Audio tweaks and accessories were on the rise, and audiophiles had grown wary of being taken in by some of their hyperbolic gimmicks, false claims, and wild stories.

One rather famous character that fit into this mold was legendary audio engineer John G. Iverson. With a reputation for being loud, bigoted, opinionated, and a heavy drinker, he also managed to design some of the most brilliant amplification equipment of the early 1980s. Even beyond his products and the two companies he founded, Electro Research and Electron Kinetics, Iverson was among a handful of the eccentrics who seem regularly drawn to the audio arts—and like most legends, his was a mix of fact and fiction. Iverson was said to be a genius who, at the age of 18, had designed the guidance system for the NASA Lunar Module for Grumman Aircraft, though I was never able to verify that claim. Nor was I able to confirm his alleged entanglements with the FBI and the CIA, or the US government's use on him of a new technology called EEG heterodyning. The device was said to have been pointed at Iverson, to connect the neural pathways of his brain to a computer. What can be said with certainty is that on January 4, 1991, Iverson vanished without a trace. As far as I know, he was never found or heard from again.

Of all the wacky claims and schemes that I ran across, none were as audacious as those of two brothers, John and Gary Bedini. Their company, Bedini, had once made reputable audio products such as power amplifiers. I'd always respected their work and had even used some of their great circuit ideas back when Stan and I were together, such as replacing a power amp's emitter resistors with heavy power diodes, which made possible a more linear amplifying device that didn't employ huge amounts of negative feedback but still improved the sound. But the Bedini brothers were also immersed in the same sorts of paranoid conspiracy notions—being watched by government investigators, working on top-secret military projects—that John Iverson had been. Like Iverson, they were bright and gifted designers with a few screws loose.

Back in the 1980s the Bedinis had said they could eliminate the need for cables to connect loudspeakers to power amplifiers. Wireless speakers would eventually come along, but this was something different. Today's wireless speakers are powered by batteries, or are plugged into a wall socket—their wirelessness applies only to the audio signals transmitted to them via radio waves. But the Bedinis claimed to have defied the laws of physics by wirelessly transferring great amounts of power through the ether, in the same way Nikola Tesla had claimed to have done nearly 100 years earlier. Few among us gave much thought to these claims until another friend of mine, fellow designer Owen Bennett of Kinergetics Research, stopped by for a visit. He'd gotten hold of the Bedinis' invisible waveguide speaker blocks, called simply Bedini Blocks, and proceeded to explain how it worked.

The Bedini Block was a wooden block with a pair of speaker binding posts at each end. A short pair of speaker cables connected the posts at one end of the block to the power amplifier, while the posts at the other end were connected to the speakers by a tiny, underweight "guide wire," to direct the ethereal flow of electrons. Owen cut one of the blocks in half, exposing a bar of copper that connected the block's inputs and outputs—essentially, it was a very short piece of very thick wire. So much for wirelessness! We had a good laugh.

I didn't think about the Bedini blocks again until a few months later, while attending the Consumer Electronics Show in Las Vegas. The Bedinis were demonstrating their miracle technology just a few doors down from PS Audio's display room, and I couldn't resist taking a peek. The Bedinis' room was packed with people excited about the demo. The speakers were Dick Sequerra's wonderful Metronomes, and the system sounded excellent. Soon the demo was over, and John Bedini began extolling the virtues of his wireless speaker cables. I had had enough and began to quietly leave, but John spotted me and called out to me.

"Yes," he said, pointing at me, "Paul McGowan, PS Audio. You heard the demo. What did you think?"

Every eye in the room turned in my direction. Not wanting to cause him any trouble, I answered as honestly as I could. "John, the demo sounded excellent."

"There!" he crowed. "Even Paul McGowan agrees—this new technology works."

That was too much. "Whoa whoa whoa!" I said. "I never said I bought the technology, John. I just said it sounded great. If you want to prove the technology, do an A/B for us, with and without those magic boxes."

John waved his hands and began sputtering about disbelievers and naysayers.

I went on. "A friend of mine sawed your wooden block in half and found nothing more inside than a copper bar, John. Maybe help us understand how this all works?"

I left as quickly as I could, feeling bad about my outburst. I just couldn't let John's load of bullshit stand as fact in my name. Later that day, John appeared in the doorway of our display room, trembling with rage.

"You're going to die," he said, pointing his glowing cigarette at me. "Radiation poisoning. Terrible way to go."

"Huh?"

"Radiation poisoning," he said. "You cut that block in half, and inside is a Plinth design transistor we grew in a radioactive environment. Deadly. That's why it was encased."

He was sweating, and deep drags on his cigarette weren't calming him down.

"Well," I said, "first off, it wasn't me who cut it open, so I'm not the one who's going to die. And second, how does wood stop radiation? I'm no physicist, but as best I remember, it takes lead to do that."

He had no answer to that. His face went red, and the veins in his neck looked ready to pop. He stumbled and stuttered for a bit, then left in a huff.

That was the kind of growing hysteria and outright BS the Power Plant had to weather before it could be accepted as a legitimate audio product. But after a few years' worth of positive reviews by audiophile writers who'd heard what a difference it could make, along with oscilloscope demonstrations quantifying at least some of those differences, we began to gain that acceptance. Eventually, our success spawned an entire new market of power conditioners for high-end audio, made by PS Audio and soon dozens of other companies.

Our Power Plant models grew so popular that it was no longer possible for Terri and me to run the company by ourselves. We'd have to make a change, in a direction that ended up being dictated by our sons: one by one, Lon, Sean, Scott, and Rob left the Vail Valley for the University of Colorado and the brighter lights along Colorado's eastern plains, near Denver—never to return to our sleepy little town.

It was time once again to pick up our sticks and move down the mountain.

CHAPTER 58

BOULDER, COLORADO, is a two-hour drive east from Vail, along I-70. All four of our sons went to college there. Terri and I had assumed that growing up in a little resort town like Vail would be heaven for our boys—and for a while, it was. Their high school had only a few hundred kids, and everyone knew everyone else. Turns out that's a problem for 18-year-olds—by the time each of our sons reached that age, he was anxious to leave. Terri and I valued and enjoyed the small-town atmosphere—it was a big change from how we'd grown up—but the boys felt trapped. As soon as they hit the big town of Boulder and, only half an hour away, the very big city of Denver—with all their nightlife, new girls, bands, drinking, and college-dorm debauchery—there was no going back. All they wanted was to wash their hands of the sleepy little life we'd imagined for them.

By 2002, the youngest of our boys, Rob, had moved to Boulder and then on to Denver. Now it was our turn. We moved PS Audio to Boulder, set up shop, sold our home in Vail, and started afresh. Good thing, too—our contract manufacturer, Rick Cullen, had started his own company to manufacture our products, and he was doing a good job but had run out of money. As I'd learned, it's not easy to run a small company by yourself, and one of the most difficult challenges is maintaining a steady cash flow of adequate size. That's where Rick stumbled, as I had so many times before, and before long his cash problems had become ours. Production faltered, and without a steady supply of Power Plants to sell, PS Audio would soon be in trouble. But try as we might, we couldn't solve Rick's problems and had to look elsewhere for a manufacturer.

In the early 2000s, American companies had begun to move the parts manufacturing and assembly of their products to China, where both could be done far more cheaply than in the US. Where one of our employees in Boulder might make $10 an hour, his or her Chinese counterpart might make $1. Even China's parts-buying abilities were enormous compared to our own. Because Chinese manufacturers dealt with really big Western companies, smaller companies could piggyback on bigger ones and take advantage of the economies of scale possible when parts are bought in large quantity. I estimated that by moving to Asia, we could cut our production costs in half and increase our volume of sales and profits.

While this economic upheaval was upsetting our own little apple-cart, the economy as a whole was being upended by events out of anyone's control. The 1990s—the longest period of sustained growth in American history—ended with the recession of 2001. The collapse of the speculative dot-com bubble, a fall in business outlays and investments, and the attacks of September 11 brought to an end a decade of growth and set many small companies like ours scrambling to make ends meet.

As if the vendor crisis and recession weren't bad enough, I'd made things worse by insisting on a complete redesign of the Power Plants. Our chief engineer, Bob Stadtherr, had figured out a new technology for regenerating AC with far greater efficiency than had previously been thought possible. The original Power Plants consumed as much energy as they produced, but this newer technology lost only 15 percent to heat. We patented his discovery, and set about reimagining and retooling a new line of products. The chance to lower production and parts costs meant that we could build a product with twice the quality and features without raising the price. It seemed too good to be true.

In less than a year, we moved our production lines from California to Shenzhen, China, and the first products they sent us were nothing short of gorgeous. The casework was the finest PS Audio had ever had: thick slabs of aluminum crafted with sweeping lines visually set our products apart from those of our competitors. Inside were more power and more features: a win-win situation for our customers and our company. Unfortunately, cracks soon began to appear. The Shenzhen plant could build a thousand units of a model in a single day, and its ability to make identical copies was remarkable—far better than we'd been accustomed to from our former, small-batch manufacturing process. But large numbers of identical products are fine only if they actually work. If an assembly error is made at the start of production, it's perfectly

337

copied a thousand times over before anyone can catch it. That's what happened in our second and third production runs from Shenzhen.

Inside the Power Plant is a critical part called a heat sensor. If, for some reason, the device's interior temperature exceeds the limit of safety, the sensor shuts down the power. This sensor had two wires that had to be insulated from each other, but a mistake had been made in the assembly instructions: instead of insulating the wires from each other, the workers had connected them. This would create an instant short circuit, disabling the heat sensor, the first time the unit was turned on. The faulty instructions would have set off an alarm in the mind of any experienced American electronics worker, but things are different in China. The problem wasn't one of intelligence or skill or experience, but culture. Westerners, particularly in the US, are encouraged to be individualists, or at least to think that they are. We're rewarded for seeing a problem, then raising a hand to tell someone about it. Asian cultures tend to put a higher value on conformity, on keeping your head down and working hard, without question.

An engineer at Bowers & Wilkins, a UK manufacturer of high-end loudspeakers that had also moved its production facilities to China, told me his own story about this. A problem with one of B&W's tweeters was plaguing their production crew in China, and B&W sent one of their top engineers from Britain to fix it. He spent weeks at the China plant, examining every aspect of their production lines, but the more he looked, the more mysterious the source of the problem became. Everything looked as if it were working just like it was supposed to: procedures were followed, and yields were as expected. But tweeters that had passed muster at final inspection were still failing.

On his last day in China, my friend watched the final testing process. The B&W engineers had built a testing chamber for their tweeters. All the operator had to do was connect two wires to the tweeter, place it in the chamber, and press a button. The computer then tested the product and reported its result: a red light for Defective, a green light for Properly Functioning. The test procedure was foolproof, except for one thing: whenever a tweeter failed the test, the worker placed it in the same carton as the tweeters that had passed. The engineer watched in disbelief

338

as this pattern was repeated over and over. Clearly, he'd discovered the problem—but why was it a problem at all? The solution seemed obvious. It turned out that no one had written down the procedure for what to do with a defective tweeter. Not knowing what to do, not wanting to break any rules, and unwilling to say anything to a superior, workers continued to do precisely no less—and precisely no more—than what they'd been explicitly told to do.

China has some of the most advanced, perfection-driven production facilities in the world. The laptop computer I'm writing this on, my smartphone, my TV, and almost all of my household appliances, are made and assembled with precision in China for big companies like Apple, IBM, Sony, and Samsung. Companies of that size can afford to spend time and money sorting out the inevitable confusions of working with partners of a very foreign culture, and they ultimately end up with the results they expect at far lower cost than they could ever manage in the West. But much smaller companies, such as PS Audio, have far less wiggle room.

The failure rate of our products soared. When Rick Cullen's company was building them, we'd managed to keep the number of failed units well below 1 percent. Now it was approaching 10 percent, and in countries with hotter climates, it got as high as 20 percent. Even worse, before we discovered what the problem was, we were replacing defective units with other defective units. Then counterfeit parts began to appear in our products: inferior, bootlegged versions of the parts we thought we'd paid for. It was becoming a nightmare—we had to pull out of China, and fast.

A company that can't produce reliable products and take care of its customers won't survive long. We managed to keep doing both, but it cost us. Any thought of savings went out the window. Within six months of the first failures appearing, we'd managed to pull ourselves out of the China mess, but the process ate up every resource we had: time, money, energy, ideas, you name it. To prevent anything like this from ever happening again, we divided PS Audio into two teams: the front-line production team worked with customers to get their units back to the factory and repaired, while the behind-the-scenes engineering team redesigned the products from the ground up to build them in Boulder, on new production lines that we now had to get up and running as soon as possible.

My bright idea of manufacturing PS Audio products in China had nearly cost us everything, and the company had only barely survived. What made the difference was the goodwill of our loyal customers, who cut us a lot of slack because they loved the brand. For that, we will be forever grateful. With production back to where it should have been in the first place — and with me feeling a lot humbler about whatever my next great idea might turn out to be — we made a lifelong commitment to build the majority of our products in the US.

CHAPTER 59

AFTER A MUTUAL SILENCE of nearly five years, Arnie Nudell and I began talking to one another again. Our anger had faded, and the wounds each of us had inflicted on the other had healed. Only the painful reality of our continued estrangement was still real—the reasons we'd fought had long since vanished. Since we couldn't remember why we'd been so angry with each other, it seemed like a good time to renew what had bound us together in the first place.

I don't remember which of us broke the ice, and it doesn't matter. For a while, in short phone calls every other week—he from his home in Vail, Colorado, and me from Boulder—we beat around the bush, not wanting to face the old wounds head on. We talked of unimportant things—world news, industry gossip. Over the course of a year, we remembered why we'd become friends, and we didn't feel the need to directly address the pain we'd inflicted on each other. Arnie had long before broken ties with Genesis, selling the company to Gary Koh, a Singaporean investor who had his own ideas about how speakers should sound and be built. Arnie told me he'd retired and was returning to his roots: physics. He'd amassed a library of reference materials and eagerly brought himself up to date on the latest thinking in string theory, the multiverse, and other barely comprehensible concepts, which Arnie had been introduced to when he attended lectures by physicist Richard Feynman at the University of California, Berkeley.

But he was still Arnie Nudell—speakers were in his blood. He could no more avoid audio than a fly can resist molasses. When I began asking him about designing a new line of speakers that PS Audio could build, his first reaction was predictable. No; he'd had enough, and would not even entertain the thought of putting himself and his designs out there again. But I knew my friend, perhaps better than he knew himself.

By this time in PS Audio's history we had regained our financial stability: we had reasonable profitability and enough cash to keep the lights on. We'd also continued design work on my ultimate company goal, building the entire audio chain from the AC wall socket to the customer's ears. That meant not only manufacturing Power Plants but expanding our product line back to building amps, preamps, DACs, and even interconnect cables. We now made every component in the audio chain except loudspeakers—a project I was anxious to engage Arnie's talents in—but first we'd have to get him reengaged in audio, slowly. If I moved too fast, the proverbial frog would jump out of the boiling water far too soon.

It took months of time, but I didn't give in, and eventually Arnie proposed an alternative—a way of our getting back in business together, but in baby steps. Arnie offered PS Audio his extraordinary hearing and grasp of the sounds of real instruments in acoustic space, to judge how close our new prototypes came to reproducing that lofty goal. This process is called voicing, a term borrowed from the tuning of pianos. It's the art of modifying and adjusting electronic designs by ear, something Stan Warren and I had learned how to do years before—but in all my years in the business, I've found no one better at voicing than Arnie. We hired him as a consultant and, from that point forward, every new PS Audio design was voiced by Arnie Nudell, a great advantage for our team and our customers.

Following the addition of Arnie to the company, the sound quality of our new products took a huge leap forward. We were finally on the right path and while finances were tough, at least we were paying our bills and managing our growth, something that had never happened in the company's nearly 40 years of business. It felt good but it was not what I had imagined. I was unsettled and dismayed to find that financial success and stability made me uncomfortable. I had just spent the last four decades of my life honing my corporate firefighting skills, and now there were no fires burning. The desperate skills I'd developed—meeting urgent design needs, drafting lifesaving plans, hatching clever get out of jail quick schemes—were no longer needed. I was relieved to be in the black financially, but I missed the design challenges. The company had always relied upon me for the rapid product innovation that would bring us a quick boost in the marketplace and keep us on the cutting edge of technological change. I was proud of our team's skills to whip up a new product from concept to production in as little as 90 days. But rapid product development comes at a cost. Scrambling to collate engineering, production, purchasing, and sales inevitably means disruption and compromise. We had earned our long sought-after financial stability by slowing down and paying attention to process. Our president, Jim Laib, our new financial whiz CFO, Keenan Haga, Terri's tireless efforts running HR, Bob Stadtherr's and Dave Paananen's engineering efforts, Scott McGowan's sales work, Bill Leeben's community outreach, and Woody Woodward's production team had brought order to the constant chaos in exchange for financial health. It was perfect in every respect, except for one thing: I was bored.

Because we'd slowed down to develop PS Audio the right way, our product design life cycles were no longer short. That's still the case. On average, our engineering team takes about a year to design a new audio component, getting everything perfect before it's handed off to the production engineers and builders. Testing the new product, then learning how to manufacture and assemble it, takes another few months. Before we know it, 18 months have passed, and customers still haven't gotten a taste of our newest creation.

For someone like me—someone with an active mind who just wants to dream up new products, designs, directions, and concepts—18 months is a long time. To keep from sitting there twiddling my thumbs as the detailed work of engineering takes its long, laborious course, I typically stay an entire product line ahead, waiting for engineering to catch up. And when that isn't fulfilling enough, I turn to improving our marketing and customer communication. I like keeping a busy, fast-paced, high-energy schedule. It's in my blood.

But there are limits to the numbers of hours and stores of energy in a life, and I was beginning to confront mine. That demanded a paradigm shift: I had to go from Paul the Everything Man to someone who devoted his finite time and energies with a bit more care and discrimination. My sons have begun to remind me that even though I still have no intention of ever retiring, life has a habit of ending—even if I can't quite believe it. The worst scenario for a business is being entirely run by one person, since it inevitably grinds to a halt as soon as that person dies. My family

343

gently pointed out that such a company is by definition selfish: it not only threatens the livelihood of its employees but dishonors its loyal customers, who are left in the lurch with worthless warranties, and no possibility of having defective products repaired. It was time for PS Audio to evolve yet again.

Up until a few years ago, all new designs at PS Audio were handled by me or by our chief engineer, Bob Stadtherr. Bob's a gifted engineer, but even he would admit that he's not the world's most acute listener or hearer. Where one of us was weaker, the other was there to fill in, and together we've come up with some innovative circuitry. But the company was growing, and it was obvious that it was time to expand our horizons of engineering design. I began to talk with friends and colleagues, letting it be known that we were open to adding to our team of designers to fulfill our growing collection of product ideas.

One night, a few weeks after I'd decided to hire more designers, Terri's and my dinner plans had to be abandoned when a good friend, mastering engineer Gus Skinas, excitedly roared up to the front of the PS Audio building in Boulder. He was breathless. "Paul! You have to come to the studio now. You can't miss this!"

Terri rolled her eyes and shook her head. "Make it quick, McGowan. I'll wait for you at the restaurant."

Gus wanted to introduce me to a friend of his, Ted Smith, who is a sort of digital genius. When Ted passed Google's entrance exam (they were luring him away from Microsoft), they realized that they had to rewrite the test: his answer was better than theirs. Now, Ted had invented a new type of digital-to-analog converter, or DAC—a device that converts the computer language of a digital audio signal into an analog signal that can then be sent to loudspeakers, which in turn produce the vibrations in air that we hear as sound and music. DACs, of course, weren't new. Every digital playback product has a DAC: your smartphone and computer, along with your Blu-ray or DVD or CD or MP3 player.

But Ted's prototype sounded so good that Gus couldn't tell the difference between his own master tapes played directly through his reference sound system and the same signal played through Ted's new DAC.

In all of Gus's many decades of mastering recordings, this had never happened before—he'd always been able to hear a difference, however small. Ted wanted someone to manufacture this DAC, and Gus knew we were looking to add to our stable of designers. It turned out to be a perfect match: Ted was a welcome addition to the PS family. Within a few more years we brought on yet another brilliant designer—Bascom King, my old friend and Arnie's most trusted engineer—to design a new line of signature products.

But about the time we brought Arnie, Ted, and Bascom aboard, new problems were looming: high-end audio dealers were closing their doors at an alarming rate, and the subscriber bases of print audio magazines were shrinking. The talk around our industry was one of doom and gloom for high-end audio. Had the growing interest in home theater and multichannel audio taken its toll? Was it the advent of big-box retailers? Mail-order catalogs? Had people changed the way they listened to music, and how they bought recordings and audio gear? The reasons for retailers' declining sales turned out to be all of those things, and more. And one thing was driving them all.

CHAPTER 60

IN MY 70 YEARS on the planet I have been fortunate to witness technology's forward march—from trains to planes, radio to television, props to jets, land lines to cell phones, typewriters to computers, black and white to color television, mono to stereo to surround audio, and vinyl to digital. But as mind-numbing and disruptive as adopting and adapting to these technological wonders continues to be, none of them compares to the rise of the World Wide Web.

The man behind it all, Tim Berners-Lee, was born in 1955 in London, England, to Mary Lee Woods and Conway Berners-Lee, both of whom worked on the first commercially built computer, the Ferranti Mark 1. Thirty-four years later, in 1989, Berners-Lee introduced to an unsuspecting planet the World Wide Web, a computer-accessible file system for a collection of documents available over the Internet, a network of networks connecting together a global system of devices.

Until the Web began to ensnare almost every aspect of modern life, audio equipment was sold through shops that now are called "bricks-and-mortar" retailers—a distinction unnecessary until the advent of online alternatives. These havens of speakers and electronics and turntables, along with the audio furniture to support and contain them, sold everything the audio shopper needed. Through the 1990s most cities had one or two high-end audio dealers, most of which carried low-cost, entry-level systems as well as ultra-expensive gear. These dealers were happy to demonstrate audio systems for anyone who walked through their doors—and if something struck a chord with a customer, most dealers were happy to set up a pair of speakers or a stack of electronics in that customer's home for a free trial. Back then, only a handful of companies—PS Audio was one of them—sold their products directly to consumers and retailers.

That all began to change in the late 1990s, as shopping habits for audio gear and most other goods and services began shifting away from bricks-and-mortar stores — first to mail-order, and later to the Web. It happened slowly, but one by one, retailers that had specialized in two-channel audio have been able to survive only by transforming themselves into sellers and/or installers of whole-home audio and home-theater systems — businesses that are less dependent on the Internet for sales — or by changing their business models in other fundamental ways, like becoming more community-oriented, offering services like the personalized audio concierge, setup expertise, running loaner programs for audio groups, or hosting live music events.

The relationship of audio dealers and audio manufacturers had long been fairly cozy. Dealers sold products at retail prices that were about twice the wholesale prices they paid manufacturers for those products, which gave dealers a profit margin that covered their rent, payroll, marketing, advertising, and service department expenses. In exchange for retailers bringing to manufacturers their customers and sales expertise, manufacturers guaranteed retailers location-based exclusivity: only those stores in that area could carry their products. If customers wanted to buy a given manufacturer's product, they could only find them in authorized stores in protected territories. But beginning in the 1990s mail-order sellers of audio gear, such as Audio Advisor, Crutchfield, and eventually Music Direct, began to get involved, with a nationwide reach that was unrestrained by the geographical territories of bricks-and-mortar dealers. Customers living anywhere in the country could pick up the phone and order what they wanted, or return for a refund goods that didn't meet their expectations. The bigger bricks-and-mortar stores and chains rebelled against this by refusing to carry the products of audio manufacturers that sold through mail-order houses.

Then came online stores and e-tailing. It didn't take online retailers long to figure out that their overheads were nothing compared to those of bricks-and-mortar retailers, and that they could quickly gain market traction with a well-established tool: the discount. The need to double products' wholesale prices to pay for overhead began to crumble, as one online stereo dealer after another slashed prices. What bricks-and-mortar retailers found a particularly bitter pill to swallow was a new form of comparison shopping: customers would spend the day at their local dealer, auditioning the equipment they were interested in, then go home and buy it online at a deep discount. Sales at bricks-and-mortar outlets slowed, then went into free fall, in a scenario repeated worldwide. Some bricks-and-mortar dealers tried to match the online sellers' discounts, but soon realized that they could never survive that way: their profit margins would soon be too slim to cover their expenses. That's precisely what happened, and bricks-and-mortar shops closed by the dozens. The race to the bottom had begun and the winners were closing their doors.

At the same time, there was a palpable shift in costs and duties from retailers to manufacturers. In any business in which profit margins are shrinking, diminishing returns mean that there's less money available to pay for expenses. In response, the first step is usually to cut those expenses, beginning with what seems the least essential. In this case the first things to go were marketing and advertising, an expensive burden that had long been carried by retailers. Previously, most retailers would promote a specific brand, because the exclusivity agreement with the manufacturer meant that the only place customers in their area could buy that brand was in their store. But when a brand of audio gear could now be bought by anyone, anywhere with only a phone call or mouse click, the money retailers spent to advertise that brand locally was wasted.

The burden of marketing and promoting—advertising—their gear now fell to manufacturers, most of whom had no idea how to do so effectively. After all, most high-end audio manufacturers were like me: engineering geeks. What did we know about getting the word out to customers by designing ads and writing ad copy? And even if we did have those skills, where would we send interested customers: to the online discounters, or to the flailing, failing bricks-and-mortar shops? Meanwhile, traditional retailers kept disappearing as more and more online dealers sprouted up on the Web.

Manufacturers divided into two camps: those who kept doing what had always worked in the past, i.e. the manufacturer-and-retailer model, and those who did something different. PS Audio was already in the latter camp—not because we were prescient, or brilliant marketers, but because we'd always been a bit of a pariah among the bigger, more established retailers. Because we sold direct from our factory and through dealers, they considered us traitors to the longstanding relationship of manufacturer and retailer—a relationship that was rapidly crumbling everywhere. Not only were these dealers uninterested in PS Audio, but the few marketing dollars they'd been spending on our behalf now vanished almost entirely.

Unfortunately, we had no advertising budget for bringing in new business. This meant that, again, we had to get creative to find a way to increase sales in a retail world that many were predicting was about to end. In the summer of 2002, I received an email from an audiophile asking for advice on how best to reach other audiophiles, and for help promoting a new idea he was working on. This man was simultaneously launching a new artist, a new recording, a new way of marketing a new digital recording format, and a new digital playback medium called SACD (Super Audio Compact Disc).

His name was Seth Godin, an author, audiophile, and music lover. He lived in Hastings-on-Hudson, a village just north of New York City, in Westchester County. Seth reveled in change—he loved throwing out the long-accepted and living for the new. We bonded almost immediately. Over the years, Seth and I discussed via email the state of high-end retailing and what it might mean for PS Audio. He encouraged me to build community by focusing on what Stan Warren and I had started in 1974, when we personally answered every letter we received from our customers. He gently steered me in a direction in which none of our competitors had yet discovered: away from what he called "interruption-based advertising" and toward what he called "permission-based marketing," something he'd first proposed in his book *Permission Marketing: Turning Strangers into Friends, and Friends into Customers*.

Traditional ads, whether in the pages of print magazines or 60-second TV commercials, are unwanted interruptions. You didn't buy the magazine or turn to that channel to see an ad. We'd all grown up accepting such interruption-based marketing as the fee we pay to read or watch what we want. After all, someone had to pay to produce the article or show. Seth's idea was the opposite of this. Instead of interrupting someone's reading or watching with unwanted content, marketers could instead provide something so compelling that people would actually invite the presenter into their lives and demand more of it. That's just what Google did—by offering information that people wanted at no cost, Google.com became the most visited website in the world. Over time, Google included ads to pay their bills, and eventually made a fortune—Google is now one of the most valuable companies on the planet. But to this day, those ads are secondary to why people continue to flock to their website.

The first permission-based marketing we launched was a free monthly newsletter. But, unlike most company newsletters filled with puffs and ads for the company's own products, ours was a collection of industry news items, interesting stories unrelated to us, tips and tricks to help subscribers get the most out of their audio systems, and one lead story of our own. This was a new idea in the industry, and at first people were distrustful of it, waiting for the other shoe to drop—perhaps a pop-up or some sort of spam. But, over time, more and more people trusted us and signed up. Within a year, the free PS Newsletter became one of the most widely read periodicals in the industry, and our community grew.

In May 2011 my son Lon, who'd moved to Seattle to start his own company (iClick) to sell such promotional goods as branded digital cameras and USB drives, sent me an email: "Your friend Seth Godin's speaking in Seattle. Wanna go?"

I knew Seth as an email friend—I'd never seen or heard him speak. Sure.

Seth's speech forever changed my life and the direction of PS Audio. I don't remember his exact words, but he described the Internet and the massive changes it had brought to the world not as disruptive threats, but as amazing opportunities for those willing to take a different view. Instead of running from the changes in retail distribution caused by the Internet—and perceived by most in the audio industry as disasters—Seth put forth the idea that the Internet was the single biggest opportunity of all time, on a par with the invention of the printing press and movable type. The World Wide Web was a sort of democracy: an opportunity for small voices to be heard over the din of millions, even without an ad budget. Here was the chance for us to magnify what PS Audio had done from the very beginning: build a community of likeminded people—people like us with a love of music and high-performing audio systems—by providing services that customers and potential customers actually wanted. Forget selling products. If we built a community based on generosity, sharing, respect, and help, sales would follow.

At the end of his talk, Seth asked the crowd: "What are you doing with this golden opportunity?" As I flew back to Boulder, his question haunted me. What was I doing with the opportunity the Web offered?

My answer frightened me. Terrified of a world we didn't understand and a marketplace that seemed to be collapsing, my fellow audio lemmings and I were running away from it as fast as we could. We didn't know what else to do. Seth's talk had shown me a way out.

A week later I launched *Paul's Post*, a short daily blog that educates, entertains, discusses, and brings new ideas to thousands of daily readers. Rarely does *Paul's Post* talk of PS Audio products. Instead, along with our online magazine, *Copper*, our daily podcasts, the monthly *PS Newsletter*, and our daily YouTube channel, it helps connect a growing community of music lovers with something they and we love: music and its quality reproduction in the home. When a customer or potential customer we communicate with is thinking of adding a stereo system or updating an existing one, they sometimes feel more comfortable reaching out to us for advice because we're like family.

The upshot of all this community outreach, customer caring, and our team's output of consistently excellent, high-value products is success. Finally, after 45 years of struggle we're a profitable, overnight hit. Our company's fortunes have turned around; we're cash positive and comfortably profitable. Our team of 50 employees and our thousands of customers are indeed family: stakeholders in a great experiment confirming that a generous, high-value, caring, sustainable enterprise

351

that benefits its constituents should and will prosper. We all march forward in the lockstep harmony of committed idealists, believing that good deeds and caring people will always trump those that place profits and shortcuts above ethics and generosity.

Change is tough, but few things in life that are worth doing are more beneficial than reaching out to a community with generosity and kindness, and growing with people who enjoy what you do.

CHAPTER 61

IN 2017, THE WORLD lost a great man. My friend and mentor, Arnie Nudell, passed away as suddenly as he'd burst on the scene 50 years before, with the Infinity Servo Static speaker. In the last few years of Arnie's life, I'd at last been able to twist his arm hard enough to renew his enthusiasm about designing some new speakers, this time bearing the logo of PS Audio. He and I would once again work together: Arnie on the speakers, me on the electronics. They would be his best effort, the culmination of a lifetime of work and learning in service to music. And once "The Arnold" got going on a speaker design, he couldn't be stopped—except by one thing.

Arnie had long suffered from back problems. They'd begun early in his life, a product of his love of playing basketball. Too many hard landings had taken their toll on his spine, compressing and fusing his vertebrae. These problems got only worse with time, and two surgeries and a series of falls in his 70s hadn't helped. But although Arnie was now 81 and using a walker, he plowed ahead with his work. We were close to a prototype of a production speaker, the latest version of a design he'd been working on for a decade: a four-way, seven-driver speaker that stood just under five feet tall and looked like a cross between a cello and an upright bass. It was Arnie's best work—in many respects the finest loudspeaker system I or anyone else who listened to it had ever heard. It even outperformed Arnie's massive Infinity or Genesis four-piece reference systems in terms of transparency. He and I could talk of nothing else.

Arnie was obsessive about everything: the wine he drank, the food he ate, the music he listened to, the systems he designed, the women he loved, and every last aspect of the cars he owned. Although his doctors had warned him not to do this sort of thing alone, one cold night in November 2017, at his home in Vail, Arnie hobbled out to the garage to check the tire pressure on his BMW, which he'd planned to drive the next morning. He fell, and not strong enough to crawl back into the house, lay there all night on the cold cement slab. He was found the next morning by our engineer Darren Myers, who'd arrived to spend the day helping Arnie continue advancing his beloved speaker design. Darren called 911, and Arnie was rushed to the hospital.

Arnie didn't regain consciousness until the next day, in the hospital. Darren was sitting next to his bed. He grabbed Darren's hand, told him of a new idea he'd had for how the tweeter should be crossed over to the midrange, and demanded that Darren bring him pen and paper, though he failed to write anything down. Then he went back to sleep. The bone-deep chill he'd caught from his night on the garage floor turned to pneumonia, and he died two weeks later. My tears for Arnie and the loss for his family were as bitter as those I'd shed for my father and mother. The world had lost a treasure. I know Arnie would have wanted us to carry on his work, to produce the speaker system on which he'd lavished everything he'd learned in an entire life devoted to sound. And that's what we are doing.

Lives end, and life goes on. Terri and I have a growing, strong company that continues to bring musical richness to music lovers around the world. To fuel our growth, we focus on building the finest two-channel audio systems we know how to design, for as broad an audience as possible. Recently that audience has included more and more twenty-and thirty-somethings — a new market for us.

PS Audio products had always appealed to customers in their 40s and older. We'd always wanted to attract younger people, but had found it a challenge. People in their 20s and 30s tend to have little disposable income, and we found that most were happy with the sound quality of their earbuds and smartphones. But with the resurgence of vinyl in the 1990s, that began to change. When the Millennials began coming of age, in their late teens and 20s, they seemed to want what every generation wants: what their parents didn't. One of those things was vinyl. To these young people, LPs were cool — something they could touch and hold, unlike ephemeral MP3s and streamed music. Their love of vinyl has proven infectious. As of this writing, nearly a billion LPs are sold each year, and turntable sales are at their highest point ever.

Into these unexpected developments stepped another McGowan: my son Scott. Scott has been part of PS Audio's core team, and a co-owner of the company, for more than a decade now, having managed our departments of purchasing, customer service, and now sales. He's passionate about music, but he's not an audiophile in the usual sense. Instead of spending his non-essential income on new speakers and high-end components for his home, he mostly buys LPs and tickets to concerts—just as I and so many other audiophiles did 40 or 50 years ago.

Not long ago, Scott came to me with a question. "I love the way music sounds on our big system in Music Room One," he said, "but there's no way I can have that at home, and neither can my friends. Would it be possible to bottle up all that great sound into a small box that people my age could afford to own?"

"Yes," I said. "But it won't be easy."

Over the next two years, Scott worked with our engineering team to build his dream: an affordable, comprehensive high-end music system no bigger than this book. He named the product Sprout—an all-in-one music player that initially retailed for $500 and needs nothing more than a pair of speakers to make music. As of this writing, Sprout has sold more units than any other model in the history of PS Audio, and it shows no signs of slowing down. Meanwhile, I've begun to reduce my own efforts in engineering and developing new products to focus more on community outreach. Eventually, Scott will step into my shoes as CEO of PS Audio. That delights me. I couldn't hope for anyone with more passion for music and for the art of our craft, or with more love of our audiophile community.

Sometimes pleasures come in pairs. While Scott was busy honing his skills, my oldest son Lon—the businessman of the family—was working behind the scenes with our PS Audio administration team. Together, they helped turn PS Audio from a marginally profitable "hobby shop" business into the real deal: a competently run "real" business that focuses on our core ideals of customer-first service and products—something Terri and I had always wanted but were never quite able to pull off. It was the strength of our family that got Terri and I through the tough times building our business. Now that same strength of family is hard at work, making sure Mom and Dad's decades of effort pay off, our customers' investments in the brand and its products are honored, and the next McGowan generation and the PS Team are ready for a new round of challenges.

Despite all of the education and outreach efforts by PS Audio and our colleagues, the possibilities and pleasures of high-end audio remain a sort of open secret. It's never been easy to spread the word of better sound out in the world. Some naysayers have suggested that's because there's little interest in quality audio—a notion that runs counter to every fiber of my being. Watching the sheer delight on the faces of newcomers to our little secret society of music lovers is enough to convince me that people haven't changed. We all like something better. Who doesn't want their music to sound live or would prefer crappy sound in their home?

We've opened our doors to everyone and anyone wishing to experience the wonders and magic of high-end audio, and most days at least one group of visitors arrives unannounced at our front door. People from all over the world make the pilgrimage to our factory and its three listening rooms. In the middle listening room visitors are treated to a pair of Arnie Nudell's Infinity IRS V speakers—one of only 58 pairs ever made of the 1.2-ton behemoths that gobsmacked Stan Warren and me at Harry Pearson's house. Next door is an even larger room with PS Audio's latest speaker creations inspired by Arnie, and next to that is a living room setup demonstrating how great affordable hi-fi can sound. Tours are informal, personal, and do not require a reservation or a thick shell: they are never sales-oriented. If you choose to visit you'll get the royal treatment: a full factory tour where you can watch the products being made, a run through our engineering department to see how they are designed and meet the designers, a visit to Gus Skinas's mastering and recording studio, and the chance to meet everyone else in the company. We're family and you're treated the same. We welcome these visits, but we also understand a trip to Boulder isn't easy or even possible for most.

Figuring out how to help people learn about high-end audio, and how to share our passion for the wonders of two-channel sound, remains an ongoing challenge, but one we heartily embrace. Stereo retailers continue

356

to vanish all over the world, while new ways of reproducing quality sound and new ideas for bringing the magic of live performances into our homes flourish in fits and starts. There are glimmers of hope, though. In the United States, and hopefully in other countries too, PS Audio ships our products directly to customers' homes and affords people a month to play with the system to make sure it fits—or arrange to send it back without charge or headache if it's not working as expected. For bigger speaker systems, we'll even send out one of our setup people.

Is there a future for high-end audio and audiophiles? Yes. There will always be those who want better sound, and who, when they hear it, will appreciate it enough to pay a reasonable premium for it. Like fine food, fine wine, fine literature, fine art, and fine music, there's audible magic being made by today's fine audio systems—more magic than ever. You just have to look and listen for it. Believe me, you'll know it when you hear it.

As for me, I continue to think and act as I always have, a rebel at heart, but also an inquisitive student of how things work. My wife Terri shakes her head with mock disdain as I begin to teach the next crop of McGowans, our grandchildren, how to laugh with the world, understand and control the adults around them, snap their fingers Curly Howard style, and revel in challenge rather than shrink from change.

My ongoing mission in life remains one of education and help, to be there when needed, to share what I can with whomever is interested in listening. Feel free to reach out to me at any time about any subject you feel comfortable sharing with me.

We're all in this world together.

ACKNOWLEDGMENTS

WRITING A BOOK for the first time is not without its challenges.

Though I have been writing daily for the past seven years—producing my daily blog, *Paul's Posts*—it is a very different discipline to unravel and write down the highlights of one's life in the form of a novel (though one of my editors bristled at that term, correcting me that this has been a memoir).

The 100 percent truth is I could not have completed this book without the generosity, hard work, and dedication of a lot of people.

I would like to offer my sincere thanks and gratitude to:

My sons Lon, Sean, Scott, and Rob, and especially my wife Terri. They encouraged me and tolerated my closed door and lack of attention for the two years it took to produce this book, and I am forever in their debt for their extraordinary understanding and patience.

Seth Godin, who inspired me to go make a ruckus. And I did.

My editors Richard Lehnert, John Acker, and Amy E. Davis, who were gracious enough not to make fun of me for my lack of ability, and who generously gave of themselves so that I might appear to have some measure of talent at writing.

Typeset by Jonathan Sturm in Avenir Next and Adobe Caslon Pro.